I RODE WITH JEB ST

I Rode with Jeb Stuart

THE LIFE AND CAMPAIGNS

OF

MAJOR GENERAL J.E.B. STUART

BY

H. B. McCLELLAN

with an Introduction and Notes by
BURKE DAVIS

DA CAPO PRESS • NEW YORK

Library of Congress Cataloging in Publication Data

McClellan, H. B.
    I rode with Jeb Stuart: the life and campaigns of Major Gen-
eral J.E.B. Stuart / by H. B. McClellan: with an introduction
and notes by Burke Davis.—1st Da Capo Press ed.
        p.   cm.
    Previously published: Bloomington, Ind.: Indiana University
Press, c1958.
    Includes index.
    ISBN 0-306-80605-3
    1. Stuart, Jeb, 1833–1864. 2. Generals—United States—Biog-
raphy. 3. Generals—Confederate States of America—Biography.
4. United States. Army—Biography. 5. Confederate States of
America. Army—Biography. 6. United States—History—Civil
War, 1861–1865—Campaigns. 7. McClellan, H. B. 8. United
States—History—Civil War, 1861–1865—Personal narratives,
Confederate. I. Davis, Burke, 1913–   . II. Title.
E467.1.S9M2 1994
973.7'3'092—dc20   94-15217
[B]   CIP

First Da Capo Press edition 1994

This Da Capo Press paperback edition of *I Rode With Jeb Stuart*
is an unabridged republication of the edition published in
Bloomington, Indiana in 1958.

Published by Da Capo Press, Inc.
A Subsidiary of Plenum Publishing Corporation
233 Spring Street, New York, N.Y. 10013

INTRODUCTION.

THIS book, which is both biography and memoir, is the richest source on the Civil War career of the plumed knight of the Army of Northern Virginia, Major General James Ewell Brown Stuart. Though it has been out of print for generations, it is still read, and has fairly won its way onto the shelf of "classics" of the war. Copies command premium prices quite out of proportion to their rarity.

Henry Brainerd McClellan is a remarkable symbol of the tragic war period. He was reared in Philadelphia by parents of distinguished New England ancestry and graduated from Williams College. His great-grandfather, General Samuel McClellan, commanded the Fifth Brigade, Connecticut militia, in the Revolution. His maternal grandfather, the Rev. Mr. Ezra Stiles Ely, donated land for Jefferson Medical College in Philadelphia, on which Henry's father, Dr. Samuel McClellan, and an uncle, Dr. George McClellan, founded that institution.

Henry was trained for the ministry, but because of his extreme youth at graduation he went to Cumberland County, Virginia, as a private tutor, in 1858. Within a little over two years he acquired the views of an impassioned Southern partisan, embraced States' Rights, and in 1861 enlisted as a private in the Third Virginia Cavalry.

One of McClellan's first cousins was George B. McClellan, twice commander of the Army of the Potomac. Four of his brothers served in the Union armies, one of them, Carswell, as adjutant general to Major General Andrew A. Humphreys, commander, II Corps, Army of the Potomac.

It was perhaps this background that gave Major McClellan's book the restraint which raised it above competitors. It is by all odds the most reliable account of Stuart and his horsemen left by Stuart's intimates. This was achieved in face of handicaps, for McClellan was not at his commander's side in the earlier phases of the war, which included some spectacular moments. Thus deprived of the authority of an eyewitness for more than half of his narrative, and intimately involved through personal relationships in the remainder, McClellan might have been forgiven a certain lack of balance. His modesty and integrity in presenting his own role are so marked, however, that only the most knowing readers can fix the moment of McClellan's actual entry into the Stuart headquarters family.

This is of importance to anyone who has sought the essence of Stuart's character among the fantasies of Major Heros von Borcke, the stirring romances of John Esten Cooke, or the galloping narrative of Captain William Blackford. In all but minor details the painstaking McClellan achieved striking accuracy, though he wrote some twenty years after the war, with many records unavailable, and most of Stuart's correspondence denied to him. Yet his is the most persuasive image of Stuart offered by a contemporary, and must be central in any recreation of the great cavalryman; the more colorful touches offered by others of Stuart's staff, lively and charming as they are, must become additions to McClellan's work.

Stuart's eye fell upon Henry early in the war, when he was rising despite his lack of military training and the potential handicap of his Northern origin. Jeb called Captain McClellan to his staff as Major and Assistant Adjutant General on April 20, 1863; McClellan had been serving as Adjutant to the Third Virginia.

Though there is no direct evidence on the point, it is probable that Stuart determined to have McClellan at his side on March 17, 1863, during the hectic and bloody engagement at Kelly's Ford, when a few of his regiments, surprised by the enemy, escaped disaster by desperate hand-to-hand fighting. The fabled cannoneer, Major John Pelham, was killed here. In the midst of this, suffering the greatest casualties in both men and horses, was the Third Virginia. Adjutant McClellan was singled out in the report of General Fitzhugh Lee on this engagement, and "particularly commended" for his gallantry.

In an official dispatch to Samuel Cooper, the Confederate Adjutant General, Stuart asked for McClellan. The document ended: "I deem it proper to state that I am influenced in this recommendation by the signal

gallantry displayed by him in the field and his efficiency and zealous devotion to duty as a staff officer.''

This was only two weeks before Chancellorsville,
where Stuart lost his Adjutant General, young Channing Price, whom McClellan succeeded. In the pro-
ceedings of the Confederate Congress, McClellan's
career on Stuart's official staff is dated from May 2,
1863. Almost without a pause the Army of Northern
Virginia moved from the slaughter pens of the
Wilderness toward the west and north, maneuvering
for the Gettysburg campaign. The changing of the
war's tides first struck the cavalry corps in these
weeks, and McClellan was in the front of the action.

Brandy Station came on June 9, 1863, the greatest
cavalry engagement of the war, and a second surprise
by the improving Federal troopers. For an hour or
so when the fate of Stuart's regiments hung in the
balance, McClellan took command on Fleetwood Hill.
In his report of the action Stuart wrote of McClellan
that "he displayed the same zeal, gallantry and efficiency which has on every battlefield, in the camp or
on the march so distinguished him as to cause his
selection for his present post.''

Between Brandy and Gettysburg Stuart's outnumbered men faced their severest test in two years
of combat as they attempted to shield Robert E. Lee's
northward-marching infantry from determined Federal riders. Obscure hill villages became memorable:
Aldie, Middleburg, and Upperville. McClellan recorded these actions and the cavalry's wide foray
into Pennsylvania with commendable clarity.

These, of course, are the crucial days of Stuart's wartime career as viewed from the present day, for the controversy over the placement of blame for the Confederate defeat at Gettysburg inevitably involves Stuart, his reaction to Lee's orders, his penchant for roving behind enemy lines, and his reputation for plunging into action at the possible expense of strategic objectives.

McClellan appreciated the meaning of the campaign, and defended Stuart's role with a vigor that never led him into such partisanship as that exhibited by Colonel John S. Mosby on the same topic. One of the shortcomings of the Major's case, and of his book, lies in his failure to uncover an order from Robert E. Lee to Stuart of June 23, 1863, a key document in any study of the campaign. McClellan assumed the document to be lost, and paraphrased it from memory. In fact it is in *Official Records* (see editor's notes, below, p. 442).

McClellan left something of equal value, perhaps, in his sketch of the scene: Stuart is asleep on the ground in a cold mountain rainstorm when, at midnight, the order arrives from Lee. McClellan is on a farmhouse porch, under orders to receive dispatches; he reads the message from Lee, fathoms its importance, rouses Stuart, reads it to him, and watches him fall asleep once more, like a child.

McClellan's prose habits will not delight every modern reader, for he sometimes introduces documents and eyewitness accounts of others at length and without subtlety, and lapses into formal sketches

of movements as if making notes for official reports.
Yet a reader who rides with Stuart through the
Gettysburg campaign, until the Confederate infantry
is safely south of the swollen Potomac, is not likely
to forget the experience. In the light of McClellan's
narrative the ancient, wearying Confederate contro-
versies over Gettysburg seem to lose a great deal of
their importance.

McClellan is muted and conservative, as usual, but
his pictures of a Stuart half asleep, dazed by fatigue
and dulled by hunger as he rides through the Maryland
rains, fending off the enemy, leave little to be desired.
The Major led his chief to and from a dinner table
when he was hardly conscious, and dealt with his
garbled attempts at dictation of dispatches. Stuart
paid his debt a good bit later in reports, praising
McClellan for "the clearness with which orders and
dispatches were transmitted," as he rode with him
"day and night." Stuart never realized his greatest
debt to Henry, of course, since he fell long before the
future biographer had matured his purpose.

McClellan's story ends with a sketch of the wounding of Stuart at Yellow Tavern and his subsequent
death in nearby Richmond. Though he was at Stuart's
side almost every hour of these two days, he resists
even here the temptation to dramatize the scenes, and
is notably self-effacing. This perhaps heightens the
interest of his account, and there are striking con-
trasts, as in the moment when the wounded Stuart
shouts to his retreating men: "Go back! I'd rather
die than be whipped!"

McClellan's subdued rendering of the death scene should be compared with that of the untrammeled raconteur von Borcke.

Two days after the death of Stuart, McClellan was called to Robert E. Lee's staff, but after three months he was assigned to the cavalry again, and served as adjutant general and chief of staff to Major General Wade Hampton, Stuart's successor. He was with the cavalry corps in North Carolina as Joseph E. Johnston surrendered to Sherman.

Major McClellan, though he technically earned the rank of lieutenant colonel, declined it afterward, saying that since it was not received until after Appomattox, he had no proper claim to it. He remained Major through postwar years in which humble men of rear ranks were miraculously elevated to the status of general officers, if not to sainthood.

His wife was Catherine Macon Matthews of Cumberland County, Virginia, whom he married in December, 1863. They had four daughters and a son, one of the girls being christened George B. McClellan.

For five years after the war the McClellans lived in Cumberland County, Virginia. A collection of his papers, rather nondescript in nature but covering sporadically the war and postwar years, is in the Virginia Historical Society at Richmond. In 1870 the family moved to Lexington, Kentucky, where McClellan opened the Sayre Female Institute. This book was written between 1880 and 1885, when he was still proprietor of the school. He died in October, 1904, just short of his sixty-fourth birthday. Not long before his death he said that he was still a Rebel, reconstructed but unrepentant.

One of his pupils at Sayre Institute was Anne Bachman, who became Mrs. Charles R. Hyde of Chattanooga, Tennessee, and served as Historian General of the United Daughters of the Confederacy. In 1958, nearing her ninetieth birthday, Mrs. Hyde could recall hearing McClellan read several chapters of his biography to her in his study. She remembered McClellan as "A handsome man who played the organ in the Presbyterian Church, and sang well." She recalled that: "The Major often told me, 'Anne, remember that George B. McClellan was a gentleman.'"

The appendix of this work includes reports on Brandy Station, an effort to illuminate a controversy which did not long survive the war.

BURKE DAVIS

Greensboro, N. C.
August 11, 1958

PREFACE.

I HAVE written this work at intervals during the past five years of a very busy life, and I fear that it may have suffered from the want of consecutive thought and labor. I believe myself to have been actuated by a sincere desire to tell the truth, and to do simple justice to the memory of one under whom I feel it an honor to have served. If it shall prove that I have failed to give due credit to the gallant men who fought on either side, it will be to me a source of lasting regret. I have not hesitated to give my personal testimony when it seemed necessary.

The story of Stuart's early life has been given to me by members of his family. The history of his campaigns has been compiled from the Official Records of both armies. I have not attempted a narrative of the Mine Run campaign, because it has not been convenient to obtain access to the Federal reports. The last chapter is, of necessity, somewhat personal in character, and is drawn largely from my own memory.

I am greatly indebted to Colonel Robert N. Scott, who presides over the War Records Office in Washington, for copies of the official reports, and for many

facts not contained in the reports, which have been
determined by special search among the archives. For
similar valuable assistance I owe thanks to the Rev.
J. William Jones, D. D., Secretary of the Southern
Historical Society, Richmond, Va.

For kind and courteous attentions, and for valuable information, I am indebted to a number of officers
of the Federal army, among whom I beg to mention
General John S. Simonson, General D. McM. Gregg,
General T. F. Rodenbough, General Wesley Merritt,
General G. K. Warren, Colonel A. C. M. Pennington,
Colonel William Brooke-Rawle, Colonel John P. Nich-
olson, and Colonel W. S. Newhall. Captain George N.
Bliss, of Providence, R. I., whose enviable reputation as
a member of the 1st Rhode Island Cavalry is well
known, has been untiring in his efforts to secure for me
information on several important points. I am also
indebted to many of my comrades in arms, whose names
are generally mentioned, in the text of the work, in
connection with the data they have supplied. Hon. M.
C. Butler, United States Senator from South Carolina,
and Colonel W. W. Blackford and Major B. S. White,
of General Stuart's staff, have given to me much of
the material contained in the chapter on the Chambersburg raid.

To the Chief of Engineers United States Army I am
indebted for the official maps of Gettysburg, Chancellorsville, the Wilderness, and other localities; and
to the Post Office Department, for maps of the postal
routes in Pennsylvania and Maryland. From these
and other reliable authorities, my maps have been

compiled by my brother, Carswell McClellan, civil engineer, formerly of the staff of Major-General A. A. Humphreys. The map of the Battle of Fredericksburg has been recently revised by its author, Colonel William W. Blackford.

CONTENTS.

———·———

LIST OF MAPS.

———·———

New maps have been specially drawn for this edition by Clark Ray, with editorial supervision by Burke Davis.

THE LIFE AND CAMPAIGNS

OF

MAJOR-GENERAL J. E. B. STUART.

CHAPTER I.

ANCESTRY, BOYHOOD AND YOUTH.

JAMES EWELL BROWN STUART was born in Patrick County, Virginia, on the 6th of February, 1833.

His ancestry is traced on his father's side to Archibald Stuart, a native of Londonderry, Ireland, but of Scotch-Presbyterian parentage, who, about the year 1726, was compelled by religious persecution to fly from his native country. He found refuge in western Pennsylvania, where he remained in seclusion for seven years. At the expiration of this period the passage of an act of amnesty rendered it safe for him to disclose his hiding-place, and his wife and children joined him in his new home. About the year 1738 he removed from Pennsylvania to Augusta County, Va., where he acquired large landed estates, which, either during his lifetime or by will, he divided among his four children.

His second son and third child, Major Alexander Stuart, was early in the Revolutionary War commissioned as major in Colonel Samuel McDowell's regiment, in which he served throughout the war. During

Colonel McDowell's illness he commanded the regiment at the battle of Guilford Court House. Two horses were killed under him in this action, and he himself, dangerously wounded, was left upon the field and fell into the hands of the enemy. He was subsequently exchanged, and his sword was returned to him. This valued relic is now in the possession of his grandson, the Hon. Alexander H. H. Stuart, of Virginia. Major Stuart was a warm friend of education, and aided liberally in the endowment of the school which afterwards expanded into Washington College, and is now known as Washington and Lee University. He was a man of large stature and uncommon intelligence. He died at the advanced age of ninety years.

Judge Alexander Stuart, the youngest son of Major Alexander Stuart, was a lawyer by profession. He resided for some years in Cumberland County, Va., but having been elected a member of the Executive Council of the State, removed thence to Richmond. He subsequently resided in Illinois, where he held the office of United States Judge; and in Missouri, where he held office as United States Judge, Judge of the Circuit Court of the State, and Speaker of the Missouri Legislature. He died in Staunton, Va., in 1832, and was there buried.

The Hon. Archibald Stuart, of Patrick County, Va., the eldest son of Judge Alexander Stuart and the father of General J. E. B. Stuart, was an officer in the United States Army in the War of 1812. He embraced the profession of law. Throughout his long and eventful life he was actively engaged in the practice of his profession and in political life. He represented, first, the county of Campbell in the Virginia Legislature, and was repeatedly elected to both branches of that body from the county of Patrick. He was a member of the Constitutional Convention of 1829–30, and of the Convention of 1850. In this latter body, he and the Hon. Henry A. Wise were two of the four members residing east of the Blue Ridge who advocated a " white basis " of representation for the State. He represented the Patrick district in the Federal Congress during the Nullification agitation, and was a strong supporter of Mr. Calhoun in that crisis. He is represented as a man of splendid talents and wonderful versatility. " A powerful orator and advocate, he charmed the multitude on the hustings, and convinced juries and courts. In addition to these gifts, he was one of the most charming social companions the State ever produced. Possessing wonderful wit and humor, combined with rare gift for song, he at once became the centre of attraction at every social gathering. Among the people of the counties where he practised his name is held in great respect, and his memory is cherished with an affection rarely equalled in the history of any public man."

He married Elizabeth Letcher Pannill, of Pittsylvania County, Va., by whom he had four sons and six daughters. Among these, James E. B. Stuart was the seventh child and youngest son.

On his mother's side the ancestry of General Stuart is not less distinguished.

Giles Letcher was descended from ancient Welsh families — the Hughses, Gileses, and Leches. He was born in Ireland, to which country one of his ancestors had removed from Wales during the reign of Charles the Second. He emigrated to the New World before the Revolutionary War, and was married in Richmond, Va., to Miss Hannah Hughes, a lady of fortune and of Welsh extraction. He settled in Goochland County, Va. He had four sons and one daughter. His eldest son, Stephen Letcher, was the father of Governor Robert P. Letcher, of Kentucky. His third son, John Letcher, married the daughter of the Hon. Sam Houston, of Texas, and was the father of Governor John Letcher, of Virginia. His second son, William Letcher, removed to Pittsylvania County, Va., where he married Elizabeth Perkins, daughter of Nicholas Perkins, who owned a considerable estate upon the Dan River. He finally settled in Patrick County, on the Ararat, a small stream which rises in the Blue Ridge and empties into the Yadkin River in North Carolina.

The settlers in that part of Virginia were greatly annoyed by the Tories, who were numerous in North Carolina, and many encounters had taken place between them and the Whigs in that border land. William Letcher had served in a volunteer company from his county that had defeated the Tories at the battle of the Shallow Ford, on the Yadkin, a place which is still considered historic in that locality. This victory had inspired the Whigs with new courage ; and William Letcher, prominent among them, had openly expressed his determination to resist the robberies and depredations of the Tories, and to hunt them down to the death. In the latter part of June, 1780, while Mrs. Letcher was in her house alone with her infant daughter, then only six weeks old, a stranger appeared at the door and inquired for Mr. Letcher. There was nothing unusual in his manner, and Mrs. Letcher replied that her husband would soon be at home. While she was speaking, Mr. Letcher entered and invited the stranger to be seated. To this courtesy the stranger (he was a Tory named Nichols) replied by presenting his gun and saying: " I demand you in his Majesty's name." Letcher seized the gun to get possession of it; the Tory fired, and Letcher fell mortally wounded. He survived a few moments, but never spoke. Nichols fled. The terror-stricken wife despatched messengers to her relatives on the Dan River, who came to her as soon as possible, and attended to the burial of her husband. Nichols committed other murders and many robberies, but was finally overtaken in the southern part of North Carolina, and expiated his crimes on the gallows.

William Letcher was a man of fine appearance, and was greatly beloved and esteemed. His widow returned to her paternal home, with her little daughter Bethenia, and there remained until her second marriage with Colonel George Hairston, of Henry County, Va. In after years Bethenia Letcher married David Pannill, of Pittsylvania County, Va. Her daughter, Elizabeth Letcher Pannill, married Archibald Stuart.

She inherited from her grandfather, William Letcher, a beautiful and fertile farm in the southwestern part of Patrick County, which was named " Laurel Hill." Here her children were born. The large and comfortable house was surrounded by native oaks and was beautified with a flower garden, which was one of the childish delights of her son James, to whom she had transmitted her own passionate love of flowers. The site commanded a fine view of the Blue Ridge Mountains, and near at hand was the monument erected to the memory of William Letcher by his daughter Bethenia.

Amid these surroundings James Stuart passed a happy boyhood. He loved the old homestead with all the enthusiasm of his nature; and one of the fondest dreams of his manhood was that he might own the place of his birth, and there end his days in quiet retirement. He writes thus to his mother from Fort Leavenworth, in 1857 : —

I wish to devote one hundred dollars to the purchase of a comfortable log church near your place, because in all my observation I believe one is more needed in that neighborhood than any other that I know of; and besides, "charity begins at home." Seventy-five of this one hundred dollars I have in trust for that purpose, and the remainder is my own contribution. If you will join me with twenty-five dollars, a contribution of a like amount from two or three others interested will build a very respectable *free* church. . . . What will you take for the south half of your plantation? I want to buy it.

A near relative writes : —

I well remember his speaking thus to his brother in 1863 : "I would give anything to make a pilgrimage to the old place, and when the war is over quietly to spend the rest of my days there."

At the age of fourteen years James Stuart was placed at school in Wytheville; and in August, 1848, he entered Emory and Henry College. During a revival of religion among the students he professed conversion, and joined the Methodist Church. Throughout his after life he maintained a consistent Christian character. Ten years later, in 1859, he was confirmed in the Protestant Episcopal Church by Bishop Hawkes, in St. Louis. The reasons for this change in his church connections were simple and natural. His mother was an Episcopalian, and had early instilled into him a love for her own church. His wife was a member of the same communion. He found, also, that a majority of the chaplains in the United States Army at that time were Episcopalian divines, and he considered that his opportunities for Christian fellowship and church privileges would be increased by the change. His spirit toward all denominations of Christians was as far removed as possible from narrow sectarianism.

In April, 1850, James Stuart left Emory and Henry

College, having obtained an appointment as cadet in the United States Military Academy at West Point, on the recommendation of the Hon. T. H. Averett, of the Third District of Virginia. During his career as cadet, Stuart applied himself assiduously to study, and graduated thirteenth in a class of forty-six members. He appears to have been more ambitious of soldierly than of scholarly distinction, and held in succession the cadet offices of corporal, sergeant, orderly sergeant, captain of the second company, and cavalry sergeant; the last being the highest office in that arm of the service at the Academy. General Fitzhugh Lee speaks thus of this period : —

I recall his distinguishing characteristics, which were a strict attention to his military duties, an erect, soldierly bearing, an immediate and almost thankful acceptance of a challenge to fight from any cadet who might in any way feel himself aggrieved, and a clear, metallic, ringing voice.[1]

The reader must not suppose from this description that Stuart was an advocate of the duel. The difficulties referred to were of such a character as are always liable to occur between boys at school, especially where, under a military organization, boys bear authority over boys. Another fellow-cadet gives the testimony that Stuart was known as a " Bible-class man," but was always ready to defend his own rights or his honor ; and that the singular feature of his encounters with his fellow-students was, that his antagonists were physically far superior to him, and that although generally worsted in the encounter, Stuart always gained ground in the estimation of his fellows by his manly pluck and endurance. What his conduct was under these circumstances may be inferred from the following extracts from letters written by his father, who was a

[1] *Southern Historical Society Papers,* vol. i. p. 100.

man of prudence and of honor. Under date of June 15, 1853, Archibald Stuart thus writes to his son : —

I am proud to say that your conduct has given me entire satisfaction. I heard, it is true (but no thanks to you for the information), of the little scrape in which you involved yourself ; but I confess, from what I understand of the transaction, I did not consider you so much to blame. An insult should be resented under all circumstances. If a man in your circumstances gains credit by submitting to insult as a strict observer of discipline, he loses more in proportion in his standing as a gentleman and a man of courage.

Again on January 5, 1854, he writes : —

I have received your letter, and much regret that you have been involved in another fighting scrape. My dear son, I can excuse more readily a fault of the sort you have committed, in which you maintained your character as a man of honor and courage, than almost any other. But I hope you will hereafter, as far as possible, avoid getting into difficulties in which such maintenance may be demanded at your hands.

The relations existing between the father and son, as revealed by their correspondence during Stuart's cadetship, were of the most admirable character. Mutual affection was founded on mutual respect. As the time of graduation approached, the minds of both were greatly exercised over the important question of a choice of profession ; and while the father seems to have preferred that his son should adopt the profession of arms, he throws the responsibility of the decision on his son, as the one most interested in, and the one most capable of making, a wise decision. The religious element in Stuart's character seems to have had a decided influence at this crisis of his life, and he was doubtless led to his decision by that Providence in which he trusted, and which was even then preparing him for his after life. During his last year at West Point he writes thus to his father : —

I have not as yet any fixed course determined upon after graduation; still I can't help but regard it as the important crisis of my life. Two courses will be left for my adoption, the profession of arms and that of law; the one securing an ample support, with a life of hardship and uncertainty, — laurels, if any, dearly bought, and leaving an empty title as a bequeathment; the other an overcrowded thoroughfare, which may or may not yield a support, — may possibly secure honors, but of doubtful worth. Each has its labors and its rewards. In making the selection I will rely upon the guidance of Him whose judgment cannot err, for " it is not with man that walketh to direct his steps."

After Stuart had fairly embarked on his military career his father writes thus : —

Before I conclude I must express the deep solicitude I feel on your account. Just embarking in military life (a life which tests, perhaps more than any other, a young man's prudence and steadiness), at an immense distance from your friends, great responsibility rests upon your shoulders. It is true that you have, to start with, good morals fortified by religion, a good temper, and a good constitution, which if preserved will carry you through the trial safely. But the temptations of a camp to a young man of sanguine temperament, like yourself, are not to be trifled with or despised. I conjure you to be constantly on your guard, repelling and avoiding the slightest approach towards vice or immorality. You have to go through a fiery ordeal, but it is one through which many great and pious men have gone unscathed. But the greater portion have not escaped unscorched, and many have perished. Your military training at West Point will strengthen you greatly in the struggle. By it you have been taught the necessity of strict subordination to superiors, and of kind and conciliatory manners toward equals; and I trust that you will carry those lessons into practice now that you have exchanged the Academy for the camp.

Words of wisdom are these ; words which the young man laid close to his heart. No stain of vice or immorality was ever found upon him.

CHAPTER II.

IN TEXAS WITH THE MOUNTED RIFLEMEN.

IMMEDIATELY after graduation Stuart was commissioned as brevet second lieutenant in the regiment of Mounted Riflemen then serving in Texas. His commission is dated July 1, 1854. Owing to the prevalence of the yellow fever in New Orleans, through which city he must necessarily pass on his way to Texas, he was unable to join his regiment until December of that year. In the mean time he was commissioned as second lieutenant on October 31, 1854.

Almost the only information concerning this portion of Stuart's career comes from General John S. Simonson, formerly major of the Mounted Riflemen, who now passes in retirement the remaining years of a life of honorable activity in the service of his country. The following letter needs no further explanation : —

CHARLESTOWN, IND., December 27, 1880.

H. B. McCLELLAN, Lexington, Ky. :

SIR, — In reply to your inquiry for information as to General Stuart's services in the expedition against the Apache Indians in the years 1854 and 1855, I have to state that J. E. B. Stuart, then a second lieutenant, joined my command at Fort Clark, Texas, in December, 1854, and continued with it until May 8, 1855, when he was relieved to take advantage of his promotion to the 1st Cavalry. In the order relieving him I gave expression to the estimation in which he was held in complimentary terms, highly creditable to his character as a soldier and a gentleman. My order-book is lost, and I have no copy of that order. A copy was furnished Lieutenant Stuart, and may be among his papers.

Lieutenant Stuart was brave and gallant, always prompt in the execution of orders, and reckless of danger or exposure. I considered him at that time one of the most promising young officers in the United States Army. The expedition continued on duty in the mountains and valleys of western Texas, the El Paso Road, and the borders of the Rio Grande, until October, 1855. A large portion of country, little known at that day, was explored, and the Muscalero Apaches made to flee across the Rio Grande into Mexico. It would take a volume to contain the history of that expedition, — its scouts, marches, skirmishes, and privations. I enclose herewith slips containing a communication of Lieutenant Stuart to the Jeffersonian, a paper I think printed in Staunton, Va. It gives a full description of the difficulties and privations encountered in one of the scouts. These slips were pasted in, and cut from, my morning-report book. Lieutenant Stuart wrote another communication, which was printed in some paper in Virginia or Texas, giving an account of a fight, at the crossing of the Peacus River, with a band of Comanche Indians, by a portion of the troops of this expedition. . . .

Very respectfully, your obedient servant,

J. S. SIMONSON.

[*For the Jeffersonian.*]
CAMP STUART, TEXAS, Major Simonson's
Command, *February* 15, 1855.

DEAR SIR, — On the 6th instant this command, of the operations and character of which you learned something in a former letter from Fort Clark, was divided into two parties, one of which, under command of Captain Elliot, was sent below Presidio del Norte, on the Rio Grande, where the Indians were reported to be ; while the main body, under command of the Major, started on the trail of a more numerous party, leading toward the Sierra Guadalupe. A few notes on this scout, though unsuccessful as regards finding Indians, yet embracing an extensive region of which but little was previously known, may not be void of interest to the readers of the Jeffersonian.

The narrow trail led in the direction of a very rugged range of mountains, a circumstance which determined the substitution of pack-mules for wagons. The trail continued for about ten miles through a narrow ravine, surrounded by precipitous ridges of a species of red sandstone, which cropped out so frequently as to leave no space for vegetation except here and there a bunch of cactus of a singular variety. This ravine was soon headed by a high mountain, up whose steep side the trail wound its serpent way. Hardly had we reached the summit when a furious storm set in, first by a few preliminary drops, then in torrents of rain and hail. Welcome as was the change from six inches of dust to a refreshing shower, this time it came most inopportunely for the command, all of whom were well drenched with rain and benumbed with cold. Our march continued in this way for several miles, the storm so blinding us that we could scarcely discern the ground; when suddenly, not only had we debouched upon a level plain, but every vestige of the storm had vanished save a few raindrops which lingered on the grass. All nature rejoiced at the change, and the gorgeous splendor of a rainbow which hung in the west was interpreted as an omen of success to the scout. Thus you see that in Texas, instead of having to follow the circuit of the seasons for variety in climate, we can have May and December in one day in February. We were obliged to camp without water, a circumstance by no means uncommon with this expedition, for its operations have been very much circumscribed on account of the great scarcity of water.

Next day we started early on the march, having a bright day and a better road than before. Proceeding thus over a diversified track, alternately rough and smooth, — now a ridge covered with scrubby pine, then a ravine skirted by muskít-wood, but all the time gradually rising upon a table-land that seemed better clad with vegetation than any of the preceding, — we were suddenly checked by finding ourselves on the crest of a stupendous precipice. Up to this time we had led our horses over rough places from choice; it now became a matter of necessity; for the weight of a man on his horse would undoubtedly have precipitated both many hundred feet below. To look at the mountain from its base, any sane man would pronounce it impassable, for it seemed a vertical ledge of rock ; yet, strange to say, the Indian trail traversed its side in a zigzag manner to the base. The descent was extremely slow, and those in the rear of the line had ample opportunity to survey the prospect before them. I was raised in the Blue Mountains of Virginia, but never have I beheld anything to compare with the grandeur of the scenery from that Comanche pass. The ridge on which we stood extended in a straight line as far as the eye could reach north and south, sloping gradually toward the rear, but in front rising in huge columns of solid rock, or in vertical ledges, to a height of two thousand feet above the level plain at its base, which extended twenty-five miles across and sixty miles in a longitudinal direction. The other side of this broad valley was terminated by a similar range, rising to an equal height, but not so precipitous or continuous. To the north, the gray and rugged peaks of the Sierra Guadalupe limited the weary vision. In the centre of the valley, which was covered with grass and sand-banks, was, in appearance, a beautiful lake covered with ice ; but it proved to be a dry salt lagune, perfectly white with incrustations of nitre and salt. Long before the rear-guard had begun the descent, the advance had dwindled away over the plain to a mere speck in the distance. Before sundown, however, we were discussing our frugal fare on the verge of the salt lagune. In the immediate vicinity were several pools of salt water and one of strong sulphur. Next day the trail, instead of keeping the valley, passed up a narrow and steep gorge, nearly opposite the other pass, obstructed at every point by huge boulders, often six feet in diameter and almost spherical. It was evident that these difficult passes were selected on purpose to elude pursuit, for the road to-day was, if possible, more difficult than that of the day before. We soon began the ascent of another ridge, where the trail scarcely furnished footing for the animals. One mule, on which the surgeon had packed the entire dispensary of the command in two panniers, lost his footing and rolled over and over to the base of the cliff, all below taking care to give him a wide berth. Thanks, however, to the efficiency of the doctor's medicine, both mule and panniers escaped uninjured. Not far from the summit of this ridge we came upon the deserted Indian village. Their dismantled lodges were in perfect preservation, and enough was left to show that they had not been gone more than ten days. The circumspect manner in which their camp was laid out would have done credit to more scientific heads. It was carefully guarded against surprise by a system of flankers and advanced posts which occupied the prominent knolls around it. The main camp was concealed from a superficial observer by a dense cluster of pines. Each lodge, formed for a family, was constructed by bending a series of twigs after the manner of the bows of an ordinary wagon, the sharpened ends being driven into the ground, and the system connected at the top by a ridge-piece. Over all was thrown brushwood and straw in quantities sufficient for shelter. We camped near this village, and started early the next day for the Guadalupe Mountains, still about thirty miles distant, leading our horses the greater part of the way. There we met with a party of the 8th Infantry, commanded by Major James Longstreet, on a mission from El Paso similar to our own. He reported that some ten days before, his guide (a Mexican) had ridden some distance in advance of the party, and was found dead on the roadside. He was killed by a small party of Indians, who, being on foot, could not be pursued. From this point (Guadalupe Spring) Major Simonson determined to push on to Delaware Creek, along the road from El Paso to Fort Chadbourne, having strong hope of finding a hostile party there. We were, however, again destined to be disappointed, for that clear and lovely stream seemed never to have been polluted by the red man's presence.

. . . .

Our bivouac that night was lighted in a deep and narrow valley or *arroyo*, clothed in luxuriant grass. We had scarcely let our horses to grass when there came down the hollow a gust of wind which scattered our fire over the grass like a tornado, setting the whole prairie in a blaze in a few moments. It swept, apparently at one breath, over the entire camp, consuming bridles, saddles, blankets, caps, overcoats, and everything else that met its devouring grasp. Many of the horses were badly singed, nor did the men escape much better, for many lost their caps and had their beards closely singed. None of those encamped in that *arroyo* escaped without some loss. The deplorable condition of many of the command caused us to steer a straight course for Camp Stuart. We descended into the same broad valley by a different and less obstructed cañon from the other, in the bottom of which was the dry bed of a stream. At places this bed was a flat slate-like rock, on which were found some singular specimens of aboriginal drawing. It was done with a deep red substance not unlike Indian red. The characters were distinctly marked, and those which I examined particularly represented three warriors, one on horseback with his bow drawn, and two others on foot, similarly equipped. Their arrows being directed up the cañon suggested the idea that at the time they were made, three warriors had gone in that direction, leaving this drawing to indicate that fact to others of their tribe. They are pretty good draughtsmen on the human figure, but make very grotesque representations of horses. Next day we arrived in camp, which really seemed like home to us, and our floorless, chairless, and comfortless tents looked luxurious after a week's shelter beneath the broad canopy of heaven.

This camp was named in honor of Captain Stuart, of South Carolina, formerly in the Mounted Riflemen, and has heretofore been the rendezvous of the expedition; the Major expects, however, in a few days to move it to Guadalupe Spring, so as to operate from that point toward the Sacramento Mountains, where the Indians must be, if anywhere in this section of country. The party despatched below Presidio have not yet been heard from. They have not had time to return, as it is some distance below Fort Davis, which is about one hundred and ten miles below this place. If they succeed in jumping the Indians in that quarter, you will be apprised of the result by   Yours truly,   S.

A fragment of a letter written to his brother, Dr. John Stuart, gives some particulars concerning his own part in the expedition which a proper modesty prevented him from making public in the above letter.

These particulars are interesting since they show that in his first experiences in active service, Stuart exhibited that perseverance and quick ingenuity in overcoming difficulties which afterwards formed one of the most prominent of his characteristics as a general. Major Simonson had placed him in charge of the artillery, which followed the advance of the mounted men as fast as circumstances would permit. Stuart thus writes : —

Next day the artillery got along so well that I began to consider my difficulties at an end ; when, as we topped a ridge, to my utter amazement there burst upon my view one of the grandest spectacles of which nature can boast. More than fifteen hundred feet below me lay a broad valley, hemmed in on both sides by abrupt precipices of naked rock. To look from below any one would pronounce that precipice impassable to a man ; yet, strange to say, the Indian trail led in a zigzag manner down its side. The descent was conducted in a very slow and cautious manner, each man leading his horse with greatest care lest both be precipitated on those below. . . . In the mean time Jack came walking up and saluted me with, " Well ! Leftenant, what you gwine to do with the cannon ? "

I told him to remain on top until I went down and picked out a road. I will be candid enough to say, however, that when I left Jack my smallest hope was to find a place to take down the cannon ; but I did hope to find at the bottom an order from Major Simonson to abandon the piece. After a time I, in turn, reached the bottom, but found no order. I hitched my horse and started back up the mountain, determined to show Jack, as well as the Major, what a little determination could do. Reaching the top, I had the mules unhitched and started Jack down with them. I told the Captain of the company of Rangers, which had been detailed to remain in rear of the artillery in case I needed their services, that with the aid of his men I could transport the cannon down ; and that, as the Major had left no orders about it, I could not and would not forsake it. The captain acquiesced in my views. I unlimbered the piece, and started him down in command of the limber and twenty-five men, having previously pointed out the route. I took charge of the piece with twenty-five men ; and down we went, lowering it by lariat ropes, and lifting it over the rocks. We reached the bottom safely, and before night were sipping our coffee at the Major's bivouac. The Major told me that I deserved great credit for my success, and said that he never expected to see me bring the artillery down that mountain.

In the spring of 1855 the 1st and 2d Cavalry regiments were organized by Jefferson Davis, who was at that time Secretary of War. Officers were selected with the greatest care, and these new regiments contained many who were destined to attain great distinction in the Civil War.[1] Stuart was transferred to the 1st regiment. U. S. Cavalry with the rank of second lieutenant. On leaving the regiment of Mounted Riflemen, Major Simonson presented to him the following testimonial : —

CAMP BURDANK, TEXAS, *May* 8, 1855.

SIR, — While relieving you from duty in order to allow you to avail yourself of the present opportunity of anticipating the arrival of orders for duty in your regiment, I have felt reluctant thus to close your connection with this expedition and with the regiment of Mounted Riflemen, without adding to the official announcement of this separation the expression of the feelings with which I regard it.

During your service with Company G, your duties have, at times, been necessarily arduous, and it has afforded me pleasure to notice that under these circumstances you have not omitted to display that cheerfulness and zeal in their performance which, if persevered in, will not fail to be appreciated by those with whom you may serve, and to secure you a favorable reputation as an officer.

A regret for the loss of your services in the regiment is

---

[1] General J. A. Early gives a complete list of these distinguished men in the *Southern Historical Society Papers,* vol. iii. p. 142 *et seq.*

therefore mingled with the pleasure with which I offer my congratulations on your promotion, and my best wishes for your
future success and happiness.   With these sentiments of es-
teem and regard,

I remain very truly your friend,

JOHN S. SIMONSON, *Major R. M. R.,*

Commanding Expedition.

To Lieut. JAS. E. B. STUART,
   1*st Cavalry.*

CHAPTER III.

In August, 1855, the 1st Regiment U. S. Cavalry, which had been organized at Jefferson Barracks, St. Louis, was ordered to Fort Leavenworth, and Stuart was appointed by Colonel Sumner regimental quartermaster and commissary at that post. About the middle of September of this year his regiment was engaged in an expedition against the hostile Indians, in which no fighting occurred, but which occupied the regiment until the 4th of November, when it returned to Fort Leavenworth. During this expedition Stuart received the intelligence of the death of his father, and his letters show what sincere and unaffected sorrow this bereavement caused him. Only a short time before, he had asked and received from his father his approval of his marriage to Miss Flora Cooke, daughter of Colonel Philip St. George Cooke, of the 2d Dragoons. Arrangements having already been made for this event, the marriage was solemnized on the 14th of November, at Fort Riley, of which post Colonel Cooke was commandant.

On the 20th of December, 1855, Stuart was promoted to be first lieutenant in his regiment. During the following year the regiment was engaged in the attempt to preserve peace between the new settlers in Kansas Territory, in that exciting period when it was as yet undetermined whether Kansas would be a free or a slave State. It was at this time that he made the acquaintance with " Osawatomie Brown " which enabled him to identify Brown at Harper's Ferry in 1859.

In the year 1857 the 1st Cavalry was actively engaged in Indian warfare. The important event of the campaign was the battle fought upon the North Fork of Solomon's River, probably within the limits of the present Norton County, Kansas. The story of Stuart's connection with this campaign is best given in his own words.

The following letter was written at intervals on the two days succeeding the battle : —

CAMP ON SOLOMON'S FORK,
July 30, 1857.

MY DARLING WIFE, — Yesterday, after seventeen days' steady march from Camp Buchanan, we overtook about three hundred Cheyenne warriors drawn up in line of battle, and marching boldly and steadily toward us. We fronted into line as soon as possible (the six companies of cavalry), the infantry being too far behind to take any part in the action, also Bayard's battery, which the colonel stopped three or four miles back, as unable to keep up. It was my intention, and I believe that of most of the company commanders, to give a carbine volley and then charge with drawn pistols, and use the sabre as a *dernier ressort ;* but much to my surprise, the colonel ordered, " Draw sabres ! charge ! " when the Indians were within gunshot. We set up a terrific yell, which scattered the Cheyennes in disorderly flight, and we kept up the charge in pursuit. I led off company G right after their main body ; but very few of the company horses were fleet enough, after the march, beside my own brave Dan, to keep in reach of the Indians mounted on fresh ponies. My part of the chase led toward the right and front, and in that direction companies G, H, and D were, in a short time, mixed together in the pursuit, so that Stanley, McIntyre, McIntosh, Lomax, and myself were, for the greater part of the time, near each other, and frequently side by side. As long as Dan held out I was foremost ; but after a chase of five miles he failed, and I had to mount the horse of a private. When I overtook the rear of the enemy I found Lomax in imminent danger from an Indian, who was on foot and in the act of shooting him. I rushed to the rescue, and succeeded in wounding the Indian in his thigh. He fired at me in return with an Allen's revolver, but missed. About this time I observed Stanley and McIntyre close by. The former said: "Wait! I'll fetch him." He dismounted to aim deliberately, but in dismounting accidentally discharged his last load. Upon him the Indian now advanced with his revolver pointed. I could not stand that; but, drawing my sabre, rushed upon the monster and inflicted a severe wound on his head. At the same moment he fired his last barrel within a foot of me, the ball taking effect in the centre of the breast, but, by the mercy of God, glancing to the left, lodging near my left nipple, but so far inside that it cannot be felt. I rejoice to inform you that the wound is not regarded as dangerous, though I may be confined to my bed for weeks. I am now enjoying excellent health in every other respect.

I was able to dismount and lie down, before which the Indian, having discharged his last load, was dispatched by McIntyre and a man of company D. Lomax, who came to my relief, had some sabres stuck in the ground, and a blanket put up for shade. Dr. Brewer was sent for, but as it was eight miles to the place where the fight began, there was great delay. In the mean time the rally was sounded, and numbers collected around me, doing everything in their power for my comfort. Soon the colonel appeared, moving up at the head of the column from the rear. He greeted me in the most affectionate terms, and had me taken on a blanket back towards the first scene of action, where he intended to camp, as his horses were too much used up to continue the pursuit.

I was carried in the blanket about three miles, when I met the doctor, who examined the wound, bandaged it, etc. Soon after, I met the sick wagon, which consisted of the two hind wheels of the ambulance, with a tongue attached, the cushions being fastened on the spring. The rest of the ambulance had broken down weeks ago, and had been left behind. Three mules hitched to this bore me off, as it were, in a car of triumph. I suffered much from this mode of transportation, but

now (July 31st) feel pretty well, though I am entirely helpless as regards locomotion.

The colonel, after resting one day to bury Privates Cade,
of company G, and Lynch, of company A, and to recuperate
the horses, starts this morning on the chase.

Captain Foote's company, Dr. Covey, and Lieutenant Mc-
Cleary are left here, with myself and the other wounded and
sick. I have every reason to believe that I will be able to resume duty in about ten days or two weeks. I have received
every attention from my fellow officers, for which I shall ever
be grateful. I send this by Colburn, in case an express is sent
in by Colonel Sumner before his return here. We will, in a
day or two, be reduced to fresh beef alone. The regiment
will return to Leavenworth, I think, certainly before the 1st of
November. See Mrs. McIntyre, and tell her all left in fine
spirits.

Fort Floyd, Cheyenne Expedition,
August 1, 1857.

After the command left yesterday I was taken on a litter to
a little field fortification built under the direction of Lieutenant
McCleary, quite respectable for the means at hand. A tent-
fly was stretched a few paces outside, and there Dr. Covey and
myself and Ben established our ranch. We have a pretty view
up the creek for about two miles, my bed being sufficiently inclined to enable me to see. It is very hot to-day. I can sit up
a little with props, and seize a moment now and then to jot a
daily token to my wife. The day drags heavily. My Prayer-
Book — which I must say has not been neglected — and my
Army Regulations are my only books. A few sheets of " Harper's Weekly " are treasures indeed. The doctor requires me
to keep very quiet. My wound does not pain me when lying
still. Dr. Covey is as kind as a brother could be. He tells
me my wound is doing finely. The wounded in the hospital,
he says, are doing remarkably well, and he has strong hope
that all will recover.

August 5th. The Cheyennes who attacked us last night were
about twenty or thirty. Before daylight this morning another
alarm. Every gun was in hand, when we could hear in the
distance " Pawnee ! Pawnee ! " and presently five men were

seen running directly toward us on foot. We immediately surmised that they were Colonel Sumner's Pawnee guides, which
proved to be true. They made signs that Colonel Sumner
had sent them with letters to Fort Kearny, and while on their
way, an hour or two ago, the Cheyennes had attacked them
and taken their ponies, and they, after killing one Cheyenne,
barely made their escape. They said they had another letter
for Captain Foote, but that the Cheyennes had torn it up.
They said that the colonel's orders were for Captain Foote to
go directly to Fort Kearny. Among the letters they had for
Fort Kearny was the one I had written July 31st, and given to
Colburn. I opened it and took possession. I have not eaten
any meat since wounded until to-day. I am able to walk
about a little.

August 6th. I am still rapidly improving. Captain Foote
held a council of war, and determined to start for Kearny on
Saturday, the 8th, the doctor deciding that the wounded
would be able to be carried then.

FORT KEARNY, N. T., *August* 19, 1857.

MY DEAREST WIFE, — I arrived here night before last,
having left Captain Foote, who has not yet arrived, three days
before. Before beginning my *letter* I will extend the narrative of our march from Fort Floyd.

August 8th. Packed up and left this forsaken region, I riding on horseback, which does not appear to fatigue me. We
are almost reduced to fresh beef alone for food. The command is, and has been, since August the 2d. The three
wounded men, who are unable to ride, are conveyed in an
affair on the Indian style, which is nothing more than two
poles lashed to a mule, like the shafts of a wagon, the other
ends dragging; having lashed across them a sort of basket-
work of strips of rawhide, in which the wounded man re-
clines in comparative comfort; men walking in rear to lift the
ends over rough places. We travel very slow. Camp ten miles
out, at a little mud hole. The Pawnee guides say that we will
reach Kearny four days after to-day. We hardly expect it.

August 9th. Went fourteen miles and encamped on a creek;
our course northeast, as well as we can tell by the stars. *No
compass in the command.*

August 14*th*. A heavy fog envelopes us this morning, and to our utter amazement and consternation we find on starting that the *Pawnees are gone.* The rascals, our sole dependence for guidance, have deserted us in this thick fog, when most needed. The wounded, particularly First Sergeant McKeown, are in great jeopardy. Yes! we are lost! lost in a fog! no compass, no guide! The sun is obscured for the day. We let the Cheyenne (a prisoner) guide us. He seems to understand what we want, and signifies that he can go to Kearny. We marched twenty miles, but no Kearny, which we were to meet to-day, according to the Pawnees. We camp by a little dry-bed stream; very little water in a hole. At night the stars, blessed stars, appear, and reveal to us the north, which we mark for to-morrow, by objects placed. To save unnecessary marching to the command, which is worn out by the hard march and scanty rations, many of the men being barefooted, I volunteer to start to-morrow with a small party to look for Fort Kearny ; and as McCleary wishes to go, I ask for him and one or two men ; among whom the captain sends a cowardly Mexican guide of Laramie. He was all the time creating discontent by contending that Fort Kearny was south of us, and secretly created discouragement among the men.

August 15*th*. The morning came, but was completely enveloped in fog. We waited until noon, and resolved to go anyhow. The suffering wounded were too strong an appeal for me to resist. We started out to go east, which Captain Foote insisted must be the course; whereas I wished to go northeast. As it was cloudy, the only way by which we could approximate the course was by keeping two of the party successively stationed on the line, the remainder trotting on the prolongation as fast as the process would allow. We got along pretty well until five P. M., when another storm came up. I established points to show our course, and waited quietly under some trees for the storm to abate. After the rain we pushed on for about half an hour, when it became so dark that I again planted stakes to mark the route, and camped for the night. We had hardly finished picketing our horses along the edge of a grassy ravine, when the storm of wind and rain, of thunder and lightning, was renewed with great violence. There we sat, every man squatted on his saddle, revealed in gloomy out-lines only by the lightning's flash, a picture I can never for-get. The night of the 13th was nothing in comparison. We were all sleepy, and were dozing through the night in this way, when a flash of lightning revealed, instead of the pretty grass plat, a large mass of water before us half way up the bodies of our horses, and rising rapidly. We ran to extricate them, and had barely time to make good our retreat with horses and saddles to higher ground.

August 16*th*. At the first dawn of day we saddled up. McCleary proposed that we should go to timber and make a big fire to warm ourselves. I told him that under such cir-cumstances we ought to endure anything rather than delay, when our speedy arrival at Kearny was of such vital im-portance to the command. To this he readily agreed. We started on the same course : the day was cloudy, but for a few moments at seven o'clock the sun dashed into view, as if by a merciful dispensation of Providence, showing that we were going south-southeast instead of east. I established an east and west line while the sun was visible, and then started northeast. I shall always suspect that the Mexican, who alter-nated with me in taking the point of direction, deflected the line toward the right according to his absurd notion of the whereabouts of Kearny. At four P. M. our course was stopped by an impassable stream, flooded, very deep, and with precipi-tous banks. We were obliged to abandon our course and pro-ceed up this stream until it could be headed. Our direction was now southeast, as well as we could guess. Soon we struck a plain wagon trail, a miracle to us. It led south-southeast, but we hoped it would take us somewhere. I surmised that it was Lieutenant Bryan's road from the Republican to Fort Kearny, and we followed it eagerly at a trot for three hours, during which it appeared that we had been going in a circle ; for a tree on our left was visible constantly, and apparently at the same distance. Dark overtook us and we encamped. Ben had two small slices of beef for each of us. I devoured one. I set a man on watch for the stars in case they should appear, in order that I might take a reckoning. I was almost in despair. I began to fear that this road was merely the trail of some hunting party, or of traders who had nothing to do with Fort Kearny; and when I thought of Captain Foote's command and the wounded sufferers, I never before felt so much anxiety and responsibility. From the first I prayed God to be my guide, and I felt an abiding hope that all would be well with us. During the night the cavalry corporal waked me to see the stars. I rejoiced to find that our course now was due north, which I knew was safe.

August 17th. At dawn we saddled up, somewhat encouraged by the prospects. We followed the trail two or three miles, when we found that the road led directly across a very considerable stream, now entirely out of its banks and very swift. I felt that we must cross that stream. I had not the most remote idea where we were, but I saw that to go around it, or to wait until it fell, would take a week. McCleary demurred; and the cowardly Mexican, who was mounted on a beautiful Indian pony, that could, I knew, swim anywhere, said, " Too deep! Me no swim." I was determined to cross it, if I crossed alone; and giving the cavalry corporal permission to swim the Mexican's pony, we started. Our animals struck out for the other bank, but the current bore them down considerably; and Dan, getting his feet entangled, fell over backwards, and unhorsed me. I swam to the opposite bank, although encumbered by my clothing. Dan came over too. The mules crossed with more or less difficulty, and then McCleary and the infantrymen swam the stream. All were now over except the Mexican, who protested that he could not get across: " Me no swim." I could not be deaf to the voice of humanity, and planned an arrangement to help him, when to our amazement the rascal swam over better than any one had done.

Meantime the cavalry sergeant had gone up the bank a short distance, and reported a plain wagon road and a fresh trail. I then knew that this stream was the Big Blue, and at least fifty miles below Kearny, on the Leavenworth road. It was now seven o'clock A. M., and cold and wet as we were, there was no time to be lost. I thanked God for the merciful deliverance, and we started for Kearny, travelling five miles an hour. About noon we met the Kearny mail for the States. We got some news and a piece of hard bread, the most delicious morsel I ever tasted. We arrived here in good time that afternoon, having travelled fifty-five measured miles since morning. We found the officers here, Marshall and Bryant and Summers, much alarmed about us. The Pawnees had come in three days before and reported us close at hand. Parties had been sent out as far as twenty-five miles in all directions to look for us, but without success. Our plans were soon formed. We sent Jeffreys, the interpreter, and the best of our Pawnees, with an ambulance and two wagons loaded with hard bread and luxuries for the sick and the well, and a sufficient escort; with instructions to go to the point where we had been deserted by the Pawnees, and thence to follow Captain Foote's trail until he was found.

The relief party sent out after Captain Foote found him without delay, and within four days the sick and wounded were brought safely to Fort Kearny.

CHAPTER IV.

THE JOHN BROWN RAID.

FROM the fall of 1857 until the summer of 1860 Stuart was stationed at Fort Riley with six companies of the 1st Cavalry, under the command of Major John Sedgwick.

In the winter of 1858–59 he invented a sabre attachment, for which he obtained a patent from the government. Having received a six months' leave of absence, he passed the summer of 1859 among his relatives in Virginia, and while attending the General Convention of the Episcopal Church, in Richmond, in October, was called to Washington to negotiate with the War Department concerning the sale of his sabre attachment. While in Washington on this business the news was received of the " John Brown Raid " at Harper's Ferry. Stuart was requested to convey to Arlington a secret communication to Lieutenant-Colonel Robert E. Lee, who had been selected to command the marines sent to suppress the insurrection. Although the facts had been carefully concealed, Stuart perceived that something unusual was transpiring, and volunteered his services as aid to Colonel Lee.

The following extracts are taken from a letter which he wrote to his mother from Fort Riley, in January, 1860. Several contemporary newspaper accounts gave to him the credit of having led the attack upon the engine house in which John Brown had taken refuge, an honor which Stuart is careful to disclaim.

Colonel Lee was sent to command the forces at Harper's Ferry. I volunteered as his aid. I had no command whatever. The United States marines are a branch of the naval force, — there was not an enlisted man of the army on hand. Lieutenant Green was sent in command. Major Russell had been requested by the Secretary of the Navy to accompany the marines, but, being a paymaster, could exercise no command; yet it was his corps. For Colonel Lee to have put me in command of the storming party would have been an outrage to Lieutenant Green, which would have rung through the navy for twenty years. As well might they send him out here to command my company of cavalry. . . .

I, too, had a part to perform, which prevented me in a measure from participating in the very brief onset made so gallantly by Green and Russell, well backed by their men. I was deputed by Colonel Lee to read to the leader, then called *Smith*, a demand to surrender immediately ; and I was instructed to leave the door after his refusal, which was expected, and wave my cap; at which signal the storming party was to advance, batter open the doors, and capture the insurgents at the point of the bayonet. Colonel Lee cautioned the stormers particularly to discriminate between the insurgents and their prisoners.

I approached the door in the presence of perhaps two thousand spectators, and told *Mr. Smith* that I had a communication for him from Colonel Lee. He opened the door about four inches, and placed his body against the crack, with a cocked carbine in his hand : hence his remark after his capture that he could have wiped me out like a mosquito. The parley was a long one. He presented his propositions in every possible shape, and with admirable tact ; but all amounted to this : that the only condition upon which he would surrender was that he and his party should be allowed to escape. Some of his prisoners begged me to ask Colonel Lee to come and see him. I told them he would never accede to any terms but those he had offered ; and as soon as I could tear myself away from their importunities I left the door and waved my cap, and Colonel Lee's plan was carried out. . . .

When *Smith* first came to the door I recognized old *Osa-*

watomie Brown, who had given us so much trouble in Kansas. No one present but myself could have performed that service. I got his bowie-knife from his person, and have it yet.

The same day, about eleven or twelve o'clock, Colonel Lee requested me, as Lieutenant Green had charge of the prisoners and was officer of the guard, to take a few marines and go over to old Brown's house, four and a half miles distant, in Maryland, and see what was there. I did so, and discovered the magazine of pikes, blankets, clothing, and utensils of every sort. I could only carry off the pikes, as I had but one wagon. The next day I was occupied in delivering the various orders of Colonel Lee, and in other duties devolving on an aid-de-camp. The night after, Colonel Lee, Green, and myself, with thirty marines, marched six miles and back on a false alarm among the inhabitants of a district called Pleasant Valley.

The prisoners having been turned over to the United States Marshal, Colonel Lee and the marines were ordered back to Washington. I went with him, and this terminated my connection with the Harper's Ferry affair.

CHAPTER V.

FIRST MANASSAS; DRANESVILLE.

In the summer of 1860 the 1st regiment U. S. Cavalry was ordered from Fort Riley to make a demonstration against the Comanche and other hostile Indians, and when on the head-waters of the Arkansas, received instructions to remain in that section and select a site for a new fort. This was done about midsummer, and the fort now known as Fort Lyon was begun. Here the regiment wintered.

In March, 1861, Lieutenant Stuart obtained a two months' leave of absence. Having resolved to direct his own course by the action of his native State in regard to secession, he wished to place himself in such position that he could either return to Virginia or remove his family to Fort Lyon when the decision of Virginia was made known. He now repaired to St. Louis, where he passed three weeks in uncertainty. Returning to Fort Riley, he there learned that Virginia had passed the ordinance of secession. His leave of absence had not yet expired, and he at once removed his family to St. Louis, and took passage on a river steamboat for Memphis. Much excitement existed in St. Louis, but keeping his own counsel, he was enabled to avoid all difficulty. When the boat landed at Cairo, Stuart forwarded to the War Department his resignation as an officer in the United States Army. Almost immediately thereafter he received the notification of his promotion to captaincy in his regiment. On the 7th of May he reached Wytheville, Va., and on the same day his resignation was accepted by the War Department. He now proceeded at once to Richmond, Va., and offered his sword in the defence of his native State.

His first commission in the Southern army was that of lieutenant-colonel of infantry, dated May 10, 1861, with orders to report to Colonel T. J. Jackson, at Harper's Ferry. This commission was issued by the State of Virginia. On July 16, 1861, he received from the same source his commission as colonel of cavalry. On the 24th of September of the same year he was made brigadier-general by the Confederate States' government, and on July 25, 1862, he was commissioned major-general by the same authority.

The cavalry under Stuart's command in June, 1861, numbered only twenty-one officers and three hundred and thirteen men present for duty,[1] and yet such was his activity that a front of more than fifty miles was efficiently watched, and every important movement of the enemy was duly reported. It was in reference to these services that General Joseph E. Johnston, when subsequently transferred to the West, wrote privately to Stuart: "How can I eat, sleep, or rest in peace without you upon the outpost?"

On July 1, 1861, Major-General R. Patterson crossed the Potomac at Williamsport and advanced into Virginia, with the intention of operating against the army of General Joseph E. Johnston, at Winchester, and of preventing him from sending reinforcements to Manassas, upon which point McDowell was about to advance. The early discovery of this movement by Stuart enabled General Johnston to send Colonel T. J.

[1] *Official Records*, vol. ii. p. 187.

Jackson's brigade to the assistance of the cavalry north of Martinsburg. Jackson was ordered to resist the advance of any small body, but to retire under cover of the cavalry if the enemy appeared in force. The result of this movement was " the affair at Falling Waters," in which Jackson, with one regiment of his brigade, numbering three hundred and eighty men, and one piece of artillery, detained the advance of Patterson's column, and compelled him to deploy an entire division for the attack. Jackson then retired beyond Martinsburg, having lost eleven men wounded and nine missing.[1]

While operating on the flank of Jackson's infantry, Stuart encountered a danger which might have been fatal to him, but which his quick courage converted into the discomfiture of others. Emerging suddenly from a thick piece of woods while riding alone in advance of his men, he found himself in the presence of a considerable body of Federal infantry, and separated from them only by a fence. Riding toward them without hesitation, he directed some of the men, who probably mistook him for one of their own officers, to throw down the fence. This was quickly done ; when Stuart ordered the whole party to lay down their arms on the peril of their lives. Bewildered by the boldness of the transaction the men obeyed, and filing them off through the gap in the fence, Stuart soon had them surrounded by his troopers. His prize proved to be forty-nine men of the 15th Pennsylvania volunteers, almost an entire company organization.

Immediately upon the withdrawal of Colonel Jackson, General Johnston moved his army forward to Darksville, and for four days offered battle to Patterson. The challenge was declined, and Johnston retired

[1] *Official Records,* vol. ii. pp. 185, 186.

to Winchester that he might be in position to reinforce Manassas. On the 15th of July General Patterson advanced to Bunker's Hill, nine miles from Winchester, and on the 17th moved to Smithfield, as if to
attack General Johnston from the south. This movement failed to deceive General Johnston, who on the
18th commenced his march from Winchester to Piedmont Station. So skilfully was this movement screened
by the dispositions which Stuart made of his cavalry,
that General Patterson does not appear to have been
aware of it until the 21st of July,[1] on which day Johnston's forces were actively engaged at Bull Run.

Johnston's infantry was transported by railroad from
Piedmont to Manassas; but Stuart's little band of horsemen made the march across the country in due time, and
actively participated in the battle. General Johnston
thus describes the supreme moment of the battle:[2] —

We had now sixteen guns and two hundred and sixty cavalry and a little above nine regiments of the Army of the
Shenandoah, and six guns and less than the strength of three
regiments of that of the Army of the Potomac, engaged with
about thirty-five thousand United States troops, among whom
were full three thousand of the old regular army. Yet this
admirable artillery and brave infantry and cavalry lost no foot
of ground. For nearly three hours they maintained their position, repelling five successive assaults by the heavy masses of
the enemy, whose numbers enabled him continually to bring
up fresh troops as their preceding columns were driven back.
Colonel Stuart contributed to one of these repulses by a well
timed and vigorous charge on the enemy's right flank with
two companies of his cavalry.

General T. J. Jackson says:[3] —

Apprehensive lest my flanks should be turned, I sent orders

[1] *Official Records*, vol. ii. p. 172.
[2] *Official Records*, vol. ii. pp. 475, 476.
[3] *Official Records*, vol. ii. p. 481.

to Colonels Stuart and Radford, of the cavalry, to secure them. Colonel Stuart, and that part of his command with him, deserve great praise for the promptness with which they moved to my left and secured the flank by timely charging the enemy and driving him back.

The Official Records give a very inadequate idea of the real service which Stuart performed on this memorable day. I am, however, permitted to make the following extract from an unpublished manuscript narrative, written by General J. A. Early in the years 1867–68, which shows that at the very crisis of the day Stuart held the turning-point of the field, and that with the insignificant force under his command he contributed in no small degree to the final victory.

General Early thus writes : —

Toward three P. M. we neared the field of battle, and began to perceive the scenes usual in the rear of an army engaged in action. On entering the road leading from the Lewis House towards Manassas, we met quite a stream of stragglers and skulkers going to the rear, and were informed by them that everything was over with us. Some of the men said that their regiments had been entirely cut to pieces, and that there was no use for them to remain any longer. It was to the encouraging remarks of this stream of recreants that my command was exposed as it moved on, but not a man fell out of ranks. I moved on, soon meeting General Johnston himself, who rode toward us when he discovered our approach, and expressed his gratification at our arrival. I asked him at once to show me my position, to which he replied that he was too much engaged at present to do that in person, but would give me directions as to what I was to do. He then directed me to move to our extreme left and attack the enemy on their right; stating that by directing my march along the rear of our line, by the sound of the firing in front, there could be no mistake ; and he cautioned me to take especial care to clear our whole line before advancing to the front, and to be particular and not fire on any of our own men, which he was sorry to say had been done in some instances.

Affairs now wore a gloomy aspect, and from all the indications in the rear, the day appeared to be going against us. . . .
Immediately in front of us was a body of woods extending
towards our left, in which there was the constant rattle of
musketry, and I moved along the rear, crossing the road from
Manassas to Sudley, and inclining to the left so as to clear
our line entirely. . . . As I approached the open space
beyond, a messenger came galloping to me from Colonel,
afterwards General, J. E. B. Stuart, who was on our extreme
left with two companies of cavalry and a battery of artillery
under Lieutenant Beckham, stating that the colonel said that
the enemy was about giving way, and if we would hurry up
they would soon be in retreat.   This was the first word of en-
couragement I had received after reaching the vicinity of the
battle-field.   I was then making all the haste the condition of
my men, who were much blown, would permit ; and I directed
my march to a field immediately on the left of the woods, and
between Stuart's position and the left of our infantry then
engaged.   The messenger from Stuart soon returned at a gallop, and stated that the colonel said the enemy had only retired his right behind a ridge now in my front, and was moving another flanking column behind said ridge still farther to
our right; and he cautioned me to look out for this new column.   The fact was that Stuart, who had been for some time
in position beyond our extreme left watching the enemy's
movements, had, by the judicious use of Beckham's guns on
his right flank, kept the enemy in check, and prevented him
from flanking Elzey, then on the extreme left of our infantry.
It was mainly by the fire poured from Beckham's guns into
the enemy, who had moved a column in front of the lower
end of the ridge mentioned, in order to flank Elzey, that that
column had been forced to retire, just as I was approaching,
behind the ridge, producing on Stuart the impression that the
enemy was about to retreat.
     Having cleared the woods entirely, I moved to the front in
order to form line against the flanking column of the enemy
which was reported forming behind the ridge in front of me.
Just at this time I observed a body of our troops move from a
piece of woods on my immediate right across an open space to
another in front of it, and this proved to be the left regiment

of Elzey's brigade. I heard a rapid fire open from the woods into which this regiment had moved, and a body of the enemy appeared on the crest of the ridge immediately in my front, preceded by a line of skirmishers. This ridge is the one on which was situated the Chinn House, so often mentioned in the descriptions of this battle and the subsequent one near the same position. It is a high ridge, sloping off to our right and terminating in front of the position occupied by Elzey. The enemy had the decided advantage, as my troops had to form in the low ground on our side of the ridge near a small stream which runs along its base. The formation of my troops was in full view of the enemy; and his skirmishers, who were about four hundred yards in front of us, opened on my men, while forming, with long-range rifles or Minie muskets. . . .

As we advanced the enemy disappeared behind the crest, and while we were ascending the slope, Lieutenant McDonald, acting aid to General Elzey, came riding rapidly towards me and requested me not to let my men fire on the troops in my front, stating that they consisted of the 13th Virginia regiment of Elzey's brigade. I said to him: "They have been firing on my men;" to which he replied, "I know they have, but it is a mistake; I recognized Colonel Hill of the 13th and his horse." This was a mistake on the part of Lieutenant McDonald, arising from a fancied resemblance of a mounted officer with the enemy to the colonel of the 13th. This regiment did not, in fact, reach the battle-field at all. This information and the positive assurance of Lieutenant McDonald caused me to halt my troops and ride to the crest of the hill, when I observed a regiment about two hundred yards to my right, drawn up in line in front of the woods where Elzey's left was. The dress of the volunteers on both sides at that time was very similar, and the flag of the regiment was drooping around the flag-staff so that I could not see whether it was the flag of the United States or the Confederate flag. The very confident manner of Lieutenant McDonald induced me to believe that this must also be one of our regiments. Colonel Stuart had advanced on my left with his two companies of cavalry and Beckham's artillery, and passing around Chinn's house had caused the battery to open fire upon the regiment I was observing. Thinking it must certainly be one of our regiments, I started a messenger to Colonel Stuart to give him the information and request him to stop the fire ; but a second shell or ball from Beckham's guns, which passed not over twenty feet in front of me, caused the regiment to face about and retire rapidly, when I saw the United States flag unfurl, and discovered the mistake into which I had been led by Lieutenant McDonald. I immediately ordered my command forward, and Kemper's and Hays' regiments advanced to the crest of the ridge. All this occurred in less time than it has taken to describe it. On reaching the crest we came in view of the Warrenton turnpike and the plains beyond, and discovered the enemy in full retreat across and beyond the turnpike. . . .

We were now on the extreme left of the whole of our infantry force and in advance of the main line. The only troops on our left of any description were the two companies of cavalry and Beckham's battery with Stuart. On my immediate right and a little to the rear was Elzey's brigade, and away farther to the right I saw our line extending towards Bull Run, but I discovered no indications of a forward movement. My troops were now very much exhausted, especially Hays' regiment, which had been marching nearly all the morning before our movement toward the battle-field ; and it was necessary to give the men a little time to breathe. Beckham's guns had continued firing on the retreating enemy until the latter was beyond their range, and Colonel Stuart went in pursuit with his cavalry, followed by Beckham's battery.

As soon as my men had rested for a brief period, I directed my brigade to advance in column of divisions along the route over which we had seen the enemy retreating, and I sent information to the troops on my right of my purpose to move along their front, with the request not to fire on us. I then moved forward, crossing Young's Branch and the Warrenton turnpike to the north side. When we got into the valley of Young's Branch we lost sight of the enemy, and on ascending to the plains north of the turnpike we could see nothing of his retreating forces. Passing to the west and north of the houses known as the Dogan House, the Stone Tavern, the Matthew House, and the Carter House or Pittsylvania House, and being guided by the abandoned haversacks and muskets, we moved over the ground on which the battle had begun with Evans' command in the early morning, and continued our march until we had cleared our right entirely. We had now got to a point where Bull Run makes a considerable bend above the Stone Bridge, and I halted, as we had not observed any movement from the main line. Nothing could be seen of the enemy, and their troops had scattered so much in the retreat that it was impossible to tell what route they had taken. Moreover, the country was entirely new and unknown to me. I therefore desisted from any farther effort at pursuit. Stuart with his cavalry and Beckham's guns had crossed the run above me, and Cocke's regiment had also moved towards a ford above where I halted.

It was this movement of mine from our extreme left along the front of our line that produced the erroneous impression, under which some newspaper correspondents wrote from the battle-field, that General Kirby Smith had gotten off the train at Gainesville, and moved directly to where the battle was raging ; as my command when first seen from our right was moving from the direction of Gainesville.

Generals Johnston and Beauregard have both attributed the turning of the tide of battle to the movement of my brigade against the enemy's right, — the former in his "Narrative," and the latter in a letter on the origin of the Confederate battle-flag. General Johnston in his "Narrative" says that on my way to attack the enemy's right I was "reinforced by five companies of cavalry commanded by Colonel Stuart and a battery under Lieutenant Beckham." Stuart had only two companies of cavalry with him, and he was in position on the extreme left when I arrived, and had been there for some time, rendering very efficient and valuable service by keeping the enemy's right in check, and thwarting the efforts to flank our left until my timely arrival. But for his presence there, I am of opinion that my brigade would have arrived too late to be of any service, as by falling upon the left and rear of Elzey's brigade, the enemy would probably have ended the battle before my brigade reached that point.

*Stuart did as much towards saving the battle of First Ma-
nassas as any subordinate who participated in it ; and yet he*

has never received any credit for it, in the official reports or otherwise. His own report is very brief and indefinite.

The force at Stuart's command was utterly inadequate to the pursuit of McDowell's routed army; but Stuart followed the fugitives for a distance of twelve miles, and until his command had been reduced to a mere handful by the sending of prisoners to the rear.

While Stuart was thus engaged on the extreme left, the 30th Virginia regiment, Cavalry, under Colonel R. C. W. Radford, rendered effective service on the right flank of Jackson's command. At the turning-point of the battle Colonel Radford charged one of the enemy's batteries, killed the horses attached to two pieces, and captured Colonel Corcoran, of the 69th New York regiment, with his colors and a number of prisoners. Colonel Radford made a second charge against a force of infantry and artillery, in which it seems that his cavalry was repulsed, but he continued to follow the retreating enemy. Lieutenant-Colonel T. T. Munford, with four companies of the 30th Virginia, aided in these movements on Colonel Radford's right. Both Colonel Radford and Colonel Munford claim that the attacks made by them caused the stampede and blockade of the enemy's vehicles near Cub Run bridge, which resulted in the capture of fourteen pieces of artillery, with wagons and ambulances.

The battle of Bull Run was succeeded by many months of inactivity to the main armies, during which the cavalry was engaged in not infrequent skirmishes and reconnoissances, the result of which was to cement the mutual confidence between Stuart and his men. Outpost duty with Stuart did not consist in the mere routine of establishing pickets and posting videttes; it was the school of instruction for his inexperienced but willing soldiers, and he himself was their ready and thorough instructor. In these early days, too, Stuart marked out for promotion more than one gallant spirit who served under him with distinction in subsequent and more important campaigns. Beckham, who handled his guns so well at Manassas, commanded the horse artillery after the death of Pelham, and proved himself no unworthy successor of that young hero. Promoted to chief of artillery of Hood's army, he laid down his life before the intrenchments at Nashville. Rosser, of the Washington Artillery, courted distinction under the eye of Stuart ; and owed his subsequent rank as much to the favor of that officer, and to the restraints which he threw about him, as he did to his own unquestioned talents, — a debt which he has of late but ill repaid by unnecessary reflections on the military character of his dead chief.

With restless activity Stuart pursued a well-directed system of annoyance against the Federal pickets, drove them from Mason's, Munson's, and Upton's hills, and established his own headquarters on Munson's Hill, with his pickets within sight of the spires of Washington. Here he maintained himself for some weeks.

On the 11th of September a reconnoissance was made to Lewinsville by a force of about 1,800 Federal infantry and cavalry, with four pieces of artillery, commanded by Colonel I. I. Stevens, of the 79th New York Infantry. This force was subsequently augmented by the arrival of other portions of the brigade under Brigadier-General W. F. Smith. The object of the reconnoissance was to examine the ground in the vicinity of Lewinsville, with a view to its permanent occupancy. Stuart was informed of this movement, and started about midday to oppose it. He took with him three hundred and five men of the 13th Virginia Infantry, one section of Rosser's battery, and two companies of the 1st

Virginia Cavalry. Before he could reach Lewinsville the enemy had been in occupation of the place for some hours, and having completed their examination of the ground, were about to retire. Stuart attacked their right flank as their skirmishers were in the act of withdrawing. It seems from the Federal reports that this attack was accompanied by the effects of a surprise, and that no vigorous resistance was offered, and no effort made to develop the strength of Stuart's attack. The Federal troops were content to have made a successful reconnoissance. They acknowledge the loss of two killed, thirteen wounded, and three missing. Stuart lost neither man nor horse.[1]

During this period Stuart was reporting to General James Longstreet, who commanded the advance forces of the Confederate army. His activity and capacity could not fail to secure the approbation of his superior officers and their united efforts for his advancement. Already, on the 10th of August, in a letter to President Davis, General Johnston had thus recommended his promotion : —

He is a rare man, wonderfully endowed by nature with the qualities necessary for an officer of light cavalry. Calm, firm, acute, active, and enterprising, I know no one more competent than he to estimate the occurrences before him at their true value. If you add a real brigade of cavalry to this army, you can find no better brigadier-general to command it.[2]

On the 24th of September, 1861, Stuart received his promotion as brigadier-general. The loss of most of the cavalry records at the close of the war renders it impossible to state with certainty the original organization of the cavalry brigade; but the " General Order-Book," which still survives, shows that in December,

---

[1] *Official Records*, vol. ii. p. 167 *et seq.*
[2] *Official Records*, vol. v. p. 777.

1861, the following regiments were under Stuart's command : —

1st Virginia Cavalry	Colonel W. E. Jones.
2d Virginia Cavalry	Colonel R. C. W. Radford.
4th Virginia Cavalry	Colonel B. H. Robertson.
6th Virginia Cavalry	Colonel C. W. Field.
1st North Carolina Cavalry . . .	Colonel R. Ransom, Jr.
Jeff Davis Legion Cavalry	Major W. T. Martin.

The most important event of this period was the battle at Dranesville, on December 20, 1861. Stuart had been placed in command of four regiments of infantry, numbering about 1,600 men, a battery of artillery, and 150 cavalry, for the purpose of covering a foraging expedition of nearly all the wagons of Johnston's army to the country west of Dranesville.

On the same morning, Ord's brigade of McCall's division, strengthened by the 1st Pennsylvania Reserve Rifles, Colonel T. L. Kane, in all numbering 3,950 officers and men,[1] and supported by the two other brigades of McCall's division, started for Dranesville, with the double purpose of driving back the Confederate pickets, which had recently been somewhat advanced, and of collecting forage.[2] General Ord's march was made with the expectation of finding a considerable body of Confederates in the vicinity of Dranesville. The Confederate pickets were driven from the town, but remained in such close observation of Ord's movements as to cause the impression that there was a considerable reserve not far distant. General Ord immediately occupied advantageous ground with his artillery and two of his regiments, and awaited the arrival of the other three regiments, all of which were placed in position before Stuart's attack was made.

[1] These figures are obtained from the records of the Adjutant-General's Office, Washington.

[2] Authority for this and subsequent statements will be found in the *Official Records*, vol. v. pp. 474–494.

In the mean time Stuart, who was entirely ignorant of these movements, had sent his cavalry in advance of his infantry, expecting to occupy Dranesville, and there cover and protect the wagons and men engaged in foraging. When Captain Pitzer, who commanded Stuart's advance guard, came within sight of Dranesville, he reported its occupation by the enemy. Nothing lay between the enemy and the foraging parties, whom Stuart was bound to protect ; and the only course to save them from destruction was to attack and delay the enemy where he was until the wagons could be withdrawn. Captain Pitzer was at once sent to gain the roads west of Dranesville, and warn and recall the wagons, while the four regiments of infantry, still three fourths of a mile distant, were hurried forward, placed in position on the right and left of the road, and advanced to the attack.

Ord's artillery was advantageously posted and admirably served. On the other hand, Stuart's battery, commanded by Captain A. S. Cutts, was, from the nature of the ground, compelled to take an exceedingly unfavorable position, where it could neither protect itself from the destructive fire of the enemy, nor make an effective reply. Courage and skill could avail but little under such circumstances, and the battery suffered most severely in men, horses, and material. One caisson was blown up ; and when the troops retired it was necessary to remove one of the guns by a detail of infantry soldiers, and to abandon one caisson and one limber, for want of horses. Another unfortunate occurrence was that the 1st Kentucky and the 6th South Carolina regiments fired into each other by mistake, and produced confusion in that part of the line. Against such an accident it was difficult to provide in the early days of the war.

After maintaining the contest for more than two hours, Stuart was satisfied that he could not move the force in his front, and that reinforcements to the enemy might place him in serious jeopardy. He therefore withdrew, first his guns and the caissons for which horses remained, and then his infantry. This movement was not made a moment too soon; for even then the two other brigades of McCall's division were moving into position, and another half-hour would have enveloped Stuart's command in an overwhelming force. As it was, the withdrawal was conducted without interference by the enemy and with success, except that one of his regiments, in regaining the road, missed the place where they had deposited their knapsacks and blankets on going into the fight, and these were left as trophies in the enemy's hands. General Ord made no advance on Stuart's position until the latter had withdrawn from his front.

Stuart retired for the night to a distance of about five miles from Dranesville. On the next morning, being reinforced by two regiments of infantry and a detachment of cavalry, he returned to the battle-field (from which the enemy had retired), buried his dead, and recovered eight or ten of his wounded. His aggregate loss in this battle was 194; that of the enemy was 68.

This was the first serious check which Stuart had received; but his conduct on the field only increased the confidence of those who served under him. His men felt that they had been overmatched and worsted in a hot fight, but the manner in which Stuart had extricated them from their danger commanded their admiration. Sergeant C. W. West, company C, 1st Kentucky Infantry, now a resident of Cynthiana, Ky., gives me the following incident: —

Captain Desha, of the 1st Kentucky, had been severely wounded early in the action, but had remained on the field with his regiment. When ordered from the field, and retiring along the road, Desha was still at the head of his company. Stuart approached. Over his horse's neck hung a quantity of harness which he had stripped from some of the dead artillery horses. Recognizing Desha and his wounded condition, he rode to him, and, urgently insisting that Desha should take his horse and ride to a place of safety, was in the act of dismounting for this purpose when prevented by Desha's firm but grateful refusal.

CHAPTER VI.

WILLIAMSBURG ; SEVEN PINES.

THE months of January and February, 1862, were marked by no events of much importance to the cavalry. Early in March the Confederates commenced the evacuation of their positions at Manassas, and on the 11th of that month the Federal army took possession of their abandoned winter quarters. On the 28th of March the Federals made a reconnoissance in force along the Orange and Alexandria Railroad as far as Bealton Station. This movement was watched by Stuart with the 1st, 2d, 4th, and 6th regiments of Virginia Cavalry, supported by a small force of infantry from General Ewell's command. No serious fighting occurred, but Stuart reports the capture of about fifty prisoners.

The work of transporting the Federal army from Washington to Fortress Monroe commenced about the middle of March, and on the 4th of April McClellan advanced upon Yorktown. Here he was confronted by the army of General Joseph E. Johnston in the works constructed by General Magruder during the previous year. Having delayed McClellan's advance for a month, the untenable position at Yorktown was quietly evacuated by the Confederates on the night of the 3d of May. The duty of covering this movement and of protecting the rear devolved on the cavalry under Stuart. Colonel Fitz Lee, with the 1st Virginia

Cavalry, was sent towards Eltham's Landing to watch the York River in that direction. The 4th Virginia Cavalry, Lieutenant-Colonel W. C. Wickham ; the Wise Legion, Colonel J. Lucius Davis ; and the cavalry of the Hampton Legion, under Major M. C. Butler, were stationed on the Telegraph Road, the direct route from Yorktown to Williamsburg. Stuart himself occupied the centre of his line at Blow's Mill, on Skiff Creek, having on his right, at Lee's Bridge, the Jeff Davis Legion, under Lieutenant-Colonel W. T. Martin. This bridge was effectually destroyed before the enemy made his appearance.

The evacuation of Yorktown was a surprise to the Federal army. Nothing was in readiness for such an event, and it was midday on the 4th before an efficient pursuit could be organized. The advance-guard of the Federal army consisted of four regiments and a squadron of cavalry, with four batteries of artillery, under the command of Brigadier-General George Stoneman. He was supported by two divisions of infantry, Hooker's and Smith's. It was expected that a rapid pursuit along the Telegraph Road would cut off and capture whatever portion of the Confederate rear-guard might be on the roads south of it, which, leading from Blow's Mill and Lee's Bridge, intersected the Telegraph Road a short distance in front of Fort Magruder, where it was expected that Stuart would concentrate his cavalry. An earlier start or a more vigorous pursuit might, perhaps, have accomplished this result. Colonel Wickham selected a strong position about four miles in advance of Williamsburg, where he checked the progress of the Federal cavalry until their superiority in artillery rendered it necessary for him to withdraw. Having dislodged Wickham from this position, General Stoneman sent General Emory, with the 3d Pennsyl-

vania Cavalry, and Barker's squadron, supported by a
battery of artillery, to gain the road from Blow's Mill,
upon which Stuart was operating. The dense woods
which covered almost the whole face of the country, and
the swampy nature of the ground, rendered active co-
operation between Stuart and Wickham impossible; and
while Stuart was slowly retiring before the languid advance on his front, General Emory had interposed his
command, and closed the road behind him. The first
notice that Stuart had of Emory's presence in his rear
was the return of a courier whom he had sent with a
despatch to the commanding general, and who narrowly
escaped capture. Thinking that his courier might
have encountered a mere scouting party, Stuart sent
Colonel Thomas F. Goode, with a portion of the 3d
Virginia Cavalry, to ascertain the true state of affairs.
A charge by Goode drove in the enemy's advance and
developed his true strength. Goode lost four men
wounded in this action, and claims to have counted
eight of the enemy's dead on the road. No route now
remained for Stuart but that along the river beach,
and without a moment's hesitation he moved his command down to it, covering his rear by the fire of
two little mountain howitzers. The enemy made no
effort to interfere with his withdrawal, and Stuart
reached Williamsburg about dark. In the mean time
Wickham had had a fierce fight on the Telegraph Road,
immediately in front of Fort Magruder, to which he
had retired in order to gain the support of artillery,
of which he was destitute. The cavalry fighting here
seems to have been extremely spirited on both sides,
the opposing squadrons meeting in well-sustained hand
to hand encounters. Aided by the Wise Legion and
the Hampton Legion, Colonel Wickham succeeded in
keeping the open ground in front of Fort Magruder

free from the enemy, who, confined within narrow
limits by the marshy nature of the ground, suffered
severely in men and horses under the fire of the artillery in Fort Magruder, and finally retired, leaving
behind them one rifle gun and three caissons. During
the action Colonel Wickham was wounded in the side
by a sabre thrust, but he remained upon the field until
the close of the day.

At daylight the next morning commenced the battle of Williamsburg. The nature of the ground rendered it impossible for the cavalry to participate in the
fighting, but it was held in reserve in rear of Fort
Magruder, exposed, throughout the entire day, not
only to a drenching rain, but also to the fire of the
enemy's artillery, from which it sustained a number
of casualties. Stuart himself was, however, by no
means an idle spectator of the scene. During the
greater part of the day he was used by General Longstreet as his medium of communication with the battle-
field.

The check received at the battle of Williamsburg,
and the immense difficulty of forwarding supplies over
the narrow and miry roads of the peninsula, prevented
the Federal army from making any further direct attempt to annoy the Confederate rear. The effort to
turn the Confederate right flank by debarking Franklin's division at Eltham's Landing, on the York River,
resulted in the spirited affair of the 7th of May, in which
two brigades of Whiting's division, Hood's and Hampton's, attacked the enemy and drove him under the
cover of the fire of his gun-boats. Major-General G. W.
Smith pays the following tribute to the cavalry : —

The affair at Eltham forms one of the most interesting incidents of the march of my command in retiring from Yorktown out of the peninsula. The route is nearly parallel to a

deep, navigable river, filled with vessels of war, gun-boats, and transports of the enemy. Along this river are many most favorable landings, and good lateral roads leading from the river, intersecting our line of march at almost every mile, and at points varying in distance between one and three miles from the river. This delicate movement has been successfully accomplished.

The comfort and quiet with which the march of the troops has been conducted on this line is largely due to the admirable dispositions and watchfulness of the cavalry rear-guard, first under Colonel Fitz Lee and more recently under Brigadier-General J. E. B. Stuart, supported from day to day by brigades detailed for this purpose.

Until Johnston's army retired into the defences of Richmond nothing more occurred on this line save a few cavalry skirmishes of so little importance as to be unworthy of mention.

On the 31st of May and the 1st of June was fought the battle of Seven Pines. The nature of the battle-field forbade the use of cavalry on either side. General Longstreet says in his report : —

Brigadier-General J. E. B. Stuart, in the absence of any opportunity to use his cavalry, was of material service by his presence with me on the field.

Major-General G. W. Smith says in his report : —

Brigadier-General J. E. B. Stuart had been for some time attached to my command, but he was during the action of the 31st principally with that portion of his cavalry attached to the three divisions on the right under General Longstreet. He gave me the first information received from the right after the close of the action, and rendered me very important assistance during the night.

CHAPTER VII.[1]

THE CHICKAHOMINY RAID.

ON the 12th, 13th, 14th, and 15th of June, Stuart prosecuted his reconnoissance to the rear of McClellan's army, which is known as " The Chickahominy Raid." This movement had been fully discussed by Lee and Stuart in a private interview, and the orders of the commanding general were conveyed in the following letter, of which the original autograph is now in the author's possession : —

HEADQUARTERS DOBB'S FARM, 11*th June*, 1862.

GENERAL J. E. B. STUART,
Commanding Cavalry.

GENERAL, — You are desired to make a scout movement to the rear of the enemy now posted on the Chickahominy, with a view of gaining intelligence of his operations, communications, etc., and of driving in his foraging parties and securing such grain, cattle, etc., for ourselves as you can make arrangements to have driven in. Another object is to destroy his wagon trains, said to be daily passing from the Piping-Tree Road to his camp on the Chickahominy. The utmost vigilance on your part will be necessary to prevent any surprise to yourself, and the greatest caution must be practised in keeping well in your front and flanks reliable scouts to give you information. You will return as soon as the object of your expedition is accomplished; and you must bear constantly in

[1] The official reports, upon which many of the statements contained in this chapter are based, can be found in the *Official Records*, vol. xi. part i. p. 1004 *et seq.*

mind, while endeavoring to execute the general purpose of your mission, not to hazard unnecessarily your command, or to attempt what your judgment may not approve; but be content to accomplish all the good you can, without feeling it necessary to obtain all that might be desired.

I recommend that you take only such men and horses as can stand the expedition, and that you use every means in your power to save and cherish those you do take. You must leave sufficient cavalry here for the service of this army, and remember that one of the chief objects of your expedition is to gain intelligence for the guidance of future movements.

Information received last evening, the points of which I sent you, leads me to infer that there is a stronger force on the enemy's right than was previously reported. A large body of infantry, as well as cavalry, was reported near the Central Railroad.

Should you find, upon investigation, that the enemy is moving to his right, or is so strongly posted as to make your expedition inopportune, you will, after gaining all the information you can, resume your former position.

I am, with great respect, your obedient servant,

R. E. LEE, *General.*

Reading this letter, as we now do, in the light of subsequent events, we are at no loss to determine that the great object of the expedition was to locate, definitely, the right wing of McClellan's army, and to ascertain whether the plan of moving Jackson upon it were feasible.

Early on the morning of Thursday, the 12th of June, Stuart commenced his movement. His force consisted of 1,200 cavalry and a section of artillery. The detachment from the 1st Virginia Cavalry was commanded by Colonel Fitz Lee; that from the 9th Virginia Cavalry, by Colonel W. H. F. Lee; and that from the Jeff Davis Legion, by Lieutenant-Colonel W. T. Martin. No field-officer of the 4th Virginia Cavalry was available for this expedition, and the detachment from that regiment was divided between the commands of Colonel Fitz Lee and Colonel W. H. F. Lee. The artillery was commanded by Lieutenant James Breathed.

Desiring to create, if possible, the impression that his force was destined to reinforce Jackson, Stuart moved northward by the Brook turnpike, and encamped that night on Winston's farm, in the vicinity of Taylorsville, twenty-two miles distant from Richmond. Early on the 13th he resumed his march. Up to this time no one but himself had any true idea of his destination ; but now, in order to secure more intelligent coöperation on the part of his regimental commanders, he made known the general purport of his orders to Colonels Fitz Lee, W. H. F. Lee, and Martin.

Scouts who had been sent out during the night had returned with the information that the road to Old Church was unobstructed, and the head of the column was turned eastward toward Hanover Court House. Reaching this point about nine o'clock A. M., it was found to be in the possession of a body of the enemy's cavalry. While occupying their attention in front, Stuart sent Fitz Lee to make a detour to the right, and to endeavor to reach their rear. But the enemy did not await the consummation of this movement. Before Fitz Lee could reach the desired position, they withdrew in the direction of Mechanicsville, and were allowed to pursue their way unmolested. A sergeant belonging to the 6th U. S. Cavalry was captured from this party. Stuart now moved forward by Taliaferro's Mill and Enon Church to Hawes' Shop, where the enemy's pickets from Old Church were first encountered. His march up to that point had not, however, been unobserved. Two squadrons of the 5th U. S. Cavalry, under command of Captain W. B. Royall,

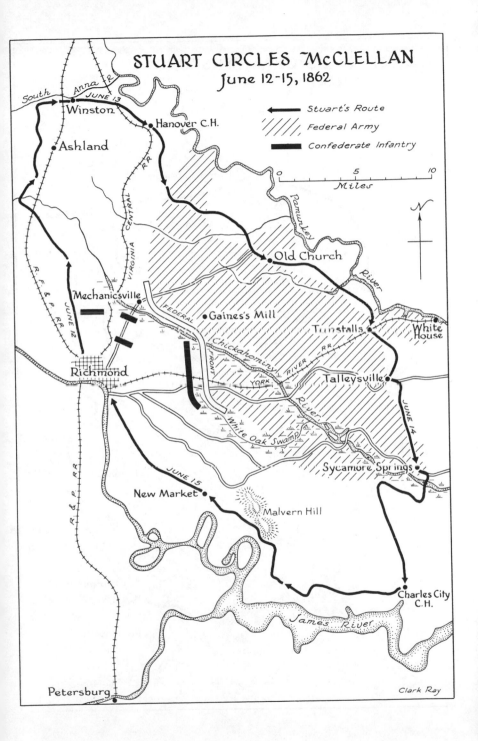

STUART CIRCLES McCLELLAN
June 12-15, 1862

Stuart's Route
Federal Army
Confederate Infantry

0   5   10
Miles

N

South Anna R.
JUNE 13
Winston
Ashland
Hanover C.H.
Pamunkey River
Old Church
VIRGINIA CENTRAL RR
R. F. & P. RR
JUNE 12
Mechanicsville
Gaines's Mill
Tunstalls
White House
FEDERAL FRONT
Richmond
Chickahominy River
YORK RIVER RR
Talleysville
JUNE 14
R. & P. RR
White Oak Swamp
York River
Sycamore Springs
JUNE 15
New Market
Malvern Hill
Charles City C.H.
James River
Petersburg

Clark Ray

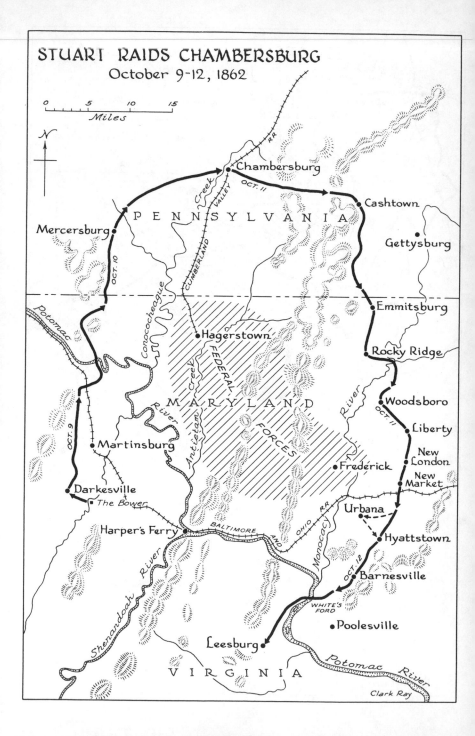

STUART RAIDS CHAMBERSBURG
October 9-12, 1862

0   5   10   15
Miles

N

PENNSYLVANIA

Chambersburg
OCT. 11

Cashtown

Mercersburg
OCT. 10

Gettysburg

Creek

CUMBERLAND   VALLEY

RR

Conococheague

Emmitsburg

Potomac

Hagerstown

Rocky Ridge

MARYLAND

Creek

Antietam

FEDERAL

River

Woodsboro
OCT. 11

River

Liberty

Martinsburg

FORCES

Frederick

New London

New Market

OCT. 9

Darkesville
• The Bower

Urbana

Harper's Ferry

BALTIMORE   AND   OHIO   RR

Monocacy   River

Hyattstown

Barnesville
OCT. 12

Shenandoah   River

WHITE'S FORD

Poolesville

Leesburg

Potomac   River

VIRGINIA

Clark Ray

were stationed at Old Church, and it was the daily duty of this command to send a scouting party northward on the road to Hanover Court House. On this morning that duty devolved on company F, under the command of Lieutenant E. H. Leib. This officer reports that he advanced to a point about a half a mile from Hanover Court House, and discovered the presence of the Confederate cavalry at about eleven o'clock A. M. He estimated the force he could observe at two squadrons of cavalry, and as this was superior to his own he retired behind the Federal picket at Hawes' Shop, where he received orders from Captain Royall to retire still further in the direction of Old Church.

The 9th Virginia Cavalry led Stuart's advance, and the advance-guard was intrusted to Adjutant Robbins of that regiment, who managed his men so well that, although the Federal picket had full warning of his approach, he succeeded in capturing several men and horses. No serious resistance was offered until the advance reached Totopotomoy Creek, where the advantages of the ground tempted Lieutenant Leib to make a stand. The road here passes through a deep ravine, whose steep banks are fringed with laurel and pine, the narrow road permitting a direct attack only in column of fours. Both north of the creek and at the bridge Lieutenant Leib halted his small command, and resisted the advance-guard, until flanking parties thrown out on either side by the 9th Virginia admonished him that he must retire. Had the whole of Captain Royall's command defended the Totopotomy bridge, Stuart's advance might have been delayed so long as, perhaps, to render his subsequent movements impossible. But Lieutenant Leib was pushed back beyond that favorable position to the junction of the road which leads by Bethesda Church to Mechanicsville. Here Captain

Royall assumed the command, and drew up his force to receive the attack.

Without hesitation Stuart charged the enemy with Crutchfield's squadron of the 9th Virginia. This squadron consisted at that time of the Mercer Cavalry, from Spottsylvania County, company E; and the Essex Light Dragoons, from Essex County, company F. Corbin Crutchfield, of company E, was senior captain, but could not accompany this expedition, having been disabled by an accident. The command devolved on Captain Latanè, of company F, who, with soldierly courtesy, declined to take the post of honor from company E, but led the charge at the head of the Spottsylvania men. The charge was made in column of fours, and with the sabre. It was received by the enemy standing in line, drawn up in the road and on either side of it, and with an almost harmless discharge of their pistols. Captain Latanè and Captain Royall met hand to hand, the one with sabre, the other with pistol, and Latanè received instant death. Royall was wounded severely by Latanè's sabre and by the men who charged close at Latanè's side, and his squadrons were driven into hurried flight. The discipline of the regular service, however, asserted itself, and within a few hundred yards the Federal cavalry wheeled into line, in beautiful order, again to receive, and again to be broken by the charge of company E. A second halt was attended by the same result.[1] These movements, and the detachments necessarily made to guard the flanks, had con-

---

[1] It is but just to Captain Royall to say that he states that his force did not exceed one hundred men, Captain Harrison, his second in command, being absent on a flag of truce with a part of his company. It is also true that the force which attacked Royall — one squadron of the 9th Virginia Cavalry — was probably smaller than his own. This squadron was, however, backed by sufficient numbers to secure success had the first onset failed.

sumed the 9th Virginia, and had brought Colonel Fitz Lee, with the 1st Virginia, to the front. The 5th United States Cavalry had formerly been designated as the 2d, and was Colonel Lee's old regiment. Numbers of the captured soldiers belonged to his former company, and in conversation with them he learned that their camp was within a short distance. Colonel Lee now begged permission from Stuart to follow the enemy and capture the camp. This Stuart readily granted, but with the injunction that Lee should return as speedily as possible. The 1st Virginia pushed rapidly forward to Old Church, where the enemy was drawn up to make a last effort in defence of their camp. Hardly awaiting the charge of the 1st Virginia, they retired toward the Federal army, and were seen no more. Fitz Lee now took possession, and the camp was speedily destroyed. It was a little removed from the road, but in full sight of it. While still there, and much to his surprise, Colonel Lee saw Stuart's column moving southward in the direction of Tunstall's Station, and as he passed, Stuart called out to Lee to follow when his work was completed. It is the opinion of General Fitz Lee, recently expressed to me, that it was Stuart's intention, after the dispersion of Royall's cavalry, to retire by the same road upon which he had advanced; but having consented that Lee should attempt the capture of the camp at Old Church he followed him to witness the result, and then changed his determination.

Stuart had now accomplished the main object of the expedition. He had ascertained that the Federal army had not extended its right wing in the direction of the railroad and of Hanover Court House; and with this as the sole result of his movement, he knew that his commander would be satisfied. But he must now determine how he could most safely convey this information within the Confederate lines.   Two courses only lay open to him : he must either return by the same road on which he had advanced, or he must make the entire circuit of the Federal army, crossing the Chickahominy at one of the lower fords.   If he returned by the same route he must, of necessity, pass through Hanover Court House, for the recent rains had rendered the South Anna River unfordable, and a *détour* northward was impossible.   The presence of the detachment of Federal cavalry which he had encountered at that point early in the morning warned him that a much larger body might be expected to be awaiting his return.   To the south and west of him lay the Federal army, some of the camps of their infantry being within five miles of the road on which he was operating, to which numerous roads leading from those camps gave easy access.   Stuart was on the outer and longer line, the enemy held the inner and shorter line.   It was now between three and four o'clock in the afternoon ; the enemy's camps had, of course, been aroused, and even should he escape their infantry, he must certainly expect to encounter their cavalry before reaching Hanover Court House, and in the darkness of the night.   If anything of perplexity existed in Stuart's mind when called upon to make his choice, nothing of it was apparent in his manner.   Everything moved forward as in accordance with a predetermined plan, and no one could suspect that the turning-point of the expedition had been reached and passed.

Let us now see how the Federal forces were occupied. Major Lawrence Williams, 6th United States Cavalry, reports that he encountered Stuart's picket, near the scene of the action with Captain Royall, at half past three o'clock.   Doubtless this picket was in the act of withdrawing when observed by Major Williams, for he occupied the road in rear of Stuart's column one half hour after it had passed on; and having sent a picket to the Totopotomoy bridge, and a scouting party to follow Stuart's column, he soon discovered the presence of the Confederates on the road to the White House. Major Williams reports the strength of the 6th Cavalry at three hundred and eighty men. He was soon joined by the 5th United States Cavalry, the 5th Pennsylvania Cavalry, Colonel Rush, and by a brigade of infantry under Colonel G. K. Warren. In the light of these reports it is evident that retreat by the Hanover Court House road was seriously impeded, if not effectually closed, at the Totopotomoy Creek, almost immediately after Stuart passed on, and certainly before Fitz Lee had completed the destruction of Royall's camp. Even then a vigorous pursuit might greatly have embarrassed Stuart, but he was favored by the uncertainty of the Federal officers as to the character of his command. Lieutenant Byrnes, of the 5th Cavalry, thought he had seen seven regiments of Confederate infantry,[1] and the first reports brought in to General P. St. George Cooke led that officer to suppose that he

---

[1] Lieutenant Byrnes says in his report : "It is proper for me to state in connection with this report, that when retreating, and when about one mile from Old Church, I saw the head of a column of infantry advancing on the road leading into the Hanovertown Ferry road. The pickets which were driven in saw the same body of infantry."

Major Lawrence Williams says : "Lieutenant Byrnes also reported, that whilst retreating from the battle-field he had seen infantry about a mile from me (five regiments, I think), on the Hanovertown road, which came on to the Old Church road about a mile ahead of me."

Brigadier-General W. H. Emory says : "He (Byrnes) had seen near Old Church five regiments of the enemy's infantry, which went to corroborate his information."

Colonel G. K. Warren says : "There was also a statement, that Lieutenant Byrnes (I believe that is the name) had seen about seven regiments of infantry at the place where the pickets were first attacked. . . . I never for a moment believed we had any evidence of an infantry force."

was about to be attacked in his camp by a greatly superior force. Major Williams and Colonel Warren seem to have been incredulous about the infantry business, but Lieutenant Byrnes' report produced its effect, and General Cooke was ordered by General Fitz John Porter to use caution in his advance, and not to attack, with cavalry alone, superior forces of the enemy. This gave Stuart all the time he needed, and before his movements could be satisfactorily determined the present danger had passed, and he was safely on his way to Tunstall's Station and the White House.

Up to this time Stuart had inflicted but little damage upon the enemy, but he was now directly upon their line of communications, and he proceeded to execute the second part of the instructions given to him by General Lee. While on the road to Tunstall's Station numbers of wagons, whose drivers were entirely unconscious of danger, fell into his hands. When he reached Garlick's, two squadrons, Knight's, of the 9th Virginia, and Hammond's, of the 1st Virginia, were sent to Putney's Ferry, and burned two large transports loaded with stores, together with a number of wagons constituting the supply train of the 17th and 44th New York volunteer regiments. The loss inflicted here was very considerable.

As Stuart approached Tunstall's Station, he sent forward rapidly a body of picked men, including his aids, Burke, Farley, and Mosby, to capture the depot, cut the telegraph wires, and obstruct the railroad. An infantry guard of fifteen men was captured at the depot without firing a gun, and the work of obstructing the railroad commenced. Before this could be done in a satisfactory manner a train of cars approached from the direction of Dispatch Station. Seeing the obstruction and suspecting its cause, the engineer refused to obey the command to halt, but crowding on steam, dashed through, running the gauntlet of the fire which was poured into the train from both sides of the road. On the cars two men were killed and eight were wounded by this attack. A few, who in fright and bewilderment jumped from the speeding train, were disabled and captured.

The great depot of the Federal army was the White House, on the Pamunkey River, less than four miles distant from Tunstall's Station. This depot was guarded by gun-boats, and by a garrison of six hundred men, including five companies of the 11th Pennsylvania Cavalry, under Colonel Harlan. Lieutenant-Colonel Rufus Ingalls, aid-de-camp, was in command of the post. As Stuart approached Tunstall's Station a scouting party of cavalry retired toward the White House. His presence was of course known, and he might reasonably expect an attack from that direction. He was still within five or six miles of the camps of McClellan's army, and the railroad could readily transport a large force of infantry to his immediate vicinity. He therefore wisely forbore to make any attack upon the White House, remembering the instructions of his commander : " Be content to accomplish all the good you can, without feeling it necessary to obtain all that might be desired." Could he have spared the time, the prize at the White House would have been rich beyond description ; but even at Tunstall's Station the property which fell into his hands was large. A wagon train, loaded and on its way to the army ; cars standing at the depot and loaded with corn and forage, were speedily destroyed, while the sutlers' stores and wagons furnished abundant rations for the hungry men. Although provided with only such implements as could be collected from the neighboring houses, the telegraph poles were destroyed to a considerable extent, and the railroad bridge over Black Creek was burned. This work occupied Stuart's command until about dark, when the head of the column was started for Talleysville, four miles distant. One who has never participated in such a scene can form but a faint idea of the careless gayety of the men. In its grimmer aspects war must always be a terrible thing, even to those most accustomed to it; but it was just such experiences as this which gave pith and meaning to Stuart's favorite song : —

> " If you want to have a good time,
> Jine the cavalry ; "

and gayest among the gay, and apparently most unconcerned among the careless, was he upon whom all the responsibility rested.

It would be a great mistake to suppose that Stuart allowed himself to drift by accident into such a position as that in which he was now situated. Every chance had been carefully calculated. The New Kent company of the 3d Virginia Cavalry furnished scouts and guides who were acquainted with every foot of the country he was now traversing, and individual scouts had carefully located many of the enemy's positions before he started. Stuart chiefly relied, in this expedition, on Lieutenant (afterwards Captain) Jones Christian and Private Richard E. Frayser, of the New Kent company, as his guides. Frayser had led the advance-guard from Old Church to Tunstall's Station, and had nearly succeeded in capturing the scouting party which occupied that place at the time of his arrival. For his invaluable services on this expedition he was promoted to a captaincy in the signal corps, and was thereafter attached to Stuart's staff. Christian led the advance from Talleysville to the Chickahominy. His home, known as Sycamore Springs, lay along the bank of the river, and it was at a private ford on this farm that Stuart expected to cross.

At Talleysville Stuart halted for three hours and a half, to give his men some rest and to allow the scattered detachments to come in. At midnight he started for the Chickahominy. It appears from the report of General J. F. Reynolds, who reached Tunstall's Station at this same hour with his brigade of infantry, that Stuart's rear-guard did not leave Tunstall's Station until about eleven o'clock. General Emory, with Rush's Lancers, arrived at Tunstall's at two o'clock. It thus appears that Stuart had the start of his pursuers only by two hours of time and four miles of distance. The 11th Pennsylvania Cavalry, from the White House, could readily have kept within sight of him, but no attempt was made to follow until daylight the next morning.

At midnight, as has already been stated, Stuart resumed his march for the vicinity of Forge Bridge, eight miles distant. The 9th Virginia Cavalry, under Colonel W. H. F. Lee, still held the advance. Day was dawning on the 14th as Lieutenant Christian led the way to the ford which, within his knowledge, had always afforded a safe, or at least a practicable, passage of the river. But the recent rains had swollen the river beyond precedent. The banks were overflowed, and an immense volume of water rushed madly on, as if mocking the weary horsemen who stood upon the bank. Colonel Lee determined not to relinquish the attempt to cross at this point, unless it were proven to be impracticable. Accompanied by a few of his men he entered the angry water and essayed to reach the opposite side by swimming. He did reach it, but only after encountering imminent peril; for beside the danger arising from the rapid current, the feet of several of the horses became entangled in the roots of trees and other obstructions on the bank, and some of them were rescued with difficulty. Colonel Lee would not consent to be separated from his regiment, and re-crossed the river by swimming; but the experiment satisfied him that the passage in this manner was impracticable for the command. Axes were now procured, and the effort was made to span the river by felling trees, upon which it was thought a temporary bridge might be laid; but as their tops reached the water the current swept them down the stream as if they had been reeds.

At this juncture Stuart reached the ford. It could not be expected that the enemy would long delay pursuit, nor did any way appear by which the river could be crossed without serious loss. Every face showed anxious care, save that of Stuart himself, who sat upon his horse, stroking his long beard, as was his custom in moments of serious thought. Having first sent a despatch by Corporal Turner Doswell to inform General Lee of his situation, and to ask that a diversion might be made in his favor on the Charles City Road, he set about to find the means to relieve his command from its unpleasant position. He soon learned that about a mile below the ford were the remains of the old bridge, where the road from Providence Forge to Charles City Court House crosses the river. Instantly he abandoned the attempt at Christian's Ford and moved to the bridge below. Enough of the *débris* of the old bridge remained to facilitate the construction of another. A large, abandoned warehouse stood near at hand, and a party was at once set to work under the direction of Captain Redmond Burke and Corporal Henry Hagan to tear down this house and convey the timbers to the river. Never did men work with more alacrity. In a wonderfully short time a foot-way was constructed, over which the cavalrymen at once commenced to pass, holding the bridles of their horses as they swam at their side. About one half of the command was sent over in this manner, while the work of enlarging and strengthening the bridge was prosecuted most industriously. Within three hours it was ready for cavalry and artillery, and by one o'clock P. M. the whole command had crossed. Fitz Lee was the last man to step upon the bridge. During these hours of earnest work he had maintained the rear-guard at such a distance as to secure the command from interruption. Once or twice the enemy had made his appearance in small force, but as Lee advanced to attack, had retired.

The greatest perils of the expedition were now safely passed, but its difficulties and dangers were by no means over. Stuart was still more than thirty-five miles from Richmond, and at least twenty of those miles lay within the enemy's lines. Until he should have passed over that distance he could not feel secure against attack. Federal gun-boats lay upon the James River, within sight of which he must pass, and General Hooker occupied the line of the White Oak Swamp, in close proximity to his road to Richmond. Nothing would be easier than to throw a force of infantry across his path from Hooker's position. But these dangers seemed as nothing in comparison with those from which they had just escaped, and the enthusiasm of the troops knew no bounds. To secure themselves from attack in the rear, the torch was applied to the newly constructed bridge, and they soon had the satisfaction of knowing that pursuit from that direction was impossible. A few Federal cavalrymen appeared on the hill beyond just as the destruction of the bridge was completed.

A short distance above the bridge a fork of the
Chickahominy leaves the main current, forming an
island in the river. This stream, ordinarily shallow,
was now both deep and rapid; but it was forded without loss, except that the pole of one of the gun-limbers was broken, and the limber was abandoned on
the north side of the river. Without halting for rest,
Stuart passed up the north bank of the Chickahominy
to the residence of Mr. Thomas Christian, and thence
to the vicinity of Charles City Court House, where he
and his staff were most hospitably entertained at the
mansion of Judge Isaac H. Christian. His command
bivouacked at Buckland, the residence of Colonel J. M.
Wilcox. For thirty-six hours the men had been continuously in the saddle, and the remainder of the day
was given to rest and sleep. At sunset Stuart turned
over the command to Colonel Fitz Lee, with orders to
resume the march to Richmond at eleven o'clock P. M.
Taking with him one courier and Frayser, his gallant
and trusted guide, Stuart hastened to report in person
to General Lee the results of his reconnoissance. The
distance from Charles City Court House to Richmond
is about thirty miles, and for two thirds of that distance he would be in danger of meeting scouting parties of the enemy. But he did not hesitate to take the
risk. Once only did he halt, at Rowland's Mill, to
drink a cup of coffee; and before sunrise on the 15th
he reached General Lee's headquarters. Having communicated the intelligence he had gained, and having
received the congratulations of his commander, he
almost immediately rejoined his command. After
reaching Richmond, and while Stuart was riding to
General Lee's headquarters, Frayser was sent to an-
nounce his safe return to Mrs. Stuart and to Governor
John Letcher, and from the governor he received a

handsome sabre in recognition of his valuable services.

The results of the expedition were important and satisfactory. One hundred and sixty-five prisoners were turned over to the provost-marshal in Richmond, and two hundred and sixty captured horses and mules were added to the quartermaster's department of the cavalry. The destruction of Federal property was great. Colonel Ingalls, commanding at the White House says : —

So far as this depot was directly concerned, it lost the two schooners and some forage, amount unknown, and in all not to exceed seventy-five wagons. There were more trains lost, probably, but they were in possession of brigade quartermasters serving with the army in front.

The greatest results, however, were those which followed from the information obtained by Stuart. All doubt as to the location of the Federal army was solved, and the possibility was demonstrated of those movements which, on the 27th of June, culminated in the defeat of the Federal right wing at Cold Harbor. Aside from these strategic considerations the influence of this expedition on the *morale* not only of the cavalry, but of the whole army, was most important ; and we have the authority of the Comte de Paris for the statement that by it the confidence of the North in McClellan was shaken.

The only casualty which occurred in Stuart's command was the fall of Latanè. He died as became a soldier, in the moment of victory, " With his back to the field and his feet to the foe." The concurrent testimony of Mrs. W. B. Newton and of Mr. O. F. Atkinson, who aided in the burial of Latanè, gives the following account of that mournful but interesting ceremony.

John Latanè, a member of the 9th Virginia Cavalry, remained with the body of his brother when the command passed on toward Old Church. A cart, returning from mill, carried the body to the house of Dr. Brockenborough, where John Latanè gave the dead into the kind care of Mrs. Brockenborough. A Federal guard was stationed at this house, and John Latanè of course could not remain. He at once proceeded to the neighboring house of Captain W. B. Newton, to obtain assistance and information which would enable him to escape from the enemy's lines. Mrs. Newton gave him the necessary instructions, and loaned to him her old blind horse, almost her only dependence. Mrs. Willoughby Newton, Mrs. W. B. Newton, and Mr. James Lowry, the manager of the farm, then repaired to the assistance of Mrs. Brockenborough, and the body of Latanè was made ready for burial. A coffin was procured with great difficulty. As there was no burial-ground on the plantation of Dr. Brockenborough, the body was removed on the following morning to Summer Hill, the residence of Captain W. B. Newton, and was interred in the old Page family burial-ground. The ladies were not allowed to attempt to secure the services of a clergyman; but the burial-service of the Episcopal Church was read at the grave by Mr. R. E. Atkinson, at the request of Mrs. W. B. Newton. Thus did tender hands and sympathizing hearts perform the last kind offices for this brave young man.

It is proper to record the names of those whose conduct on this expedition won the especial commendation of their commander. General Stuart says in his report : —

I am most of all indebted to First Lieutenant D. A. Timberlake, 4th Virginia Cavalry; Second Lieutenant Jones R. Christian, and Private R. E. Frayser, 3d Virginia Cavalry, who were ever in advance, and without whose thorough knowledge of the country and valuable assistance I could have effected nothing.

The following paper accompanied General Stuart's report : —

HEADQUARTERS CAVALRY BRIGADE, *June* 17, 1862.

GENERAL, — I have the honor to append to the report of the Pamunkey expedition the following recommendations, which were suggested more particularly by the distinguished services rendered then : —

1st. Colonel Fitzhugh Lee, 1st Virginia Cavalry, for promotion as brigadier-general of cavalry. In my estimation no one in the Confederacy possesses more of the elements of what a brigadier of cavalry ought to be than he.

2d. Colonel W. H. F. Lee, rivalling his cousin in daring exploits on this expedition, has established a like claim to promotion to the same grade.

3d. Lieutenant-Colonel W. T. Martin to have Shannon's and two other companies added to the Legion, so as to be colonel, a grade which he has fairly won.

4th. Assistant-Surgeon J. B. Fontaine to be surgeon of his regiment, 4th Virginia Cavalry, now without one. Dr. Fontaine is a man of signal military merit, and an adept in his profession.

5th. M. Heros von Borcke, a Prussian cavalry officer, has shown himself a thorough soldier and a splendid officer. I hope the department will confer as high a commission as possible on this deserving man, who has cast in his lot with us in this trying hour.

6th. First Lieutenant Redmond Burke to be captain for the important service rendered by him on this occasion.

7th. Captains W. D. Farley and J. O. Mosby, without commissions, have established a claim for position which a grateful country will not, I trust, disregard. Their distinguished services run far back towards the beginning of the war, and present a shining record of daring and usefulness.

8th. First Lieutenant W. T. Robbins, Adjutant of the 9th

Virginia Cavalry, would be a valuable addition to the regular army. I have the honor to be, general,

Your most obedient servant,

J. E. B. STUART,

Brigadier-General commanding Cavalry.

To General R. E. LEE,
    Commanding Departments of Virginia and Carolinas.

General Lee's congratulatory order is as follows : —

HEADQUARTERS DEPARTMENT OF NORTHERN VIRGINIA,

June 23d, 1862.

GENERAL ORDERS, No. 74.

The commanding general announces with great satisfaction to the army the brilliant exploit of Brigadier-General J. E. B. Stuart, with part of the troops under his command. This gallant officer, with portions of the 1st, 4th, and 9th Virginia Cavalry, a part of the Jeff Davis Legion, with whom were the Boykin Rangers, and a section of the Stuart Horse Artillery, on the 13th, 14th, and 15th of June made a reconnoissance between the Pamunkey and Chickahominy rivers, and succeeded in passing around the rear of the whole of the Union army, routing the enemy in a series of skirmishes, taking a number of prisoners, and destroying and capturing stores to a large amount.

Having most successfully accomplished its object, the expedition recrossed the Chickahominy almost in the presence of the enemy, with the same coolness and address that marked every step of its progress, and with the loss of but one man, the lamented Captain Latanè, of the 9th Virginia Cavalry, who fell bravely leading a successful charge against a superior force of the enemy. In announcing the signal success to the army, the general commanding takes great pleasure in expressing his admiration of the courage and skill so conspicuously exhibited throughout by the general and the officers and men under his command.

In addition to the officers honorably mentioned in the report of the expedition, the conduct of the following privates has received the special commendation of their respective commanders : Private Thomas D. Clapp, Co. D, 1st Virginia

Cavalry, and J. S. Mosby, serving in the same regiment; privates Ashton, Brent, R. Herring, F. Herring, and F. Coleman, Co. E, 9th Virginia Cavalry.

By command of General Lee,

R. H. CHILTON, A. A. G.

CHAPTER VIII.

THE SEVEN DAYS' BATTLES AROUND RICHMOND.

In order that the movements of the Confederate cavalry during the " Seven Days' Battles around Richmond " may be understood, it is necessary to relate the operations of those divisions of Lee's army with which it was in immediate connection.

The order of battle issued by General Lee on the 24th of June assumed that Jackson's command would be able to reach the vicinity of the Central Railroad on the 25th, and be in position to turn the enemy's right flank early on the 26th. Jackson's march was, however, delayed to such an extent that he only reached the vicinity of Ashland on the night of the 25th. Here he was joined by Stuart with the 1st, 4th, and 9th regiments of Virginia Cavalry, the Cobb Georgia Legion, the Jeff Davis Legion, and the Stuart Horse Artillery. The 3d and 5th regiments of Virginia Cavalry, the Hampton Legion, and the 1st North Carolina Cavalry were stationed on the right of the Confederate army, observing the country between the White Oak Swamp and the James River. The 10th Virginia Cavalry was held in reserve on the Nine Mile Road.

The positions held by the Federal army on the 25th of June were nearly the same as at the time of Stuart's reconnoissance. The three divisions of the 5th corps under General Fitz John Porter, occupied the north bank of the Chickahominy. Taylor's brigade of Franklin's corps, which had constituted the extreme right at

Mechanicsville, was withdrawn on the 19th, and replaced by McCall's division of the 5th corps. This appears to have been the only change on the Federal right wing since the 15th of June. The remainder of McClellan's forces extended south of the Chickahominy to the White Oak Swamp. Generals Stoneman and Emory observed the country north of Mechanicsville towards Atlee's Station and Hanover Court House with cavalry. The official reports do not show what cavalry was under General Stoneman's command, but on the night of the 25th he was reinforced by two regiments of infantry from Morell's division — the 18th Massachusetts and the 17th New York. Colonel H. S. Lansing, of the 17th New York, states that the cavalry force under General Stoneman consisted of two regiments and a light battery.[1]

Leaving Ashland early on the 26th, Jackson pursued the Ashcake Road and crossed the Central Railroad about ten o'clock A. M. Here he met the first Federal cavalry picket or scout. Stuart covered his left flank by the march of his column and by scouts as far north as Hanover Court House. At Taliaferro's Mill, Stuart encountered a cavalry picket, which retired before him, skirmishing, by way of Dr. Shelton's, to the Totopotomoy. A part of Stuart's command scouted the road past Enon Church to Hawes' Shop. At Dr. Shelton's, Stuart awaited the arrival of Jackson's column, having sent one squadron to seize the bridge over the Totopotomoy. The enemy, however, had burned this bridge, and held the opposite bank until the arrival of the Texas brigade of Whiting's division, whose skirmishers crossed the stream and drove them away. The bridge was rebuilt, and Jackson's march was continued. His divisions rested for the night in the vicinity of Pole

[1] *Official Records*, vol. xi. part ii. p. 332.

Green Church and Hundley's Corner, his left still covered by Stuart's cavalry.[1]

General Lee's plan of battle had contemplated an attack upon the enemy's positions in the vicinity of Mechanicsville at an early hour on the 26th, in which Jackson was to play the all-important part of turning the Federal right in their strong position on Beaver Dam Creek. But as we have already seen, Jackson's march had been unexpectedly delayed; and although nothing had been heard from him since early in the day, General A. P. Hill, at three o'clock P. M., crossed the Chickahominy at Meadow Bridge, with five of his brigades, and drove the enemy back upon their impregnable line on Beaver Dam Creek. This movement uncovered the bridge at Mechanicsville for Longstreet, who had been waiting since early in the morning for an opportunity to cross.

The Federal position on Beaver Dam was to be approached only by two roads; the one leading from Mechanicsville northward to the Pamunkey, the other crossing the creek lower down at Ellyson's Mill, and leading

---

[1] Brigadier-General H. C. Whiting says, in his report : "Discovered an advance post of cavalry west of the Totopotomoy, which fled at our approach. At three o'clock reached the creek, found the bridge in flames, and a party of the enemy engaged in blocking the road on the opposite side. The Texan skirmishers gallantly crossed and engaged. Reilly's battery being brought up, with a few rounds dispersed the enemy ; the bridge was rebuilt and the troops crossed, continuing on the road to Pole Green Church, or Hundley's Corner. Here we united with Ewell's division, and, night coming on, bivouacked. A furious cannonade in the direction of Mechanicsville indicated a severe battle." — *Official Records,* vol. xi. part ii. p. 562.

Brigadier-General Isaac R. Trimble says in his report : "On the 26th we moved with the army from Ashland in a southerly direction, passing to the east of Mechanicsville in the afternoon, and at four P. M. heard distinctly the volleys of artillery and musketry in the engagement of General Hill with the enemy. Before sundown the firing was not more than two miles distant, and in my opinion we should have marched to the support of General Hill that evening." — *Official Records,* vol. xi. part ii. p. 614.

towards Cold Harbor. Field's, Archer's, and Anderson's brigades, of A. P. Hill's division, attacked the upper position, while Pender's brigade, aided by Ripley's, of D. H. Hill's division, assailed the lower. Neither effort was attended with success, and after sustaining heavy losses, the Confederate lines withdrew, at nine o'clock, from the unavailing contest. Early the next morning the attack was renewed ; but without more favorable results. After two hours of fighting, the Federal troops were withdrawn to take position at Gaines' Mill. This movement was the necessary result of the march of Jackson's command, which now rendered the position at Beaver Dam untenable. It seems from General Trimble's report that Jackson might have reached this same point on the previous evening, and that it was within his power to have rendered efficient aid to the troops which were there engaged. The Federal line on Beaver Dam was held, mainly, by two brigades of McCall's division, who, protected by their works, inflicted upon their assailants a loss probably ten times as great as they themselves suffered. The withdrawal of McCall on the morning of the 27th under fire, and in the presence of a superior force of the enemy, was conducted in a manner worthy of praise.

During the morning of the 27th Longstreet and A. P. Hill moved down the Chickahominy towards Gaines' Mill, while D. H. Hill moved by way of Bethesda Church to Cold Harbor. Jackson crossed Beaver Dam Creek early in the morning, and advanced to Walnut Grove Church ; then bearing to his left, moved on Cold Harbor. Finding his road obstructed, he was compelled to make a still wider *détour* to the left, which threw him in the rear of D. H. Hill.

Meantime Stuart had covered the left of Jackson's march, and having thoroughly scoured the country toward the Pamunkey as far as Old Church, had advanced by way of Beulah Church, and had taken position on Jackson's left, in readiness to intercept the enemy should he attempt to retreat to the Pamunkey by way of Old Cold Harbor. The battle at Gaines' Mill was opened by A. P. Hill at about 2.30 P. M., and soon extended from right to left along the whole Confederate line. On Jackson's line there was no opportunity to use artillery during the earlier part of the battle. Stuart was the first to find a suitable position. Observing, late in the evening, a movement of the enemy's artillery on the road from Grapevine Bridge, two of Pelham's guns, a twelve-pounder Blakely and a Napoleon, were ordered forward to meet it. The Blakely gun was disabled at the first fire, leaving the Napoleon to encounter alone the two batteries to which it was opposed. Pelham maintained the unequal contest with the same courage which subsequently, at Fredericksburg, called forth the praise of Lee and Jackson. By the personal efforts of General Jackson, whose attention was called to the position occupied by Pelham, he was reinforced by the batteries of Brockenborough, Carrington, and Courtney.

The design of the Federal commander was not yet manifest, and it was still deemed possible that he might attempt to retreat toward the Pamunkey River. When the Federal lines had been forced at Gaines' Mill and Cold Harbor, Stuart proceeded three miles still further to his left, to intercept any movement in that direction; but finding no evidences of a retreat, he returned the same night to Cold Harbor. Early the next morning, the 28th, General Ewell's division was sent down the Chickahominy to Dispatch Station, and the 9th Virginia Cavalry constituted his advance-guard. With his main body Stuart pursued a parallel route to the left, and pushing ahead of Ewell's column, surprised a squadron of the enemy's cavalry at Dispatch Station. The enemy retreated in the direction of Bottom's Bridge. Ewell remained at Dispatch Station during the rest of the day, and on the 29th moved to Bottom's Bridge. On the following day he rejoined his corps.

After Ewell had taken position at Dispatch Station on the 28th, Stuart determined to advance toward the White House. General Stoneman and General Emory had retired in that direction, and had occupied Tunstall's Station on the evening of the 27th, stationing pickets on the roads towards Dispatch Station. Stuart advanced to Tunstall's Station. Here he found that a field-work commanding the approaches to the station had been constructed since his recent visit on the 13th, which gave proof by its presence that one of the results desired in his late reconnoissance had been accomplished, and that a considerable force of the enemy had been detached to guard his communications. Immediately beyond Tunstall's Station the enemy had destroyed the bridge over Black Creek, and there awaited Stuart's advance, with cavalry and artillery posted on the hills beyond. The fire of Stuart's guns dispersed the cavalry, and Captain Farley, having gained the opposite bank with a few dismounted men, drove off the sharpshooters who commanded the bridge. Captain Blackford at once proceeded to rebuild, but it was after dark before a practicable crossing could be made.

Meantime Stoneman had sent his infantry to the White House, where, with all the infantry of General Casey's command, it was received on board transports and gun-boats, and moved down the river. At dark the evacuation of the White House Landing was completed. So far as their hasty departure permitted, the government property was destroyed by the Federal

troops, and, last of all, the torch was applied to the
home of Colonel W. H. F. Lee. It is but just to General Casey to state that he says in his report that this
last act was performed without his knowledge and
against his express orders.

Early the next morning, the 29th, Stuart moved
cautiously toward the White House. He had reason to
think that it was held by a considerable force of the
enemy; nothing, however, was in sight but a Federal
gun-boat, the Marblehead, which occupied a threatening position in the river. Imagination had clothed the
gun-boat with marvellous terrors, and at this stage of
the war there was nothing which inspired more of fear
than the screech of its enormous shells. Stuart determined to illustrate to his command its real character.
Leaving his main body about two miles in the rear, he
advanced with seventy-five men selected from the 1st
and 4th Virginia Cavalry and the Jeff Davis Legion.
These men were armed with rifle carbines. Deployed
in pairs, with intervals of forty paces, they advanced
across the open ground to attack the boat, from which
a party of sharpshooters was promptly sent on shore to
meet them. A lively skirmish ensued, during which
Stuart brought up one of Pelham's howitzers and
placed it in position to command the gun-boat. Pelham's shells were soon exploding directly over her
decks. To this fire she was unable to reply; for while
her guns might throw shot far inland, they could not
be brought to command that point of the bank where
the howitzer was posted. The skirmishers were soon
withdrawn to the boat, and under a full head of steam
she disappeared down the river, followed as far as was
practicable by the impudent and tormenting howitzer.

Although the destruction of Federal property at the
White House had been great, it was by no means com-

plete, and sufficient remained to supply both men and
horses of Stuart's command. Having sent Colonel Fitz
Lee with the 1st Virginia Cavalry to observe the Chickahominy from Bottom's Bridge to Forge Bridge, Stuart
remained at the White House for the rest of the day.
The information which he had been able to send to
General Lee was of importance, for it was demonstrated
that the enemy had abandoned his base on the Pamunkey, and was seeking a new one on the James.

Late in the afternoon of the 29th Magruder engaged
the enemy at Savage Station. Jackson's route lay to
the flank and rear of this position, but he was unable
to participate in the battle, being delayed by the necessity of rebuilding Grapevine Bridge, which the enemy
had destroyed on his retreat. He succeeded in crossing the Chickahominy during the night, and by noon
on the 30th had advanced to White Oak Swamp.

On the 29th a reconnoissance was made on the
Charles City Road by five companies of the 1st North
Carolina Cavalry and the 3d Virginia Cavalry, under
the command of Colonel L. S. Baker, of the 1st North
Carolina. The enemy's cavalry was discovered on the
Quaker Road, and a charge, the 1st North Carolina
leading, drove it back to Willis' Church. Here the
head of the column was greeted by a fire of artillery
and infantry, and Colonel Baker was forced to retire,
having sustained a loss of sixty-three in killed, wounded,
and missing. His charge had led him unwittingly into
the presence of a large force of infantry.

During the 30th Stuart moved his command to Long
and Forge bridges, and at the latter place he bivouacked that night. At half past three the next morning, July 1, he received orders to cross the Chickahominy at Grapevine Bridge, and connect with Jackson.
He moved at once up the Chickahominy, but on reach-

ing Bottom's Bridge, discovered that the army had passed on to the south, and that the only practicable way for him to connect with Jackson was to retrace his steps and cross at one of the lower fords. Turning the head of his column about, he returned to Forge Bridge, where he found the 2d Virginia Cavalry, Colonel T. T. Munford, which at that time belonged to the Valley cavalry, and had accompanied Jackson's command. Fording the river at this point Stuart pressed on past Nance's shop to Rock's house, near which he encountered a picket, which he pursued until within sight of the camp-fires of a large body of the enemy. Here he encamped for the night.

While Stuart was thus occupied, Longstreet and A. P. Hill had fought the bloody battle of Frayser's Farm, or Glendale, on the afternoon of the 30th. Could Jackson have participated in this battle the result must have been fatal to the Federal army. He had reached White Oak Swamp at midday, but found the bridge destroyed and the passage disputed by a large force of infantry and artillery. After sending Munford's regiment of cavalry across, Jackson decided that the passage was impracticable.[1] The Rev. Dr. Dabney

---

[1] I have received from General T. T. Munford an interesting letter, under date of August 4, 1884, which describes the action of his regiment, the 2d Virginia Cavalry, on this day. I am permitted to make the following extract : —

"My recollection is very distinct in regard to what happened on that day. On the evening before, 1 had heard of some forage and provisions which had been left by the enemy at a point about four miles on our left ; and as we had no quartermaster and no wagons, I started to carry my regiment over to this place to get food for man and beast. When I left him, General Jackson ordered me to be at the cross-roads at sunrise the next morning, ready to go in advance of his troops. The worst thunderstorm came up about night that I ever was in, and in that thickly-wooded country it became so dark that one could not see his horse's ears. My command scattered in the storm, and I do not suppose any officer ever had a rougher time in any one night than I had to endure. When the first gray dawn appeared I started couriers, adjutant, and officers, to blow up the scattered

seems to be of the opinion that this was, perhaps, the
sole occasion on which the great " Stonewall " did not

regiment ; but at sunrise I had not more than fifty men, and I was half
a mile from the cross-roads. When I arrived, to my horror, there sat
Jackson waiting for me. He was in a bad humor, and said : ' Colonel,
my orders to you were to be here at sunrise.' I explained my situation,
telling him that we had no provisions, and that the storm and the dark
night had conspired against me. When I got through he replied : ' Yes,
sir. But, colonel, I ordered you to be here at sunrise. Move on with
your regiment. If you meet the enemy drive in his pickets, and if you
want artillery, Colonel Crutchfield will furnish you.'

"I started on with my little handful of men. As others came straggling
on to join me Jackson noticed it, and sent two couriers to inform me that
my ' men were straggling badly.' I rode back and went over the same
story, hoping that he would be impressed with my difficulties. He listened
to me, but replied as before, ' Yes, sir. But I ordered you to be here at
sunrise, and I have been waiting for you for a quarter of an hour.'

" Seeing that he was in a peculiar mood, I determined to make the best
of my troubles, sent my adjutant back, and made him halt the stragglers and
form my men as they came up ; and, with what I had, determined to give
him no cause for complaint. When we came upon the enemy's picket we
charged, and pushed the picket every step of the way into their camp,
where were a large number of wounded and many stores. It was done so
rapidly that the enemy's battery on the other side of White Oak Swamp
could not fire on us without endangering their own friends.

" When Jackson came up he was smiling, and he at once ordered Crutchfield to bring up sixteen pieces of artillery, and very soon one or two batteries were at work.

" After the lapse of about an hour my regiment had assembled ; and while
our batteries were shelling those of the enemy, Jackson sent for me and
said, ' Colonel, move your regiment over the creek and secure those guns.
I will ride with you to the swamp.' When we reached the crossing we
found that the enemy had torn up the bridge, and had thrown the timbers
into the stream, forming a tangled mass which seemed to prohibit a crossing. I said to General Jackson that I did not think we could cross. He
looked at me, waved his hand, and replied, ' Yes, colonel, try it.' In we
went, and you never saw such a time as the first squadron had ; but we
floundered over, and before I had formed the men, Jackson cried out to me
to move on at the guns. Colonel Breckinridge started out with what we
had over, and I soon got over the second squadron, and moved up the hill.
We reached the guns, but they had an infantry support which gave us a
volley ; at the same time a battery on our right, which we had not seen,
opened on us, and back we had to come. I moved down the swamp
about a quarter of a mile, and recrossed with great difficulty by a cow-
path. I sent General Jackson a despatch telling him where I had crossed,
but his engineers thought they could cross better above than below. A di-

accomplish all that lay within his power.[1]   On the afternoon of the next day, July 1, Jackson, D. H. Hill, Huger, and Magruder fought the battle of Malvern Hill.

Early on July 2, Stuart took position at Gatewood's on Jackson's left; but as soon as it was known that the enemy had abandoned the position at Malvern Hill, Stuart started down the river to ascertain his location. Lieutenant-Colonel W. T. Martin, of the Jeff Davis Legion, was sent in advance.   To his command the 4th Virginia Cavalry had been temporarily added, because all of the field officers of that regiment were disabled. When opposite Haxall's, Colonel Martin and a few of his men proceeded to the river bank, where, in full sight of the Monitor and the Galena, which were lying in the river not one hundred yards distant, he captured a sailor belonging to the Monitor, drove off thirty mules from the open field, and, scouring the adjacent woods, retired in safety with one hundred and fifty prisoners. Privates Volney Metcalf and William Barnard are especially mentioned by Colonel Martin for boldness in this affair.

At the Cross Roads near Shirley, Stuart found the rear-guard of the enemy in such force that he was unable to move it.   He spent the remainder of the day in collecting prisoners toward Malvern Hill, and in reconnoitring toward Charles City Court House.   Having ascertained that the enemy had not moved in that direction, Captain Pelham was sent with one howitzer and Irving's squadron, of the 1st Virginia Cavalry, with orders to take position in the vicinity of Westover, and shell

vision of infantry was put in above the bridge, and hammered away all day, but did not get over.   I never understood why he did not try the ford where I had crossed.   He sent me a little slip of paper saying, 'I congratulate you on getting out,' or words to that effect.   He held on to the idea of crossing above the bridge."

[1] Dabney's *Life of Jackson*, p. 466.

the enemy should he attempt to move down the river road during the night. Pelham discovered the position of the Federal army at Westover, and informed Stuart of the advantages which might possibly be gained by occupying Evelington Heights, a plateau which commanded the enemy's encampment. Pelham's report was received during the night, and Stuart at once moved his command, as it suggested, having forwarded the information to the commanding general, through General Jackson, and occupied the heights at about nine o'clock in the morning of the 3d. He had been informed that Longstreet and Jackson were moving to his support, and believing that Longstreet was close at hand, he opened with Pelham's howitzer on the Federal camps on the plain below. Artillery and infantry were moved to confront him, but he maintained his ground until nearly two o'clock in the afternoon, when, having exhausted his ammunition, and having learned that Longstreet had advanced no further than Nance's Shop, he withdrew.

Colonel Walter H. Taylor, in his valuable work, "Four Years with General Lee," says, on page 41 : —

Without attempting an account of any one of the severe engagements embraced in the seven days' battles, so fully described in General Lee's official report, I cannot forbear mention of a maladroit performance just before their termination, but for which I have always thought that McClellan's army would have been further driven, even " to the wall," and made to surrender ; a trifling matter in itself, apparently, yet worthy of thoughtful consideration. General McClellan had retreated to Harrison's Landing; his army, supply, and baggage trains were scattered in much confusion in and about Westover plantation ; our army was moving down upon him, its progress much retarded by natural and artificial obstacles ; General Stuart was in advance, in command of the cavalry. In rear of and around Westover there is a range of hills, or elevated ground, completely commanding the plains below. Stuart,

glorious Stuart! always at the front and full of fight, gained
these hills. Below him, as a panorama, appeared the camps
and trains of the enemy, within easy range of his artillery.
The temptation was too strong to be resisted; he commanded
some of his guns to open fire. The consternation caused
thereby was immediate and positive. It frightened the enemy, but it enlightened him.

Those heights in our possession, the enemy's position was
altogether untenable, and he was at our mercy; unless they
could be recaptured, his capitulation was inevitable. Half a
dozen shells from Stuart's battery quickly demonstrated this.
The enemy, not slow in comprehending his danger, soon advanced his infantry in force, to dislodge our cavalry and re-
possess the heights. This was accomplished: the hills were
fortified, and became the Federal line of defence, protected
at either flank by a bold creek which entered into James River,
and by heavy batteries of the fleet anchored opposite. Had
the infantry been up, General Lee would have made sure of
this naturally strong line, fortified it well, maintained it
against assault, and dictated to General McClellan terms of
surrender; and had the attention of the enemy not been so
precipitately directed to his danger by the shots from the little
howitzers, it is reasonable to presume that the infantry would
have been up in time to secure the plateau.

Colonel Taylor's criticism is based on the assumption that the Federal commander was ignorant of the
necessity of occupying a position which commanded his
camp until his attention was drawn to the fact by the
fire of Stuart's guns. This seems improbable, both from
the character of General McClellan and from the fact
that at 5.30 P. M., on the 2d of July, he thus wrote to
President Lincoln from Harrison's Landing: "If not
attacked during this day I will have the men ready to
repulse the enemy to-morrow."[1] But even if General
McClellan had been so culpably ignorant, can we believe
that there was not one among his able subordinates who

[1] *Official Records*, vol. xi. part iii. p. 288.

would have seen and suggested the necessity of securing so obvious and vital a position?

Again, Colonel Taylor assumes that the Confederate infantry would have been in position to make an irresistible attack had it not been for Stuart's precipitate action. The facts of the case do not, however, justify this assumption; for the movements of the Confederates had been greatly retarded by the severe storm of July 2, and neither Jackson nor Longstreet, who approached Harrison's Landing by different roads, were able to reach that vicinity until late in the afternoon of the 3d, and after Stuart had retired from the plateau, which he had occupied for five hours. The supposition that McClellan would have allowed the whole of the 3d to pass without guarding against assault from that position cannot be entertained.

Again, Colonel Taylor assumes that the position on Evelington Heights could have been fortified and maintained by the Confederates against assault aided by the fire of the flotilla of gun-boats, which lay on the river within effective range, in front, and completely enfilading the whole line from the mouth of Herring Creek. At least seven gun-boats guarded the flanks of the Federal army on July 2, and on the 4th Flag Officer Goldsborough informs the Secretary of the Navy that seventeen are at the scene of action.[1] Perhaps the picture which Colonel Taylor presents might have been realized, but, in the light of these facts, it by no means assumes the proportions of a certainty, hardly of a probability.

[1] *Official Records*, vol. xi. part iii. pp. 287, 295.

CHAPTER IX.

THE SECOND MANASSAS CAMPAIGN.

On the 25th of July, 1862, Stuart received his commission as major-general. On the 28th of the same month the cavalry was organized into two brigades as follows : —

First brigade, Brigadier - General Wade Hampton commanding : —

1st North Carolina Cavalry, Colonel L. S. Baker.

Cobb Legion Cavalry, Lieutenant-Colonel P. M. B. Young.

Jeff Davis Legion, Lieutenant-Colonel W. T. Martin.

Hampton Legion Cavalry, Major M. C. Butler.

10th Virginia Cavalry, Lieutenant-Colonel Z. S. Magruder.

Second brigade, Brigadier - General Fitzhugh Lee commanding : —

1st Virginia Cavalry, Colonel L. Tiernan Brien.

3d Virginia Cavalry, Colonel Thomas F. Goode.

4th Virginia Cavalry, Colonel W. C. Wickham.

5th Virginia Cavalry, Colonel T. L. Rosser.

9th Virginia Cavalry, Colonel W. H. F. Lee.

A month of inactivity succeeded the " Seven Days' Battles." The Federal army remained within its strong position at Harrison's Landing, and the Confederate army was withdrawn nearer to Richmond. Stuart's two brigades of cavalry were placed alternately on picket duty on the Charles City front, and in camp of instruction at Hanover Court House. Meantime a Federal army, fifty thousand strong, and commanded by General Pope, had been concentrated east of the Blue Ridge, between the two branches of the Rappahannock; and on the 13th of July Jackson, with his own and Ewell's divisions, was sent to Gordonsville to observe and oppose its movements. On the 27th of July Jackson was still further reinforced by A. P. Hill's division. General Pope's advance had now been pushed forward as far as the Rapidan River. On the 2d of August Colonel W. E. Jones with his regiment, the 7th Virginia Cavalry, was placed in command of Jackson's outposts, and had a spirited fight with the enemy's cavalry at Orange Court House, in which, although at first successful, he was driven back by superior numbers. On the 7th Jackson advanced from Gordonsville, and on the 9th another victory crowned his arms at Cedar Run. The cavalry of the Army of the Valley, under the command of Brigadier-General B. H. Robertson, participated in this battle. On the morning of the 10th General Stuart arrived on a tour of inspection which he had been ordered to make of all the cavalry under General Lee's command; and by request of General Jackson took command of a reconnoissance to ascertain the position and strength of the enemy. The information obtained by Stuart determined General Jackson not to attempt to follow up his victory, but to await the attack of the enemy, should he be disposed to make it.

Stuart had just returned from an expedition of some importance, which had occupied him from the 4th to the 8th of August.

The occupation of Fredericksburg by the enemy was a standing menace to the Central Railroad. A body of Federal cavalry had already penetrated to Beaver

Dam Station, where they captured Captain J. S. Mosby, who was awaiting the arrival of the train. Some damage was inflicted upon the railroad. It was important to counteract such raids, if possible, and on the 4th of August Stuart started from Hanover Court House with Fitz Lee's brigade and a battery of horse artillery, marched to Bowling Green, thence to Port Royal, and passing by Morse's Neck, encamped at Grace Church on the night of the 5th. On the next morning he learned that two brigades of infantry, under Generals Gibbon and Hatch, with some cavalry, had encamped the previous night at Massaponax Creek, and were then marching down the Telegraph Road toward the railroad. This was evidently another and more determined attempt to break the communications of General Lee's army. Stuart struck the Telegraph Road at Massaponax Church, between which place and the crossing of the Po River he captured a number of wagons and straggling infantry. At the Po River he attacked the rearguard of the enemy, and drove it in upon the main body, whose advance was arrested to meet this unexpected assault from the rear. As the enemy moved back against him, Stuart retired, contesting the ground with artillery until he reached the hills north of the Ny River. Here he turned off toward Bowling Green, and the enemy attempted no pursuit. Stuart captured eighty-five prisoners, eleven wagons and teams, and fifteen cavalry horses. He lost two men mortally wounded. He mentions Colonel S. D. Lee, temporarily in command of the 4th Virginia Cavalry, Lieutenant-Colonel J. T. Thornton, Captain Berkeley, and Lieutenant George D. White, of the 3d Virginia Cavalry, as distinguished by conspicuous gallantry.

This expedition was, however, only partially successful. Stuart drew back the main body of the enemy and prevented their reaching the railroad ; but although his scouts reported the presence of a body of Federal infantry at Spottsylvania Court House on the 6th, he did not know, and could not learn, that it was the rear-guard of another column which had pressed on toward the railroad that same morning ; for Colonel Cutler, of the 6th Wisconsin Infantry, with his own regiment, eight companies of the 2d New York Cavalry, and a section of artillery, had left Spottsylvania Court House late on the previous evening, and, reaching Frederickshall Station on the afternoon of the 6th, had torn up about two miles of the railroad and destroyed some other property ; after which, by a forced march, he recrossed the South Anna River the same night.

On the 16th of August the evacuation of Harrison's Landing, which had been commenced on the 11th, was completed, and McClellan's army was on its way to reinforce Pope. On the 13th of August Longstreet was ordered to Gordonsville to join Jackson, and Anderson's division soon followed to the same point, Hampton's cavalry being left to watch the Charles City and Fredericksburg front.

On the 16th of August Stuart went by the cars to Orange Court House for consultation with General R. E. Lee. He had given instructions to Fitz Lee's brigade to move toward the Rapidan, where he proposed to meet it on the evening of the next day. Stuart expected Fitz Lee to march on the 17th from Beaver Dam to the vicinity of Raccoon Ford, a distance of about twenty-seven miles. From some cause explicit directions had not been conveyed to Fitz Lee, and he was ignorant of Stuart's expectations. This misunderstanding nearly resulted in the capture of Stuart and his staff. Fitz Lee's command was out of rations. He therefore marched on the 17th to the depot at Louisa Court House, and having filled the haversacks of his men, resumed his march the next day, leaving his wagons to follow. Meantime Stuart reached Verdiersville on the evening of the 17th, and hearing nothing from Fitz Lee, sent his adjutant, Major Norman R. Fitz Hugh, to meet him and ascertain his position. A body of the enemy's cavalry had, however, started on a reconnoissance on the previous day, and in the darkness of the night Major Fitz Hugh rode into this party and was captured. On his person was found an autograph letter from the commanding general to Stuart, which disclosed to General Pope the design of turning his left flank. The fact that Fitz Hugh did not return aroused no apprehensions, and Stuart and his staff imprudently passed the night on the porch of an old house on the Plank Road. At daybreak he was aroused by the noise of approaching horsemen, and, sending Mosby and Gibson, two of his aids, to ascertain who was coming, he himself walked out to the front gate, bareheaded, to greet Fitz Lee, as he supposed. The result did not justify his expectations. In another instant pistol shots were heard, and Mosby and Gibson were seen running back, pursued by a party of the enemy. Stuart, Von Borcke, and Dabney had their horses inside of the enclosure of the yard. Von Borcke gained the gate and the road, and escaped unhurt after a long and hard run. Stuart and Dabney were compelled to leap the yard fence and take across the fields to the nearest woods. They were pursued but a short distance. Returning to a post of observation, Stuart saw the enemy depart in triumph with his hat and cloak, which he had been compelled to leave on the porch where he had slept. He bore this mortification with good nature. In a letter of about that date he writes: "I am greeted on all sides with congratulations and 'Where's your hat?' I intend to make the Yankees pay for that hat." And Pope did cancel the debt a few nights afterward at Catlett's Station.

In his report of this circumstance Stuart is unjustly severe on Fitz Lee. Had the latter understood that he was expected at Raccoon Ford on the evening of the 17th he would have been there, full or hungry. But his orders indicated nothing of the exigencies of the case, and he deemed himself fully at liberty to provide his men with the necessary rations. He was made aware of Stuart's strictures; but manfully preferred to rest under an injustice rather than engage in controversy with his commander. He was always more fond of fighting than of writing, and to this day has never appeared publicly to justify himself.

Stuart's division had now been augmented by the addition of Robertson's brigade, which then consisted of the 2d Virginia Cavalry, Colonel T. T. Munford; the 6th Virginia Cavalry, Colonel P. S. Flournoy; the 7th Virginia Cavalry, Colonel W. E. Jones; the 12th Virginia Cavalry, Colonel A. W. Harman; and the 17th battalion Virginia Cavalry, Major O. R. Funsten.[1]

It was the intention of the commanding general that the cavalry should cross the Rapidan on the 18th, and endeavor to gain the enemy's rear on the railroad, and destroy the bridge over the Rappahannock; while Jackson advanced by Orange Court House and Longstreet by Raccoon Ford. This movement was delayed

---

[1] Ashby's original command consisted of twenty-six companies without regimental organization. After his death the 7th and 12th regiments and the 17th battalion were organized from these companies; other companies were soon added to the 17th battalion, which became the 11th regiment Virginia Cavalry, under Colonels L. L. Lomax and O. R. Funsten. For these facts I am indebted to Captain W. K. Martin, A. A. G. under General W. E. Jones.

until the 20th, and in the mean time Pope had withdrawn his army across that river.

Having previously detached Munford's regiment to guard the upper fords of the Rapidan, and to operate on Jackson's left, Stuart crossed the Rapidan early on the 20th, with Fitz Lee's brigade and the remainder of Robertson's. Fitz Lee proceeded by Willis Madden's to Kelly's Ford, where he drove the enemy's cavalry across the river, capturing a flag and some prisoners. Stuart himself with Robertson's regiments turned northward at Stevensburg and moved on Brandy Station. The 7th Virginia Cavalry held the advance, and soon encountered the 2d New York Cavalry (the Harris Light), under Lieutenant-Colonel J. Kilpatrick, which it pressed back upon its support at Brandy Station, while Robertson, with his remaining regiments, was sent to make a *détour* by Barbour's house, with a view of attacking its right and rear. The Federal cavalry at this point was commanded by General George D. Bayard, and consisted of five regiments, the 1st New Jersey, the 2d New York, the 1st Pennsylvania, the 1st Maine, and the 1st Rhode Island. Two of these regiments, the 1st Maine and the 1st Rhode Island, had retired toward the river, but three remained to confront Colonel Jones and the 7th Virginia as they emerged from the woods in the vicinity of the station. General Robertson had been misled, and had made a wider *détour* than was expected; he was therefore unable to render immediate assistance to the 7th, which charged and routed the New York and New Jersey regiments. The arrival of Robertson with his other regiments completed the victory, and the Federal cavalry was pushed, almost without a pause, to the protection of their guns on the opposite bank of the Rappahannock. Stuart reports the capture of sixty-four prisoners, many of them wounded. His own loss was three killed and thirteen wounded. This was the first time that these Valley regiments had served under Stuart's eye, and he highly compliments them and their commander.

The advance of Jackson's corps reached Brandy Station on the evening of the 20th, and Stuart was reinforced by the 1st and 5th regiments from Fitz Lee's brigade; but as the enemy held the opposite bank of the Rappahannock in force, nothing further could be accomplished by the cavalry. At daybreak on the 21st Colonel Rosser, with the 5th Virginia Cavalry, was sent to secure the crossing at Beverly's Ford. His dash at the ford was so sudden that the infantry picket left their muskets standing in stacks, and fled to the adjacent woods. Stuart soon arrived with two pieces of artillery furnished to him by General Jackson, and for several hours maintained his position, expecting that the army would follow. Robertson had crossed at an upper ford, and had there also prepared the way for an advance. This was not, however, the intention of the commanding general, and the cavalry was withdrawn to the south side of the river. On the afternoon of this day Fitz Lee joined Stuart with the 4th and 9th regiments, the 3d having been left in observation on Longstreet's right at Kelly's Ford. On the 22d and 23d Jackson moved northward to the Warrenton Springs Ford, and crossed the river with a considerable portion of his command. A violent rain, however, rendered the river impassable, and threatened to divide his corps: he therefore, on the night of the 23d, by means of a temporary bridge, withdrew that portion of his troops which had crossed, before the arrival of the Federal forces, which quickly concentrated at that point with the expectation of crushing him.

General Stuart had proposed to General R. E. Lee to allow him to take his cavalry to the rear of Pope's army, and endeavor to interrupt his communications by the railroad. General Lee gave his consent; and on the morning of the 22d Stuart crossed the Rappahannock at Waterloo Bridge and Hart's Ford with all of his command except the 7th and 3d Virginia Cavalry. Two pieces of artillery accompanied the expedition. Marching by way of Warrenton, Stuart reached Auburn, in the immediate vicinity of Catlett's Station, after dark; and, having captured the enemy's pickets, was soon in the midst of their encampments. But now that he had reached the desired point it seemed impossible to accomplish anything; for the rain fell in torrents, and the night was so dark that it was impossible to tell where an attack should be directed, or to distinguish friend from foe. Fortunately a captured negro, who had known Stuart in Berkeley County, recognized him, and offered to lead him to the place where the wagons belonging to General Pope's headquarters were parked. Under the guidance of this man, the 9th Virginia Cavalry attacked the camp and captured a number of officers belonging to General Pope's staff, together with a large sum of money, the despatch-book and other papers of General Pope's office, his personal baggage and horses, and other property. While this attack was being made, the 1st and 5th Virginia Cavalry moved against another part of the camp, and Captain W. W. Blackford, of the engineers, attempted the destruction of the railroad bridge over Cedar Run. It was found impossible to set fire to the bridge on account of the rain which was falling, and the heavy timbers defied the attack of the few axes which could be found in the darkness. The enemy also opened fire from a cliff on the opposite side. After exhausting all

the means at his disposal, Stuart was compelled to acknowledge that the destruction of the bridge was beyond his power; and as the immediate return of his
cavalry was imperative, he withdrew before daylight,
and returned to Warrenton Springs on the 23d, bringing with him more than three hundred prisoners. For
many days thereafter General Pope's uniform was on
exhibition in the window of one of the stores on Main
Street, in Richmond, and Stuart felt that he had been
fully repaid for the loss of his own hat and cloak at
Verdiersville.

The swollen condition of the river now enabled General Pope to concentrate his army between Warrenton
Springs and Waterloo; but while Longstreet and A.
P. Hill occupied his attention on that front, Jackson
crossed the Rappahannock four miles above at Hinson's
Mill, on the 25th, and by a forced march reached
Salem on the night of the same day. On the 26th he
passed the Bull Run Mountain at Thoroughfare Gap,
and marching by way of Gainesville reached the railroad at Bristoe Station on the same evening. At
Gainesville he was joined by Stuart with Robertson's
and Fitz Lee's brigades, except the 3d Virginia Cavalry, which had been left at Brandy Station as rear-
guard to the army, to watch the fords of the Rappahannock, and to forward stragglers and convalescents.
The 2d Virginia Cavalry was assigned to special duty
as the advance-guard of Jackson's corps. Colonel
Munford had seen much service in the Valley under
Jackson, and had performed this same duty for him
during the battles around Richmond.

As he approached Bristoe Station Jackson sent Colonel Munford forward to surprise and capture the place.
In this Munford succeeded. He approached within one
hundred yards before the enemy was aware of his

presence, dispersed a cavalry company which constituted a part of the guard, and captured forty-three infantry, killing two and wounding seven. While thus engaged a train of cars approached, and succeeded in making its escape before Munford could sufficiently obstruct the track. The arrival of the Louisiana brigade soon after placed an efficient force on the railroad, and two large trains were captured.

But the main depot of the Federal army was at Manassas Junction, still seven miles distant. Here immense supplies of clothing and provisions were stored, and it was important that no time should be lost, lest the enemy, alarmed by the reports of the fugitive cavalry which Munford had driven from Bristoe, or by notice given by the train which had escaped capture, should apply the torch and destroy that of which Jackson's half-famished men stood so much in need. Although the night was exceedingly dark, and the troops had marched more than twenty-five miles since daybreak, Brigadier-General I. R. Trimble volunteered to undertake the capture of the Junction with two of his regiments, the 21st North Carolina and the 21st Georgia, numbering in all about five hundred men. General Jackson says in his report: —

In order to increase the prospect of success, Major-General Stuart, with a portion of his cavalry, was subsequently directed to move forward, and, as ranking officer, to take command of the expedition.

The sequel shows that General Jackson failed to notify General Trimble that Stuart had been placed in command, and from this circumstance there arose a controversy which demands some notice, because it has been made the occasion of unjust criticisms.[1]

---

[1] See *The Army of Virginia from Cedar Mountain to Alexandria*, by Major-General George H. Gordon, p. 138 *et seq.*

In examining the reports of General Stuart and General Trimble we notice, first of all, that the controversy is begun by General Trimble, and, apparently, without cause. In his report, dated February 28, 1863, General Stuart thus refers to the capture of Manassas Junction : —

As soon as practicable I reported to General Jackson, who desired me to proceed to Manassas, and ordered General Trimble to follow with his brigade, notifying me to take charge of the whole. The 4th Virginia Cavalry (Colonel Wickham) was sent around to gain the rear of Manassas, and with a portion of Robertson's brigade not on outpost duty I proceeded by the direct road to Manassas. I marched until challenged by the enemy's interior sentinels, and received a fire of canister. As the infantry were near, coming on, I awaited their arrival, as it was too dark to venture cavalry over uncertain ground against artillery. I directed General Trimble, upon his arrival, to rest his centre directly on the railroad and advance upon the place, with skirmishers well to the front. He soon sent me word that it was so dark he preferred waiting until morning, which I accordingly directed he should do. As soon as day broke the place was taken without much difficulty, and with it many prisoners and millions of stores of every kind, which his [Trimble's] report will doubtless show.

There is certainly nothing in this extract to excite the jealousy of General Trimble. Stuart states that, under the circumstances, his cavalry was inadequate to the capture of the place, and he therefore awaited the arrival of the infantry. He does not even claim that his cavalry participated in the attack, and only asserts that, as commanding officer, charged with the conduct of the undertaking, he gave general instructions to General Trimble, which he (Trimble) carried into successful execution. He even assumes that Trimble took charge of the prisoners and captured stores, as a duty and honor to which he was justly entitled, and that he had made report of the same to his division or corps commander. Stuart makes no parade of his own services, nor does he in the slightest degree depreciate the services of General Trimble. The latter, however, in his report, which bears date of January 6, 1863, uses the following language : —

> In this successful issue of the night's work I had no assistance from artillery or from any part of General Stuart's cavalry, a regiment of which arrived some hours after the attack was made, and commenced an indiscriminate plunder of horses. General Stuart himself did not arrive until seven or eight o'clock in the morning.

Let it be borne in mind that these words were penned before General Trimble had seen General Stuart's report, and it is apparent that General Trimble not only lays claim to the sole honor of this undertaking — an honor which had not been denied him — but that he unnecessarily *makes* an occasion to cast injurious reflections upon the cavalry and its leader. It is an uglier exhibition of the same spirit which causes him to complain, in a subsequent sentence of his report, because the hungry soldiers of Hill's division paid no respect to the guards which he had placed over the captured stores, but regaled themselves to satiety on the rare dainties provided by the Federal sutlers.

It appears from the Official Record that on the 9th of April, 1863, General Trimble's attention was called to the discrepancies between his report and that of General Stuart, by a note from General Jackson's headquarters, and that he was at the same time furnished with a copy of General Stuart's remarks. In his reply to this note General Trimble maintains his self-imposed position of antagonism to General Stuart in a still more offensive manner, and again asserts that General Stuart was not upon the field, that he received no orders from him, that he sent to Stuart no message in regard to waiting until the morning, and that the attack was made at about half past twelve o'clock at night. This reply was referred to General Stuart. A few extracts from the addition which he made to his report, on the 25th of April, will show the spirit in which Stuart received these strictures.

Human memory is frail, I know; and while in what I have said or may say on this subject my recollection is as vivid as upon any other contemporaneous event about which there is no difference, I lay no claim to infallibility, and I am very far from imputing to the veteran General Trimble any improper intention or motive in what he has said. . . . The idea which, strange to say, never entered General Trimble's head, never for one moment left mine, that he was under my command on that occasion, it is hard to account for; and yet I remember that he sent me no message upon the capture of Manassas, but sent it direct to General Jackson; and besides, he failed to submit to me his official report, which he should have done. I attributed these omissions to a certain jealousy of authority, which officers older in years are apt to feel toward a young superior in rank, and never suspected that the question of my being in command was involved in any kind of doubt in his mind. I received instructions from General Jackson, and was told by him that Trimble's brigade would be sent to me. I pushed on with the cavalry to surprise the place, but the train which ran the gauntlet at Bristoe put the garrison on the alert. I awaited Trimble's arrival to make the attack, as well as to give Wickham more time with his regiment to seize the avenues in rear of Manassas, which he did in a very creditable manner, as shown in his report.

Now, as to the interview when General Trimble came up, he says: "It was arranged between General Stuart and myself that I should form line," etc. How arranged? I was a major-general, he a brigadier; I was assigned specially to this duty, and was notified that General Trimble would report to me. It is true that I am not in the habit of giving orders, particularly to my seniors in years, in a dictatorial manner, and my manner very likely on this occasion was more suggestive than imperious; indeed, I may have been content to satisfy myself that the dispositions which he himself proposed accorded with my own ideas, without any blustering show of orders to do this or do that. My recollection is clear that I indicated that the centre should rest on the railroad. The cavalry under Wickham had already been sent, long before Trimble's arrival, to seize the avenues of escape and await events. Wickham, Eliason, and myself have corresponding impressions, *without conference,* as to the events of the night. Wickham says he carried out his instructions to the letter, and reported to General Trimble as soon as the place was taken. He says the first fire occurred about twelve o'clock, and that it was about two A. M. before any further firing was heard, and then the place was taken. General Trimble says the place was taken at 12.30 A. M. Eliason thinks it was even later than two o'clock: so do I. All accounts agree — General Trimble's too — that the place was taken without difficulty. General Trimble remarks that he admits that it was taken without difficulty so far as my executions contributed to its capture. I certainly could not have participated more than I did, without officiously interposing to assist Brigadier-General Trimble to command two regiments of his brigade in an enterprise attended with so little difficulty. I commanded in the capture of Manassas quite as much as either General Jackson or General Lee would have done, had either been present. . . .

General Trimble says I did not reach the place until seven or eight o'clock. I was in plain view all the time, and rode through, around, and all about the place soon after its capture. . . .

When matters follow each other so closely, it is difficult in a report written some time after to fix the order of time, but General Trimble does the cavalry injustice in his report. There seems to be a growing tendency to abuse and underrate the services of that arm of service by a few officers of infantry, among whom I regret to find General Trimble. Troops should be taught to take pride in other branches of service than their own. Officers, particularly general officers, should be the last, by word or example, to inculcate in the troops of their commands a spirit of jealousy and unjust detraction towards other arms of service, where all are mutually dependent and mutually interested, with functions differing in character, but not in importance.

These extracts sufficiently refute the insinuations made against Stuart. It may, however, be well to consider what were the probabilities in regard to the time at which the attack was made. In his official report General Trimble states that he received General Jackson's order at about nine o'clock in the night. General Jackson states in his report that the distance to Manassas Junction was about seven miles, and that General Trimble's regiments would have marched more than thirty miles since dawn before reaching the Junction.[1] It is not an easy matter to arouse soldiers who are weary and footsore from a long day's march, and if General Trimble started within an hour after receiving the order, he did well. Moreover, three miles per hour is rapid marching for troops in the daytime, and over unobstructed roads. Jackson had not accomplished as much on this day, and all regard his movement as one of unusual celerity. Tired soldiers could not accomplish two miles an hour in the darkness of the night, and over an unknown road, and it speaks volumes for the *esprit du corps* of Trimble's regiments that they acccomplished this undertaking with such spirit and success as they did. When we take into consideration the time necessarily consumed in the march, in changing from march by the flank to line, in throwing out a line of skirmishers, in arranging passwords so that friends might be distinguished from foes,

---

[1] The actual distance between the two stations is four and three quarters miles, but it may have been that Trimble's brigade was some distance from Bristoe Station at the time the order was given. Both General Jackson and General R. E. Lee state the distance at seven miles.

and in regulating the advance of the two regiments, which were separated by the railroad embankment (and General Trimble states that he did all this), it must be acknowledged that two hours and a half were not sufficient for its accomplishment; and that, although General Trimble's watch may have marked 12.30 A. M. at the time of the attack, it was probably much nearer the hour as stated by Stuart, namely, two o'clock.

It may be asked why Stuart did not communicate with General Trimble at an earlier hour. The answer is furnished by the circumstances themselves. Stuart says, " I reported to General Jackson, who desired me to proceed to Manassas, and ordered General Trimble to follow with his brigade." Again, in the addendum to his report, he says : " I was assigned specially to this duty, and was notified that General Trimble would report to me." And again : " I received instructions from General Jackson, and was told by him that Trimble's brigade would be sent to me." It is therefore plain either that Stuart and Trimble pursued different routes, or else that although Trimble received his orders first, Stuart was first upon the road, and pushed on in advance, thinking that he might effect a surprise; failing in this, he awaited Trimble's arrival, taking it for granted that Jackson had ordered Trimble to report to him. Jackson failed to do this, and the opportunity was seized by General Trimble to make the remarks contained in his report.

The capture of Manassas Junction placed immense stores of food and clothing in Jackson's hands. Eight guns, fully equipped, and three hundred prisoners, were captured. Leaving Ewell's division at Bristoe, Jackson moved the rest of his corps to the Junction, upon which a gallant attack was made by General G. W. Taylor's New Jersey brigade, which had been sent

on that morning by railroad from Alexandria to hold
the bridge over Bull Run. General Taylor pressed
the attack with great vigor, but was soon compelled
to retire, himself being mortally wounded and carried
from the field. His brigade moved back the same
evening to Fairfax Court House, where it encountered
Fitz Lee, who, with three regiments, had been sent to
harass the rear. Stuart mentions the fact that during
the attack made by Taylor's brigade, Mr. Louis F. Ter-
rill, volunteer aid to General Robertson, performed valuable service, extemporizing lanyards, and working the
captured guns with detachments of infantry as cannoneers.

On the afternoon of the same day heavy columns of
the Federal army attacked General Ewell at Bristoe
Station, and after repulsing several attempts to carry
his position, Ewell withdrew while yet under fire toward
Manassas Junction. During this movement his rear
was covered by the 2d and 5th Virginia Cavalry, under Colonels Munford and Rosser. After supplying his
troops with all that they needed from the captured
stores at the Junction, and having destroyed what he
could not remove, Jackson evacuated the place on the
night of the 27th, and on the following day concentrated his three divisions at Groveton, north of the
Warrenton and Alexandria turnpike. During this
movement his rear and flanks were covered by Stuart's
cavalry, and he received correct information concerning the Federal forces, which were now rapidly concentrating upon him with the hope that he might be
crushed by superior numbers before Longstreet could
bring him aid. At sunset on the 28th Jackson attacked
the enemy with two of his divisions, and after a fierce
battle, which lasted until nine o'clock, remained master
of the field. Two of his division commanders, General

Ewell and General Taliaferro, were wounded in this engagement. On the morning of the 29th Jackson awaited the enemy's assault, which commenced about ten o'clock and continued until nine o'clock P. M., and although the fighting was of the most desperate character, maintained his lines intact. During the day Longstreet arrived and took position on his right.

Having followed the same line of march pursued by Jackson on his advance, Longstreet reached Thoroughfare Gap at three o'clock on the 28th, and finding a considerable body of the enemy in possession, was unable to force a passage until late in the evening. Early the next morning he resumed his march, and reached Groveton in time to participate in the battle of that day.

On the 28th General Stuart learned from despatches which he had captured that the enemy's cavalry was ordered to concentrate at Haymarket, under the command of General Bayard. With Jackson's consent, Stuart proceeded thither with a small part of his now widely scattered command, and engaged the enemy in the afternoon in a brisk skirmish, but without decided result. From his position the fight in which Longstreet was engaged at Thoroughfare Gap was plainly visible, but being unable to effect a successful diversion, Stuart withdrew to cover the right of Jackson's battle, having first sent a trusty messenger to communicate with Longstreet. On this same day the horse artillery took important part in the battle. General Jackson says in his report : —

Owing to the difficulty of getting artillery through the woods, I did not have as much of that arm as I desired at the opening of the engagement ; but this want was met by Major Pelham, with the Stuart Horse Artillery, who dashed forward on my right and opened upon the enemy at a moment when his services were much needed.

On the morning of the 29th General Stuart again set out to open communication with Longstreet. He had proceeded but a short distance on the Sudley road when he encountered a force of the enemy which had penetrated to the rear of Jackson's line, and endangered his trains. Jackson at once sent infantry to meet this attack, but before its arrival the enemy was repulsed by the fire of Pelham's guns. Major William Patrick, commanding the 17th battalion of Virginia Cavalry, was left in charge of this position, and at a later hour in the day was attacked by a stronger force. He repulsed the enemy, but fell mortally wounded at the head of his men. General Jackson says : —

At a later period Major Patrick, of the cavalry, who was by General Stuart intrusted with guarding the train, was attacked, and though it was promptly and effectually repulsed, it was not without the loss of that intrepid officer, who fell in the attack while setting an example of gallantry to his men well worthy of imitation.

General Stuart says of Major Patrick : —

He lived long enough to witness the triumph of our arms, and expired thus in the arms of victory. The sacrifice was noble, but the loss to us irreparable.

After effecting a junction with Longstreet's command Stuart placed his available cavalry on his right toward Bristoe Station, where Rosser, with the 5th Virginia Cavalry, was already operating. Fitz Lee, with the rest of his brigade, remained on Jackson's left, and both flanks of the army were thus guarded during the remainder of the 29th.

On the 30th Stuart obtained an important post of observation on the right, from which the movements of the enemy, as he concentrated a force against Jackson's corps, were plainly visible. The attack, thus anticipated, was made at about four o'clock in the afternoon. At the proper moment Longstreet moved forward to the relief of Jackson. Stuart had obtained control of four batteries, Stribling's, Rogers', Eshleman's, and Richardson's, and having placed them under the command of Colonel T. L. Rosser, who was detached from his regiment for this service, pressed forward in advance of Longstreet's right to obtain an enfilading fire upon the enemy's lines. Although, as Rosser narrates, at one time nearly half a mile in advance of Longstreet's right, and unsupported even by cavalry, these batteries maintained their position in spite of the attempt made by a force which was sent to dislodge them; and they contributed in no small degree to the repulse of that portion of Pope's army against which Longstreet advanced.

While Rosser was thus occupied Robertson had advanced his brigade to the vicinity of the Lewis House, in order that he might, if opportunity offered, strike the enemy's rear near the Stone Bridge. Here he met Buford's cavalry brigade in one of the handsomest cavalry fights of the war, the honors of which fairly belong to Munford and the 2d Virginia Cavalry. Observing at the first only a small portion of the Federal cavalry, Lieutenant-Colonel J. W. Watts was sent forward with one squadron. His charge developed the fact that he had attacked the advance-guard of a brigade, which was advancing to battle in column of regiments. Munford formed the 2d regiment in line, and was retiring to gain the advantage of a better position, when he heard the order given to the enemy's column, " Forward! trot! march! " He instantly wheeled by fours, and charged at full gallop. The impetuosity of the charge carried his regiment entirely through the first line of the enemy, with whom his men were thoroughly intermingled in hand to hand fight.

For a moment his position was critical, for he had engaged perhaps four times his number; but General Robertson rapidly brought forward the 7th regiment, under Captain S. B. Myers, and the 12th regiment, under Colonel A. W. Harman, whose supporting charge drove the enemy across Bull Run. The 2d regiment stopped at the ford, but the 7th and the 12th continued the pursuit until the enemy were driven beyond the turnpike at the Stone Bridge. Adjutant Harman and Sergeant Leopold, both of the 12th Virginia Cavalry, are mentioned for conspicuous courage. The 2d Virginia Cavalry lost three men killed and four officers and twenty-eight men seriously wounded. Among the wounded were Lieutenant - Colonel J. W. Watts and Major C. Breckinridge. Colonel Munford himself was dismounted by a sabre stroke, and his horse was killed. The entire loss in Robertson's brigade was five killed and forty wounded. More than three hundred prisoners were captured, together with a large number of horses, arms, and equipments.

During these days Stuart sustained a severe loss in the death of his signal officer, Captain J. Hardeman Stuart, whom he had sent on the 25th to attempt the capture of the Federal signal station on View Tree, an eminence overlooking Warrenton, and, if possible, to establish his own flag in its place. Captain Stuart was unable to surprise the station, and the force under his command was insufficient to effect its capture. He had dismounted for the purpose of reconnoitring the enemy, and had given his horse to a man to hold. For some unaccountable reason this man left his post, carrying with him the captain's horse, and leaving him to make his way out as best he could. In this Captain Stuart succeeded, and, joining the march of Longstreet's command, shouldered a musket and fought in

the ranks as a private soldier. General Stuart says of
him : —

He was killed at the storming of Groveton Heights, among
the foremost. No young man was so universally beloved or
will be more universally mourned. He was a young man of
fine attainments and bright promise.

The battle of the 30th was continued until ten o'clock
at night, when darkness closed the pursuit and covered
the retreat of Pope's army across Bull Run. A heavy
rain, which fell during the night, impeded the movements of Lee's army and gave the enemy opportunity
to recover. While Longstreet remained on the field
of battle to bury the dead and collect the captured
arms, Jackson crossed Bull Run at Sudley's Ford, and
moved toward the Little River Turnpike. Early on
that morning Stuart had preceded Jackson, and had
concentrated his two brigades on the same road, near
Chantilly. The Federal army was in full retreat toward Centreville, its flanks feebly guarded by some
small bodies of cavalry, two companies of which surrendered almost without firing a shot. Pressing down
toward the Centreville road, on which the enemy was
retreating, Stuart obtained a commanding position, and
about dark attacked their trains with his artillery as
they were moving on toward Fairfax Court House.
On the morning of this day, Colonel Rosser, with the
5th Virginia Cavalry, was sent to reoccupy Manassas
Junction, where he captured about four hundred stragglers, some arms, and medical stores.

On the 1st of September Jackson fought the battle
of Ox Hill. On the next day Fitz Lee's brigade occupied Fairfax Court House. On the same day the 3d
regiment of Virginia Cavalry rejoined its brigade, having moved up from Brandy Station, and Hampton's
brigade reached the front, after having guarded the

removal of the army from Richmond. A reconnoissance by Hampton on this day developed the position
of the enemy at Flint Hill.

Having driven Pope's army to a secure position behind the defences of Washington, General Lee turned
northward to the Potomac, and began the first Maryland campaign. While this movement was in progress
Stuart covered the front toward Washington. He had
learned that an irregular body of cavalry under a certain Captain Means was harassing the citizens in the
vicinity of Leesburg, and on the 2d of September he
sent Colonel Munford, with the 2d Virginia Cavalry,
to that point. On approaching Leesburg, Munford
learned that it was occupied by Means' company, and
that he was supported by about two hundred men
under Major Cole, of Maryland. Munford's regiment
numbered only about one hundred and sixty men; but,
approaching Leesburg by an unexpected direction, he
effected a surprise, and after a heavy skirmish completely routed Means' party, and pursued him to Wa-
terford, a distance of seven miles. He captured forty-
seven prisoners, and killed or wounded twenty. An
interesting incident of this fight was that Edward, the
servant of Private English, of company K, followed his
master in the charge, and shot one of the Means party
who had made himself especially obnoxious.

On the 5th of September Brigadier-General B. H.
Robertson was relieved of the command of his brigade,
and was ordered to the department of North Carolina,
where (in the words of the order) " his services are in-
dispensably necessary for the organization and instruction of cavalry troops of North Carolina." Colonel
Munford was assigned to the command of the brigade,
and served in that capacity until the latter part of October, when Colonel W. E. Jones was appointed brigadier-general.

CHAPTER X.

FOLLOWING the march of the main army, Stuart's cavalry crossed the Potomac at Leesburg on the afternoon of the 5th of September, and extending itself from the river to the Baltimore and Ohio Railroad covered the front toward Washington. Fitz Lee occupied the left at New Market, Hampton the centre at Hyattstown, while Munford covered the signal station on Sugar Loaf Mountain, and extended his pickets as far as Poolesville. Stuart's headquarters were in rear of the centre of this line at Urbana. This position was maintained until the 11th, Hampton being engaged in some unimportant skirmishes near Hyattstown, and Munford in more serious fighting near Poolesville. Upon leaving Virginia the 6th regiment had been detached from Munford's brigade to collect arms and guard the captured property on the battle-field at Manassas ; and the 17th battalion had also been assigned to detached service. Three regiments only remained to Munford, and upon these the casualties of the campaign had fallen heavily. The 12th regiment had been reduced to seventy-five men, and the 2d regiment numbered less than two hundred.

On the 7th of September Pleasonton's cavalry drove in Munford's pickets at Poolesville, and on the following day the 8th Illinois and the 3d Indiana Cavalry, with two pieces of artillery, advanced to occupy that place and establish pickets beyond. As the Federal cavalry entered the town Munford approached it from the north with the 7th and 12th regiments and two guns. He had hardly taken position outside of the town when he was charged by the enemy. The 7th regiment under Captain Myers met and repulsed that charge which was directed against Munford's advance gun; but despite the example of gallantry set by Colonel Harman, a part of the 12th regiment behaved badly, and the other gun was with difficulty extricated from an exposed position. Munford retired on the road toward Barnesville, near which place the advance of the enemy was checked by the sharpshooters of the 2d regiment. His total loss in this affair was ten men, eight of whom were from the 12th regiment. On the following day, the 9th of September, the 12th regiment was again somewhat roughly handled, in an affair near Monocacy Church, in which General Pleasonton claims to have captured the regimental flag. On the 10th, Pleasonton attempted to dislodge Munford from his position guarding Sugar Loaf Mountain, but although now reinforced by the 6th U. S. Cavalry he found the position too strong to be assailed. On this day Munford's force was still further weakened by the detachment of the 7th Virginia Cavalry, which was sent to aid Jackson's movement on Harper's Ferry. On the 11th, Franklin's corps advanced upon Munford, causing him to uncover Sugar Loaf Mountain and retire to a point about three miles from Frederick, on the Buckeystown road.

Until the 10th of September General Lee's army had been concentrated in the vicinity of Frederick. He had anticipated that his advance into Maryland would lead to the evacuation of Harper's Ferry; but as this result did not follow, it became necessary to dislodge the large Federal army which occupied that place and Martinsburg, before his own could with safety be concentrated west of the mountains. On the morning of the 10th of September Jackson's corps left the vicinity of Frederick to accomplish this object. Marching by way of Boonsboro' Jackson recrossed the Potomac at Williamsport, and occupied the Baltimore and Ohio Railroad northwest of Martinsburg on the evening of the next day. The Federal garrison at Martinsburg was made aware of his approach, and evacuating the town on the night of the 11th, retreated to Harper's Ferry, thus postponing their surrender for a short time. On the 12th Jackson passed through Martinsburg, and by noon on the 13th had placed his corps in front of the position occupied by the enemy on Bolivar Heights. In the mean time McLaws' division, reinforced by six brigades under Major-General Anderson, had been sent to drive the enemy from Maryland Heights, north of the Potomac; while Walker's division recrossed the river to the Virginia side, and was ordered to gain possession of Loudon Heights east of the Shenandoah. General Lee's order for these movements anticipated that McLaws and Walker would be in position to cooperate with Jackson on Friday the 12th, and that Jackson himself would complete the investment of Harper's Ferry west of the Shenandoah on the morning of the 13th. The advance division of Jackson's corps was in position before Bolivar Heights at the time specified; but McLaws had encountered many obstacles and strong resistance, and was only able to gain possession of Maryland Heights on the afternoon of the 13th; while Walker's division, which had been engaged in incessant duty for two days and nights, reached the summit of Loudon Heights at about the same time. The investment of Harper's Ferry was now complete;

but some time was consumed in establishing communications and securing coöperation between the Confederate forces, which were separated by the Potomac and Shenandoah rivers. This was not accomplished until the afternoon of the 14th; for before his artillery could be placed in position to command Harper's Ferry and Bolivar Heights, it was necessary for McLaws to cut a road along the top of the ridge to the bluff which overhangs the river. This work occupied the morning of the 14th. At dawn on the 15th Jackson attacked the garrison from the Virginia side, and within two hours received the surrender of an army of eleven thousand men, seventy-three pieces of artillery, thirteen thousand stand of small arms, and large stores and munitions of war.

Until the 13th of September the utmost uncertainty in regard to Lee's movements and intentions had existed in the Federal army and at Washington. The fact that Jackson had recrossed the Potomac at Williamsport was telegraphed by Governor Curtain to President Lincoln on the 12th; but so far from divining the real object of this movement, the Federal authorities were only able to see in it an indication of the retreat of Lee's army, or of a possible attack upon Washington from the south side of the Potomac. General McClellan's movements were much embarrassed by this uncertainty, and by the timidity of those in Washington who so largely controlled him. His right wing under Burnside rested on the Baltimore and Ohio Railroad, while his left under Franklin extended to the Potomac. On the 11th of September the left wing was thrown forward, and, as we have already seen, drove away Munford's party from Sugar Loaf Mountain. On the 12th a general advance along his whole line compelled Stuart to withdraw from his position at

Urbana and Hyattstown. Fitz Lee crossed the Monocacy above Frederick, while Hampton retired through
that place toward Middletown. Munford was at the
same time drawn back to the gap in the Catoctin range
at Jefferson. As Hampton was withdrawing through
the streets of Frederick, the enemy pressed so closely
upon his rear with infantry and artillery that he found
it necessary to check their pursuit in order to insure
the orderly withdrawal of his brigade. The enemy
had planted a gun in the suburbs of the city, and were
firing along the street through which Hampton must
pass. This gun was supported by the 30th Ohio Infantry and by two companies of cavalry. Colonel M. C.
Butler, of the 2d South Carolina Cavalry, was directed
to attack. Lieutenant Meighan's squadron made the
charge, supported by the brigade provost guard of
forty men, under Captain J. F. Waring. Lieutenant Meighan rode over the gun, dispersed its support,
and captured the officer in command, Colonel Moore of
the 30th Ohio, and seven other prisoners. He might
have brought off the gun had not five of its horses
been killed in the fight. This sharp action protected
Hampton's rear, and his brigade was slowly withdrawn
to Middletown, leaving the Jeff Davis Legion and two
guns, under Lieutenant-Colonel W. T. Martin, to hold
the gap in the Catoctin Mountain.

Early on the 13th Stuart returned with Hampton's
brigade to the position occupied by Colonel Martin at
the gap. He had not yet been able to determine
whether he was opposing a reconnoissance, or whether
the army of McClellan was advancing. The orders
which he, in common with the other subordinate commanders, had received contemplated the reduction of
Harper's Ferry on the 12th or 13th; and after that
event no importance would attach to the mountain

gaps. But no intelligence had been received from Harper's Ferry ; and in order to gain time and to develop the enemy, Stuart determined to hold the gap beyond Middletown ; while Fitz Lee, from his position on the left, was sent to gain the enemy's rear, and endeavor to ascertain his real force. Although attacked by Pleasonton's cavalry, Hampton held the gap until about two o'clock in the afternoon, when the advance of Rodman's division of infantry compelled him to withdraw toward Middletown, near which place he made a second and a third stand, checking each time the progress of the enemy.

Having assured himself that Turner's Gap, where the Boonsboro' road crosses the South Mountain, was held in force by the infantry of D. H. Hill's division, and having posted Rosser with the 5th Virginia Cavalry and the horse artillery at Braddock's Gap, on the right of Hill's position, Stuart withdrew Hampton from contact with the enemy and sent him to reinforce Munford at Crampton's Gap, which he now considered the weakest portion of the line. The Jeff Davis Legion was detached from Hampton for service at the Boonsboro' Gap.

Munford's two regiments had not been allowed to remain idle on this day. The enemy pressed upon his position at Jefferson by three roads, and followed him closely with cavalry as he retired toward Burkittsville, or Crampton's Gap. Colonel Harman with the 12th regiment was sent hurriedly to gain position at Burkittsville and to secure the wagons of the brigade, while Munford with the sharpshooters of the 2d regiment, under Captain Holland, disputed the enemy's advance. Finding himself heavily pressed, Captain Holland made a dash at his pursuers with a mere handful of mounted men, and checked them until an advantageous position had been secured for the artillery on the mountain side. At this opportune moment Hampton was approaching from the north, but all unaware of the pressure under which Munford was laboring. Observing a regiment of the enemy's cavalry on a road parallel to the one on which he was moving, Hampton took the Cobb Georgia Legion across to charge it. Lieutenant-Colonel P. M. B. Young led the charge, dispersed the party, and captured prisoners from the 3d Indiana and 8th Illinois Cavalry. Hampton states that the published accounts of the enemy acknowledged the loss of thirty men killed and wounded in this fight. His own loss was four killed and nine wounded. Among the latter was Lieutenant-Colonel Young. This attack upon the enemy's rear brought the much needed relief to Munford, although he was at the time unaware of the real cause. Menaced by this new danger the enemy retired from Munford's front, giving the road to Hampton, who, approaching from the direction from which Munford anticipated attack, was not recognized by him. Waiting until the head of Hampton's column was within easy range, Munford's guns were shotted and the lanyards applied; when fortunately Hampton perceived the intention, and raising a white flag made himself known as a friend.

The situation of the Confederate army on the morning of the 14th of September was critical in the extreme. Jackson's corps and three divisions of Longstreet's were concentrated at Harper's Ferry, and were separated from the rest of the army by the Potomac River. This was practically the case even with McLaws' command on Maryland Heights; for he was eventually compelled to cross the river into Virginia and recross at Shepherdstown before he could rejoin the army at Sharpsburg. Four divisions of infantry and a

part of the cavalry alone remained with General Lee.
The mountain passes at Turner's and Crampton's gaps
were held by mere rear-guards: D. H. Hill's division, of
less than five thousand men, occupying the important
point at Turner's Gap, while Hampton and Munford,
with their cavalry, held Crampton's Gap. In his advance on the 13th the enemy had not exposed much
of his force, and Stuart was still uncertain as to the
character of the movement he had been opposing, especially as Fitz Lee had been unable to gain the enemy's rear. Naturally anxious not to overestimate the
force he had encountered, Stuart reported to D. H. Hill
and to McLaws only what he had seen, and this was
not enough to cause serious apprehensions. Nevertheless Harper's Ferry had not yet surrendered, and until
this did take place and give opportunity for the concentration of the Confederate army, the gravest peril
existed that McLaws might be overpowered at Maryland Heights, and that the four divisions with General Lee might be called upon to face the greater part
of the Federal army. It was therefore imperative
that the mountain passes should be held for at least a
day longer; and to effect this Longstreet was recalled
from Hagerstown to Boonsboro' by a forced march, and
Cobb's brigade was sent by McLaws to reinforce the
two brigades he had left near Crampton's Gap. But
so great was the uncertainty produced by the inactivity
of the enemy on the 13th that D. H. Hill did not
move to the front two of his brigades, Ripley's and
Rodes', until he was actually attacked; and McLaws
did not send Cobb's brigade to reinforce the gap in his
rear until noon on the same day.

Stuart left the vicinity of Boonsboro' early on the
morning of the 14th and rode rapidly to Crampton's
Gap. The enemy had as yet made no demonstration

at this point, and Stuart deemed it necessary to send Hampton to guard the road next to the river at the end of the mountain ridge, lest an attempt should be made to relieve Harper's Ferry from that direction. Leaving Munford at Crampton's, with his own two regiments of cavalry and two fragments of infantry regiments from Mahone's brigade, and having instructed Munford to hold the gap at any cost, Stuart himself proceeded to McLaws' position to procure additional force, and to acquaint himself with the state of affairs.

Leading westward from Burkittsville two practicable roads cross the mountain at points about a mile distant from each other. The southern passage is known as the Browersville Gap, the northern, as Crampton's. General McLaws had advanced on Maryland Heights through the Browersville Gap, and it was here that he had left General Semmes with his own and Mahone's brigade. Semmes' position was four miles distant from Maryland Heights, and Crampton's Gap was five miles. The roads east of the mountain leading to both these gaps were within sight of each other, and a force advancing upon either was exposed to artillery fire from both.

The inactivity of the Federal army on the 13th and the early part of the 14th of September will, perhaps, be excused by the historian on account of the demoralized condition in which that army was left by the disastrous campaign under General Pope. It possessed, however, at this time every incentive for active exertion. On the 13th General McClellan was authoritatively informed of General Lee's plans and movements; and the exposed condition of his army was as well known to him as to us at the present day. Through the fatal carelessness of some one, that copy of the order of march issued by General Lee on the 9th of September and addressed to General D. H. Hill, which revealed the movement of every part of Lee's army, was left at Frederick and fell into General McClellan's hands. No general could hope for a greater advantage over his adversary; and yet the mountain gaps were not forced until the evening of the 14th. In calculating the results which might have ensued had the Federal army moved with greater celerity, it must not be forgotten that both Hill and McLaws had abundant time to make more effective dispositions for the defence of the gaps, and that these dispositions were not made, simply because the small force developed by the enemy on the 13th did not seem to require them. For the same reason Hampton's brigade of cavalry was moved on the morning of the 14th from Crampton's Gap, where its services would have been of inestimable value, to a point which the sequel showed to be of but little importance.

The battle at Turner's Pass began at about seven o'clock on the morning of the 14th. As the record does not show that the cavalry was actively engaged in this battle, it is only necessary for this narrative to state the general result. General D. H. Hill maintained his position unsupported and without sustaining any serious reverse until four o'clock in the afternoon, although assailed by the two corps which constituted the right wing of the Federal army. At four o'clock Longstreet arrived at the gap, which was held until darkness put an end to the conflict. But both the right and left of the Confederate line had been turned by the superior numbers of the enemy, and the position was no longer tenable. Longstreet and Hill were therefore withdrawn during the night, and on the next morning were placed in position beyond the

Antietam at Sharpsburg. The withdrawal of these troops was covered by Fitz Lee's cavalry brigade, which, on the morning of the 15th, was hotly engaged in a manner which will hereafter be described.

The gallant defence made by Colonel Munford at Crampton's Gap demands a more extended notice. Munford had selected a strong position for his men behind a stone fence near the eastern base of the mountain. In his rear was a body of woods, and in his front a large open field over which the enemy must advance to the attack. Every available cavalryman was dismounted and placed in line of battle to strengthen the two regiments of infantry under his command. Chew's battery of horse artillery and a section of navy howitzers from the Portsmouth battery were placed in position near this line, but were subsequently removed to a more commanding point higher up the mountain. Not until skirmishing had actually begun was Munford reinforced by the two remaining regiments of Mahone's brigade under Colonel Parham. These regiments hardly numbered three hundred men, and the whole force under Munford's control could not have amounted to as many as eight hundred. At noon his pickets at Burkittsville were driven in, and the enemy soon after appeared in force at the base of the mountain. The first demonstration was directed toward the lower gap, the one held by General Semmes; but being met by the artillery fire from both gaps, the assault concentrated on Munford. At three o'clock in the afternoon a column of attack was organized consisting of the three brigades of Slocum's division strengthened by two brigades of Smith's division. Although assailed by such superior numbers Munford held his position for three hours. The action was in full view of General Semmes, but from him he received no further assistance. The infantry under Colonel Parham and the dismounted cavalry vied with each other in the steadiness of their fire, and there was no break in their ranks until after the arrival of Cobb's brigade. Munford's report says: —

After much delay, and some four couriers had been sent, General Cobb, with two regiments of his brigade, came up to my support. When the general himself came up, I explained the position of the troops, and of course turned over the command to him. At his request I posted the two regiments. The first troops, having exhausted all their ammunition, began to fall back as soon as their support came up, Colonel Parham having already partially supplied them with ammunition. When the two other regiments of General Cobb's brigade came up, he again requested me to put them in position, but they behaved badly and did not get in position before the wildest confusion commenced, the wounded coming to the rear in numbers, and more well men coming with them. General Cobb attempted to rally the men, but without the least effect, and it would have been as useless as to attempt to rally a flock of frightened sheep. Had General Cobb's brigade given the support to the first troops engaged which they deserved, the gap would have been held. The cavalry horses were on the road leading to Boonsboro', and having previously retired the artillery on the Harper's Ferry road (every round of ammunition having been fired for some time before), I formed my command and moved down the mountain, the infantry still running in great disorder on the Harper's Ferry road, followed at a short distance by the enemy, who were then between them and the cavalry, who had to go for their horses. The enemy was at the forks of these roads before many of the cavalry, who were the last to give up their position. Had General Cobb come up in time the result might have been otherwise. There were two stone walls at the base of the mountain parallel to each other, and one commanding the other, which could have been held against great odds had the troops been in position.

It affords me great pleasure to commend Colonel Parham as

a gallant and efficient officer, who did everything in his power to hold his position. His little command fought splendidly. Colonel Parham's loss must have been heavy, as he was a long time engaged and the firing was as heavy as I ever heard.

General Slocum acknowledges a loss of 511 in his division. He claims to have captured over 300 prisoners, 700 stand of arms, and one piece of abandoned artillery.

Having regained his horses, Munford retired towards Boonsboro', and on the next day took position covering the approaches to Keedysville. As the enemy closed down upon the line of the Antietam, Munford retired to Sharpsburg, and was assigned to the right of Lee's line of battle, guarding the lower crossings, where he was engaged in active skirmishing on the 17th and 18th.

Munford's gallant fight had transpired while Stuart was on Maryland Heights. The knowledge which he had gained of the country during the John Brown raid led him to believe that he could render valuable assistance at that point; and with this object in view, as well as to gain the information necessary for the proper direction of his own command, he had joined General McLaws while the enemy appeared inactive at Crampton's Gap. He urged that the road leading from Harper's Ferry, by the Kennedy Farm, toward Sharpsburg, be occupied, lest any of the enemy should escape thereby. The neglect of this precaution was followed by serious results. On the night of the 14th, Colonel B. F. Davis, of the 8th New York Cavalry, marched out from Harper's Ferry by this very road, at the head of fifteen hundred horsemen; and, meeting with no opposition, he not only delivered the cavalry from the surrender of the following morning, but inflicted serious loss on the Confederates by capturing a portion of Longstreet's ordnance train near Sharpsburg. General Lee acknowledges the loss of 45 wagons. Colonel Voss, of the 12th Illinois Cavalry, claims the capture of 60 wagons and 675 prisoners.

As soon as Stuart was informed of the fight at Crampton's Gap he returned thither, but only in time to meet the disorganized fugitives of Cobb's brigade as they were streaming down Pleasant Valley. They reported that the enemy was immediately in their rear and in overwhelming force. Aided by the presence of General McLaws, some portions of the brigade were rallied and a line was formed across the road. Reconnoitring parties were sent back toward the gap, but found no enemy within a mile. The approach of night had prevented the enemy from following up the signal advantage which he had gained, and gave time for dispositions to dispute his progress. All of McLaws' command except one regiment and two guns was withdrawn from Maryland Heights, and was moved back toward the mountain passes, in anticipation of a battle on the following morning, but the early surrender of Harper's Ferry relieved McLaws of his most serious embarrassment, and the excellent position of his line of battle in Pleasant Valley caused the enemy to pause. McLaws withdrew his command to Harper's Ferry at two o'clock P. M., and marching by way of Shepherdstown, reached Sharpsburg at sunrise on the 17th, in time to participate in the battle of that day. During this movement his rear was covered by the cavalry under Hampton, which on the 17th occupied position on the right of the Confederate line on the Antietam.

Stuart was on McLaws' line of battle in Pleasant Valley when Harper's Ferry surrendered. The news was at once communicated to the troops, and produced wild demonstrations of joy. Stuart reported in person to General Jackson, and was by him requested to convey the information to the commanding general at Sharpsburg. Leaving his staff to follow at a more moderate pace, he took with him one courier, and proceeded at full speed upon this mission. He reached the town soon after the arrival of Longstreet and D. H. Hill, whose troops were greatly strengthened and encouraged by Jackson's success.

On the night of the 14th, after the battle at Turner's Pass, Fitz Lee was ordered to cover the withdrawal of the infantry from the mountain, and to resist and retard as much as possible the advance which it was anticipated the enemy would make on the following morning. He took position east of Boonsboro', where he could command the road as it descended from the mountain. A good position was secured for his artillery, and dismounted skirmishers were thrown out well to the front. A mounted force on either side of the road supported the guns.

Soon after daylight a column of the enemy's infantry debouched from the gap. Fitz Lee's skirmishers were soon engaged, and fell back slowly until the position occupied by his guns was uncovered. He withheld their fire until the head of the enemy's column was within easy range, when shells were exploded in it so rapidly and accurately as to cause a halt. A second attempt to advance was attended with a like result. Lines of battle were now formed extending beyond both of Fitz Lee's flanks, and he was compelled to retire toward the town. His guns had been sent back to a new position, and his mounted men were in the act of withdrawing, when the lines of the enemy's infantry opened and let out a force of cavalry, which came charging down the road.

The 3d Virginia Cavalry was called on to meet this charge, and responded so handsomely that the Federal cavalry was driven back to their infantry. But the pressure upon Lee's rear was soon renewed, and became so heavy as he was passing through Boonsboro' that it was necessary to make a stand with one of his regiments to insure the orderly withdrawal of the remainder. This difficult duty devolved upon Colonel W. H. F. Lee and the 9th Virginia Cavalry. The street through which he necessarily passed was so narrow that his regiment could only be operated in column of fours. A sufficient interval was, however, preserved between his squadrons, which were employed successively in charging the head of the enemy's advancing column. As one squadron retired from the charge, to form again in rear of the regiment, the one next in front took up the battle. By a rapid series of well executed attacks the 9th regiment thus covered the retreat of the remainder of the brigade and gave it time to take position west of Boonsboro'.

The contest in the streets of the town was fierce and protracted. The Union sentiment here was strong, and Colonel Lee's squadrons were assailed not only by an open enemy, but concealed foes shot at his men from the windows of the houses. The 9th regiment was of course pushed back steadily through the town. In retiring from a charge, one squadron was compelled to cross a narrow bridge. The enemy was pressing close behind. At the entrance to the bridge Colonel Lee's horse fell in the road. The press of men and horses permitted no attempt at recovery. In an instant he was overridden by his own men and by a portion of the enemy. Captain Haynes, who commanded the squadron next in position, charged and recovered the bridge, and raising Colonel Lee's horse from the ground, called upon him to mount and escape. He was, however, so stunned and bruised as to be incapable of moving hand or foot; and before others of his men could come to his rescue Captain Haynes was driven back across the bridge by a fresh charge of the enemy, and was compelled to leave his colonel to his fate. For some time he lay on the roadside, dazed and helpless, as the enemy's cavalry, infantry, and artillery passed by within a few feet of him. No one, however, noticed him. At length the thought entered his mind that escape was not impossible. By slow and painful movements he crawled to a copse of woods which skirted the field adjacent to the road. Here he was so fortunate as to meet two or three Confederate soldiers, who had become separated from their commands. By them he was raised to his feet and supported to a farm-house, where a horse was procured. Avoiding the roads and pressing westward, he succeeded in crossing the Antietam before night, and was soon afterwards in the hands of his friends, who welcomed him as one restored from the dead.

Having brought his command through Boonsboro', Fitz Lee made another stand at the intersection of the Keedysville road, where he was again successful in delaying the enemy for a considerable time. In withdrawing from this position he retired on the road leading directly west, hoping to draw the enemy after him on this, which was, for them, the wrong road. He thus occupied their attention during the greater part of the day, and finding, at length, that he was no longer pursued, he moved his command to Sharpsburg, and placed it on the left of the Confederate line, guarding the upper fords of the Antietam.

It was not until late in the afternoon of the 16th that the Federal army was so far concentrated west of the Antietam as to warrant the beginning of an attack. The Confederate line of battle rested its right upon Antietam Creek, covering the two bridges by which alone Sharpsburg could be approached in that direction, and extended thence northward for a distance of about two and a half miles, nearly parallel with the course of the Antietam. The right was held by Longstreet, the centre by D. H. Hill, and the left by two small divisions of Jackson's corps, commanded by General Lawton. The Confederate left was prolonged by the cavalry under Stuart, and was somewhat retired, in a westerly direction, toward the Potomac River. Any attack upon the Confederate right or centre must of necessity be preceded by a severe struggle for the possession of the narrow stone bridges which there spanned the Antietam; but on the Confederate left there were bridges and practicable fords across which an undisputed passage could be made. This consideration determined McClellan's plan of battle, which was to cross the Antietam at the points above Sharpsburg where it was undefended, and attempt to crush the Confederate left wing, which being accomplished would make easy the attacks which should be subsequently directed against the centre and right. The effort against the Confederate left was made by three corps, those of Hooker, Mansfield, and Sumner. Hooker crossed the Antietam on the afternoon of the 16th, and pressed southward and eastward. Timely notice of this movement was given by Stuart, and two brigades of Hood's division were sent forward to meet it. They encountered Hooker's troops in the woods east of the Hagerstown turnpike, and opposite the Dunkard Church, around which the battle must rage so fiercely the following day. Night had now fallen. The sharp contest between Hooker's troops and Hood's brigades had lasted but a short time, and had resulted in no advantage to either side. Both parties lay down upon their arms, ready to resume the battle at the dawn of day. During the night Hood was replaced by Lawton's and Trimble's brigades from Jackson's command. On the other side Mansfield's corps had crossed the Antietam and lay within supporting distance of Hooker, while Sumner was close to the Antietam, ready to cross at daybreak.

I borrow the following description of this part of the field of battle from Swinton's " Decisive Battles of the War " : —

If leaving the town of Sharpsburg the pedestrian walks northward by the Hagerstown road, he will, at the distance of a mile, reach a small edifice, known as the Dunker Church, situate on the road, hard by a body of woods. This wood, which has a depth of about a quarter of a mile, runs along the Hagerstown road for several hundred yards, entirely on the left hand side as you proceed from Sharpsburg. Then there is a field, the edge of which runs at right angles to the road for about two hundred yards, thus making an elbow in the woods. The field then turns to the right, and runs along the woods parallel to the Hagerstown road for a quarter of a mile, when the wood again turns square to the left and extends back about half a mile, making at this point again an elbow with the strip of woods running along the road from the church. The timber ground is full of ledges of limestone and small ridges, affording excellent cover for troops. It was here that Jackson's troops were posted. The field from the timber to the Hagerstown road forms a plateau, nearly level, and in higher ground than the woods, which slope down abruptly from the edges of the plateau. The field, however, extends not only *to* the Hagerstown road, but for a considerable distance to the east side of it, when it is again circumscribed by another body of timber, which we may call the " east woods." The woods around the Dunker Church, the " east woods," and the open field between them formed the arena whereon the terrible wrestle between the Union right and Confederate left took place, — a fierce flame of battle, which, beginning in the "east woods," swept back and forth across the field, burst forth for a time in the woods around the Dunker Church, and which left its marks everywhere, but in most visible horror on the open plain.

The advance of Hooker's corps, which had been interrupted by nightfall, was resumed at the dawn of day. His first onset fell upon the three brigades of Ewell's division, Lawton's, Trimble's, and Hays', under the command of General Lawton, which numbered only twenty-four hundred men. Early's brigade had been sent to support the artillery with which Stuart, on the left, maintained a severe enfilading fire upon the enemy's right. After sustaining the unequal contest for an hour, this little band of heroes was forced back across the open field east of the turnpike, and into the woods in which is situated the Dunkard Church. Here, still fighting, they were reinforced by Jackson's other division, commanded by General Starke, and the battle was renewed with almost unparalleled ferocity. Before seven o'clock A. M. Jackson had lost one half of his men in killed and wounded, and Hooker's corps had been so completely shattered that General Sumner stated that when he came upon the field he saw nothing of it at all.

As the Confederate line retired, Stuart's position became too much exposed, and the direction of his fire now endangered his friends. He therefore withdrew more to the rear of the Confederate left, where he was better able to participate in the contest, which still raged around the Dunkard Church. At the same time Early was recalled to assume the command of Ewell's division, after General Lawton was wounded; and leaving one regiment, the 13th Virginia, to support Stuart's artillery, he returned toward the position he had first occupied that morning. At half past seven o'clock Mansfield's corps reinforced Hooker's shattered line, but he was met and disastrously repulsed by Hood's division, which pursued the retreating enemy east of the turnpike, until the ground was recovered on which the battle had begun at daybreak. But here again the tide of battle turned, for Sumner's corps had now advanced to the front, and attacking with fresh strength troops already exhausted, Hood's division was forced back across the open field, now ghastly with the dead and dying, and into, and even beyond, the woods surrounding the Dunkard Church. While this last attack was transpiring Early was moving his brigade into position in this body of woods, which he had just regained after leaving Stuart. The advance of Sumner was pursued so far that Early was entirely separated on his right from the rest of Jackson's command, and was at the same time threatened with attack by a force which was advancing across the open field toward his left. At the moment when the success of Sumner's attack was such as seemingly to threaten the destruction of the Confederate left, McLaws' division arrived in place, and, joining with Early in a sweeping charge, drove Sumner back through the woods and across the open field east of the turnpike, and into the woods in which the battle first began.

In such a battle there was no opportunity to use the little body of cavalry which followed Stuart to support his guns. But Stuart himself was ceaselessly active. The positions which he occupied were indeed of the greatest importance. Between the left of Jackson's line and the sharp elbow which the Potomac makes just beyond was an open space, through which, if left unguarded, the enemy might easily have penetrated to

Jackson's rear. The rising ground gave admirable positions for artillery, and had these hills fallen into the possession of the Federals, Jackson's divisions must have been driven back upon the Confederate centre. The historian Swinton blames Hooker because, after his first success in driving back Lawton's three brigades to the Dunkard Church, he did not at once order up Mansfield's corps, and occupy this ground. He says : —

There is a commanding eminence to the right of where Hooker's flank rested, which would thus have been occupied ; and as it is the key of the field, taking *en revers* the woods with the outcropping ledges of limestone where Jackson's reserves lay, its possession would, in all likelihood, have been decisive of the field. Hooker failed to perceive this; but he advanced his line to reap the fruit of his first advantage, thrusting forward his centre and left over the open fields toward the woods west of the Hagerstown road.[1]

This very position which Swinton thinks might have been occupied by Mansfield was the one which Stuart guarded. Behind his guns at the time of Hooker's first success lay Early's brigade of infantry and Fitz Lee's brigade of cavalry. Mansfield might have gained these heights, but certainly not without a struggle ; for not only was the horse artillery brought into action by Stuart, but other guns from Jackson's command served with him under Pelham. Poague, Pegram, and Carrington, with others, were there. The last assault made by Sumner's corps brought it under the musketry fire of the 13th Virginia Infantry, which supported these guns. In speaking of the final repulse of this corps General Early says : —

Major-General Stuart, with the pieces of artillery under his charge, contributed largely to the repulse of the enemy, and

[1] *Decisive Battles of the War*, p. 165.

pursued them for some distance with his artillery and the 13th
Virginia regiment under the command of Captain F. V.
Winston.

General Jackson says, in reference to a proposed
movement against the enemy's right, on the afternoon
of the 17th : —

In this movement Major-General Stuart had the advance,
and acted well his part. This officer rendered valuable service
throughout the day. His bold use of artillery secured for us
an important position, which, had the enemy possessed, might
have commanded our left.

The repulse of Sumner's corps closed the serious
fighting on that flank. Attempts were made to force
the right and centre of the Confederate line, but they
were repulsed ; and night closed down upon this hard-
fought field. With four thousand men Jackson had
sustained the attack of Hooker's powerful corps, and
had reduced it to the condition described in General
Sumner's words. When Hooker was reinforced by
Mansfield's corps, Hood's division came to Jackson's assistance. Then followed McLaw's charge and the final
repulse of Sumner's corps. Two divisions of Jackson's
corps, aided by two divisions from Longstreet's, in all
less than ten thousand men, had met and shattered
three corps of the Federal army, which outnumbered
them four to one.

On the 18th the two armies confronted each other
in sullen silence. The scene can never be forgotten
by those who rode along Jackson's attenuated line.
There appeared to be hardly one man to a rod of
ground, and it seemed that a compact regiment must
pierce such a line at any point, should the attempt be
made. But a bold front and an over-cautious enemy
saved the Confederates from such an unequal contest ;
and during the night General Lee safely transferred

his forces to the south bank of the Potomac. Fitz Lee's brigade again covered the withdrawal of the infantry. Munford, who had been skirmishing with the enemy on the extreme right, along the bank of the canal, made a somewhat narrow escape. The messenger sent by Fitz Lee to notify him to withdraw had failed to find him ; and it was not until he rode in person to Sharpsburg, and there met General Fitz Lee, that he was made aware of the isolated situation of his command. However, a rapid ride brought his brigade to Shepherdstown in time to cross the river in the presence of the enemy, and under the cover of the friendly guns on the southern bank. General Munford relates an incident which occurred at the ford, and which is worth preservation. As he reached the river bank he found there General Maxey Gregg with about one hundred men, the rear of the infantry. At the edge of the river, and in the water, stood an ambulance filled with wounded men. The cowardly driver had unhitched his horses, crossed the river, and had left his suffering comrades to the mercy of the foe. The poor fellows begged piteously to be carried to the other side. General Gregg lifted his hat, and said to his soldiers, —

" My men, it is a shame to leave these poor fellows here in the water ! Can't you take them over the river ? "

In an instant a dozen or more strong men laid hold on the ambulance and pulled it through the water, in most places waist deep, amid the shouts of the rest, who sang, —

" Carry me back to Old Virginia."

General Munford also states that Lieutenant W. O. English, of company K, 2d Virginia Cavalry, was the last Confederate who crossed the ford at Shepherdstown. He blew up two abandoned caissons with a slow match, and then crossed under fire.

Munford's brigade now took position on the right of the Confederate line, near Boteler's Ford. On the evening of the 19th four regiments of the 5th corps crossed the river at this ford, and attacked the reserve artillery, which was supported by Lawton's and Armistead's brigades. These two brigades did not number more than 600 men. They gave way before the attack of the enemy, and permitted the capture of four pieces of artillery. The retreat of the infantry and artillery was covered by Munford's brigade, and greater loss was prevented by the efficiency with which the cavalry was handled. The enemy retired to the Maryland side during the night, but renewed the attempt to harass the Confederate rear on the following morning. Two brigades of Sykes' division and one from Morell's, in all thirteen regiments, numbering about 3,500 men, crossed the river at an early hour, and advanced toward Shepherdstown. They were met by A. P. Hill's division, and were driven back across the river with a loss of 331 men. In this action only three brigades of Hill's division were engaged. His total loss was 261.

While these events were transpiring on the right of the Confederate army, Stuart, with Hampton's brigade and some small detachments from several infantry regiments, had ascended the Potomac on the afternoon of the 18th to Williamsport, for the purpose of making a demonstration which might give aid to the army in retiring across the river on the 19th. Two sections of artillery accompanied this movement. Stuart maintained a threatening position on the Maryland side during the 19th and 20th. On the latter day he was engaged in skirmishing with Couch's division, which had been sent to dislodge him. At night on the 20th he withdrew to the Virginia side without loss.

General Lee's army now moved back beyond Martinsburg, and for about six weeks enjoyed much-needed rest. The cavalry covered the front of the army, and protected it from annoyance. On the 1st of October, General Pleasonton, with seven hundred cavalry and a battery of artillery, made a reconnoissance as far as Martinsburg, retiring within his lines on the same day. This affair was attended with but little result on either side.

CHAPTER XI.[1]

DURING the period of rest which succeeded the battle of Sharpsburg, the cavalry headquarters was located under the magnificent oaks which beautify the lawn of "The Bower," — the residence of Mr. A. S. Dandridge, near Charlestown. The open-hearted hospitality, the pleasant and ennobling social intercourse of those days, can never be forgotten by those who participated in them.

For a few days before the 9th of October a more than usual stir at cavalry headquarters aroused suspicion on the part of those who were somewhat behind the scenes. On the afternoon of the 8th Stuart ordered his acting adjutant, Lieutenant R. Channing Price, to prepare all official papers which required his attention. The evening, until eleven o'clock, was spent in the society of the ladies of "The Bower." Retiring to his tent Stuart then consumed two hours in closing up the business of his office. This done, the banjo, fiddle, and bones were awakened, and a parting serenade was given to his kind friends.

On the morning of the 9th everything was astir. Eighteen hundred cavalry were to rendezvous that day at Darksville. Six hundred of the best mounted and most reliable men had been selected from each of the

---

[1] Reports and correspondence, verifying most of the statements contained in this chapter, will be found in *Official Records*, vol. xix. part ii. p. 26 *et seq*.

three brigades of Hampton, Fitz Lee, and Robertson, and these detachments were commanded respectively by Brigadier-General Wade Hampton, Colonel W. H. F. Lee, and Colonel William E. Jones. Major John Pelham commanded the four guns which accompanied the expedition.

When the troops had assembled at the rendezvous, Stuart issued to them the following address: —

Soldiers! You are about to engage in an enterprise which, to insure success, imperatively demands at your hands coolness, decision, and bravery; implicit obedience to orders without a question or cavil; and the strictest order and sobriety on the march and in bivouac. The destination and extent of this expedition had better be kept to myself than known to you. Suffice it to say, that with the hearty coöperation of officers and men I have not a doubt of its success, — a success which will reflect credit in the highest degree upon your arms. The orders which are here published for your government are absolutely necessary, and must be rigidly enforced.

The orders which controlled the action of the troops were in substance as follows : each brigade commander was required to detail one third of his command to seize horses and other property of citizens of the United States subject to legal capture, while the remainder of his command was held at all times in readiness for action. It was required that receipts should be given to all non-combatants for every article taken from them, in order that they might have recourse upon the Federal government for damages. Individual plundering was prohibited in the strongest manner. The arrest of public functionaries, such as magistrates, postmasters, and sheriffs, was ordered, that such persons might be held as hostages for citizens of the Confederacy who had been arrested and imprisoned. The seizure of private property in the State of Maryland was prohibited.

Every nerve of every man responded to Stuart's address. The secrecy of the movement added zest to it. Many a trooper in that company had ridden with him around McClellan's army, on the Chickahominy, and all felt that they could safely follow where Stuart led the way. Hampton took the lead from Darksville. It was necessary to conceal the presence of the troops from the signal station on the Maryland side of the river, and Hedgesville was approached after dark. Here the command bivouacked for the night, during which Hampton personally selected the place where a chosen body of twenty-five men, under Lieutenant H. R. Phillips, of the 10th Virginia Cavalry, was to cross the river on foot above the ford at McCoy's, and attempt the surprise and capture of the Federal picket. Colonel M. C. Butler, of the 2d South Carolina Cavalry, who led Hampton's advance, added to this party Lieutenant Robert Shiver, an experienced scout, and six picked men from his own regiment.

Before daylight every man was in the saddle. Butler, at the head of Captain John Chestnut's company, was at the ford, listening for some token of Shiver and his men. Soon it came. Shiver had not succeeded in surrounding the picket; but he drove it in so rapidly that the fugitives were cut off from their reserve, and were unable to report the attack made upon them. One Federal soldier was wounded and several horses were captured.

At the first sound from the opposite side Butler plunged into the river and secured the ford; and the whole command made a quick and quiet crossing. The advance was immediately pressed forward to the National Turnpike, which joins Hagerstown and Hancock, near which, upon Fairview Heights, was established a Federal signal station. Along this road, between three

and five o'clock that morning, had passed General Cox's
division of infantry. Butler reached the turnpike so
close to their rear that he captured ten stragglers from
that command. The heavy fog which covered the
river valley obscured all movements, and General Cox
proceeded on his march to Hancock ignorant of the
presence of the Confederate cavalry in his rear.

Twenty men were now sent to capture the signal
station on Fairview. They approached it within a few
rods before they were discovered. The two officers in
charge of the station succeeded in making their escape;
but two privates and all the equipments of the station
were captured.

Stuart's march was not, however, unobserved. Captain Logan, of the 12th Illinois Cavalry, who had charge
of the pickets in the vicinity, was apprised by a citizen
as early as half past five o'clock that the enemy was
crossing at McCoy's Ferry; and he immediately moved
out his reserve to the support of his interior pickets,
which had been attacked but not surprised. He remained in observation of Stuart's column until nine
o'clock A. M., when, finding that Stuart was marching
towards Mercersburg, he moved his pickets around to
guard the roads leading from the north. At half past
seven o'clock General Kenly at Williamsport was aware
of the raid, and at ten o'clock A. M. had communicated
the direction of Stuart's march to General Brooks at
Hagerstown. But there was no force of cavalry available to check its progress, and the column pressed
steadily forward toward Mercersburg.

Although McClellan's army was now on the lookout
for the invading cavalry, there was no suspicion of
their presence on the line of march, which was remote
from telegraph and railroad. The Pennsylvania people
could not believe it possible that the rebel cavalry had

invaded the security of their farms, and when the truth was forced upon them, their surprise and consternation were the occasion of many incidents highly amusing to the Confederates. Butler's advance - guard was completely equipped with boots and shoes at the expense of a Mercersburg merchant, who had no suspicion of the character of his liberal customers until payment was tendered in the form of the receipt required by General Stuart's orders. One old gentleman, who was despoiled of a large sorrel mare which he was driving to a cart, protested that the impressment of horses had been forbidden by orders from Washington. He refused to be convinced that he had fallen into the hands of the rebels; but threatened the vengeance of the general government upon those who had disregarded its orders.

The terms of Stuart's orders were strictly enforced during the whole march. Nothing whatever was disdisturbed on the soil of Maryland ; but when once the Pennsylvania line was crossed, the seizure of horses was prosecuted with system and diligence. Six hundred men scoured the country on either side of the line of march, and as far as scouts could extend the country was denuded of its horses. With his usual courtesy toward ladies, Stuart gave orders that, whenever they might meet his column, they should be allowed to pass in their conveyances without molestation. So strict was the enforcement of orders that the men were not even allowed to seize provisions for themselves. They sometimes, however, obtained by stratagem what they were not permitted to take by force. On the second day's march some hungry cavalrymen approached a house whose male defenders had fled, leaving the women and babies in possession. A polite request for food was met by the somewhat surly reply that there was none in the house. Casting a wolfish glance upon the babies, a lean fellow remarked that he had never been in the habit of eating human flesh, but that he was now hungry enough for anything; and if he could get nothing else he believed he would compromise on one of the babies. It is hardly necessary to say that the mother's heart relented and a bountiful repast was soon provided.[1]

Stuart reached Chambersburg about eight o'clock on the evening of the 10th, in the midst of a drizzling rain. Two pieces of artillery were placed in position commanding the town, and Lieutenant Thomas Lee, with nine men from Butler's regiment, was sent forward to demand an unconditional surrender within thirty minutes, under penalty of a cannonade. No resistance was made, and the troops were immediately marched into the town and drawn up on the public square. Colonel Butler was ordered by Stuart to enter the bank and obtain whatever funds were on hand. Accompanied by a suitable guard Butler took possession of the building. The cashier assured him that the funds had been sent away that morning, and he opened the vault and drawers for inspection. Butler was soon satisfied that the statement of the cashier was correct. Doubtless he had been warned from Hagerstown of possible danger, and had prudently provided against it. Reassured by the courteous deportment of Colonel Butler, the cashier, now that the search for money was ended, summoned the ladies of his family, and voluntarily brought forth food for the men, who, though hungry, had made no demand on him for the supply of their personal wants. Hampton was constituted military governor of the town, and placed Butler in

[1] This incident has been claimed by other Confederates ; but it is original with a member of the 9th Virginia Cavalry, and on this raid.

immediate command. The strictest discipline was enforced, and quiet reigned throughout the entire night.

The conduct of the Confederate cavalry in Chambersburg was so exemplary that it deserves especial commemoration. The testimony on this point comes almost exclusively from Federal sources, and bears the greater weight because given voluntarily. Colonel A. K. McClure, now proprietor of the Philadelphia "Times," was at that time a resident of Chambersburg, and was one of the committee of three citizens who formally surrendered the city to General Hampton. Colonel McClure wrote at the time a most interesting account of the "day of rebel rule in Chambersburg," from which extracts are given which show its true character. It will be well, however, to relate first one incident which has come to light within recent days.

Hugh Logan, one of Stuart's trusted guides and scouts, had been for years a resident of Pennsylvania. To him Colonel McClure had, in former days, rendered some professional services which Logan remembered with kindness. The present circumstances placed it in Logan's power to pay his debt of gratitude. He recognized Colonel McClure at the time of the surrender of the city; and knowing that he was subject to capture as an officer of the United States, he advised him to go to his home and there remain quietly, in the hope that he might escape identification and arrest. At the same time he assured Colonel McClure that if he should be discovered and arrested, he would take means to secure his release. Influenced by these and other considerations Colonel McClure determined to share the fate of his fellow-citizens. He thus describes the scenes of that night.

After travelling a mile westward we were brought to a halt by a squad of mounted men, and were informed that General

Hampton was one of the party, to whom we should address ourselves. It was so dark that I could not distinguish him from any of his men. Upon being informed that we were a committee of citizens, and that there was no organized force in the town, and no military commander at the post, he stated, in a respectful and soldier-like manner, that he commanded the advance of the Confederate troops, that he knew resistance would be vain, and he wished the citizens to be fully advised of his purpose, so as to avoid needless loss of life and wanton destruction of property. He said that he had been fired upon at Mercersburg and Campbellstown, and had great difficulty in restraining his troops. He assured us that he would scrupulously protect the citizens, — would allow no soldiers to enter public or private houses unless under command of an officer upon legitimate business, — that he would take such private property as he needed for his government or troops, but that he would do so under officers who would allow no wanton destruction, and would give receipt for the same if desired, so that claim might be made therefor against the United States government. All property belonging to or used by the United States, he stated, he would use or destroy at his pleasure, and the wounded in hospitals would be paroled. Being a United States officer myself, I naturally felt some anxiety to know what my fate would be if he should discover me, and I modestly suggested that there might be some United States officers in the town in charge of the wounded, stores, or of recruiting offices, and asked what disposition he would make of them. He answered that he would parole them, unless he should have special reasons for not doing so ; and he instructed us that none such should be instructed by us to leave the town. Here I was in an interesting situation. If I remained there might, in General Hampton's opinion, be " special reasons " for not paroling me, and the fact that he had several citizens of Mercersburg with him as prisoners did not diminish my apprehensions. If I should leave, as I had ample opportunity afterward to do, I might be held as violating my own agreement, and to what extent my family and property might suffer in consequence, conjecture had a very wide range. With sixty acres of corn in shock, and three barns full of grain, excellent farm and saddle-horses and a number of best blooded cattle, the question of property was worthy of a thought. I resolved to stay, as I felt so bound by the terms of surrender, and take my chances of discovery and parole.

. . . .

I started in advance of them for my house, but not in time to save the horses. I confidently expected to be overrun by them, and to find the place one scene of desolation in the morning. I resolved, however, that things should be done soberly, if possible, and I had just time to destroy all the liquors about the house. As their pickets were all around me, I could not get it off. . . . I finished just in time, for they were soon out upon me in force, and every horse in the barn, ten in all, was promptly equipped and mounted by a rebel cavalryman. They passed on towards Shippensburg, leaving a picket force on the road.

In an hour they returned with all the horses they could find, and dismounted to spend the night on the turnpike in front of my door. It was now midnight, and I sat on the porch observing their movements. They had my best corn-field beside them, and their horses fared well. In a little while one entered the yard, came up to me, and after a profound bow, politely asked for a few coals to start a fire. I supplied him, and informed him as blandly as possible where he would find wood conveniently, as I had dim visions of camp-fires made of my palings. I was thanked in return, and the mild-mannered villain proceeded at once to strip the fence and kindle fires. Soon after a squad came and asked permission to get some water. I piloted them to the pump, and again received a profusion of thanks.

Communication having been opened between us, squads followed each other closely for water, but each called and asked permission before getting it, and promptly left the yard. I was somewhat bewildered by this uniform courtesy, and supposed it but the prelude to a general movement upon everything eatable in the morning. It was not a grateful reflection that my beautiful mountain trout, from twelve to twenty inches long, sporting in the spring, would probably grace the rebel breakfast-table ; that the blooded calves in the yard beside them would most likely go with the trout ; and the dwarf pears had, I felt assured, abundant promise of early relief from their golden burdens.

About one o'clock, half a dozen officers came to the door, and asked to have some coffee made for them, offering to pay liberally for it in Confederate scrip. After concluding a treaty with them on behalf of the colored servants, coffee was promised them, and they then asked for a little bread with it. They were wet and shivering, and seeing a bright, open wood-fire in the library, they asked permission to enter and warm themselves until their coffee should be ready, assuring me that under no circumstances should anything in the house be disturbed by their men. I had no alternative but to accept them as my guests until it might please them to depart, and I did so with as good grace as possible.

Once seated around the fire all reserve seemed to be forgotten on their part, and they opened a general conversation on politics, the war, the different battles, the merits of generals of both armies, etc. They spoke with entire freedom upon every subject but their movement into Chambersburg. Most of them were men of more than ordinary intelligence and culture, and their demeanor was in all respects eminently courteous. I took a cup of coffee with them, and have seldom seen anything more keenly relished. They said that they had not tasted coffee for weeks before, and that then they had paid from six to ten dollars per pound for it. When they were through they asked whether there was any coffee left, and finding that there was some, they proposed to bring some more officers and a few privates who were prostrated by exposure, to get what was left. They were, of course, as welcome as those present, and on they came in squads of five or more, until every grain of browned coffee was exhausted. Then they asked for tea, and that was served to some twenty more.

In the mean time a subordinate officer had begged of me a little bread for himself and a few men, and he was supplied in the kitchen. He was followed by others in turn, until nearly a hundred had been supplied with something to eat or drink.

All, however, politely asked permission to enter the house, and behaved with entire propriety. They did not make a single rude or profane remark even to the servants. In the mean time, the officers who had first entered the house had filled their pipes from the box of Killickinick on the mantel, — after being assured that smoking was not offensive, — and we had another hour of free talk on matters generally. . . .

At four o'clock in the morning the welcome blast of the bugle was heard, and they rose hurriedly to depart. Thanking me for the hospitality they had received, we parted, mutually expressing the hope that should we ever meet again, it would be under more pleasant circumstances. In a few minutes they were mounted and moved into Chambersburg. About seven o'clock I went into town.

. . . .

General Stuart sat on his horse in the centre of the town, surrounded by his staff, and his command was coming in from the country in large squads, leading their old horses and riding the new ones they had found in the stables hereabouts. General Stuart is of medium size, has a keen eye, and wears immense sandy whiskers and moustache. His demeanor to our people was that of a humane soldier. In several instances his men commenced to take private property from stores, but they were arrested by General Stuart's provost-guard. In a single instance only, that I heard of, did they enter a store by intimidating the proprietor. All of our stores and shops were closed, and, with a very few exceptions, were not disturbed.

Certainly this was a remarkable scene. It did, however, but illustrate the control which Stuart had over his men. They were accustomed to feel his hand upon them in the camp as well as on the field of battle ; and they knew that when occasion required that hand was a heavy one. Orders were issued to be obeyed, and not as an empty sound. And then, the ranks of Stuart's regiments were largely filled by men from the highest class of Southern society, — men who intelligently appreciated the importance of obedience, and who yielded it as readily as they did their lives at their country's call.

Stuart, with his staff and escort of couriers, bivouacked outside of the town, at the toll-gate on the Gettysburg road. Night had settled down upon him with a drizzling rain, which had since increased to a steady, continuous dropping.

Rain! rain! rain! Will it never cease? Dangers are multiplying around him. Troops are concentrating to oppose him. Cavalry is marching to intercept him. Scouts are threading every road to ascertain his movements and direct attack upon him. And then this rain! It is easy enough to penetrate into the enemy's country, but can he as easily escape from it?

His plan of return is fixed in his mind; but what if the river should rise beyond fording, and thus cut off the last hope of escape?

Captain B. S. White, of his staff, was a former resident of Poolesville, Md., and on him Stuart relied as his principal guide on the return. Three times during that anxious night, while his soldiers slept the sleep of the weary and the careless, did Stuart arouse White and ask whether he thought that the rain would at once raise the river. Each time White assured him that his troopers could march as fast as the water would flow, and that he would have ample time to cross the river before the rain now falling on the mountains could cause a swell at the lower fords. But oh! how slowly passed the hours! The plashing rain invited thought, and there was nothing of action to banish apprehension. The command must rest until morning to prepare for the supreme effort which lay before them; and their leader could only wait and long for daylight. How heavy the responsibility which drove sleep from the eyes of that light-hearted cavalryman!

Day dawned at last, and the head of the column started toward Gettysburg. While riding between his advance-guard and his main body, Stuart called to his side his engineer officer, Captain W. W. Blackford. For some moments he rode in silence. At length he spoke with deep feeling : —

"Blackford, I want to explain to you my reasons for selecting this route for return ; and if I do not survive, I want you to vindicate my memory."

Taking out his map, he proceeded : —

"You see, the enemy will be sure to think that I will try to recross above, because it is nearer to me and further from them. They will have all the fords strongly guarded in that direction, and scouting parties will be on the lookout for our approach, so that they can concentrate to meet us at any point. They will never expect me to move three times the distance and cross at a ford below them and so close to their main body, and therefore they will not be prepared to meet us down there.

"Now, do you understand what I mean ? And don't you think I am right ?"

Blackford assured him that he understood and approved his reasons, and that, should the necessity arise, he would make them known.

This momentary unbending brought to Stuart's mind the needed relief, and soon the cloud of thought was lifted from his brow, and his joyous, confident habit resumed its sway.

Colonel Butler, who had held the advance on the previous day, now brought up the rear with the 2d South Carolina and a detachment from the 1st North Carolina Cavalry, under the gallant Captain W. H. H. Cowles. He was ordered to destroy the ordnance store-house, which contained a large amount of ammuni-

tion and other army supplies. Having made all necessary arrangements, he started his own regiment on the
march, retaining with him only Cowles' detachment.
He then notified the residents in the immediate vicinity
of his intention to fire the building, applied the match
to the slow-burning fuse, and retired to the edge of the
town to await the result. A loud explosion announced
that the fire had reached the fixed ammunition, and in
another instant the whole building was wrapped in
flames. Satisfied that his work was accomplished, Butler hurried on to rejoin the command, which he overtook at Cashtown, seven and a half miles from Gettysburg. He did not leave Chambersburg until nine
o'clock A. M., and from this hour the duration of the
return march is fairly to be computed.

Stuart followed the direct road from Chambersburg
to Gettysburg until he had crossed the Catoctin Mountain. At Cashtown he turned southward and marched
through Fairfield, on the road to Emmittsburg. All
day long the details had been busy collecting horses ;
but when the Maryland line was reached the command
was halted, compactly closed up, and the order was
again issued that no horses should be taken from the
State of Maryland.

The detachment from Fitz Lee's brigade commanded
by Colonel W. H. F. Lee, had held the advance since
leaving Chambersburg. A squadron of the 1st Virginia
Cavalry, under Captains C. R. Irving and F. W. Southall, constituted the advance - guard. Captain B. S.
White was now placed at the head of this squadron, as
guide, and with Logan and Harbaugh, the other guides,
led the command forward to Emmittsburg, which they
entered about sunset, amid the most extravagant demonstrations of joy and welcome from the inhabitants,
who brought out bountiful provisions for the hungry

men during the few minutes they were allowed to remain in their midst.

Let us now follow the movements of the Federal forces in their endeavors to intercept the raiders.

The cavalry which guarded the right of McClellan's army had given early and accurate reports of the movements of Stuart's column on the morning of the 10th of October. By ten o'clock that night Stuart's arrival at Chambersburg was telegraphed by Governor Curtin to General Wool, at Baltimore, and from that city troops were sent out for the protection of Harrisburg and Gettysburg, at which latter place they arrived about the time that Stuart was recrossing the Potomac at White's Ford. Doubtless these troops could have been moved more expeditiously if they had only known where to move them ; but it required all of Saturday, the 11th, for General Wool and Governor Curtin to decide upon what point Stuart would be most likely to move.

His march as far as Chambersburg was of course definitely known at the headquarters of the Army of the Potomac on the same night ; but General McClellan wisely refrained from sending his cavalry on the fruitless task of following on the trail of the raiders, but waited until Stuart's march from Chambersburg was sufficiently developed to enable him to act with some degree of certainty. Accordingly General Pleasonton and his cavalry were held in readiness near Knoxville during the 10th, and on the 11th, at four o'clock A. M., were ordered to Hagerstown, which they reached before noon. Here Pleasonton received false intelligence which caused him to think that Stuart was endeavoring to retrace his steps and recross the Potomac at one of the upper fords, and he immediately started westward toward Clear Spring. He had not marched more than four miles when he was halted by orders from army headquarters, and at half-past one o'clock was turned back with orders to proceed towards Emmittsburg and Gettysburg. At noon General McClellan had received intelligence of the direction of Stuart's march toward Gettysburg, intelligence which had been forwarded from Chambersburg to Governor Curtin by Colonel McClure, as early as half-past seven o'clock, by the way of Shippensburg. Conjecturing that Stuart might attempt to recross the river near Leesburg, McClellan ordered Stoneman, at Poolesville, to be on the lookout, and turned back Pleasonton to intercept him if possible near Emmittsburg or Mechanicstown.

But Pleasonton had lost nearly two hours of precious time, and had made an unnecessary march of eight miles — hours that might have placed him in position to confront Stuart, and miles every foot of which would tell against his weary horses during the night which was to follow. He reached Mechanicstown, which is hardly less than twenty miles from Hagerstown, at half-past eight o'clock that evening, — an excellent march when it is remembered that he had already travelled thirty miles on the same day. Stuart was even then passing within four miles of him; but Pleasonton did not know it, and his scouts seem to have brought him but tardy information, for he himself states that he was not aware of Stuart's movements until midnight. He then immediately set out for the mouth of the Monocacy, which he reached about eight o'clock on the morning of the 12th. But his extraordinary march of over seventy-eight miles within twenty-eight hours had left him with but a fragment of his command, and he could do little more than observe Stuart's crossing.

Stuart reached Emmittsburg near sunset on the 11th, having marched thirty-one and a half miles since leav-

ing Chambersburg. He was now forty-five miles from
the Potomac. One hour before his arrival at Emmittsburg, four companies of the 6th Pennsylvania Cavalry,
Colonel Rush's Lancers, numbering one hundred and
forty men, had passed through the town on a scout
toward Gettysburg. Some stragglers from this command were chased by Stuart's advance-guard as it entered the town. After enjoying the hospitalities of the
citizens for a few minutes, the march was resumed at a
rapid trot on the road leading southward toward Frederick. Southall commanded the advance platoon.
With him rode Pelham, throughout the night, as a com-
panion. Stuart accompanied Southall for a short distance, to regulate the rate of the march, and, on leaving him, ordered him to keep that gait throughout the
night, and to ride over anything which might oppose
him. Soon after dark a courier was captured bearing despatches from Frederick to the scouting party of Rush's
Lancers. From him and from his papers Stuart learned
that the enemy was still unaware of his locality, although using every means to intercept him. He learned
that Colonel Rush held Frederick with a force sufficient
for its protection,[1] and that General Pleasonton, with
eight hundred men, was rapidly approaching Mechanicstown, only four miles from his line of march. He perhaps
also learned the fact that two brigades of infantry occupied the railroad crossing of the Monocacy, in cars,
the engines with steam up, ready to convey them in
either direction at a moment's warning.[2] To avoid
these dangers, the head of the column was ordered to
turn eastward at Rocky Ridge, and strike the Woods-

---

[1] The records of the A. and I. G. Office show that Colonel Rush had at
Frederick the 6th Pennsylvania Cavalry, the 1st Maine Cavalry, Cole's Maryland battalion of Cavalry, the 5th Connecticut Infantry, the 29th Ohio Infantry, and Battery K, 1st New York Light Artillery.

[2] McClellan's Report.

boro' road, two miles distant. At Rocky Ridge the
advance-guard met a small scouting party of Federal
cavalry which must have come from Pleasonton's command. This party retired at once towards Mechanicstown. This incident, which is given to the author by
Captain B. S. White, who guided the advance-guard,
could not have occurred much later than nine o'clock
P. M., for at half-past ten o'clock a company of the 6th
Pennsylvania Cavalry, sent out from Frederick by
Colonel Rush, observed the march of Stuart's column
through Woodsboro', more than eight miles distant
from Rocky Ridge, and transmitted this information to
Colonel Rush by midnight, sending it at the same time
to General Pleasonton, at Mechanicstown. It is hard
to understand how more than three hours could have
been consumed in sending intelligence from Rocky
Ridge (which must be the place called Middletown in
Pleasonton's report) to Mechanicstown, only four miles
distant; but whatever the cause of the delay, the hours
were well improved by Stuart. Everything now depended upon the rapidity of his march, for his route to
the Potomac was necessarily longer by many miles than
the road which lay open to Pleasonton. Throughout
the whole of the night the head of his column was kept
at a trot, and by daylight on the 12th the advance-
guard entered Hyattstown, which is thirty-three and a
half miles from Emmittsburg. Within twenty hours
Stuart had marched sixty-five miles, and had kept up
his artillery. Horses for the guns and caissons there
were in abundance; and as fast as one team was broken down the horses were turned out and others were
substituted. Three or four times during the night did
the drivers change their horses, and the march was
made without delay or interruption. But at Hyattstown he was still more than twelve miles from a place

of safety. General Stoneman, who was stationed at Poolesville, guarded all the lower fords with three brigades of infantry and Colonel Duffié's cavalry, and Pleasonton was rapidly closing down upon the mouth of the Monocacy. It seemed hardly possible that he could escape these dangers. Even at this day we can almost justify General McClellan in saying : " I did not think it possible for Stuart to recross, and I believed that the capture or destruction of his entire force was perfectly certain." [1]

Up to the time when the command reached Hyattstown Logan and Harbaugh had aided in guiding the advance ; but now that all-important duty devolved solely upon Captain B. S. White, whose long residence at Poolesville had rendered him perfectly familiar with the country. His courage and capacity had often been tried ; nor was he found wanting on this occasion. Upon his well-laid plans the final success of the expedition now largely depended.

Until nine o'clock on the morning of the 12th General Stoneman had been led to believe, by despatches from army headquarters, that Stuart would endeavor to pass between him and the river, and cross at Leesburg. While not neglecting other points, Stoneman's expectations and dispositions were largely based on this information. All that could be learned of Stuart's movements tended to confirm this idea ; and, indeed, Stuart directed his march from Hyattstown with the intention, if possible, thus to deceive his enemy. From Hyattstown he moved to Barnesville, which he reached just after it was vacated by a company of Duffié's cavalry. Thence he pushed boldly southward toward Poolesville. He took it for granted that Sugar Loaf Mountain was occupied by a signal station, and that his every move-

[1] McClellan's Report.

ment would be telegraphed thence, and cause a concentration of forces at Poolesville. When he had
marched a little more than two miles in that direction,
the road entered a large body of woods which enveloped his command and concealed his movements. Here
he found, as White had predicted, a road long disused,
but easily reopened by throwing down a few fences.
Turning abruptly to the west, this road led, within a
mile and a half, to the road between the mouth of the
Monacacy and Poolesville, and entered that road about
three miles from the mouth of the Monocacy. When
Stuart's advance-guard reached the last-named road
they immediately turned northward.

Meanwhile General Pleasonton had reached the
mouth of the Monocacy with that portion of his command which had survived the night's march from Mechanicstown. It was now eight o'clock in the morning. Pleasonton had four hundred cavalry and two of
Pennington's guns in hands. He was pleased to have
occupied the ford which he had selected in his own
mind as the point at which Stuart intended to cross.
As yet nothing had been heard from the raiders, and
Pleasonton moved on toward Poolesville by the very
road now occupied by Stuart, whose advance-guard had
hardly cleared the woods and gained the road, when
the Federal cavalry came in view. The night had
been cold, and the morning was chilly and damp, and
the Confederates had not yet put off the blue overcoats
with which they had provided themselves at Chambersburg. Stuart was riding at the head of his advance-
guard, side by side with Captain Irving and Captain
Southall. The Federal cavalry could not be sure that
this was not a party of their friends. Noticing their
hesitation Stuart restrained his men until a nearer
approach gave him a more complete opportunity for a

surprise. Then the charge was ordered. The Federal squadron stood only long enough to fire one volley, and then turned and ran back to their main body. Captain Irving's horse was wounded by this fire, but no other casualty resulted to the Confederates; nor does it appear that the Federal squadron allowed their enemies to approach sufficiently near to inflict any serious damage upon them. This charge was, however, of the greatest importance to Stuart. By it he occupied the road up to the Little Monocacy, where a high bluff, extending nearly to the river, protected his left flank, and screened his subsequent movements from observation. He also gained a commanding position a quarter of a mile in advance of the road by which Captain White expected to approach White's Ford. Thus far all was well. Unless White's Ford were occupied by the enemy Stuart was safe. Instantly Pelham with one of his guns was hurried forward, and, supported by dismounted men, opened a rapid fire across the Little Monocacy upon Pleasonton's command. At the same moment Colonel W. H. F. Lee, with the leading brigade and the led horses was turned off to the left by a farm road to the ford, which was two miles distant. Lee was followed by Colonel W. E. Jones' command. Hampton held the rear. Stuart's demonstration so impressed Pleasonton with the idea that he wished to advance and cross the Potomac at the mouth of the Monocacy, that he made no effort to attack until reinforced by the arrival of the two remaining guns of Pennington's battery, and by four companies of infantry,[1] which had been stationed at

[1] I have followed General Pleasonton's statement as to the number of companies of infantry, although the report of Colonel E. Walker, commanding the 3d and 4th Maine Infantry, seems to show that both of these regiments were engaged at this point.

the ford behind him. Here again Stuart gained more than two hours, — hours that insured his safety.

As Colonel Lee approached White's Ford it seemed that the worst fears were about to be realized. A large body of Federal infantry had it in possession. Posted on a precipitous quarry bluff, and separated from the ford only by the width of the canal, it seemed a desperate undertaking to attempt to dislodge this force if any serious resistance should be made. But something must be done, and that quickly. The situation seemed so dangerous that Colonel Lee sent a messenger to Stuart requesting his presence at the ford; but Stuart only replied that he was fully occupied where he was, and that the ford must be gained at all hazards. Nothing remained for Lee but to make the attack. His plan was to assail the quarry bluff in front and from his left flank, while a strong party of cavalry made a dash at the ford and endeavored to cross in spite of and through the fire of the enemy. He hoped thus to gain the opposite bank with one gun, and thence open fire upon the enemy's rear. It seemed like a forlorn hope, but there was no escape from it.

While making his dispositions for the attack, Colonel Lee concluded to try the effect of a little bravado. He wrote a note to the Federal commander, stating that General Stuart with his whole command was in his front, and that the hopelessness of making successful resistance must be apparent: to avoid unnecessary bloodshed he was called upon to surrender: fifteen minutes were granted for compliance with this demand, at the expiration of which his line would be charged.

A courier with a handkerchief tied to his sabre conveyed this note to the Federal skirmishers. The fifteen minutes passed, and yet there was no sign of a white flag along the enemy's line. Lee opened with his artillery and ordered his regiments to advance. In another moment he expected to receive the fire of the enemy.

" Is it possible ! " exclaimed several voices. " They are retreating ! They are retreating ! "

It seemed too good to be true ; and yet it was true. With flags flying, drums beating, in perfect order, with skirmishers well out to the rear, the Federal infantry abandoned their strong position without an effort at resistance, and marched eastward down the river. A wild cheer arose from the Confederate ranks when they realized this unexpected deliverance. Glad were they to allow their enemy an unmolested retreat; for the ford was now secure, and safety was within their grasp.

Down into the dry bed of the canal, up its steep bank, and across the rugged ford, one piece of artillery was hurried, and soon crowned the bluff on the Virginia side. The other gun was stationed to sweep the tow-path and other approaches to the ford, while the stream of cavalrymen and the long train of captured horses passed rapidly through the water.

Pelham maintained his position in Pleasonton's front until all but the rear-guard had passed, when he too was gradually withdrawn from one position to another toward the ford. He was making his last stand on the Maryland side, firing now up, now down the river, at the enemy approaching from both directions. Everything was ready for the final withdrawal except that the rear-guard — Butler's regiment and the North Carolinians — had not arrived. Courier after courier had been sent to hasten Butler toward the ford, but no tidings of him had been received.

Captain Blackford had been stationed by Stuart at

the ford to urge on the crossing and to prevent the men from stopping to water their horses. Stuart approached him, and said with evident emotion, —

"Blackford, we are going to lose our rear-guard!"

"How is that, General," asked Blackford.

"Why, I have sent four couriers to Butler, and he is not here yet; and see! there is the enemy closing in behind us!"

"Let me try it!" said Blackford.

Stuart paused a moment, and then, extending his hand, said, —

"All right! and if we don't meet again good-by, old fellow!" and in an instant Blackford was speeding on his mission.

Colonel Butler had brought up the rear the whole distance from Chambersburg. He had assigned the rear-guard to Captain Cowles and the North Carolina detachment. Before his rear had cleared the Poolesville road, Cowles notified Butler that the enemy had overtaken him and was pressing upon him. Butler halted at once, and being entirely ignorant of what was transpiring at the front, made disposition of his regiment and his one gun to resist or delay the further advance of the enemy. While thus engaged, Blackford, who had passed in succession the couriers sent in search of Butler, arrived in hot haste with the news from the front, and all excitement with the intensity of the occasion.

"General Stuart says, 'Withdraw at a gallop, or you will be cut off!'"

"But," replied Butler, with his own inimitable coolness, "I don't think I can bring off that gun. The horses can't move it!"

"Leave the gun," said Blackford, "and save your men."

" Well, we 'll see what we can do!" replied Butler.

To the amazement of all, the broken-down horses responded to whip and spur, and the gun went whirling down the road, followed by Butler and his men. As he rounded the turn of the road toward the ford, Pennington saluted him with his guns; and as he approached the ford he was subjected to the distant and scattering fire of the infantry approaching from Poolesville and the lower river. Ten minutes later, and he could hardly have cut his way through, even with the loss of his gun; but now a rapid dash through the ford, and the last man was safely landed on Virginia soil.

Stuart's joy at the successful termination of his expedition was unbounded. The enemy made no attempt at further pursuit, but approached the ford sufficiently near to receive a few shots from Pelham's guns, and to hear the exulting cheers with which his men greeted Stuart as he rode along their lines.

His march from Chambersburg is one of the most remarkable on record. Within twenty-seven hours he had traversed eighty miles,[1] although encumbered by his artillery and captured horses, and had forced a passage of the Potomac under the very eyes of forces which largely outnumbered his own. His only casualty was the wounding of one man. Two men, who for some reason dropped out of the line of march, were captured.

After a short breathing-spell the troops moved on to Leesburg, ten miles distant, where they bivouacked for the night and enjoyed well-earned repose. Thence by

---

[1] The map shows that Stuart's route from Chambersburg to White's Ford is seventy-seven miles in length. The details of the roads, which the map cannot show, may reasonably be estimated at three miles. Both McClellan and Pleasonton state the length of Stuart's march at ninety miles.

easy marches they returned to their camps west of the mountains.

The amount of public and railroad property destroyed in Chambersburg was estimated by Colonel McClure at about two hundred and fifty thousand dollars. Two hundred and eighty sick and wounded prisoners were paroled. About thirty United States government officials and other citizens of prominence were captured and forwarded to Richmond, to be held as hostages for citizens of the Confederacy imprisoned by the United States authorities. Of the number of horses brought over to Virginia there is no official record; but private memoranda state it at about twelve hundred. The remounts obtained by the Southern cavalry were, however, generally less valuable for the cavalry service than many of the horses that were of necessity abandoned on the march. Stuart himself lost two valuable animals — Lady Margrave and Skylark — which were in charge of his servant Bob. The temptation of drink was too strong for Bob's constancy. He imbibed enough to make him sleepy, fell out of the line to take a nap, and awoke to find himself and his charge in the hands of the enemy.

Not the least important of the results of this expedition was its effects on the physical and moral condition of the Federal cavalry. As to its physical results, General McClellan sufficiently describes them when he says in his report, that it was necessary for him to use all of his cavalry against Stuart, and that " this exhausting service completely broke down nearly all of our cavalry horses and rendered a remount absolutely indispensable before we could advance on the enemy." On the 6th of October General McClellan had received positive orders " to cross the river and attack the enemy." He was unable to execute these orders until

the last days of that month.   His correspondence with
General Halleck shows that the condition of his cavalry was one of the chief causes of this delay.   Perhaps
even more important was the fact that confidence in
the cavalry of the Army of the Potomac was seriously
impaired, not only among the people generally, but
even in the highest circles of the Federal government.
That this statement is no exaggeration appears from
the following letter of President Lincoln.   If *he* could
have given expression to such opinions, what must
have been the sentiment among the people at large!

EXECUTIVE MANSION, WASHINGTON,
October 26, 1862 (Sent 11.30 A. M.).

MAJOR-GENERAL McCLELLAN, — Yours, in reply to mine
about horses, received.   Of course you know the facts better
than I ; still, two considerations remain.   Stuart's cavalry out-
marched ours, having certainly done more marked service on
the Peninsula and everywhere since.   Secondly, will not a
movement of our army be a relief to the cavalry, compelling
the enemy to concentrate, instead of foraying in squads everywhere ?   But I am so rejoiced to learn from your dispatch to
General Halleck that you begin crossing the river this morning.   A. LINCOLN.

The effect upon the Federal cavalry itself may be
inferred from the fact that on the 31st of October,
Stuart felt able, with one thousand men, to throw himself between Pleasonton at Purcellville and Bayard at
Aldie, both of whom commanded forces superior to his
own, causing Bayard to retire toward Washington ;
and holding Pleasonton in check for three days between Philemont and Paris, a distance hardly exceed-
ing ten miles ; although Pleasonton was operating with
two brigades of cavalry and one of infantry.

It is interesting to inquire what were the elements
of success which brought Stuart safely through those

combinations of his enemies which to General McClellan's mind appeared certain to result in the capture or destruction of his command.

First, we must notice that General Stuart himself reverently ascribes his success to the guiding hand of a protecting Providence. To the pious mind, the narrow escape from conflict with Pleasonton south of Emmittsburg; the capture of the courier near Rocky Ridge, with information which showed what dangers were to be avoided; and the retreat of the Federal infantry from White's Ford, must seem to be interpositions of Providence in his behalf.

General Williams C. Wickham relates the following incident. When his command was mounted at Chambersburg on the morning of the 11th, his regiment was formed fronting westward, with the expectation of retracing the march of the previous day. He was, however, soon ordered to change front and move toward Gettysburg. In a conversation held with Stuart months after these events, Wickham inquired what caused his determination to make the circuit of McClellan's army. " Was it intuition ? " asked Wickham. " No," replied Stuart, " rather say judgment." Stuart then repeated to Wickham, substantially, the reasons stated in the conversation with Blackford, which has already been related.

The swiftness of Stuart's march, and the uncertainty of the enemy as to his intentions, were, humanly speaking, the strongest elements of success in the expedition. After the direction of his march toward Gettysburg was determined, it seemed reasonably certain that he would endeavor to cross the river somewhere in the vicinity of Leesburg : but between that place and the Point of Rocks there were several practicable fords, any one of which he might select, and all of which must be observed by the Federal forces. It would have been a rare chance which had concentrated at any one of these fords sufficient force to resist the attack of twelve hundred fighting men, within sight of safety, and under such leadership. And then the other route could not be neglected; for it was by no means certain that, after occupying Gettysburg, Stuart would not retrace his steps, and attempt some of the upper fords. He chose, however, the boldest and the safest plan. The ford which he had selected was so near the main body of the Federal army that it seemed improbable that he would there attempt a passage; and although his presence was detected at an early hour, his movements were so bold and so swift, that he altogether avoided any serious collision with his foes.

Again: at the time and place of danger Stuart was always present. He habitually rode with his advance-guard, and was ever ready to seize and improve an opportunity. He could " trust in Providence " with an honest and sincere faith: but he also *kept his powder dry*.

The management of the Federal infantry at White's Ford invites criticism. From General Stoneman's report we learn the dispositions which he made on the 11th of October, when informed of the possibility that Stuart might attempt to cross the Potomac in his vicinity. He tells us that the 3d and 4th Maine Infantry, 600 strong, were posted at the mouth of the Monocacy; the 99th Pennsylvania and the 40th New York Infantry, 700 strong, at White's Ford; the 10th Vermont Infantry at Seneca Creek; the 39th Massachusetts Infantry at Edward's Ferry; and the reserve, consisting of the 38th and 101st New York and 57th Pennsylvania Infantry and the 1st Rhode Island Cavalry, 950 strong, at Poolesville. It appears, however, from the report of Colonel H. G. Staples, commanding brigade, that the 40th New York had been sent on the morning of the 11th on a reconnoissance towards Leesburg, in support of a portion of the 1st Rhode Island Cavalry, and that it returned to camp near Conrad's Ferry on the same night.

The 99th Pennsylvania was, therefore, the only regiment at White's Ford at the time of Stuart's arrival. Lieutenant-Colonel Edwin R. Biles, who commanded this regiment on this occasion, states that the 99th was extended along the river "from near Conrad's Ferry, on the left, to some three hundred yards above White's Ford, on my right, a distance of about four miles." He had two reserves, — one, of three companies, at White's Ford ; and another, of one company, at Weedin's Ford, a mile and a half below. Company A had been sent on the night of the 10th to relieve a company of the 40th New York at the mouth of the Monocacy. The remainder of the regiment was distributed along the river at various picket posts. Colonel Biles does not mention the fact that company A rejoined him on the morning of the 12th ; but Colonel E. Walker, of the 4th Maine, states that he found a company of the 99th Pennsylvania at the Culvert Bridge, and ordered it to rejoin its regiment at White's Ford ; and Colonel Biles states, incidentally, that, having withdrawn from White's Ford, and having reached Weedin's Ford, his regiment was " now together." It would seem, therefore, that company A was not absent.

About nine o'clock on the morning of the 12th, Colonel Biles discovered that the enemy was advancing upon him. He immediately stationed his reserve on the hill commanding the ford, and drew in his nearest pickets. He was joined by one company which had been on his left. He now commanded five entire companies (if company A be included), to which were doubtless added pickets from other companies. He states that his force was " about one hundred men." It is difficult, however, to accept this estimate; for, according to the records of the adjutant-general's office, his regiment numbered, on the 30th of September, an aggregate present for duty of 477. If only four companies were present, they should have numbered nearly 200 men. Stuart states that about 200 infantry occupied the ford. General W. H. F. Lee considers that this is an underestimate. Whatever may have been his force, it was certainly a matter of extreme and grateful surprise to the Confederate cavalry that Colonel Biles was content to abandon so strong a position without a contest. That he occupied a post of danger was certainly true. Some men, out of just such circumstances, have won for themselves undying fame.

One other characteristic incident of this expedition may be noted. During the first Maryland campaign, while his headquarters were at Urbana, Stuart had received many acts of kindness and courtesy at the hands of the ladies of the family of Mr. Cockey. As he bade them good-by when his cavalry fell back before McClellan's advance, he had laughingly promised these ladies that he would call upon them again before very long. When he reached New Market on the night of the 11th, he, with a few of his staff and couriers, left the route of his column, rode to Urbana, aroused the family from slumber, paid his compliments to the ladies while yet on horseback, reminded them of his promise, and begged that they would accept this as the fulfilment of it. He then rode on and rejoined his column before daylight.

CHAPTER XII.

ONLY two days of rest were allowed to Stuart's command after his return from Chambersburg. At daylight, on the 16th of October, two columns of the Federal army advanced: one, under Brigadier-General A. A. Humphreys, from Shepherdstown to Smithfield; the other, under Brigadier-General W. S. Hancock, from Harper's Ferry to Charlestown. General Humphreys commanded 6,000 infantry, 500 cavalry, and six pieces of artillery. General Hancock commanded his own division, 1,500 men from other divisions, four regiments of cavalry, and four pieces of artillery. He does not state the numerical strength of his command, but it was probably greater than that of the other column. Stuart's raid seems to have suggested many possibilities to the Federal authorities; hence this reconnoissance in force, the object of which was to determine whether General Lee's army was yet in the Valley of Virginia.

The advance of General Humphreys' column was opposed by Stuart in person with Fitz Lee's brigade. At Kearneysville, six and a half miles from Shepherdstown, Stuart was reinforced by Winder's brigade of infantry, which happened to be at that point engaged in destroying the railroad. A determined attack was necessary to dislodge him from this position. This occurred about sunset. On the following day Hampton's brigade joined Stuart, who so closely covered General Humphreys' movements that he was unwilling to trust his cavalry beyond the support of his infantry. He estimated Stuart's force at 7,000 men; and as his object was to obtain information rather than to bring on a fight, he pushed forward cautiously as far as Leetown, whence he sent a scouting party of twenty-five cavalry to Smithfield. Having thus accomplished his object, he retraced his steps on the same day. General Humphreys particularly acknowledges " the assistance received from Major Lovell, commanding the brigade of regulars ; Major Curtis, commanding the cavalry ; Captain McClellan, my assistant adjutant-general ; Lieutenant Ash, commanding detachment of 5th U. S. Cavalry ; and Lieutenant Hazlett, commanding the artillery."

The advance of General Hancock's column was opposed by Colonel T. T. Munford with the 6th, 7th, and 12th Virginia Cavalry, and a portion of the 2d Virginia Cavalry, supported by one gun from Chew's battery of horse artillery, and three guns from the Richmond Howitzer Battalion, under Captain B. H. Smith, Jr. Munford offered stubborn resistance, and compelled the enemy to deploy three brigades of infantry to support his advance cavalry; but he was pushed back to Charlestown, which the enemy occupied about one o'clock P. M.[1] Colonel Munford makes special mention of the gallantry of Captain B. H. Smith, who lost a foot and was captured in Charlestown as his last piece was retiring from the field. He also commends Lieutenant J. W. Carter, of Chew's battery, who, although wounded early in the day, returned to his gun as soon as his wound was dressed.

General Hancock remained in occupation at Charles-

[1] Report of Col. S. K. Zook, *Official Records*, vol. xix. part ii. p. 94.

town until the afternoon of the 17th, when he also
withdrew his command to his former position at Harper's Ferry.[1]

Having ascertained by means of this reconnoissance
that the army of General Lee was yet in the Valley,
General McClellan rapidly completed his preparations
for an advance, and on the 26th of October crossed the
Potomac below Harper's Ferry with two divisions of
the 9th corps and Pleasonton's cavalry, and pushed
back the Confederate pickets east of the mountains as
far as Snicker's Gap. By the 2d of November the
whole of his army had crossed the river and was advancing into the interior of Virginia. Stuart was, of
course, informed of the earliest of these movements,
and while Lee's army was preparing to march, he
crossed the mountains into Loudon County, by way of
Snicker's Gap, with Fitz Lee's brigade and six pieces
of artillery. General Fitz Lee was disabled from service, and Colonel W. H. F. Lee had not recovered from
the severe injuries received at Boonsboro'. The command of the brigade devolved on Colonel W. C. Wickham, of the 4th Virginia Cavalry. A troublesome disease, known as the " greased heel," had prevailed
among the horses, and the number of men for duty in
this brigade had been reduced to less than one thousand. On the night of the 30th of October Stuart bivouacked near Bloomfield. A picket consisting of
three companies of the 1st Rhode Island Cavalry had
been established by the enemy at Mountsville, where
the Snickersville turnpike crosses Goose Creek.[2] Having ascertained their position, Stuart determined to

---

[1] Quotations from reports and other statements made in this chapter may
be verified by reference to the *Official Records*, vol. xix. part ii. p. 102 *et
seq.*

[2] *Sabres and Spurs: the History of the 1st Regiment Rhode Island Cavalry.* By Rev. F. Denison, Chaplain, p. 169.

attempt their capture. Moving early on the morning of the 31st, he approached Mountsville by an unfrequented road, surprised the party, captured their camp, and drove the whole into rapid flight. Lieutenant L. D. Gove, of the 1st Rhode Island, was killed, and fifty prisoners were captured, including one commissioned and nine non-commissioned officers.[1] The attack was made by the 9th Virginia Cavalry, supported by the 3d. The latter regiment continued the pursuit as far as Aldie, where it encountered Bayard's brigade of cavalry, from the defences of Washington,[2] and, retiring to the hills west of the village, awaited the arrival of the rest of the command. The advance was now given to the 4th Virginia Cavalry, which moved toward Aldie, meeting midway a column of the enemy charging up the narrow lane. A conflict between the heads of the opposing columns resulted in the retreat of the Federal cavalry to the cover of their artillery, posted on the hills east of the village. Stuart's artillery had not been able to keep up with his rapid advance, but, arriving after a time, was placed in position and engaged the enemy. Stuart's advance to Aldie was made with the full knowledge that he thereby exposed his rear to attack from the direction of Pleasonton's command ; but, trusting to the vigilance of his scouts, he remained in General Bayard's front until nightfall, when he withdrew and bivouacked a few miles west of Middleburg. General Bayard seems to have believed that he was opposed by a largely superior force. He states his own numbers at two thousand men, but says that one half of his command was absent on picket duty. He

---

[1] *Sabres and Spurs,* p. 170.

[2] Bayard's brigade consisted of the 1st New Jersey, 2d New York, 10th New York, and 1st Pennsylvania regiments of Cavalry, and Whiting's company, D. C. Cavalry. A battery from Sigel's corps was present. To this force add about one hundred fugitives from the 1st Rhode Island Cavalry.

acknowledges that, being so far from any support, he retired two miles to a more secure position, leaving eight of his dead on the field. During the night he retired still further, to his camp near Chantilly.

While these movements were in progress, D. H. Hill's division had moved through Ashby's Gap, and was now encamped in the vicinity of Paris and Upperville. On the following morning, the 1st of November, Stuart's command was disposed so as to cover his front. Learning that the enemy was advancing upon Philemont, Stuart moved through Union to meet him. The fighting on this day was of comparatively little moment, but its connection with the events of the two succeeding days gives it an importance that cannot be overlooked. After stating that he met the enemy a short distance in advance of Union, Stuart says in his report: —

The enemy spent the remainder of the day in reconnoitring, displaying very little force, and in the skirmishing which took place our lines were advanced to the vicinity of Philemont.

General Pleasanton says in his report: —

On November 1st the command moved forward and occupied Philemont, several hundred of Stuart's cavalry leaving about the time we entered. Colonel Gregg, with the 8th Pennsylvania and 3d Indiana Cavalry, pursued this cavalry and drove it very handsomely from some woods it attempted to hold; but, the enemy bringing up his artillery, no further advance was made, except to silence the rebel guns by the fire of Pennington's battery. The rebels left five dead upon the field. Our loss was one killed, and one officer and thirteen men wounded.

A fair interpretation of these extracts is, that Pleasonton drove Stuart's advance-guard back upon his main body, which he declined to attack. Pleasonton's loss in so small a skirmish seems to have been unusually severe. We are inclined to discredit the number of rebel dead, because similar estimates made by General Pleasonton on other occasions are so evidently excessive. The " silencing " of " hostile guns " by a destructive reportorial fire is an easy achievement, of·which both Confederate and Federal generals were far too fond. Stuart as well as Pleasonton is open to this charge. Perhaps we should forgive them readily, for they wrote amid the heat and smoke of the conflict.

Stuart retired at nightfall to feed his men and horses, but resumed the same line of battle early the next morning, the 2d of November. The second cavalry brigade, with which General Pleasonton was operating, consisted of four regiments, and was supported by Pennington's battery. Among his regimental commanders were Colonel B. F. Davis, of the 8th New York, and Colonel D. M. Gregg, of the 8th Pennsylvania Cavalry. The brilliant career of Colonel Davis was cut short at the battle of Fleetwood, on the 9th of June, 1863; but Colonel Gregg and Lieutenant Pennington survived to attain distinction — the one, in command of a cavalry division, the other, of a cavalry brigade. General Pleasonton did not lack in efficient subordinates. His command was reinforced on this day by the 2d brigade of Doubleday's division of infantry, under Lieutenant-Colonel J. W. Hofman, of the 56th Pennsylvania Volunteers. This brigade consisted of four regiments, three of which numbered, according to Colonel Hofman's statement, 700 men. It is fair to conclude that the brigade was not less than 900 strong. The 1st New Hampshire Battery accompanied it, and, added to Pennington's guns, gave Pleasonton the preponderance of artillery. When it is remembered that Stuart crossed the mountains on the 30th of November with less than 1,000 men, it is apparent that he was on this day opposed by forces more than double his own in numbers, — forces which were led by some of the best officers in the Federal cavalry service.

The successful resistance which Stuart was enabled to oppose to the Federal advance was in great measure due to the skilful handling of his artillery. Two spirits more congenial than Stuart and Pelham never met on the field of battle. Stuart's fondness for the use of artillery was almost excessive; Pelham's skill in its management amounted to genius. Stuart and Pelham imparted to the horse artillery an independency of action and a celerity of movement which characterized it to the end of the war, and which was nowhere equalled or imitated, except in the same arm of the Federal service. The achievements of the batteries attached to both the Federal and Confederate cavalry are worthy of a separate record and of the careful attention of military men.

The general agreement of the official reports of Generals Stuart and Pleasonton and of Colonel Hofman is somewhat unusual. General Pleasonton says : —

On November 2d my advance came up with the enemy at Union. They had some infantry supporting their guns, and very soon some sharp fighting began, which resulted in the blowing up of one of their caissons, by which a number of their men were killed, and their retreat for several miles on the road to Upperville.

Lieutenant-Colonel Hofman, with a small brigade of infantry and a battery, reported to me for duty this morning from Doubleday's division.

The fighting did not cease until after dark, the rebels giving way at every point. Their loss must have been considerable. One of their officers was left dead upon the field, and ten wounded fell into our hands, besides a number of prisoners. My loss in my own brigade was one man killed and twenty-six wounded. The infantry brigade lost five men killed and thirty wounded.

Colonel Hofman corrects the statement of his loss by giving it at five men killed and twenty-three wounded. This makes Pleasanton's total loss fifty-five men. Of course General Pleasonton is in error in stating that Stuart was supported by infantry; and the fact that he mistook Stuart's dismounted men for infantry may be regarded as a compliment to the steadiness of their conduct. Colonel Hofman's report corrects General Pleasonton's in several important particulars. He says : —

I found General Pleasonton engaged with the enemy in front of the town of Philemont. The enemy were throwing shell with considerable rapidity. We, however, sustained no loss. General Pleasonton directed that two regiments of my brigade should skirmish through the wood on the left of the road leading to the town of Union. The 56th and 95th regiments were detailed for this duty. They were soon recalled, and I was directed by General Pleasonton to take the brigade to the front, advance through the town, and then hold it. The enemy had his cavalry posted in the town at the time, and had his artillery in front of it. After fording the creek and ascending the hill in our front, the brigade was formed in line of battle, and, with skirmishers thrown out, we advanced upon the town. We had proceeded about two hundred yards when General Pleasonton sent for a regiment to support a battery on our left and rear. The 76th regiment was detailed for this purpose. The line, now consisting of 700 men, passed on through the town, the enemy retiring, on our approach, to a hill one mile beyond the town. After passing through the town, I sent the 95th regiment and two companies of the 56th to take possession of a strip of wood on the left of the road and about three hundred yards to our front. Two companies of the 7th Indiana regiment were then sent to picket the roads leading into the town. I then sent a request to General Pleasonton to send forward a battery of artillery. General Pleasonton soon arrived in person, and brought the artillery with him. He directed me to again move the brigade to the front, leaving the 76th regiment to picket the roads. As we advanced on the enemy they again opened on us with shell, one of which struck the line of the 7th Indiana, killing the color sergeant and one color corporal and wounding a number of others. We then took possession of a wood beyond the church, on the left of the road, and awaited the arrival of the artillery. The enemy in the mean time continued throwing shell, causing a number of casualties. After our artillery had thrown a few shots at the enemy, they again retired to a position three fourths of a mile further on. toward the turnpike leading to Upperville. We crossed the ravine in our front, and again advanced in line of battle upon the enemy, who soon reopened on us with shell. As we were crossing an open field, a shell struck the line of the 56th regiment Pennsylvania Volunteers, killing two men of company G and mortally wounding two others.

I would be doing injustice to this regiment to omit mentioning the prompt manner in which the gap formed by the loss of four men was closed ; not a single man left the line until permission to do so had been given.

The brigade was placed in rear of a stone wall, and our artillery soon replied to the enemy. The 95th regiment was ordered to go to the left and front, to support a section of artillery. They were soon reinforced by the 56th regiment. The enemy were now soon driven from their position, and it being quite dark the firing ceased on both sides.

In the light of these reports Stuart's will be read with the greater interest. The difference in the estimates of General Stuart and Colonel Hofman as to the distance over which Stuart retired is not unnatural or irreconcilable, while General Pleasonton's statement that Stuart retreated " several miles on the road to Upperville " is as evidently inaccurate as many others which he has allowed to escape from his pen. General Stuart says : —

About eight o'clock the enemy began to deploy in our front

both infantry and cavalry, with six or eight pieces of artillery. Our dispositions were made to receive him by posting artillery advantageously, and the cavalry dismounted behind the stone fences, which were here very numerous and consequently afforded the enemy as good shelter as ourselves. Having to watch all the avenues leading to my rear, my effective force for fighting was very much diminished, but the Stuart Horse-Artillery, under the incomparable Pelham, supported by the cavalry sharpshooters, made a gallant and obstinate resistance, maintaining their ground for the greater part of the day, both suffering heavily, one of our caissons exploding from the enemy's shot. It was during this engagement that Major Pelham conducted a howitzer some distance beyond support to a neighboring hill, and opened a masked fire upon a body of the enemy's cavalry in the valley beneath, putting them to flight, capturing their flag and various articles, — their arms, equipments, and horses, as well as some prisoners, — sustaining in this extraordinary feat no loss whatever. The enemy finally enveloped our position with his superior numbers, both infantry and cavalry, so as to compel our withdrawal; but every hilltop and every foot of ground was disputed, so that the enemy made progress of less than a mile during the day. The enemy were held at bay until dark at Seaton's Hill, which they assailed with great determination, but were each time signally repulsed by the well-directed fire of the horse artillery. Major Pelham, directing one of the shots himself at the color bearer of an infantry regiment, struck him down at a distance of eight hundred yards. During this withdrawal Captain Bullock, of the 5th Virginia Cavalry, by great presence of mind and bravery saved himself from capture in a very perilous position.

At night I bivouacked the command east of Upperville, with the view of occupying as a line of battle the ground along the creek below the town. Some few of our wounded, who were so much disabled that they could not be moved, were left in hospital near Union, with surgeons and nurses.

On the following day, the 3d of November, General Pleasonton was still further reinforced by the 1st Cavalry brigade, under General Averell, and by Tidball's battery, but no fresh troops came to Stuart's assistance. His only reinforcement was a battery loaned by General D. H. Hill, who had withdrawn from Upperville, and had moved his division through the gap toward Front Royal. A reconnoissance made by Captain W. W. Blackford, engineer officer, disclosed the fact that McClellan's whole army was in motion southward. Stuart's instructions were, in such a case, to retire along the east side of the mountains, observing and delaying the enemy; but, upon the urgent request of General D. H. Hill, who visited him at Upperville, Stuart determined to divide his command, and, sending a portion of it toward Piedmont, retire with the remainder to Ashby's Gap, where he expected to meet Hampton's brigade, thus keeping the gap open for the movement of Jackson's corps, for which General Hill desired to provide.

Pleasonton advanced upon Stuart's new position at about nine o'clock A. M. He was met by Stuart in the manner of the previous day, and it was late in the afternoon before he gained possession of Upperville. As Stuart retired from this place he sent the 1st, 4th, and 5th Virginia Cavalry on the road to Piedmont, to constitute a rear-guard for his trains, and moved his two remaining regiments, the 3d and 9th, back toward Paris and Ashby's Gap. General D. H. Hill had left in the gap a small force of infantry, supporting a Whitworth gun and some other pieces of artillery under Captain Hardaway. The Whitworth gun opened an effective fire on the enemy at long range. General Pleasonton mentions this gun, but calls it a ten-pounder Parrott. This same gun, under the same commander, was stationed on the extreme Confederate right at the battle of Fredericksburg, and greatly annoyed Burnside's troops on the plain below. By one of its shells

General George D. Bayard, of the Federal cavalry, was killed.

While retiring toward Upperville Colonel W. C. Wickham, commanding the brigade, was wounded in the neck, by a fragment of a shell. The command now devolved on Colonel T. L. Rosser, of the 5th Virginia Cavalry.[1]

---

[1] However valuable the Comte de Paris' history may be as a treatise on military strategy, the greatest inaccuracies in regard to the details of the movements he narrates are apparent even to a careless student of the records. The following is the account which he gives, in his second volume, page 552, of Stuart's movements on the 2d and 3d of November.

"Stuart pressed the latter [the Federals] very closely, sometimes remaining on the crest of the Blue Ridge, where he could perceive their long columns from a distance, at other times descending into the valley which stretched out below him, and boldly disputing the ground with them whenever he found an opportunity. His battery of artillery, almost entirely served by Europeans, was of powerful assistance to him in this kind of warfare, and was remarkable for its precision of aim ; a very rare thing in the Southern armies. But, since the time when the inexperience of the Federal cavalry made Stuart's task an easy one, his adversaries had learned much. Pleasonton and his brigade, who cleared McClellan's march, asked nothing better than to measure strength with the Confederate cavalry and revenge themselves for not having been able to catch them in their raid across Maryland. A favorable opportunity for accomplishing this presented itself to the Union troops on the 2d of November. While the 2d corps was occupying Snicker's Gap Pleasonton pushed forward in the direction of Ashby's Gap. At Union village he met a brigade of the enemy's cavalry, which he dislodged after a sharp fight. The next day, having been reinforced by Averell, he continued his march. Stuart was waiting for him with his entire division, in front of the village of Upperville, determined to resist as long as he could, in order to defend the pass of Ashby's Gap. But the Federals attacked him so vigorously that he was soon overthrown and driven in disorder through Upperville as far as the village of Paris, at the very entrance of the pass."

There are some expressions in this extract, and others on the page which follows the one from which this is taken, which clearly show that the noble author had read Stuart's report; and yet, with an utter disregard of the facts presented in it, he asserts that Stuart's " entire division " was present at Upperville, when in reality less than one thousand men from Fitz Lee's brigade were there. A comparison of Colonel Hofman's report with General Stuart's shows that on the 2d of November this same little band resisted the advance of a brigade of infantry, a brigade of cavalry, and two batteries of artillery, and that in a fight which commenced at eight o'clock in

After Pleasonton had occupied Upperville he showed but little disposition to advance upon the gap beyond. Averell's brigade was, however, sent to Piedmont, following the road pursued by the three regiments which Stuart had sent to the same point. Anticipating such a movement, and fearing for the safety of his trains, Stuart sent Rosser with his two remaining regiments, the 3d and the 9th, after nightfall, by way of Paris to Piedmont. Major B. B. Douglass, of the 5th Virginia Cavalry, commanded the three regiments which had been sent in the same direction from Upperville. Stuart retained with him only a picket, under Captain W. B. Wooldridge, of the 4th Virginia Cavalry. He expected Hampton to reinforce him on this day, and knew that he could not be far distant. Finding that Jackson's troops were not in motion, and that Jackson himself was at Millwood, Stuart repaired thither to ascertain what change of plans had been made. He was informed by General Jackson that instead of following Longstreet's march he should remain in the valley, so as to be on McClellan's flank. It was now no longer necessary for Stuart to hold Ashby's Gap, and he therefore ordered D. H. Hill's infantry and

the morning and lasted until dark Stuart did not give up more than two miles of ground. Surely during this long day the Federal cavalry might have been given opportunity to cross sabres with the Confederates had Pleasonton been so anxious for it as the Comte de Paris represents. From Colonel Hofman's report one might even be led to suspect that *his infantry* did most of the fighting, and that the Federal cavalry were content to observe the field, or to advance dismounted side by side with his line of battle.

The statement that Stuart's artillery was "almost entirely served by Europeans" will be a surprise to the surviving members of that organization. Pelham, Henry, Hart, Breathed, McGregor, and Johnston were certainly not of any European nationality, and the only foundation for this statement is, that one detachment of Pelham's original battery consisted so largely of Frenchmen that it was known as the "French Detachment."

The Comte de Paris' narrative of the fight at Upperville on the 3d, and at Barbee's Cross Roads on the 4th, is as erroneous as the above.

artillery to rejoin his division at Front Royal, while Captain Wooldridge remained to picket the gap, with orders to retire in the same direction upon the advance of the enemy. Hampton's brigade reached Millwood on the evening of the 3d, and was ordered to Markham's Station on the morning of the 4th, while Stuart himself, unaccompanied except by his staff, rode by a nearer but much more exposed route toward the same point.

On the evening of the 3d, Major Douglass had occupied Piedmont, but through a misunderstanding of his orders had retired toward Markham's on the approach of Averell's brigade. As Rosser approached Piedmont in the night he found the town in the possession of the enemy, and was compelled to make a detour toward Markham's, between which place and Manassas Gap he found the regiments commanded by Major Douglass. Having thus reunited the brigade, Rosser moved forward to Markham's on the morning of the 4th, and offered battle to Averell. The reports of this affair are meagre. Stuart refers to it only by saying that the enemy advanced upon Rosser in such force that he was compelled to withdraw, but without suffering any serious loss; and that the battery of horse artillery under Captain Henry behaved with conspicuous gallantry. Stuart was not present at this fight, and his report was written many months after its occurrence. Rosser made no report of it. But we can glean some interesting items from the despatches of General Pleasonton, who, at 3.45 P. M. on this day, thus writes to General McClellan : " General Averell has sent for assistance at Markham, and reports having had a hard fight with Stuart. I am moving forward to reinforce him. It would be well to send some infantry here to-night."

An hour later he again writes: "I have sent Colonel Gregg and the 6th Cavalry to reinforce Averell at Markham. . . . Averell sends me word he had two guns and three hundred prisoners of Stuart's at one time, and then lost them. I expect he has had a hard fight, and as they can so easily throw infantry upon him through the gap, and the country is bad, I have advised him to be very careful."

An hour still later he thus writes: "Averell's command is, I fear, a good deal crippled, from his report. He does not give me his killed and wounded, but tells me one of his squadrons was overwhelmed by superior numbers."

This is all that we can learn from the Official Records. There is, however, the unwritten tradition, among the Southern cavalry, that on this occasion two of the guns of Henry's battery, — one of which was the Napoleon afterwards distinguished at Fredericksburg, and manned by "The French Detachment," — were surrounded by the Federal cavalry, and attacked at the same time both in front and rear; and that these gallant fellows, all the while singing the *Marseillaise Hymn*, fought their guns with unfaltering courage until relieved from their peril by a successful charge of one of Rosser's regiments. We give the story for what it is worth. Perhaps some of Averell's men may corroborate it.

Rosser retired to Barbee's Cross Roads, where he was joined by Stuart and by Hampton's brigade on the night of the 4th. Here Stuart determined to give battle. He thus describes his position: —

The crest of the hill immediately north of the town was occupied by our artillery and sharpshooters, with a view to rake the enemy's column as it moved up the road; but the main position for defence was just at the Cross Roads, where the main body was held in reserve.

Toward nine A. M. the enemy advanced, and a fierce engagement of artillery and sharpshooters ensued, lasting some hours. The enemy at length approached under cover of ravines and woods, and my command held the position near the Cross Roads, where our artillery had complete control of the approaches. At this juncture I received information that the enemy was in Warrenton. This information, together with the delay and lack of vigor in the enemy's attack at this point, led me to believe that this was only a demonstration to divert my attention from his move on Warrenton. I accordingly gave orders to Hampton and Rosser to withdraw, the former by the Flint Hill road, the latter by the Orleans road, as the withdrawal of both by the same route would have been next to impossible. In withdrawing there was a sharp conflict between the 1st North Carolina Cavalry, under Lieutenant-Colonel J. B. Gordon, and the enemy on the left, that regiment suffering a good deal. . . . The enemy made no pursuit.

Colonel Gordon tells the story of this action as follows : —

I sent a courier to General Hampton reporting the position of the enemy. As he came up a squadron of Yankee cavalry dashed up along a stone fence in front. I asked him if I should charge them, stating to him at the same time that there was a large body of the enemy upon my right behind a stone fence, and that they had sharpshooters also posted there. He replied, No, there was no fence there ; that he had been there during the morning, and that it was open. He then ordered me to charge, the regiment being in a column of squadrons. I asked him if I should charge in squadron form. He replied, Yes, and that he would support me with the 2d South Carolina regiment. I ordered the charge. The men moved out promptly, going at the men we could see. The enemy fled rapidly as soon as they discovered that we were charging them, passing through a narrow opening in the stone fence and going over a hill in rear. As we got near the fence we encountered a broad ditch, concealed by grass and weeds, into which a number of horses fell, dismounting the riders. I ordered the men in front to pass through the opening in the fence in pursuit. A few only had passed when we received a withering fire from one hundred and fifty dismounted men and one piece of artillery placed behind the stone fence on our right flank, running at right angles to the one in front. From this fire a number of men and horses were shot down. Seeing no chance to get at the enemy, and being exposed to a terrible fire from the sharpshooters and artillery, which were near by, I ordered the regiment to retire from that position by the left about wheel. As the squadrons were wheeling, to my surprise I saw a large body of cavalry charging upon us from the right, which had been concealed from view by a hill. The regiment fell back across the hill to the point from which it started, where it reformed, with the exception of some men who went into the road against orders. The enemy dashed up boldly, but did not enter the column, except three who were captured or killed. The 2d South Carolina regiment did not come to my support as promised. I have since learned that it was blocked in the road by the Cobb Legion. Major Deloney, of the Legion, came up with a few men, and he, in connection with Captain Cowles and Lieutenant Siler, of my command, made a dash at the enemy, when they ran back.

I lost in this affair four men killed, seventeen wounded and captured. The captured men were dismounted at the ditch. The enemy report a loss of four men killed."

General Pleasonton thus describes the same affair : —

By this time I had advanced two sections of artillery to the position held by the rebels, where they first opened, and I soon discovered that Colonel Davis, of the 8th New York Cavalry, had a much superior force to his own to contend with, and that they were about to charge him in column of squadrons. I ordered the 3d Indiana to reinforce Davis, and opened a fire on the enemy's squadrons. Before, however, much was effected, Davis saw his situation, and dismounted one of his squadrons behind a stone wall, while he gallantly led the remainder of his regiment against the enemy to meet their charge. The result was very successful. The carbines of the dismounted squadron gave a galling flank and front fire, while the attack of the 8th New York routed the enemy, and

sent them flying in all directions. Thirty-seven of the rebel
dead were left on this field, and more than that number of
arms, horses, and prisoners were captured. This part of their
command retreated towards Chester Gap, and that from Barbee's Cross Roads took the Warrenton road.

On this occasion the second brigade had contended with two
rebel brigades (Hampton's and Lee's), the whole commanded
by Stuart, and had driven them in confusion from their positions with a severe loss. My own loss was five killed and
eight wounded.

On November 7 moved, with the first and second brigades,
to Amissville, and was opened on by the rebels with artillery,
on the Little Washington road, and also on the Jefferson road.
Drove the rebels out of Jefferson and captured two guns ;
also, three officers and ten men.

The capture of these guns seems to have been accomplished without any difficulty. General Stuart,
however, makes mention of no such circumstance.
Moreover, in his report of the battle near Middleburg,
on June 19, 1863, Stuart distinctly states that the
Blakely gun which he was compelled to abandon on
that field was the first which the horse artillery had
lost during the war. This and other evidence [1] compels
us to believe that the two guns mentioned by General
Pleasonton belong to the same category with the thirty-
seven dead North Carolinians found by him on the field
at Barbee's Cross Roads.

General Pleasonton continued to drive the rebels
before him on the 8th and 9th of November, and further states that, —

On November 10, the enemy from Culpeper attacked me in

[1] I have in my possession the diary of Lieutenant-Colonel W. R. Carter,
of the 3d Virginia Cavalry, in which the losses sustained during these days
of November, 1862, are recorded with much minuteness. He makes no
mention of the loss of any artillery. Surviving officers of the Stuart Horse
Artillery deny General Pleasonton's claim, and reaffirm General Stuart's
statement.

force with a brigade of infantry, one of cavalry and artillery, and at Corbin's Cross Roads drove in my pickets, and compelled me to concentrate my whole force to resist him. Several prisoners taken say that it was Longstreet making a reconnoissance to find out where our army lay. He did not succeed, as he was repulsed late in the afternoon with severe loss. Our loss was two men mortally and two severely wounded. General Sturgis, who was stationed at Amissville, quickly sent several of the regiments of his division to the right of the enemy to outflank them. This movement, doubtless, had great effect in inducing the enemy to withdraw.

General Stuart's explanation of this attack is as follows : —

The enemy moved over two brigades of infantry to Jeffersonton, and kept a large force of cavalry with a strong infantry support at Amissville. With a view to dislodge the latter I concerted a simultaneous attack with Hampton's and Lee's brigades on the enemy there, supported by two regiments of infantry, under Colonel Carnot Posey, of the 16th Mississippi. Hampton did not receive the orders in time to coöperate, but the remainder of the force advanced on the enemy, dislodging him from his position, and he was rapidly retiring when a large force of infantry came to his relief. The command was, therefore, leisurely returned to camp.

The conduct of the Southern cavalry during this brief campaign was certainly creditable. General Stuart makes no undue claim when he says : —

In all these operations I deem it my duty to bear testimony to the gallant and patient endurance of the cavalry, fighting every day most unequal conflicts, and successfully opposing for an extraordinary period the onward march of McClellan.

The Stuart Horse Artillery comes in for a full share of this praise, and its gallant commander, Major John Pelham, exhibited a skill and courage which I have never seen surpassed. On this occasion I was more than ever struck with that extraordinary coolness and mastery of the situation which more

eminently characterized this youthful officer than any other
artillerist who has attracted my attention. His *coup d'œil* was
accurate and comprehensive, his choice of ground made with
the eye of military genius, and his dispositions always such
in retiring as to render it impossible for the enemy to press us
without being severely punished for his temerity.

These words were penned nearly a year after the
death of Pelham, and form no uninteresting tribute to
the memory of one who seems to have won the hearts
of all with whom he came in contact. Certainly no
similar organization in the Army of Northern Virginia
contained more officers who were distinguished by excessive daring than did the cavalry division: yet, much
as Stuart valued and admired them all, no one could
to him supply the place of his " incomparable Pelham."

While Stuart had been operating on the front of
Lee's army in the movements which have just been
described, the country between Warrenton and Fredericksburg had been occupied by a force of cavalry under
Colonel J. R. Chambliss, of the 13th Virginia Cavalry,
who, in addition to his own regiment, appears to have
commanded the 15th Virginia Cavalry and the 2d
North Carolina Cavalry, the latter regiment temporarily under the command of Lieutenant-Colonel W. H.
Payne of the 4th Virginia Cavalry. These regiments
had not as yet been assigned to Stuart's command.[1]

[1] On the 10th of November, 1862, the cavalry brigades were reorganized
by Special Orders No. 238, from the Headquarters of the Army of Northern Virginia. This order may be found in the *Official Records*, in the preliminary print of Confederate reports of that date, page 626. The brigades
were arranged as follows : —

HAMPTON'S BRIGADE.
1st South Carolina Cavalry,
2d South Carolina Cavalry,
1st North Carolina Cavalry,
Cobb Georgia Legion,
Phillips Georgia Legion.

FITZHUGH LEE'S BRIGADE.
1st Virginia Cavalry,
2d Virginia Cavalry,
3d Virginia Cavalry,
4th Virginia Cavalry.

On the 7th of November General McClellan was relieved of the command of the Army of the Potomac, and General Burnside was appointed in his place. This change of commanders produced a short period of inaction, after which the Federal army was moved toward Fredericksburg only to find itself again confronted by its vigilant adversary. W. H. F. Lee's brigade guarded the lower Rappahannock, while Hampton and Fitz Lee picketed the river above. The interval of time which elapsed before the battle of Fredericksburg furnished the opportunity for some successful reconnoissances by the cavalry.

On the 27th of November Brigadier-General Wade Hampton, with two hundred and eight men from his brigade, crossed the Rappahannock at Kelly's Ford, and proceeded through Morrisville toward Hartwood Church or the Yellow Chapel. His march was made by unfrequented country roads, and avoided all of the

W. H. F. LEE'S BRIGADE.	W. E. JONES' BRIGADE.
5th Virginia Cavalry,	6th Virginia Cavalry,
9th Virginia Cavalry,	7th Virginia Cavalry,
10th Virginia Cavalry,	12th Virginia Cavalry,
15th Virginia Cavalry,	17th Battalion Virginia Cavalry,
2d North Carolina Cavalry.	35th Battalion Virginia Cavalry.

The Jeff Davis Legion Cavalry was detached from Hampton's brigade for service with General Longstreet, but returned to its proper place within a few weeks. Colonel W. H. F. Lee, of the 9th Virginia Cavalry, was promoted as brigadier-general. Colonel T. T. Munford, who had so ably commanded Robertson's brigade since the Second Manassas, was transferred with his regiment to Fitzhugh Lee's brigade. Colonel W. E. Jones, of the 7th Virginia Cavalry, was promoted as brigadier-general, and assigned to Robertson's brigade. Jones' brigade remained in the Valley of Virginia until the following May, and only rejoined the cavalry division in time to participate in the battle of the 9th of June, 1863. At this latter date the 17th battalion had been increased to a regiment, and was then and afterwards known as the 11th Virginia Cavalry, under Colonels L. L. Lomax and O. R. Funsten. In a subsequent arrangement the 15th Virginia Cavalry was taken from W. H. F. Lee's brigade, and was replaced by the 13th Virginia Cavalry, Colonel J. R. Chambliss.

enemy's pickets. He thus succeeded in reaching at nightfall a point within two miles of Hartwood Church, where was stationed the reserve of the Federal pickets, who, though warned that an attack was probable, were entirely ignorant of his proximity. At four o'clock on the morning of the 28th Hampton moved out from his noiseless bivouac, and, gaining the rear of the Federal squadrons, surprised them in their camp and captured the entire party without the loss of a man. Four Federal soldiers were left in the camp so badly wounded that they could not be removed; but eighty-two prisoners, including five commissioned officers, with their horses and equipments, were securely landed within the Confederate lines. The Federal picket consisted of two squadrons of the 3d Pennsylvania Cavalry, commanded by Captain George Johnson. General Averell's report confesses the full magnitude of this disaster, and indignantly blames Captain Johnson for it. At the same time he estimates Hampton's force at seven or eight hundred men, and states that he marched through the country, avoiding all pickets and roads. Under these circumstances Captain Johnson was perhaps more to be pitied than blamed.

On the 1st of December, Major T. Weller, of the 9th Virginia Cavalry, crossed the Rappahannock near Port Royal, with sixty men from his regiment, and captured a Federal picket consisting of two commissioned officers and forty-seven men.

On the 10th of December General Hampton started from his camp in Culpeper County with five hundred and twenty men, on a reconnoissance to the north of Fredericksburg. His object was to reach Dumfries and then sweep the road northward to Occoquan. This expedition was successful, although it was accomplished under circumstances which severely taxed the strength and endurance of his troops. Snow lay on the ground to the depth of several inches, and for three days and nights Hampton's men were exposed to severities of winter such as they had never before experienced.

Having marched sixteen miles before daylight on the morning of the 12th, Hampton surprised Dumfries and captured over fifty prisoners and twenty-four sutler's wagons. His further progress toward Occoquan was arrested by the discovery that General Sigel's corps occupied that road. Leaving Dumfries with his captures at eight o'clock in the morning, Hampton returned to Morrisville, where he encamped for the night, after his long march of forty miles. On the following morning everything was safely brought across the Rappahannock. No loss or casualty occurred during this expedition.

On the 17th of December General Hampton made another successful reconnoissance in the same direction. Crossing the Rappahannock at the railroad bridge, he bivouacked at Cole's Store on the night of the 17th, and reached Neabsco Creek at daylight on the 18th, where he surrounded and captured two picket posts. Dividing his command into three columns, Hampton rapidly moved upon Occoquan, where he found a train of wagons belonging to Sigel's corps in the act of crossing the river from the north side. Lieutenant-Colonel Martin, of the Jeff Davis Legion, dismounted some men, and forced the wagon guard, who were on the north side, to surrender and come over on the ferry-boat. Having effected this capture the work of bringing over the wagons was at once commenced. This was, however, necessarily slow, as there was but one small boat at the ferry, and the approaches to the river on either side were bad. While thus engaged the enemy appeared on the north side. The 17th Pennsylvania Cavalry and two companies of the 6th Pennsylvania Cavalry, under the command of Colonel R. H. Rush, of the 6th Pennsylvania, were on the march from Washington to the Army of the Potomac, and at this moment approached the Occoquan. A part of this force threatened the ferry, while the larger part attempted to force a passage at Selectman's Ford, and thus gain Hampton's rear.[1] But Selectman's Ford was held by Captain T. H. Clark, of the 2d South Carolina Cavalry, with forty men from his own regiment and from the Phillips Legion, and the efforts of the enemy to dislodge him were not successful. The work of ferrying over the captured wagons was, however, so slow that Hampton felt that he would incur unjustifiable risk in attempting to complete it. He therefore withdrew from the town, bringing with him one hundred and fifty prisoners, twenty wagons laden with valuable stores, thirty stands of infantry arms, and one stand of colors. Captain Clark held his position at Selectman's Ford for one hour after the rest of the command had retired, and although followed by the enemy, successfully protected the rear of Hampton's column. On the 19th Hampton returned to his camp without the loss of a man.

The battle-field of Fredericksburg offered but little opportunity for the use of cavalry. Hampton was, as we have seen, engaged on his expedition to Dumfries. Fitz Lee's brigade watched the fords of the Rappahannock on the Confederate left, above Fredericksburg. W. H. F. Lee's brigade extended the Confederate right as far as Massaponax Creek. To this part of the line, as being of the greater importance, Stuart gave his personal presence. Neither he nor any of his subordinate commanders made report of this battle. The following extract from a letter written to his

[1] *Annals of 6th Penn. Cavalry.* By Rev. S. L. Gracey, Chaplain, p. 119.

mother on the 17th of December, by Lieutenant R. Channing Price, of Richmond, Va., furnishes the most interesting and perhaps the most accurate narrative of General Stuart's movements which it is possible to obtain at this day. At the time of this battle Lieutenant Price was aid-de-camp to General Stuart. He was subsequently promoted to the position of major and assistant adjutant-general of the cavalry division. He was wounded on the 1st of May following, near the Old Furnace, during Jackson's movement around Hooker at Chancellorsville, and died within an hour after receiving the wound. General Stuart thus wrote to his bereaved mother: —

The dear boy fell at my side, displaying the same devotion to duty and abnegation of self which signalized his whole career. As an adjutant-general he had no superior, and his reputation as an able and efficient staff-officer had already spread through the army. Many have been the expressions of regret and sympathy from officers of all grades, even the highest.

Channing Price's letter presents so vivid a picture of the battle-field from an unmilitary stand-point that on this account alone it would be worth preservation.

Thursday morning (the 11th), sometime before day, I was aroused by the heavy cannonading in the direction of Fredericksburg, it having commenced some time before I heard it. About sunrise we got up, and, as soon as we could get breakfast, started for the front, General Stuart having gone on a little before us to General R. E. Lee's headquarters. We found Generals Lee, Longstreet, Stuart, and some others, on a very commanding hill to the right of the Telegraph Road, and the fog was so dense that we could only conjecture what was going on from the other side of the river. After a while the fog began to lift, and just then General Stuart sent me back to headquarters to get more couriers. On my return everything was perfectly clear, and soon afterward commenced the grand bombardment of the town. Such a cannonading I never heard before, one hundred or more guns to the minute. All the batteries were in full view, and until nearly night this continued — the whole being done to drive out one brigade (Barksdale's), which was keeping them from getting across. A little before sunset they succeeded in getting a number of troops across in boats, and Barksdale, not being able longer to hold the bank, withdrew his men to this side of the town, having inflicted a tremendous loss on the enemy, and having made him show his desire to cross at Fredericksburg. They had succeeded also in getting two bridges over below the town, and we went to headquarters to sleep, knowing that the enemy were crossing in heavy force.

Friday morning (the 12th) we went out again to our same position, but the fog was very thick. About the middle of the day, General Stuart having gone towards our right wing, I rode along the lines in that direction to find him. After passing Pickett's, McLaw's, and Hood's divisions, we came upon the left of Jackson's corps (which had come up during the night), consisting of Pender's brigade of A. P. Hill's division. I rode to the position of the Letcher Battery. Generals Lee and Jackson were there, watching the troops who were marching from the bridges and taking position on the left as they came up. General Lee told me that General Stuart had gone out to our skirmish line to examine the enemy more closely, and pretty soon he came galloping back and joined General Lee. We then rode back to General Hood's position. Before returning to camp I wrote a note to General Fitz Lee (between Spottsylvania Court House and Beaver Dam) to bring the main portion of his command and unite with General W. H. F. Lee during the night on the Bowling Green and Fredericksburg road near Hamilton's Crossing. Next day (the 13th) we had breakfast sometime before daylight, and made our way to Hamilton's Crossing, near which we found the cavalry. The enemy were very near the junction of the Bowling Green and Hamilton's Crossing roads, as we found out by riding in the field, when their sharpshooters opened on us. We then went on the hill to the left of the Crossing (A. P. Hill's extreme right), where were Pegram's battery and Jim Ellett's section. While there the fog rose and revealed the enemy coming up in beautiful style, forming line of battle, planting batteries, etc. I then galloped out to where General Stuart was (at the junction of the two roads named above), and there Major Pelham had come up with one gun of Henry's horse artillery. The enemy were in dense masses advancing straight towards our line of battle, and Pelham was exactly on their left flank with his gun, with no support whatever. He opened on them with solid shot, and though most of them went amongst the infantry, one blew up a caisson for the Yankees. They now opened about fifteen or twenty guns on Pelham; but he had splendid shelter, and only had one man wounded, I think. He kept up his fire until he was ordered to cease so that they might come up closer. Not a gun in our long line from Fredericksburg to Hamilton's Crossing had yet fired; only Pelham with his Napoleon, and soon afterwards a Blakely nearer the railroad. General Lee expressed his warm admiration for Major Pelham's distinguished gallantry, but said that the young major-general (alluding to Stuart) had opened on them too soon. Everything was now quiet along our line. The rest of Jackson's corps (D. H. Hill's division and Brown's artillery) had gotten up and were in reserve. The enemy's field batteries and his heavy guns across the river commenced to shell in every direction to find our position. The hill on which Pegram and Ellett were came in for a large share of the shelling; and it was now that Jim Ellett was killed, long before his battery had fired a gun. I saw his body at the Crossing soon after. All of us except the general now got out of the way to the right of the railroad until the fight should commence in earnest. General Stuart remained where he could see plainly when the enemy began to move, so that he might know when to begin his work, which was to bring to bear a large number of guns and break the left flank of the enemy. So soon as they began to advance, Lindsey Walker's guns on the hill opened on their infantry, and Pelham moved into the field to the right of the railroad, with twelve or fifteen rifle guns, and opened an enfilading fire. We now all joined the general, who was near Pelham, and the fight began in earnest. Time and again we strained over the field to Gen-

eral Jackson, the Lees, and Pelham. Once when I galloped
into Major Pelham's batteries to order him to advance his
guns and enfilade the enemy, who was now recoiling from the
fierce shock of A. P. Hill's gallant men, I recognized the boys
at the old gun which I have assisted so often to work. In a
minute they pulled off their caps and cheered me until I left
the place. Pelham was standing between White's and Wake-
ham's guns, and the shells were crashing in every direction.
This was the last time I saw poor Jim Utz, as he was struck
soon afterwards and instantly killed. Pelham continued to advance his guns as the enemy retreated, pouring in an enfilading
fire all the time. After reaching the protection of their batteries, the enemy were reorganized by bringing up fresh lines, and
again presented their front. A Parrott gun of the 2d Howitzers
and one of the Powhatan battery now crossed the Bowling
Green road and opened a very destructive fire on their flank
(under the direction of Colonel Rosser), Major Pelham commanding the others. I went to General Jackson to apprise
him of this change, and when I returned, the neighborhood of
those two guns was, I think, the hottest place from artillery
fire that I have ever been in. Just as I entered the field (a
caisson having been blown up a few minutes before), when
going up a slippery bank, a shell struck very close to my
horse, and, rearing up, he rolled over me in the ditch. For a
moment I thought he was struck ; but he soon recovered himself and I found it was merely fright. Galloping to the general, I found him looking on with his usual coolness. He soon
started towards the Crossing, and on our way met the two
Parrotts I have mentioned above leaving the field. The general was very much displeased at first, but Colonel Rosser
made matters all right by telling him that it was useless to
stay there, a great many horses having been killed, men
wounded, and ammunition nearly exhausted.

.   .   .   .

Sunday we were up before day and off for the field.
Everything was quiet ; the enemy lay in full view and reach
of our guns all day ; but not a shot was fired from us,
General Lee hoping that they would again make the attack.
Monday the same programme was carried out, and I spent

most of the day with the boys of the rifle section of my old corps.

The gallantry and efficiency of the services rendered by Major John Pelham in this battle have been considered worthy of especial commendation. General R. E. Lee and General Jackson were present together on the extreme Confederate right, and were eye-witnesses of the contest between Pelham's Napoleon and the Federal batteries. Both of these great generals in their reports bestow distinguished praise upon the young artillerist. The immediate effect of his fire was to stop the advance of Meade's division, whose ranks he enfiladed, until the arrival of Doubleday's division, which, facing to the left, advanced to protect the flank of Meade. The Federal reports show that the fire of not less than five batteries, attached to Meade's and Doubleday's divisions, was turned upon this one gun;[1] but Pelham maintained his ground for at least an hour, and retired only when ordered to a new and more important position, where a large number of guns was placed under his command.[2] John Esten Cooke has recorded the incident, which is no doubt authentic, that, on the day following the battle, Jackson said to Stuart:[3] "Have you another Pelham, General? If so, I wish you would give him to me!"

[1] Meade's, Doubleday's, Lieutenant Stewart's, Lieutenant Edgell's, and Captain Reynolds' reports.

[2] Sergeant Reuben B. Pleasants, of the second company of the Richmond Howitzer Battalion, has, in a publication entitled *Contributions to a History of the Richmond Howitzer Battalion*, claimed for a gun belonging to his company the honor which has been accorded to Pelham's Napoleon. This claim has been sufficiently refuted in the *Southern Historical Society Papers*, vol. xii. p. 466. Sergeant Pleasants has, however, done well in calling attention to the fact, which is also mentioned in Channing Price's letter, that his gun and another were, at a later hour, advanced by Rosser to a position not far from and probably in advance of the spot where Pelham opened the battle with his Napoleon.

[3] *Surry of Eagle's Nest*, p. 373.

Although the Federal army had been warned by Hampton's expeditions of the danger to which their line of communications along the Potomac was exposed, Stuart determined to keep up the system of irritation. He therefore organized an expedition, known among his men as the *Dumfries Raid,* which, although unproductive of any great material results, illustrates the facility with which a bold leader may move a large body of cavalry in an enemy's country, striking heavy blows where weak points present themselves, and avoiding dangers which are too serious to be encountered.

The line of communication between Fredericksburg and Alexandria was no longer insecurely guarded, as when Hampton made his last descent upon it. A brigade of infantry and detachments from two cavalry regiments under Colonel A. Schimmelfennig occupied Aquia where the Telegraph Road crosses Aquia Creek. A brigade of cavalry under Colonel De Cesnola lay within supporting distance of the same place. Scouting parties from this post reached as far west as Stafford Springs, and Colonel Schimmelfennig was aware of the presence of Confederate patrols at that point on the 24th and 25th of December. At Dumfries, Colonel Charles Candy commanded a brigade of infantry, together with the 1st Maryland Cavalry and six companies of the 13th Illinois Cavalry and a battery of artillery. Patrols and pickets from this post were sent out southward to Chopawamsic Creek and westward toward Brentsville. A brigade of infantry occupied Wolf Run Shoals,[1] and the line of the Occoquan eastward from this point was guarded by the 2d and 17th Pennsylvania Cavalry. To this force was intrusted the safety of the road from Neabsco Creek to the Occoquan. The remainder of the cavalry brigade to which these regiments belonged, and which was com-

---

[1] Colonel R. Butler Price's Report.

manded by Colonel R. Butler Price, extended a line of
pickets from Wolf Run Shoals to Manassas Junction,
where it connected with the pickets of the brigade of
cavalry commanded by Colonel Percy Wyndham, who
was encamped at Chantilly, and who in turn connected
with another force of cavalry at Dranesville. Within
this line of outposts a brigade of infantry was posted at
Union Mills, another at Fairfax Court House, while a
considerable force of infantry occupied the railroad at
Fairfax Station. As soon as the news of Stuart's attack
upon Dumfries was known at Washington, three regiments of infantry, with cavalry and artillery, were
moved from the vicinity of Alexandria to Annandale,
and a similar force was stationed midway between
Fairfax Court House and Falls Church. Around and
between these numerous posts Stuart led his command,
avoiding forces which would have endangered him, and
quickly overpowering such resistance as he chose to encounter.

On the afternoon of the 26th of December, 1,800
cavalry, commanded by Generals Hampton, Fitz Lee,
and W. H. F. Lee, crossed the Rappahannock at
Kelly's Ford, and encamped for the night at Morrisville. Early on the following morning the command
moved toward the Potomac. Stuart's plan was to
strike the Telegraph Road at three points between
Aquia Creek and the Occoquan; then, sweeping northward, to reunite his forces wherever the events of the
day might determine. Fitz Lee was accordingly directed to strike the Telegraph Road north of the Chopawamsic and move northward to Dumfries, while W. H.
F. Lee was sent directly to the latter place. Hampton
was directed upon Occoquan. A march of more than
twenty miles was necessary before any serious contact
with the enemy could be expected, and the larger part

of the day was expended before any of the detachments reached the points of attack. Fitz Lee struck the Telegraph Road just north of Chopawamsic Creek, and moved toward Dumfries, capturing wagons and prisoners. W. H. F. Lee reached Dumfries, having captured a number of pickets. He found the place strongly defended, but caused the enemy to withdraw all of his forces to the north bank of the Quantico. When Fitz Lee arrived, Stuart at first determined to make a serious attack. The 2d and 3d Virginia Cavalry were directed to move against the front of the enemy by the Telegraph Road, while the 1st and 5th Virginia Cavalry crossed the fords above and engaged in a mounted charge. Before this movement became serious, Stuart discovered that the statements of the prisoners whom he had captured were correct, and that the town was held by a force of infantry and cavalry whose numbers exceeded his own at this point. Fitz Lee's attack was therefore converted into a demonstration which should occupy the attention of the enemy until darkness might cover withdrawal and prevent pursuit. In this affair the detachment from the 5th Virginia Cavalry was principally engaged. Early in the action, Captain J. N. Bullock, who had led the dismounted men, received mortal wounds, and was carried from the field. Lieutenant James P. Bayly succeeded to the command, and, under orders from Colonel Rosser, charged across the creek, driving back the infantry skirmishers of the enemy and capturing eleven of their number. Lieutenant Bayly held the position he had gained until dark, when he was withdrawn. The whole command now moved out on the Brentsville road, and encamped for the night in the vicinity of Cole's Store. The loss inflicted on the Federal command at Dumfries, as shown by the reports, was 3 killed, 12 wounded, and 68 missing.

While the two Lees were thus occupied, Hampton had pursued his longer march to Occoquan, which he reached about sunset. Colonel M. C. Butler charged into the town, and drove from it a detachment of the 17th Pennsylvania Cavalry, capturing 8 wagons and 19 prisoners. Hampton now withdrew and joined the other brigades at Cole's Store. During the night the captured wagons and prisoners, together with two guns, whose ammunition was exhausted, were sent back to the Rappahannock, under the escort of a squadron of the 9th Virginia Cavalry.

Early on the 28th Stuart moved forward to the Occoquan. At Greenwood Church, Colonel M. C. Butler, with 150 men of the 2d South Carolina Cavalry, was detached, with orders to go to Bacon Race Church and endeavor to capture a body of the enemy reported to be at that point. Butler encountered cavalry pickets about a mile from the church and drove them back upon their support, which he found to consist of a considerable force of cavalry and two pieces of artillery. He had been instructed that the rest of the command would advance in the same direction, on a parallel road, and join him in the vicinity of Bacon Race Church. He therefore maintained his position in front of the force he had engaged, although exposed to a severe fire from the enemy's artillery. But events had carried the larger part of the Southern cavalry in another direction, and Butler in vain awaited the attack which he momentarily expected to be made by his friends, in which he was prepared to join. Not deeming it prudent longer to remain in his isolated position, he attempted to withdraw toward Brentsville by the same road on which he had advanced. He had moved but a short distance when he found this road occupied by a large force of the enemy. Thus enclosed in front and rear, his position was critical; but by making a *détour* of three or four miles he eluded his enemies and safely rejoined his brigade at Selectman's Ford. Both Stuart and Hampton bestow praise on Butler for the manner in which he extricated his command.

At a short distance from Greenwood Church, where Butler had separated from the main column, the advance of Fitz Lee's brigade had encountered the enemy's cavalry. Captain Chauncey, of the 2d Pennsylvania Cavalry, and Major Reinholt, of the 17th Pennsylvania Cavalry, with about 150 men from each of these two regiments, had crossed Selectman's Ford at daylight on the 28th, to discover what had become of the enemy who had attacked Occoquan on the previous evening. It appears from the reports that Captain Chauncey was in command of this party. He followed the trail made by Hampton's command until he reached the vicinity of Greenwood Church, where he was charged by the 1st Virginia Cavalry. Colonel R. Butler Price, commanding brigade of Federal cavalry, states in his report that the 2d Pennsylvania was deserted by the 17th Pennsylvania at the first fire, and that the whole command was routed and pursued for two miles north of Selectman's Ford. Stuart claims to have captured more than 100 prisoners, while the incomplete Federal returns show a total loss of 115.

At Selectman's Ford the enemy was tempted by the narrow and difficult nature of the ford to make a stand. Dismounted men were posted on the north bank, and an effort was made to hold the ford. The long chase from Greenwood Church had now brought the 5th Virginia Cavalry to the front. Without hesitation Colonel Rosser ordered his regiment to cross the creek. The charge was of necessity made by file; but it was executed with such spirit that Rosser suffered no loss, and quickly dispersed the enemy. The 3d Virginia Cavalry now took the lead, and continued the pursuit until the camp of the 3d Pennsylvania Cavalry was uncovered. This was speedily destroyed by the regiments which followed the 3d.

When the whole of his command was collected north of the Occoquan, Stuart sent a detachment, under Hampton, toward the village of Occoquan, which encountered and drove back a small party of the enemy. The pursuit was not continued on account of the darkness. Captain Dickenson, of the 2d Virginia Cavalry, was sent toward Wolf Run Shoals. He met a patrol of Major Stagg's cavalry command, captured a wagon and three prisoners, and drove the enemy back upon the infantry at the Shoals.

Stuart now directed his march northward to the railroad, which he struck at Burke's Station. The telegraph office was surprised and captured before the operator could give the alarm. Stuart always carried with him an accomplished telegraph operator, and he now had the satisfaction of receiving official information from General Heintzleman's headquarters in Washington concerning the dispositions which were being made to intercept him. After gaining the information he needed, he caused his operator to send a message to General M. C. Meigs, Quartermaster-General, at Washington, in which he complained that the quality of the mules recently furnished to the army was so inferior as greatly to embarrass him in moving his captured wagons. Having thus revealed his locality, the telegraph wire was cut, and he moved on. While waiting at Burke's Station General Fitz Lee was sent to destroy the railroad bridge over the Accotink. He took with him Lieutenant John Lee and Surgeon J. B. Fontaine of his staff, and ten men. He destroyed the bridge and safely rejoined his brigade, bringing with him a lieutenant and three men, captured from one of the enemy's pickets.

From the information he had received Stuart conceived that it might be possible to surprise and capture the post of Fairfax Court House. He therefore marched direct to that point; but when within about a mile of the town his advance was stopped by a volley from infantry and artillery, which showed that the enemy was in force and on the alert.[1] While still maintaining the semblance of an attack, he turned off the rear of his column to the right without the least delay, and crossing the turnpike between Fairfax Court House and Annandale, marched to Vienna. Here he turned westward to Frying Pan, which he reached at daybreak, and fed and rested for some hours. Thence by easy marches he returned through Middleburg and Warrenton to Culpeper Court House, which he reached on the 31st of December.

His loss on the expedition was 1 killed, 13 wounded, and 14 missing. The captured sutlers' wagons proved capable of inflicting nearly as much damage as the rifles of the enemy. The Federal loss exceeded 200 men. About twenty wagons and sutlers' teams were captured.

[1] The following extract from the *Diary of Lieutenant-Colonel W. R. Carter*, of the 3d Virginia Cavalry, will be recognized as a correct picture by those who participated in this affair : —

"Reaching the Little River Turnpike, the division turned down toward Fairfax Court House, and on arriving within a mile of that place the enemy's infantry, in ambush, opened on the head of our column, fortunately killing only two horses and wounding one man very slightly. We made no reply to their fire, and only withdrew out of musket-range; whereupon the enemy, not knowing how to interpret it, and thinking it might be a party of their own men, sent a flag of truce to ask whether we were friends or foes. They were told that they would be answered in the morning. On this being reported back they began to shell the turnpike; but in the interim we had built camp-fires, as if about to encamp for the night, and had left, taking a cross-road towards Vienna.

CHAPTER XIII.

KELLYSVILLE.

It has been customary to designate the battle near Kelly's Ford, on the 17th of March, 1863, as the first of the *battles* between the horsemen of the Army of the Potomac and those of the Army of Northern Virginia. As regards the Southern cavalry this battle differed from those of the previous fall in that it was fought almost entirely on horseback, and in the earlier part of it entirely without the support of artillery. As regards the Federal cavalry, the novel features were, that a larger force than usual was concentrated under one commander, and that an advance was made into the enemy's country beyond the hope of assistance from their infantry. That they should have returned from such an expedition without suffering serious loss, and after having crossed sabres with their adversaries in hand to hand fight, was considered a matter of congratulation, and perhaps justly; for up to this time the Federal cavalry certainly labored under such stigma as was placed upon it in President Lincoln's letter to General McClellan, which has been quoted in a previous chapter. The expedition itself was barren of results, unless, as some claim, it improved the *morale* of the Federal cavalry. It certainly added nothing enviable to the reputation of the brigadier-general in command, whose conduct has even called forth a weak animadversion from that most partial of historians M.

le Comte de Paris.[1] A candid examination of the facts as disclosed in the official records will justify these statements.

On the 9th of February Fitz Lee's brigade broke up camp in Caroline County, where it had been stationed since the battle of Fredericksburg, and moved to Culpeper Court House, where, on the 12th, it relieved Hampton's brigade, and assumed the duty of picketing the upper Rappahannock. On the 24th General Fitz Lee crossed the Rappahannock at Kelly's Ford with 400 men from the 1st, 2d, and 3d regiments, to make a reconnoissance on the Falmouth road, under orders from General Stuart. It will be sufficient to say, that in executing his orders General Lee advanced to Hartwood Church, where he encountered the enemy's cavalry, which he attacked and drove before him until he came within sight of the camps of the 5th corps. He captured 150 prisoners, representing seven regiments, with their horses, arms, and equipments. Among the prisoners were five commissioned officers. He returned to his camp on the 26th, having sustained a loss of 14 in killed, wounded, and missing.[2]

[1] *History of the Civil War in America*, vol. iii. pp. 17, 18.

[2] The diary of Lieutenant-Colonel W. R. Carter, of the 3d Virginia Cavalry, has been placed in my hands by the kind confidence of his venerable mother. It narrates some incidents of this reconnoissance, which, although they may not interest the general reader, will certainly be appreciated by the survivors of his old command. Colonel Carter was one of the most promising officers of his rank in Stuart's cavalry. Always cool and collected, always provident for the wants of his men even to the minutest details, he commanded their confidence and respect. He was frequently in command of his regiment, and always fought it well. He fell, mortally wounded, at the battle of Trevillian's Station, in June, 1864. I make the following extracts from his diary : —

February 24*th.* Colonel Owen being sick, I deferred my departure on furlough and took the regiment on the scout, — about one hundred and fifty officers and men, — with three days' rations and as much corn as the men could well carry on their horses. We marched at nine o'clock A. M. through Culpeper Court House and Stevensburg, and crossed the Rappahannock

On the 16th of March Brigadier-General W. W. Averell left the main body of the Army of the Potomac with the intention of crossing the Rappahannock at Kelly's Mill. On account of eighteen inches of snow the roads were miserable, almost impassable. No ambulances with the command. Encamped near Morrisville, Fauquier County. We got plenty of hay for our horses, and notwithstanding the snow the men spent a very agreeable night by scraping it away and making beds with brush and straw near large log fires. The river was so high as to swim low horses at the ford.

February 25th. Marched at eight o'clock A. M., 1st regiment in front, down the Falmouth road, passing Grove Church, Deep Run Mill, Franklin Gold Mines, and Hartwood Church, in Stafford County. Came upon the enemy's pickets below Hartwood, and charged them, the 1st regiment being in front and the 3d in rear. In the first charge the 1st regiment and a part of the 2d pursued the enemy to the left of Wallack's house, on the ' Poplar Road,' while the remainder of the 2d regiment, under Major Breckinridge, with the 3d in reserve, pursued them down the Falmouth road. After charging several miles General Lee had the rally sounded and ordered the 1st and 2d regiments to form behind the 3d. We had then pursued about a mile beyond Hammett's house, and having captured a number of prisoners, and having accomplished our purpose, we began to retire by *echelon.* The 2d regiment formed in line of battle at Hammett's house, and the 1st went to form in a field in their rear. Captain Randolph, of the Black-Horse Troop, having thrown out his company as sharpshooters to my front, I was ordered by General Lee to withdraw and form behind the 1st regiment. On moving back to execute this order I was met by several couriers looking for General Lee to inform him that a regiment of Yankees was in the woods on the right of the road facing Falmouth. I moved up quickly to support Colonel Drake, of the 1st. As I did so I saw an officer on the right of the road as aforesaid waving his handkerchief to me. Learning from some stragglers that the party probably belonged to the enemy, and thinking that it might be a *ruse* for the purpose of disentangling his men from the woods, I threw the regiment 'left into line,' to be ready to meet them in case they charged, and then advanced myself to meet the flag of truce. Whereupon Lieutenant Wetherell, of the 5th Pennsylvania Cavalry, surrendered himself and twenty men to me. Eight or ten others came out and surrendered to Colonel Drake. This proved to be the party supposed to be a regiment of the enemy, and I immediately informed General Lee to that effect. While this was transpiring the enemy had advanced their sharpshooters within carbine range of Hammett's house, and commenced firing on the 2d regiment, which was ordered to retire and form behind the 1st and 3d, which were stationed near Coakley's house. The enemy continuing to press, our sharpshooters were placed in the edge of the woods three hundred yards in advance of Coakley's house, on both sides of the road. In a very few moments the enemy drove in our sharpshooters and commenced following them up with a cheer, their skir-

at one of the upper fords and provoking a battle with
the Southern cavalry. Something more than a mere
reconnoissance was in view, for General Averell tells us
that he was ordered "to attack and rout or destroy"
Fitz Lee's brigade of cavalry, which was reported to be
in the vicinity of Culpeper Court House. The Confederate scouts had been very active north of the Rappahannock, and by their operations had created the impression that a considerable force was located in the
vicinity of Brentsville, against which General Averell
was warned in his orders that he must provide. He
accordingly detached 900 men from his command to
guard his rear at Morgansburg, Elk Run, and Morrisville, and with 2,100 men and his artillery advanced
to Kelly's Ford, which he reached, according to his
report, at eight o'clock on the morning of the 17th.
A wide discrepancy is to be noticed between the reports
of General Averell and General Lee as to the hour of
the attack upon the ford. General Lee states that the
attack was made at five o'clock A. M., three hours earlier than the time given by General Averell. For sufficient reasons, we adopt as correct the hour stated by
General Lee.[1] He had been notified by telegram from

---

mishers being supported by a column in the road with sabres drawn.
General Lee ordered me to charge them with a yell, which the regiment did
in most gallant style, striking at the column advancing along the road, and
disregarding the skirmishers on the flanks. The enemy continued to move
on until we came within thirty yards of them, when they broke, and fled
in perfect confusion. We pursued them for a quarter of a mile, killing
and capturing several of them, when, thinking that we had pursued as far
as prudence would permit, or as far as was in accordance with the designs
of General Lee, I halted the column, formed it front into line, and immediately received orders to retire to the edge of the woods and form in line
facing the enemy. Retiring from this position, and coming within speaking
distance of General Lee, he highly complimented the regiment for the gallant charge it had made, which praise the men received with loud cheers.
After this charge the enemy made no further effort to pursue.

[1] *Sabres and Spurs*, p. 208, Captain George N. Bliss, 1st Rhode Island

General R. E. Lee, at eleven o'clock on the previous day, that a large body of cavalry had left the Federal army, and was marching up the Rappahannock. The scouts which he sent out the same day correctly located the enemy at Morrisville and at Bealton. He was therefore uncertain whether the enemy would cross at Kelly's Ford or at the railroad bridge, or whether they would pursue their march toward Warrenton. Under these circumstances he strengthened his picket of twenty carbines at Kelly's Ford with forty more, and ordered the rest of the sharpshooters of the brigade, under Major W. A. Morgan, of the 1st Virginia Cavalry, to be stationed at daylight at the point where the road to Kelly's Ford leaves the railroad, that they might be in readiness to reinforce either place. Captain James Breckinridge, of the 2d Virginia Cavalry, commanded the picket at Kelly's Ford. There was no more efficient officer of his rank in either army, and had he been properly supported on this occasion, he would probably have succeeded in preventing General Averell from crossing at that point. His picket consisted of twenty men, of whom only fifteen at most were available for fighting, because every fourth man must be a horse-holder. General Lee says that only eleven or twelve men were stationed in the rifle-pits at the ford at the time of the attack. The horse-holders of the forty men sent to reinforce Breckinridge were stationed too far in the rear, and the dismounted men, although hurried forward, did not reach the ford in time to gain the shelter of the pits. This occasion, as well as many others, demonstrated the fact that the horse-holders in a cavalry

Cavalry, states that the attack was made about daylight. The diary of Lieutenant-Colonel W. R. Carter states that "boots and saddles" was sounded in the 3d Virginia Cavalry at seven o'clock, A. M., and that the regiment, moved out immediately, from its camp near Culpeper Court House, toward Kelly's Ford.

fight should be the coolest and bravest men in the company. "Number Four" has no right to be exempt from the perils of the battle. He holds the horses of his comrades only in order that they may more efficiently fight on foot; and he should always be near at hand to give whatever aid the occasion demands. In the present instance several brave men were captured simply because their horses were so far distant.

The brunt of the fight fell upon Breckinridge's little band of about a dozen men. General Lee says that he detained the enemy at the ford for an hour and a half. General Averell says that he dismounted two squadrons and endeavored to cross his advance-guard under their fire, but failed. Two similar attempts made by his pioneers met with the same result. An effort was made to find a place for crossing below the ford; but the swollen stream, four feet deep at the ford, was impassable elsewhere. Major Chamberlaine, chief-of-staff to General Averell, now selected sixteen men and placed them under the command of Lieutenant S. A. Brown, of troop G, 1st Rhode Island Cavalry, and ordered him to cross the river and not return. Lieutenant Brown gallantly executed this order, and opened the way for the remainder of his regiment, which followed immediately. Captain Breckinridge escaped capture, but twenty-five dismounted men, who could not reach their horses, were the trophies of Brown's brave dash. It is a noteworthy fact that General Lee reports a loss of twelve horses captured in this battle, and that not one was lost by the 2d Virginia Cavalry, to which Captain Breckinridge belonged. It would seem, therefore, that as a prudent officer he had his horses near at hand, and thus provided for the safety of his men. General Averell's loss at the ford was one officer and two men killed, two officers and five men wounded, and fifteen horses killed and wounded.

After the resistance at the ford had been overcome, two hours were consumed in crossing over the command.[1] The river was deep and swift, and the caissons and limbers of the guns were submerged. It was necessary that the cavalrymen should carry across the artillery ammunition in the nose-bags of their horses. Having watered his horses by squadrons, and having gotten his command well in hand on the south side of the river, General Averell was prepared to advance, as he states, at twelve M. Captain Bliss, 1st Rhode Island Cavalry, names the hour at ten o'clock A. M., doubtless with greater accuracy.[2]

In the mean time General Fitz Lee was awaiting news from the front in his camp near Culpeper Court House. At half past seven o'clock he received his first intelligence, which was that the enemy had crossed at Kelly's Ford, driving back his picket and capturing twenty-five of their number. He immediately moved his regiments at a rapid trot to Miller's house, about a mile and a half below Brandy Station. Finding that the enemy delayed, General Lee moved rapidly down the road toward Kelly's Ford and met Averell's troops before they had advanced as much as a half-mile from the ford. General Averell was correct when he wrote : " From what I had learned of Lee's position, and from what I knew personally of his character, I expected him to meet me on the road to his camp." . . . The distance passed over by either command, from the crossing at the ford to the time of meeting, is suggestive. When General Lee met him, Averell's right rested on the river near Wheatley's Ford, and his left extended a short distance beyond Brooks' house. He had a force of sharpshooters posted behind a stone fence which connected these two places, while his mounted reserves

[1] *Sabres and Spurs*, p. 210.   [2] *Ibid.*

were drawn up in the fields and woods in the rear, on both sides of the road which branches off from Wheatley's to Kelly's Ford. On his right was the 4th New York, on his left the 4th Pennsylvania, both regiments deployed to use carbines, and supported by two sections of artillery.

Fitz Lee approached with his 3d regiment in front, preceded by the sharpshooters of the brigade under Major W. A. Morgan, of the 1st regiment. Major Morgan immediately engaged the enemy with effect, as we learn from General Averell's report; for he says: "The 4th Pennsylvania and the 4th New York, I regret to say, did not come up to the mark at first, and it required some personal exertions on the part of myself and staff to bring them under the enemy's fire, which was now sweeping the woods." While this was transpiring, the 3d regiment threw down the fence and entered Wheatley's field about one hundred yards below Brannin's house, and moved back to form near Brown's house in the same field. From this point General Lee ordered the 3d to charge. The order was executed in column of fours. The regiment swept down the line of the stone fence which separated them from the enemy in the woods beyond, delivering the fire of their pistols. The enemy's line wavered throughout its length, and the utmost exertions of the Federal officers were required to keep their men from flight. But no outlet could be found through the stone fence, and the 3d regiment turned across the field to its left and moved down toward Wheatley's ice-house.

As adjutant of the 3d, it was made my duty by Colonel Owen, who led the charge in person, to see that the column of the regiment was kept well closed up. When about midway of the column, I saw Major John Pelham rushing to its head with the shout of battle on

his lips. After the rear of the regiment had passed
through a small enclosure near Wheatley's house, I
saw a single cavalryman struggling to place the body
of a comrade across the bow of his saddle. I approached to assist, and recognized Pelham. He had
been struck in the head by a piece of a shell, and life
was extinct. By this narrow chance was his body
preserved from falling into the hands of the enemy.

As the 3d regiment moved down toward Wheatley's,
endeavoring to find an outlet by which to attack the
enemy's right flank, McIntosh's brigade, the 16th and
4th Pennsylvania Cavalry, moved forward to the
same point, and having occupied Wheatley's house
and garden, opened a severe fire, by which several
men were wounded. The 3d was now joined by the
5th regiment, under Colonel T. L. Rosser, and the
two regiments endeavored to force the enemy near
the house of G. T. Wheatley. While retiring from
this unsuccessful attempt, Major Fuller, of the 5th
regiment, was killed. The 3d and 5th regiments now
drew back to the remainder of the brigade, which,
mean time, had not been idle. Colonel Duffié had advanced his three regiments, the 1st Rhode Island, the
4th Pennsylvania, and the 6th Ohio, in front of the
left of Averell's line, and General Lee moved forward
the 1st, 2d, and 4th regiments to meet him. In the
charges which followed, Colonel Duffié's three regiments were aided by two squadrons of the 5th U. S.
Cavalry and by McIntosh's command, which advanced
upon Lee's left as soon as the 3d and 5th regiments retired. If we may credit General Averell's report, " The
enemy were torn to pieces and driven from the field in
magnificent style." General Averell, however, pro-
ceeds to explain why he could not improve this rout of
his opponents, and why he did not capture three to five

hundred prisoners, "because the distance was too great for the time, the ground was very heavy, and the charge was made three minutes too soon, and without any prearranged support." In point of fact, in these combats General Lee found himself largely outnumbered and was compelled to withdraw; but he retired in such manner that Averell was able to gain no advantage over him. In one of the charges, Major Cary Breckinridge, of the 2d Virginia Cavalry, leaped his horse across a wide ditch which separated him from the enemy. His horse was killed, and Major Breckinridge was compelled to surrender to Lieutenant James M. Fales, of the 1st Rhode Island Cavalry. The 1st Rhode Island, however, lost in this charge eighteen men captured, and among them Captain Thayer and Lieutenant Darling.[1]

It should not be forgotten that all this fighting occurred in the immediate vicinity of Kelly's Ford ; nor should the great disparity in numbers be unnoticed. According to his own account, Averell commanded not less than twenty-one hundred men and six pieces of artillery. General Lee could not bring eight hundred men into line, and his advance to Kelly's Ford had been so rapid that his battery could not reach him until after this part of the battle was over. Surely Averell should have felt himself able to " rout or destroy " that small force, especially when he had them " torn to pieces and driven from the field."

Having thus compelled the enemy to display his superior numbers, General Lee deemed it prudent to retire to a stronger position, where he could receive assistance from his artillery. He accordingly withdrew through Miss Wheatley's farm (occupied by Lumpkin) to the road leading from Brandy Station to Kelly's

[1] *Sabres and Spurs*, p. 210.

Ford, and formed his line across that road, near Carter's Run, on the farm of James Newby. Here an open field, not less than five or six hundred yards wide, extended for a considerable distance on either side of the road. Gently sloping toward the centre, the southern side of this field was enclosed by thick woods, while the opposite hill was skirted by a thin growth of old-field pines, which terminated the view in that direction. Captain James Breathed's battery now crowned the hill on the north side, and Fitz Lee's brigade was drawn up in line across the road in the open field, with his mounted skirmishers in front. After considerable delay, the enemy made his appearance in the edge of the opposite woods, and opened fire at long range with his carbines and with a battery of four pieces.[1] The 2d and 4th regiments, which numerically constituted more than half of Lee's brigade, held the field on his right of the road; the 1st, 3d, and 5th regiments held the left. Fitz Lee endured the enemy's fire for a time, but seeing that Averell showed no disposition to advance, he ordered his brigade to charge in line, commencing on the right. This was a serious movement. Not a squadron was left to reinforce the charge when broken on the enemy's lines, and there was nothing behind which his regiments could rally, if unsuccessful, except the four guns of Breathed's battery. A year later in the war Lee would hardly have ventured on such a charge, but at this time he was probably influenced by what he " *knew personally of his* [Averell's] *character.*" From the very beginning of the charge Lee's regiments were subjected to the fire of the enemy's carbines, and of shell, spherical case, and double-shotted canister from his artillery. Midway across the field the charge of the 4th

---

[1] General Averell says three guns, but Lieutenant George Brown, Jr., commanding the battery, says four guns.

regiment was interrupted by a rail fence, which was, however, so soon thrown down that the regiment immediately recovered its alignment. On the left of the road the 3d regiment was compelled to change from line into column of fours, to cross the run which flowed through the bottom of the valley; but the line was reformed on the other side without a halt. Captain Bliss, of the 1st Rhode Island Cavalry, tells us that the right of General Averell's line was held by the 3d Pennsylvania and the 5th Regulars, and that the 1st Rhode Island and a squadron of the 6th Ohio held the left.[1] Everything gave way before the charge of Lee's left. The enemy disappeared in the dense woods, and made no show of resistance, except by a desultory fire of carbines at long range. Could a fresh regiment have supported this charge, Averell's guns would certainly have fallen into Lee's hands; but these guns were all on the left of Averell's position, and between them and Lee's left were two strong fences which lined either side of the road. It was impossible, under the circumstances, to pursue the advantage farther, and the 1st, 3d, and 5th regiments, broken by the charge into little squads, retired across the field to reform on the ground whence they had started.

On the right, the 2d and 4th regiments met with more resistance. They pressed their charge so close to the enemy's battery that the gunners fled from their guns. The 1st Rhode Island, however, came to the rescue, and a hand to hand fight ensued. The contemporary writer on either side would doubtless have recorded that his adversaries were " *driven in headlong flight and scattered in every direction.*" The facts are that the 2d and 4th regiments did not and could not reach the guns, though they were silent; and that the

[1] *Sabres and Spurs*, p. 211.

1st Rhode Island did not feel itself strong enough, after its encounter, to follow or molest these regiments as they retired to reform on the other side of the field.

Now, indeed, there was an opportunity for General Averell to " rout or destroy " Fitz Lee's brigade. He had a large force in reserve; and two fresh regiments, one on either side of the road, could have swept that field beyond the hope of recovery. He could have ridden over Breathed's guns before the brigade could possibly have formed to protect them. Why did he not do it? Let us turn to his report for information. Near the beginning of his report, General Averell says : —

On the night of the 16th the fires of a camp of the enemy were seen from Mount Holly Church by my scouts between Ellis' and Kelly's fords, and the drums, beating retreat and tattoo, were heard from their camps near Rappahannock Station.

And thus it appears that the phantom of " rebel infantry " was conjured up before General Averell's imagination at the very outset of his expedition. Further on he says : —

Here the enemy opened three pieces, two ten-pounder Parrotts and one six-pounder gun, from the side of the hill, directly in front of my left. No horses could be discovered about these guns, and from the manner in which they were served it was evident that they were covered by earthworks. It was also obvious that our artillery could not hurt them. Our ammunition was of miserable quality and nearly exhausted. . . . Theirs, on the contrary, was exceedingly annoying. Firing at a single company or squadron in line, they would knock a man out of ranks very frequently. . . . Their skirmishers again threatened my left, and it was reported to me that infantry had been seen at a distance to my right, moving towards my rear, and the cars could be heard running on the road in rear of the enemy, probably bringing reinforcements. It was 5.30 P. M., and it was necessary to advance my cavalry upon their intrenched positions, to make a direct and desperate attack, or to withdraw across the river. Either operation would be attended with imminent hazard. My horses were much exhausted. We had been successful thus far. I deemed it proper to withdraw.

It is hardly necessary to state that there was no Confederate infantry nearer to Fitz Lee's brigade than the camps of the army in the vicinity of Fredericksburg.

We may thus sum up the results of this battle. With 2,100 men and six guns, between the hours of five o'clock A. M. and 5.30 P. M., General Averell advanced less than two miles on the road to Culpeper Court House, his avowed destination. He was turned back by General Fitz Lee with 800 men aided by a well served battery of four guns, and reinforced by imaginary " *drums beating retreat and tattoo . . . near Rappahannock Station;* " by imaginary " *earthworks* " and " *rifle-pits, which could not easily be turned,* " but which must be approached by " *a direct and desperate attack;* " by imaginary " *infantry . . . seen at a distance to my right, moving towards my rear;* " and last, but not least, by imaginary cars " *heard running on the road in rear of the enemy, probably bringing reinforcements.* "

We cannot excuse General Averell's conduct. He ought to have gone to Culpeper Court House.

Among numerous instances of personal gallantry there were two which seem worthy of permanent record. After three attempts to force a passage at Kelly's Ford had failed, Lieutenant Simeon A. Brown, of the 1st Rhode Island Cavalry, charged the deadly pass at the head of sixteen men. The lieutenant was the first to reach the opposite bank, but only two of his men followed him. His horse was wounded in two places, and he himself received three bullets through his clothing. Sergeant Kimborough, of company G, 4th Virginia Cavalry, was wounded early in the action. He refused to leave the field. In the last charge he was the first to spring to the ground to throw down the fence which obstructed the way; remounted, and dashed on at the head of his regiment; was twice sabred over the head; had his arm shattered by a bullet; was captured and carried over the river, but made his escape, and, on the same night, walked back twelve miles to the camp of his regiment.

General Lee reports a loss of 11 killed, 88 wounded, and 34 taken prisoners. Of the latter, 25 were captured at the ford; only 9 were lost in the subsequent fighting. This fact is in itself an eloquent commentary on the conduct of this brigade. General Lee reports a loss of 71 horses killed, 87 wounded, and 12 captured. In his address on the Battle of Chancellorsville he calls attention to the large proportion of horses killed, as showing " the closeness of the contending forces."

General Averell reports an aggregate loss of 80. Out of this number, 41 casualties occurred in the 1st Rhode Island Cavalry. This regiment fairly carried off the honors of the day on the Federal side.

General Stuart was present at this battle, but, as it were, by accident. He did not assume command, and accords all the honor of the battle to General Lee. Stuart and Pelham had been attending the session of a court-martial in Culpeper Court House as witnesses. They had expected to return to Fredericksburg on the morning of the 17th, but learning that the enemy was advancing, both borrowed horses and joined Lee's brigade. Pelham could not remain inactive on the battlefield. Having no guns to occupy his attention, he rode forward to aid in leading the charge of the 3d regiment, and met his fate.

CHAPTER XIV.

CHANCELLORSVILLE.

EARLY in February, 1863, the cavalry of the Army of the Potomac was consolidated into one corps under the command of Brigadier-General George Stoneman, who soon afterwards received the rank of Major-General. Thus organized, the cavalry constituted a command of which any general might have been proud. On the 28th of February General Stoneman reported the strength of his corps at about 12,000 men and 13,000 horses present for duty; and the monthly report of the Army of the Potomac for the 30th of April, 1863, shows that the force of cavalry "actually available for the line of battle" was 11,079. Upon this splendid body of troops General Hooker depended for the successful opening of the campaign he had planned against Lee's army at Fredericksburg. It was intended that General Stoneman should cross the Rappahannock River at the fords west of the Orange and Alexandria Railroad with all of his command except one brigade; and after dispersing the small force of Confederate cavalry in Culpeper, a force which General Hooker estimated at not over 2,000 men,[1] that he should interpose his command between Lee's army and Richmond. He was expected to destroy communication along the line of the Central Railroad, to capture the supply stations at Gordonsville and Char-

[1] *Preliminary print of Federal Reports*, vol. xiv. p. 830.

lottesville, and to inflict all possible damage along the
Pamunkey River as far as West Point. But the main
object of the expedition was to penetrate to the Richmond and Fredericksburg Railroad, along the line of
which it was anticipated that General Lee would retreat; and by breaking up that road and by destroying
the bridges over the North and South Anna, to sever
direct communication between Lee's army and Richmond. General Stoneman was assured that he might
rely upon the fact that General Hooker would be in
connection with him before his supplies were exhausted; for it was further intended that the Army of the
Potomac should pass around the left of Lee's army,
and, compelling the evacuation of the strong fortress
at Fredericksburg, cause the Confederates to retreat
toward Richmond by the direct line, or to withdraw
through Spottsylvania toward Gordonsville. In either
event General Stoneman would be in position to harass
and delay the movements of the defeated army. The
instructions which General Stoneman received closed
with this solemn injunction: —

It devolves upon you, general, to take the initiative in the
forward movement of this grand army, and on you and your
noble command must depend in a great measure the extent
and brilliancy of our success. Bear in mind that celerity,
audacity, and resolution are everything in war, and especially
is it the case with the command you have and the enterprise
upon which you are about to embark.

General Stoneman received his orders on the 12th of
April. On the night of the 13th his command was
concentrated at Morrisville, ready to cross the Rappahannock on the following morning. In order that his
movement might be unimpeded, a brigade of infantry
and a battery of artillery from the 11th corps was
directed to take possession of Kelly's Ford. On the

same day the Army of the Potomac was ordered to prepare eight days' rations in haversacks, so that it might be ready to move when the cavalry had performed the part assigned to it.

To oppose the movement of this heavy column of cavalry Stuart had only the 9th and 13th regiments of Virginia Cavalry, 116 mounted men of the 2d North Carolina Cavalry, and 143 dismounted men (men whose horses had been lost in the service) of the same regiment. Two batteries of horse artillery were present. Fitz Lee's brigade had been moved northward toward Salem, and could not return in time to meet the enemy.[1] During the night of the 13th General W. H. F. Lee was informed by his scouts of the presence of the enemy at Morrisville, and he promptly reinforced his picket at Kelly's Ford by Captain S. Bolling's company of sharpshooters from the 9th Virginia Cavalry. Captain Bolling's force at the ford amounted to about 150 men. He was subsequently strengthened by one gun from Moorman's battery, and by the larger part of the 13th Virginia Cavalry, under Colonel J. R. Chambliss.

At daylight, on the 14th, General John Buford, commanding the Cavalry Reserve (U. S. Regulars), made his appearance and attempted to force a passage of the ford under cover of a large party of riflemen; but meeting with strong resistance the attempt was abandoned and was not renewed. General Buford's report

---

[1] Extract from the diary of Lieutenant-Colonel W. R. Carter, 3d Virginia Cavalry : —

April 14th. Started to move camp nearer to Salem on Manassas Gap Railroad, but hearing that a large force of Yankee cavalry was at Morrisville, preparing to cross at Kelly's Ford and attack General W. H. F. Lee's force, we were ordered to move back to Amissville, where we encamped for the night.

April 15th. Rainy and cold all day. Ordered to start for Culpeper Court House. Having marched two miles, the order was countermanded, and we returned to the same camp, with no dry place to pitch a tent.

states that his object at Kelly's Ford was merely to make a demonstration which should favor the passage of the rest of the corps at the upper fords; and this was undoubtedly the plan marked out in the orders which had been given to General Stoneman.

While General Buford was thus observing Kelly's Ford, General D. McM. Gregg's division was moved up to the ford at the railroad bridge. This point was defended by a few dismounted men (it does not appear from what regiment), who held a block-house which commanded the bridge; and by twenty men of company D, 13th Virginia Cavalry, under Lieutenant W. T. Gary, who occupied the adjacent rifle-pits. The 9th Virginia Cavalry and two sections of artillery, one from Moorman's and one from Breathed's battery, supported these riflemen. One hundred and sixteen mounted men of the 2d North Carolina Cavalry, commanded by Captain J. W. Strange, supported a Whitworth gun which was stationed one mile east of Brandy Station.

A party from General Gregg's command was allowed to cross at the bridge without opposition from the block-house, while at the same time a mounted party crossed the ford. Lieutenant Gary was outflanked and retired from the rifle-pits; but he soon gained position in the block-house, and without loss, except that he himself was wounded. When the 9th Virginia Cavalry moved down to attack, the Federals retired to the north bank of the river, and the remainder of the day was consumed in a desultory fire between the sharpshooters and the artillery on either side. General Gregg sent a squadron to Beverly's Ford, two miles above the bridge, and ascertained that a force of dismounted Confederates held the south bank. Nothing further was attempted on this day. From early morning the Federal cavalry had threatened the fords which were then entirely practicable. A determined effort on the part of General Gregg's command could not have failed to secure the passage of his division at the railroad and at Beverly's Ford; and success at these points would have caused the withdrawal of the Confederates at Kelly's Ford. General Stoneman, however, deferred a serious attempt until the following morning, and lost his opportunity. We are not surprised to read the following tart despatches which were sent by General Hooker to General Stoneman on the following day : —

HEADQUARTERS ARMY OF THE POTOMAC,
April 15, 1863.

GENERAL STONEMAN, — Despatches of April 15th, from ——, signed by the chief of your staff, have been received. The commanding general desires me to call your attention to your letter of instruction. The tenor of your despatches might indicate that you were manœuvring your whole force against the command of General Lee, numbering not over two thousand men. The commanding general does not expect, nor do your instructions indicate, that you are to act from any base or depot. When any messengers are coming this way please acknowledge the receipt of the despatch concerning the telegram from General Peck, sent for your information.

JOS. HOOKER,
Major-General commanding.

HEADQUARTERS ARMY OF THE POTOMAC,
April 15, 1863.

GENERAL STONEMAN, — Your despatches of 9 and 10.35 o'clock, of this date, are received. As you stated in your communication of yesterday that you would be over the river with your command at daylight this morning, it was so communicated to Washington, and it was hoped that the crossing had been made in advance of the rise of the river. If your artillery is your only hindrance to your advance, the major-general commanding directs that you order it to return and proceed to the execution of your orders without it. It is but reasonable to suppose that if you cannot make use of that arm of the service the enemy cannot. If it is practicable to carry into execution the general instructions communicated to you on the 12th instant, the major-general commanding expects you to make use of such means as will, in your opinion, enable you to accomplish it, and that as speedily as possible. This army is now awaiting your movement. I am directed to add that, in view of the swollen condition of the streams, it is not probable, in the event of your being able to advance, that you will be troubled by the infantry of the enemy.

> S. WILLIAMS,
> *Assistant Adjutant-General.*

On the same day President Lincoln thus wrote to General Hooker: —

> MAJOR-GENERAL HOOKER, — It is now 10.15 P. M. An hour ago I received your letter of this morning, and a few moments later your despatch of this evening. The letter gives me considerable uneasiness. The rain and mud, of course, were to be calculated upon. General S. is not moving rapidly enough to make the expedition come to anything. He has now been out three days, two of which were unusually fair weather, and all three without hindrance from the enemy, and yet he is not twenty-five miles from where he started. To reach his point he still has sixty to go, another river (the Rapidan) to cross, and will be hindered by the enemy. By arithmetic, how many days will it take him to do it? I do not know that any better can be done, but I greatly fear it is another failure already. Write me often, I am very anxious.
>
> Yours truly,   A. LINCOLN.

The failure which President Lincoln feared had already been consummated when this letter was written. At 6.30 A. M. on the 15th, Buford's cavalry, which had moved up from Kelly's Ford, was at the railroad bridge and ready to cross. He was ordered to await further instructions. It seems that some Federal cavalry had been sent early in the day to Welford's Ford, where the small Confederate picket was easily driven back, and a crossing was effected. Moving rapidly down the river this party approached Beverly's Ford, to which General Gregg's division had been moved, and surprised the dismounted men who, under Lieutenant-Colonel M. Lewis, guarded that point. But although surprised, this picket was not to be captured without a fight. Colonel Lewis and Lieutenant G. W. Beale, of the 9th Virginia Cavalry, boldly charged the advance of the enemy, and thus gained time to withdraw in safety. It seems strange that any could have escaped from such a position. They were cut off from their horses and lost them all, twelve in number; but the loss in men was only one killed and five captured.

As soon as this news was received, General W. H. F. Lee moved the 9th and 13th regiments to the threatened point. The enemy had partly recrossed the river, but Colonel Chambliss, at the head of about fifty men, charged their rear-guard and drove them into the stream. One lieutenant and twenty-four men, of the 3d Indiana Cavalry, were captured, and some were drowned in the rapid waters. The 9th Virginia Cavalry was also engaged in this charge. It is noticeable that the Federal reports are silent concerning this affair.

Thus ended this expedition. The bold action of two small cavalry regiments, aided by a swollen stream, thwarted the plans of the Federal commander and delayed for a fortnight the advance of the Grand Army of the Potomac.

The meaning of such a concentration of the enemy's cavalry as had just been witnessed could not be mistaken, and General Stuart was especially charged by his commander to do all in his power to prevent a foray upon his communications. Therefore, as soon as the flood had subsided, Fitz Lee's brigade was brought back from Sperryville to Culpeper Court House. The force under Stuart's command was painfully small in comparison with the services demanded of it. It is impossible at the present day to give exact numbers, but General Hooker's statement that Stoneman was opposed by not over 2,000 cavalry is probably correct.[1] With this small force Stuart was required to cover a front of more than fifty miles, maintaining pickets at the fords of both the Rappahannock and the Rapidan.

For some days prior to the 28th of April, the north bank of the Rappahannock, at Kelly's Ford and at the railroad bridge, had been held by Federal infantry pickets, and this unusual appearance had placed the Confederates fully on the alert. On the afternoon of the 28th three corps of the Federal army were concentrated near Kelly's Ford, and at six o'clock in the evening a strong party crossed the river in boats below the ford, severing communication with the pickets lower down the river, and driving back the picket at the ford. A pontoon bridge was laid, and the passage of the 11th and 12th army corps was effected during the night. No effort was made to extend the advance further than was necessary to accommodate these troops for the night.

Stuart received notice of these movements by nine o'clock P. M., at Culpeper Court House. His scouts

---

[1] In his Chancellorsville Address General Fitzhugh Lee estimated his own brigade at 1,500 men, and that of W. H. F. Lee at 1,200 men. This estimate is based on the monthly report of March 31, 1863, and is probably an over-estimate. On the 30th of April, 1863, the Federal cavalry reported an effective total of 11,079. But the reports of Generals Stoneman and Averell show that only about 6,900 men were engaged in the "Stoneman Raid"; and yet this was *all* of the cavalry of the Army of the Potomac except one brigade, which General Pleasonton calls a "small brigade," which was left with the main body of the army. If we apply the same ratio of discount to the Confederate cavalry, General Fitzhugh Lee's 2,700 men will be reduced to about 2,000.

had detected, and he had already reported to General
R. E. Lee, the movement of a large force of infantry
and artillery up the river from Falmouth, and unless
the telegraph line was closed, he must have reported
these facts also.   It must be remembered, however,
that the magnitude of the enemy's force was concealed
by darkness, and that no forward movement was made
until the following morning.   Unless the most urgent
necessity required it, Stuart had no right to move his
command from a position where it would be able to confront the enemy's cavalry, which he had abundant reason to believe would now attempt to reach the interior
of the State.   So far as he could observe, the present
advance might be intended solely as a diversion in favor of such a movement.   He accordingly ordered that
the enemy be enveloped with pickets, and, concentrating his command near Brandy Station, awaited the developments of the morning.   At four o'clock A. M. on
the 29th, the 12th corps advanced toward Germanna
Ford, followed by the 11th corps, while the 5th corps
commenced the passage of the pontoon bridge at eleven
o'clock A. M., and moved at once on the road to Ely's
Ford.   To cover this movement, a force of infantry
was sent out toward Brandy Station, and with these
troops the 13th Virginia Cavalry was engaged in skirmishing during a considerable part of the morning.

Early in the afternoon Stuart learned that the enemy's column was moving toward Germanna Ford, and
to ascertain the truth of the report he moved the larger
part of his command to Willis Madden's, where he
pierced the marching column and captured prisoners
from the 11th, 12th, and 5th corps.   The intentions of
the enemy were now well developed, and this information was at once telegraphed to the commanding general.   In reply, Stuart was not only instructed to swing

around to join the left wing of Lee's army, but he was also charged to give the necessary orders for the protection of public property along the railroads. To accomplish this latter purpose, General W. H. F. Lee was ordered to proceed by way of Culpeper Court House to the Rapidan, and endeavor to cover Gordonsville and the Central Railroad. Two regiments, the 9th and 13th Virginia Cavalry, constituted the whole of his command. Fitz Lee's brigade was put in motion as soon as possible for Raccoon Ford. Before leaving the position he had gained at Madden's, Stuart detached a strong party of sharpshooters from the 4th Virginia Cavalry, who were ordered to remain at that point and annoy the enemy's trains and marching columns as much as possible ; and, when driven away, to follow the brigade to Raccoon Ford. The reports of General Howard and of Colonel Devin show that this party occupied the attention of the 17th Pennsylvania Cavalry during the remainder of that day and during the night of the same, and prevented it from taking an active part in the advance of the army.

After marching more than half the night, Fitz Lee's brigade crossed the Rapidan and rested for a few hours. The 3d Virginia Cavalry, under Colonel Thomas H. Owen, was sent on without stopping, and early the next morning interposed between the enemy and Fredericksburg, at Wilderness Run.[1] The darkness of the

---

[1] The conduct of General Stuart on the present occasion has been criticised by the Hon. William E. Cameron, of Petersburg, Va., in the Philadelphia *Weekly Times*, of the 5th of July, 1879, as wanting in the vigor and watchfulness which usually characterized him. An examination of the Official Records will not establish the justice of this criticism. The roads leading southward from Kelly's Ford to the Rapidan were not left unobserved. Pickets were placed upon them, and this was all that could be done *or ought to have been done*, for no one will venture to assert that, with the facts which were before him on the night of the 28th, Stuart would have been justified in separating any portion of his small command from the apparently paramount

night and the excessive fatigue of his men produced a
separation of several companies from Colonel Owen's
regiment, and he was able to oppose only the smaller

duty of guarding the railroads. Moreover, General Howard states that the
11th corps commenced the passage of the pontoon bridge at Kelly's Ford
only at ten o'clock on the night of the 28th ; and General Slocum states
that the advance of the 12th corps began on the following morning at four
o'clock. Superhuman penetration and personal ubiquity, but nothing less,
might have enabled Stuart to ascertain these facts in time to interpose cavalry on the roads leading to Ely's and Germanna fords. But Slocum's advance instantly closed access to the former road, and although Stuart sent
couriers to notify the pickets on the Rapidan, they were captured and
failed to reach their destination.

The march of Slocum's column was not, however, unopposed. We have
the testimony of his report for the fact that " during the entire march from
the Rappahannock to the Rapidan, the advance-guard, consisting of the 6th
New York Cavalry, Lieutenant-Colonel McVicker commanding, was opposed by small bodies of cavalry." What officer was in command of this
Confederate picket does not appear ; nor can it be stated why he failed to
notify the Ely's Ford picket; nor why he failed to communicate his movements to General Stuart. It is reasonable, as well as charitable, to suppose
that he made the effort to perform these evident duties, but that his couriers also were captured.

There is one portion of the Hon. Mr. Cameron's criticism which produces
an unpleasant impression. He brings forward General R. E. Lee as a witness to the tardiness of his lieutenant. He says : —

" But Major-General Anderson arrived at Chancellorsville at twelve
o'clock on Thursday night, the 29th of April, having been sent by General
Lee ' *as soon as he had intelligence of the enemy's movement.*' This proves
that the Confederate commander received his first notice of the great events
maturing on his left late in the afternoon of the 29th, and then Slocum and
Meade were within easy striking distance."

The words which I have italicized appear as if quoted from General Lee's
report. It seems impossible to put any other construction upon them. And
yet, neither these words nor anything like them can be found in that report. On the contrary, after acknowledging that he had been informed by
General Stuart, on the 28th, that a large body of infantry and artillery was
moving up the river, General Lee says : —

" During the forenoon of the 29th that officer reported that the enemy
had crossed in force near Kelly's Ford on the preceding evening. Later in
the day he announced that a heavy column was moving from Kelly's toward
Germanna Ford, on the Rapidan, and another towards Ely's Ford, on that
river."

Toward the close of his report, General Lee gives the following explicit
testimony to the vigilance and energy of his cavalry : —

" The cavalry of the army, at the time of these operations, was much re-part of his force to the advance of the 6th New York Cavalry on the morning of the 30th. He made, however, a spirited fight for the possession of the bridge over Wilderness Run, as is testified by Colonel Devin, who commanded the cavalry brigade operating with the right of Hooker's army ; and when forced away, retired skirmishing toward Chancellorsville. Stuart, with the remainder of Fitz Lee's brigade, reached the Germanna road in the vicinity of the Wilderness Tavern soon after Colonel Owen had retired, and opened on the enemy's column with artillery and dismounted men. Stuart claims that he delayed the enemy at this point until midday. General Slocum states that he sent two regiments to oppose this attack, but that his " main body continued its march." It is clear, however, that some delay occurred ; for the distance from Germanna Ford to Chancellorsville is less than ten miles, and although Slocum's advance division left the ford at daylight, it did not reach Chancellorsville until two o'clock P. M. Meantime Colonel Owen had discovered and reported that the 5th corps, under Meade, had reached Chancellorsville by the Ely's Ford road. Stuart therefore withdrew from the Wilderness Tavern, and directed his march by way of Todd's Tavern toward Spottsylva-

---

duced. To its vigilance and energy we were indebted for timely information of the enemy's movements before the battle, and for impeding his march to Chancellorsville. It guarded both flanks of the army during the battle at that place, and a portion of it, as has already been stated, rendered valuable service in covering the march of Jackson to the enemy's rear."

These quotations may be verified by reference to pages 258 and 266 of the preliminary print of Confederate Reports from November 15, 1862, to June 3, 1863, issued by the War Records Office, Washington, D. C.

I should have thought it unnecessary to answer the criticisms of Mr. Cameron were it not for the fact that Major I. Scheibert, of the Prussian army, who is, I am persuaded, an admirer of General Stuart, has thought Mr. Cameron's paper of sufficient importance to translate it into the German language.

nia Court House.   Night had fallen when the command
reached Todd's Tavern.   Here Stuart proposed that his
troops should bivouac, while he himself, with his staff,
rode to army headquarters to receive instructions.   A
bright moon was shining.   Stuart had not proceeded
far on his way when he found himself confronted by
the enemy's cavalry.   The 6th New York regiment,
under Lieutenant-Colonel McVicker, had been sent on
a reconnoissance toward Spottsylvania Court House,
and was now returning.   Stuart's party readily yielded
the right of way to this regiment, while he sent for aid
to the brigade, which fortunately had not yet dismounted.   The 5th Virginia Cavalry, being nearest,
advanced against the enemy, who, warned of danger
by contact with Stuart's staff, had left the road and
were drawn up in line in Hugh Alsop's field.   The 5th
regiment kept the road past this field.   The 6th New
York charged upon the rear of the column of fours as
it passed on, took some prisoners, gained the road in
rear of the 5th regiment, and moved on to occupy the
forks of the road, which it was necessary for them to
hold in order to make good their way to Chancellorsville.   Here they met that portion of the 3d Virginia
Cavalry which had rejoined the brigade under Lieutenant-Colonel W. R. Carter.   The 3d regiment charged
with vigor, and a scene of indescribable confusion ensued.   Many of the 5th regiment were mingled with
the 6th New York, some unrecognized, and some as
prisoners ; and as soon as the heads of the two columns
closed, the cry arose, " Don't shoot ! don't shoot ! we 're
friends ! "   The place where the encounter occurred
was shaded by woods on one side of the road, and the
light was insufficient to distinguish between friends and
foes.   The 6th New York scattered for the moment
in the woods, and, all uncertain whether he had not

made a mistake and charged one of our own regiments, Colonel Carter withdrew his men a short distance and awaited further developments. This gave the 6th New York the road to Chancellorsville, and they speedily availed themselves of it, leaving at the forks of the road a picket, which was soon afterward captured by the 2d Virginia Cavalry. The 3d regiment lost one man wounded in this affair. During the fight all of the prisoners which had been taken from the 5th Virginia Cavalry made their escape. Lieutenant-Colonel McVicker was killed at the head of his regiment. His body was carried off by his friends; but several of his men were buried on the field on the following day.

While these events were transpiring on his left flank, General R. E. Lee was moving the larger part of his army from Fredericksburg toward Chancellorsville, and at eight o'clock A. M. on the 1st of May had concentrated near that point all of his force except Early's division of Jackson's corps and Barksdale's brigade of McLaws' division, which remained at Fredericksburg. At eleven o'clock A. M. Anderson's and McLaws' divisions advanced, and were soon engaged in severe fighting, the result of which was that the Federal army fell back within the strong defensive line which later surrounded their position at Chancellorsville. During the movements of this day the 4th Virginia Cavalry, under Colonel Williams C. Wickham, and a portion of the 3d Virginia Cavalry, under Colonel Thomas H. Owen, guarded the right flank of the Confederate army from the Mine Road to the Rappahannock, while the remainder of Fitz Lee's brigade protected the left flank. At about six o'clock in the evening, Wright's brigade of Anderson's division was engaged at Welford's Old Furnace. Having no artillery, General Wright requested Stuart

to aid him in this respect. Four guns belonging to the
horse artillery battalion, under the immediate command
of Major R. F. Beckham, were sent to General Wright,
and were soon engaged with a superior force of the enemy's artillery.   Major Beckham states that " One gun
from McGregor's battery, commanded by Lieutenant
Burwell, had every man about it wounded, except one.
The axle of another gun of the same battery was cut
nearly in two." General Stuart himself was present on
this occasion, and it was here that he sustained an irreparable loss in the death of his assistant adjutant-general, Major R. Channing Price.   A piece of a shell cut
an artery, and before medical assistance could be procured he had bled beyond recovery.   He had won his
promotion from the rank of lieutenant and aid-de-camp
under the eyes of his own general, to whom he had
made himself a necessity.   His years were few, but his
character was strong and mature.

   During the 2d of May that part of the cavalry which
was on the Confederate left was engaged in the delicate operation of screening from view the movement
of Jackson's three divisions around the Federal right
wing.   The 1st Virginia Cavalry marched in advance
of Jackson's column, while the 2d and 5th regiments
and part of the 3d interposed between the enemy
and its right flank.   After the rear of A. P. Hill's division had passed the Furnace, and while Jackson's
ordnance train was on the road, the enemy made another determined attempt to pierce the line at this
point.   Two divisions of the 3d army corps, under the
personal command of General D. E. Sickles, penetrated
to the Furnace, and ultimately gained possession of the
road upon which Jackson's corps had passed.   Lieutenant-Colonel W. R. Carter, of the 3d Virginia Cavalry, commanded the picket at the Furnace; and by

his activity a sufficient force was obtained to check the attack. Colonel J. Thompson Brown furnished two guns from his battalion of artillery; two companies of the 14th Tennessee Infantry, under Captain W. S. Moore, who had just been relieved from picket, were induced to move immediately to the point of danger; and General Archer, when notified by Colonel Carter of the attack, moved back his own brigade and Thomas', and engaged the enemy. Sickles' advance was checked until the last of Jackson's train had passed in safety; when General Archer, having been relieved by troops from McLaws' division, moved on to join his corps.

Meanwhile General Fitz Lee, who commanded in person the cavalry which preceded Jackson's column, had reached the plank road, and had halted his command to await the arrival of the infantry. To improve the time he made a personal reconnoissance, which revealed the fact that a force advancing on the turnpike would take in reverse the right of the enemy's line of battle. Fully appreciating the importance of the discovery he had made, General Lee hurriedly returned along the line of march until he met General Jackson, whom he conducted in person to the same point of observation. " Below, and but a few hundred yards distant, ran the Federal line of battle. There was the line of defence, with abatis in front, and long lines of stacked arms in rear. Two cannon were visible in the part of the line seen. The soldiers were in groups in the rear, laughing, chatting, smoking ; probably engaged, here and there, in games of cards, and other amusements indulged in when feeling safe and comfortable, awaiting orders. In the rear were other parties driving up and butchering beeves.[1] "

General Jackson immediately ordered his troops to

[1] General Fitzhugh Lee's Chancellorsville Address.

cross the plank road and take position on the turnpike. At six o'clock P. M. everything was ready for the attack, and before dark the right of Hooker's army had been hurled back upon the position at Chancellorsville. The only artillery employed in this attack was from the battalion of horse artillery, under the command of Major R. F. Beckham, who thus modestly describes the part taken by his guns : —

Under instructions from Major-General Stuart I had placed two pieces in the turnpike, under the command of Captain Breathed, and held them in readiness for the advance of our infantry. Two other pieces, immediately in rear, were kept as a relief to Breathed from time to time, the width of road not allowing more than two pieces in action at once. Captain Moorman's battery was still farther in rear, to be brought up in case of accident. I was directed by the major-general commanding as our line started forward to advance with them, keeping a few yards in rear of our line of skirmishers. This we did not entirely succeed in doing, owing to the narrow space in which the pieces had to be manœuvred and the obstructions encountered at various points along the road. I am glad, however, that I can report that we were able to keep up almost a continuous fire upon the enemy from one or two guns, from the very starting-point up to the position where our lines halted for the night.

Major Beckham reaped a rich reward for his services. His conduct attracted the attention of General Jackson. Meeting him in the road at the first pause of the battle, Jackson leaned forward on his horse, and extended his hand to Beckham, with the words, "Young man, I congratulate you." [1]

The two sections of Breathed's battery were commanded by Captain James Breathed and Lieutenant (afterwards Major) P. P. Johnston. While the front section was engaged in firing, the section in rear was

[1] This incident was related to the author by Major Beckham.

limbered up and ready to move. When the infantry had advanced beyond the guns, the front section ceased firing, and the rear section was moved forward at a gallop, often taking position in advance of the infantry. The strain upon the gunners was excessive, and Breathed's men were aided by volunteers from Moorman's battery in the rear, who came forward to supply the places of those who fell from exhaustion.

Finding no room for the use of his cavalry on the field of battle, Stuart asked permission of Jackson to take it and a small force of infantry, and hold the road to Ely's Ford. The permission was readily granted, and the 16th North Carolina Infantry was placed under his orders. Stuart reached the hills adjacent to the ford and found there Averell's division of cavalry. While making dispositions for an attack, he received the information, through Captain Adams, of General A. P. Hill's staff, that both Jackson and Hill had been wounded, and that the command of Jackson's corps devolved on him. The 16th North Carolina had already been deployed in line. Stuart ordered the officer commanding this regiment to fire three rounds into the enemy's camp, and then retire and rejoin his brigade. Without awaiting the result of this attack, and leaving Fitz Lee and his cavalry to guard the road from Ely's Ford, he hastened to assume the responsibility which had so unexpectedly devolved upon him.

The circumstances under which General Stuart took command of Jackson's corps were of a trying nature. It was about midnight when he reached the line of battle. The fact that Jackson had been borne wounded from the field could not be concealed; and there was unmistakable evidence that the troops were shaken by the great disaster. Stuart had no information from the commanding general concerning his plans for the movement which Jackson had commenced; and he was of course ignorant of the positions of the troops and the condition of the field. There was no possibility of receiving immediate instructions from General Lee; and when he requested suggestions from General Jackson he received the reply: "Tell General Stuart to act upon his own judgment and do what he thinks best; I have implicit confidence in him." [1] He was even denied the assistance of a staff who could work efficiently under these trying circumstances; for none of General Jackson's staff reported to him except Colonel A. S. Pendleton; and his own staff made almost their first personal acquaintance with the commanders of Jackson's corps during that night and the following day. Moreover, the fall of Jackson developed the fact that no one of his subordinates had received from him the least intimation of his plans and intentions; and that every one was ignorant of the topography of the battle-field. The enemy's artillery, of which a large force was concentrated near the Chancellorsville House, commanded the plank road, and ever and anon swept it with a fearful fire. A part of A. P. Hill's division, now thrown in advance and formed at right angles to the road, presented a solid front to the enemy; but Rodes and Colston had become mingled in great confusion by the ardor with which they had pursued the defeated enemy, and had been withdrawn to reform. On the right this confusion was greatly increased by an attack which had thrown back that flank until it rested nearly upon and parallel with the plank road. These facts were duly presented to Stuart by the infantry commanders, and he decided to defer further attack until morning.

In order that the situation in which Stuart found

---

[1] Cooke's *Life of Jackson*, p. 430.

Jackson's corps may be understood, it is necessary to enter somewhat minutely into the details of the movements of the brigades which composed it, as they are presented in the Official Reports.

It has already been indicated that Jackson's march toward the right of the Federal army had been observed at the point where his column passed near the Welford Furnace. This movement was interpreted by the Federal commander as the beginning of a retreat toward Gordonsville; and as early as twelve o'clock General Sickles, commanding the 3d army corps, was ordered to push forward two of his divisions on a reconnoissance. Three regiments of cavalry, under General Pleasonton, accompanied him. General Sickles advanced beyond the Welford Furnace, and gained the road upon which Jackson had passed. To oppose this movement, and to secure Jackson's trains, Archer's and Thomas' brigades, of A. P. Hill's division, which were at that time about two miles from the Furnace, moved back and checked Sickles' advance until they were relieved by some of McLaws' troops. This delay prevented these brigades from taking any part in the battle of the evening of the 2d. General Sickles was well pleased with the early success of his reconnoissance. He had advanced nearly two miles; had captured a number of prisoners; and, having made satisfactory disposition of his forces, was about to advance to fresh conquests, when he was informed of the disaster which had overtaken the 11th corps. His own position was now precarious. Jackson's advance threatened to enclose his rear and cut off his retreat. General Sickles immediately commenced to withdraw his two divisions; and, in order to gain time, requested General Pleasonton to check the enemy as much as possible with his cavalry and with artillery. The 8th Pennsylvania Cavalry, under Major Keenan, was ordered to interpose if possible between Jackson and the fugitives of the 11th corps. Major Keenan reached the plank road with a portion of his command, and made a gallant charge, which, it is claimed, checked for a short time the advance of Jackson's men.[1] The interval was improved by General Pleasonton, who succeeded in massing twenty-two pieces of artillery on a clearing about eight hundred yards from the plank road,[2] and in such position as to command the front and right flank of the advancing Confederates. The importance of this position, which is designated in many of the reports as Fairview, but which is properly known as Hazel Grove, will appear as our narrative advances. To this place General Sickles conducted his two divisions. Although exposed to the demoralizing influence of the panic-stricken fugitives of the 11th corps, Sickles' troops maintained an unbroken formation; and to them and to the artillery under General Pleasanton must be ascribed the honor of placing the first check upon Jackson's advance. This is made clear in the reports of Lieutenant-Colonel D. R. E. Winn and Colonel J. T. Mercer, commanding the 4th and 21st Georgia regiments of Doles' brigade. Colonel Winn states that when he reached this place he found himself in charge of about two hundred men of various commands, and facing two regiments of the enemy, which, with artillery, were posted on the cleared ridge obliquely to his left. While forming his line for attack, an officer, whom he supposed to be the commander of the Fed-

---

[1] Captain J. E. Carpenter, of the 8th Pennsylvania Cavalry, has described this charge in the Philadelphia *Weekly Times*, 29th of June, 1878. He says : " Five officers rode at the head of the column — Major Huey, Major Keenan, Captain Arrowsmith, Adjutant Haddock, and the writer. Of these only two escaped with their lives, and Huey alone came out with horse and rider uninjured."

[2] General Pleasonton's report says three hundred and eighty yards.

eral troops in his front, rode toward his line. His men were ordered not to fire; but when the officer had approached within a hundred yards, two men shot at him; whereupon he returned to his lines, and a heavy artillery and infantry fire was opened. Colonel Winn returned this fire until his ammunition was exhausted. When his fire ceased, that of the enemy ceased also; and without having been relieved or reinforced his command retired, after dark, to the plank road. General Pleasonton describes this same incident. Being uncertain whether the troops in sight were Confederates or a portion of the 11th corps, he sent his aid, Lieutenant Thompson, of the 1st New York Cavalry, to clear up the doubt. Lieutenant Thompson was induced to approach within fifty yards of the Confederate line, along which no color was visible except an American flag in the centre battalion. In another moment " the whole line in a most dastardly manner opened on him with musketry, dropped the American color, and displayed eight or ten rebel battle-flags." Lieutenant Thompson escaped unhurt, and Pleasonton opened on the Confederates with his guns. " This terrible discharge staggered them and threw the heads of their columns back on the woods, from which they opened a tremendous fire of musketry, bringing up fresh forces constantly, and striving to advance as fast as they were swept back by our guns."

The importance of the position held by Pleasonton can hardly be exaggerated; but he over-estimated the troops opposed to him. Two hundred men, under Lieutenant-Colonel Winn, supported on their left by the 21st Georgia regiment, under Colonel Mercer, were the only troops attacking that point. In this same connection it is worthy of notice how small a portion of Rodes' division operated on his right of the road. Colquitt's and Ramseur's brigades had been diverted, early in the action, by a reported advance on their right flank; and were, as General Rodes states, "deprived of any active participation." The brunt of the battle on the right fell on Doles' brigade, with which was mingled a portion of Colston's brigade from the second line. As we have now seen, these were the troops which were confronted and checked by Pleasonton and Sickles.

Night had now come on. The confusion in Rodes' and Colston's divisions was so great that an advance seemed inadvisable. General Rodes says:—

I at once sent word to Lieutenant-General Jackson, urging him to push forward the fresh troops of the reserve line, in order that mine might be reformed. Riding forward on the plank road, I satisfied myself that the enemy had no line of battle between our troops and the heights of Chancellorsville, and on my return informed Colonel S. Crutchfield, chief of artillery of the corps, of the fact, and he opened his batteries on that point. The enemy instantly responded by a most terrific fire, which silenced our guns, but did little execution on the infantry, as it was mainly directed down the plank road, which was unoccupied except by our artillery. When the fire ceased General Hill's troops were brought up, and as soon as a portion were deployed in my front as skirmishers I commenced withdrawing my men under orders from the lieutenant-general.

It had not been an easy matter for A. P. Hill's division to maintain its formation and still keep pace with the pursuit in which Rodes and Colston had been engaged; and we find that only one of the four brigades present in this division was ready immediately to take the place of Rodes' men. This brigade was Lane's. General Lane says:—

Here General A. P. Hill ordered me (at dark) to deploy one regiment as skirmishers across the road, to form line of battle in rear with the rest of the brigade, and to push vigorously forward. In other words, we were ordered to make a night attack and capture the enemy's batteries in front if possible. Just then they opened a terrific artillery fire, which was responded to by our batteries. As soon as this was over I deployed the 33d North Carolina troops forward as skirmishers, and formed line of battle to the rear, — the 7th and 37th to the right, and the 18th and 28th to the left, — the left of the 37th and the right of the 18th resting on the road.

It is manifest from the reports both of General Lane and of General Rodes that the fire of the Federal artillery from the Chancellorsville hill delayed the movements of Hill's division in relieving Rodes' line ; and that Rodes' division was withdrawn, by order of General Jackson, before even one brigade had completely deployed in its front. Lane's brigade, being at first required to occupy both sides of the road, could not, and did not cover the line from which Rodes withdrew. Confirmation of this is to be found in the reports of the officers commanding the 4th and 21st Georgia regiments of Doles' brigade, which show that these regiments were withdrawn from the position confronting Pleasonton and the two divisions of Sickles' corps, without having been replaced by any other troops. More interesting proof of the same fact is found in the following extract from a letter written to the author by General James H. Lane, under date of May 14, 1885 : —

I was not in line, but was ordered to move along the road by the right flank, immediately in rear of the artillery commanded by my friend, Stapleton Crutchfield. When this artillery halted in the road near the last line of breastworks from which the enemy had been driven, I was immediately behind it, and was kept standing in the road a short time. Here, about dark, I was ordered by General A. P. Hill in person to form my brigade, as described in my official report, for a night attack. As General Hill rode off I called my command to attention; and just then our artillery opened fire down the plank road in the direction of Chancellorsville. This drew a most terrific fire from the enemy's artillery in our front, and I at once ordered my men to lie down, as they were enfiladed, and I thought it would be madness to attempt to move them under such circumstances, in the dark, and *through such a woods*. Not long afterwards I heard Colonel Palmer, of General Hill's staff, inquiring for me, as it was too dark for him to recognize me, though we were not far apart. I called him; and he informed me that General Hill wished to know why I did not form my command as I had been ordered. I requested him to tell General Hill, if he wished me to do so successfully, he would have to order our artillery to cease firing, as I thought the enemy's fire was in reply to ours. The message was delivered, and Hill at once ordered Braxton, through Palmer, to cease firing; and as I expected, the enemy also ceased.

When I threw forward my first regiment as skirmishers, I ordered them to go well to the front, as we were to make a night attack; and to be very careful not to fire into any of Rodes' men, whom we would relieve. When the colonel commanding this regiment reported to me after the deployment, he informed me that there were none of Rodes' men in my front.

As soon as I had formed my whole command as ordered, I rode back from the right to the plank road, to know of General Hill if I must advance at once or await orders. On reaching the road I met General Jackson, who, strange to say, recognized me first, and remarked: "Lane, for whom are you looking?" (I was a cadet at the Virginia Military Institute under the old hero.) I told him, and for what purpose; and then remarked that as General Hill was acting under his orders, and I did not know where to find him, it would save time were he to tell me what to do. He replied: "Push right ahead, Lane!" accompanying his order with a pushing gesture of his right hand in the direction of Chancellor's house, and then rode forward. I at once rode to the right to put my line in motion; when the colonel on that flank advised me not to move, as his men had heard the talking and movement of troops on their flank.

Lieutenant Emack and four men were sent out to reconnoitre, and they soon returned with the 128th Pennsylvania regiment, commanded by a Lieutenant-Colonel Smith. Emack, on encountering them, put on a bold front and advised them to throw down their arms, as they were cut off by Jackson's corps. I was present when the lieutenant marched them in from the right, between my line of skirmishers and the main line, and they were without arms. Soon after they were halted in front of my right regiment, some one rode up from the front to the right of my skirmish line, and called for General Williams. Instead of capturing this individual, some of my skirmishers fired upon him, and he escaped unhurt, as far as we know. This seemed to cause a fire along the skirmish line, and the enemy's artillery again opened a terrific fire. It was then that General Jackson was wounded, as I have always thought, by the 18th regiment, of my brigade. This regiment undoubtedly fired into Hill and his staff; and they were not to blame, as I had told them that the enemy only were in their front, and that they must keep a sharp lookout. They were formed in low, dense, scrubby oaks, on the left of the road, and knew nothing of these generals having gone to the front. When the skirmish and artillery fire caused them and their staffs to turn back, there was a loud clattering of horses' hoofs, and some one cried out, "Yankee cavalry!"

From that unknown person's riding up, and calling for the Yankee General Williams, it is evident that they had a line in our front, possibly at the edge of the woods, Chancellorsville side, where they had their breastworks the next morning. My skirmish line was in the woods on the crest of the hill, and my main line on the right of the works last captured by Rodes. My line on the left was further advanced. General Pender rode into the woods inquiring for me just as I had ordered my right forward, and advised me not to advance, as Generals Jackson and Hill had both been wounded, and it was thought by my command. I did not advance; and was subsequently ordered by General Heth to withdraw that part of my brigade on the left of the road and prolong my line on the right.

This, then, seems to have been the exact position of

the troops when Jackson was wounded: Rodes' and Colston's divisions had been withdrawn, incapable of action on account of the disorder consequent on the victory which they had won. Of A. P. Hill's brigades, Lane's alone was formed in line of battle, and in such position that any immediate advance would have exposed his right flank and rear, now uncovered by the withdrawal of Doles' brigade. Heth, Pender, and McGowan were on the plank road, marching through the confused regiments and brigades of Rodes and Colston; while Archer and Thomas were still some miles in the rear, hurrying on to overtake their division, from which they had been separated by the necessity of meeting Sickles at the Welford Furnace.

It is proper now to notice the location of the Federal troops. The position of the two divisions of the 3d corps, which were with General Sickles, has already been described. The 1st division of the 12th corps, commanded by Major-General A. S. Williams, had been sent forward early in the afternoon to coöperate with General Sickles' attack at the Welford Furnace. Upon the first intelligence of the defeat of the 11th corps, Williams' division was ordered to return to its former line. Before it could reach this point the Confederates had it in possession, but this division did reach the plank road in time to form line of battle on the south side of that road before dark. The 2d division of the 3d corps, Hooker's old division, commanded by Major-General Berry, together with one brigade of the 2d corps, had been held in reserve near Chancellorsville. These troops were now moved forward through the tide of the fugitives of the 11th corps, and formed line of battle on the north side of the plank road, connecting with General Williams. This line of battle was formed on the Chancellorsville side of the woods in which the

Confederate advance had halted, and in which the battle was renewed on the following morning. About five hundred yards in rear of this line Captain C. L. Best, chief of artillery of the 12th corps, had massed thirty-four pieces of artillery. The official reports leave no reasonable doubt that all of these troops were in the positions indicated at the time when Lane's brigade formed line of battle, with orders to "push right ahead."

While Jackson was being carried from the field, Heth's brigade was approaching, marching by the flank. General Heth says : —

On reaching the position on the road occupied by General Hill, he directed me to deploy two regiments — one on the right the other on the left of the road — to check the enemy, who were then advancing. These movements had not been completed before the enemy opened heavily upon the 55th Virginia regiment. It was here that gallant and promising officer, Colonel F. Mallory, was killed. Soon after, General Hill informed me that he was wounded, and directed me to take command of the division. General Lane's brigade at this time was in line of battle on the right of the road, occupying the breastworks from which the enemy had been driven. I directed General Pender to form his brigade in line of battle on the left of the road, occupying the deserted breastworks of the enemy. Before the remaining brigade could be placed in line of battle, the enemy, under General Sickles, advanced and attacked General Lane's right.

The " remaining brigade " to which General Heth refers was McGowan's, which, we learn from the reports of General Rodes and Colonel D. H. Hamilton, had been halted to guard one of the roads leading from the plank road to the position held by Pleasonton and Sickles.

As soon as Heth's and Pender's brigades came into position, Lane withdrew his two regiments, which had been on the left of the road, and with them extended his right flank. Even then he was not able to occupy

the whole of the line from which Doles' brigade had
been withdrawn.   General Lane says : —

General A. P. Hill being wounded, the night attack was not
made, as at first contemplated.   I withdrew the left wing of
the 33d, which formed on the right of the 7th, and extended
our line still further to the right with the 18th and 28th regiments, the right of the 28th resting on a road running obliquely to the plank road, with two of its companies broken
back to guard against a flank movement.   Between twelve and
one o'clock that night the enemy could be heard marshalling
their troops along our whole front, while their artillery was
rumbling up the road on our right.   Soon after, their artillery
opened right and left, and Sickles' command rushed upon us
with loud and prolonged cheering.   They were driven back on
our left by our skirmishers, but the fight was more stubborn
on the right, which was their main point of attack.   The 18th,
28th, and left wing of the 33d engaged them there and gallantly drove them back, although they had outflanked us, and
encountered the two right companies of the 28th, which had
been deflected in anticipation of such a movement.   A subsequent attack made about half an hour later was similarly repulsed.   The 28th captured a staff officer.   The colors of the
3d Maine volunteers were taken by Captain Niven Clark's
company, of the same regiment.   The 18th also captured an
aid to General Williams.   A number of field and company
officers and a large number of men were captured along our
whole line.   After the enemy were repulsed, General McGowan
was ordered forward with his brigade and took position on our
right.

General Sickles claims as the result of this night attack that " all of our guns and caissons and a portion
of Whipple's mule train were recovered, besides two
pieces of the enemy's artillery and three caissons captured."   General Sickles also claims to have reached
the plank road with a portion of his command.   In the
last statement General Sickles is certainly in error ;
for the plank road was closely occupied with troops as

far back as Melzi Chancellor's, and none of them were aware of his presence. But there can be no doubt that he made the recoveries, and perhaps even the captures he claims; and this circumstance reveals to us in the strongest light the extremely hazardous position of Jackson's corps so long as Hazel Grove was in the possession of the enemy. Had Sickles actually thrown a heavy force as far forward as the plank road, he would have divided Jackson's corps. But this much praised night attack seems to have been of short duration and feeble character. On his right, General Sickles' troops made no impression on the firm lines of Lane's brigade; on his left, they were content to regain the lines which had been carried in the evening by Doles' brigade, and abandoned soon after dark. The heavy artillery fire which accompanied the night attack penetrated to the plank road and caused many casualties; but Lane's brigade was the only body of Confederate troops which was assailed. The reports from Colquitt's brigade, which relieved McGowan's, concur in stating that the brigade was moved forward to support a battery, and was subjected for a short time to a severe artillery fire, and even to musketry fire; but that no engagement ensued.

Stuart's report seems to be at fault as to the hour when he took command of Jackson's corps. He states that he reached the front at ten o'clock P. M., but his subsequent description of the positions in which he found the troops shows that he was not on the field until after the attack made by Sickles, which a majority of the reports locate at midnight. General Rodes' report agrees with this. He says : —

Soon after this occurrence I was informed that Lieutenant-General Jackson was wounded, and also received a message from Major-General Hill that he likewise was disabled, and that the command of the corps devolved on me. Without loss of time I communicated with Brigadier-Generals Heth and Colston, commanding respectively the divisions of A. P. Hill and Trimble, and made the necessary arrangements for a renewal of the attack in the morning, it being agreed that the troops were not in condition to resume operations that night. Just at this time (about twelve o'clock) the enemy made an attack on our right, but, being feeble in its character and promptly met, it lasted but a short time. Very soon after, Major-General J. E. B. Stuart, who had been sent for by Major A. S. Pendleton, assistant adjutant-general of Lieutenant-General Jackson, arrived on the ground and assumed command.

The report of General A. P. Hill confirms General Rodes' statements, and both of these reports show that before Stuart's arrival the judgment of the ranking officers of Jackson's corps was opposed to any further advance on that night.

Such was the situation when Stuart reached the field. The details have been thus minutely described in order that an intelligent opinion may be formed as to whether his action was all that the occasion demanded.

Soon after Stuart assumed command he directed Colonel (afterwards Brigadier-General) E. P. Alexander, upon whom the command of Jackson's artillery had devolved when Colonel Crutchfield was wounded, to make reconnoissance of the field of battle, and post artillery in readiness for an attack early in the morning. General Alexander's report contains the following accurate description of the ground on which the fighting occurred on the 3d of May: —

A careful examination showed that our attack must be made entirely through the dense wood in front of us, the enemy holding his edge of it with infantry protected by abatis and breastworks, supported by a numerous and powerful artillery in the fields behind, within canister range of the woods.

There were but two outlets through which our artillery could
be moved — one on the plank road, debouching within four
hundred yards of twenty-seven of the enemy's guns protected
by breastworks and enfiladed for a long distance by a part of
them, as well as by two guns behind a breastwork thrown up
across the road abreast of their line of abatis and infantry
cover; the second outlet was a cleared vista or lane through
the pines (a half mile south of the plank road) some two hundred yards long by twenty-five wide. This opened on a cleared
ridge, held by the enemy's artillery, about four hundred yards
distant. This vista was reached from the plank road by two
small roads: No. 1 leaving the plank road near our infantry
lines and running parallel with and close behind them to the
head of the vista, where it crossed them and went perpendicu-
larly down the vista to the enemy's position; thence it bore
to the left and north, and, crossing a ravine, came upon the
plateau in front of Chancellorsville at the south end of the enemy's line of artillery breastworks. Road No. 2 left the
plank road a half mile behind our lines and ran into Road No.
1 at the head of the vista.

It is hardly necessary to say that the " cleared ridge "
of which General Alexander speaks was Hazel Grove,
the position held by Pleasonton and Sickles on the evening of the 2d, and that Road No. 1 was the outlet by
which the 8th Pennsylvania Cavalry gained the plank
road and charged upon Iverson's brigade. Colonel Alexander's reconnoissance convinced Stuart that Hazel
Grove was the key to the Federal line; and to this
part of the field Stuart directed a large share of his
personal attention on the morning of the 3d.

Jackson's men had eaten nothing for twenty-four
hours except such provisions as they had obtained from
the haversacks of the 11th corps Rations were on
hand for a part of the command, and some of the general officers were urgent that the men be allowed time
to eat. But Stuart had received orders just before day,
from General Robert E. Lee, to begin the attack as

soon as possible. Before sunrise the right flank, which had been thrown back during the night, was advanced to bring it parallel with the rest of the line, and the battle opened at once with great fury. It is unnecessary to describe with minuteness the movements of this morning. Immediately on the plank road the battle assumed the phase of an infantry duel, and the opposing lines stood for hours delivering steady volleys into each other's faces. On the Confederate left there was greater activity. Charges were made, and ground was gained, lost, and retaken. The deciding contest was all this time raging on the Confederate right, where Pender's and McGowan's brigades, of A. P. Hill's division (Heth's command), parts of Rodes' and Iverson's brigades, of D. H. Hill's division (Rodes' command), and Colston's, Jones', and Paxton's brigades, of Trimble's division (Colston's command), united in the attack upon Hazel Grove, where the Federal artillery and infantry were posted in force. The contest here was of the most desperate nature, but the ridge was at last carried, and its great importance was apparent at a glance. Nearly the whole of the Federal line about Chancellorsville was enfiladed from this ridge, and a position was gained which commanded the Federal artillery about the Chancellorsville House. Stuart immediately ordered thirty pieces of artillery to occupy the ridge, and, aided by their fire, his whole line was advanced. A desperate struggle now ensued for the possession of the Chancellorsville clearing. Two unsuccessful charges were made upon the Federal entrenchments. They were carried by the third charge; connection was made with Anderson on the right, and the whole Federal force was swept back into the woods north of Chancellorsville.

The personal bearing of Stuart created great enthusiasm among the troops. General Lane says in his report that Stuart led two charges which were made by the 28th North Carolina regiment, and in the letter from which an extract has already been made he says: —

That afternoon, when the 28th rejoined me on the left, where I had been ordered to support Colquitt, its colonel, Thomas L. Lowe, was perfectly carried away with Stuart. He not only spoke of his dash, but he told me he heard him singing, "Old Joe Hooker, won't you get out of the wilderness!" and he wound up by saying, "Who would have thought it? Jeb Stuart in command of the 2d army corps!"

The imagination of the people of the South has drawn a picture of the annihilation of Hooker's army on this field, as a catastrophe which was averted only by the fall of Jackson. The real foundation of this opinion is perhaps to be found in that valuable work, "The Life of Lieutenant-General Jackson," by the Rev. R. L. Dabney, D. D., whose distinguished abilities, as well as the confidential relations he held with General Jackson as major and assistant adjutant-general on his staff, entitle his statements to the fullest credence. On page 699 Dr. Dabney says: —

But we are not left in doubt concerning General Jackson's own designs. Speaking afterwards to his friends, he said that if he had had an hour more of daylight, or had not been wounded, he should have occupied the outlets toward Ely's and United States fords, as well as those on the west. (It has already been explained that of the four roads diverging from Chancellorsville, the one which leads north, after proceeding for a mile and a half in that direction, turns northwestward, and divides into two, the left-hand leading to Ely's and the right-hand to United States Ford. And the point of their junction, afterwards so carefully fortified by Hooker, was on Saturday night entirely open.) General Jackson proposed, therefore, to move still further to his left during the night, and occupy that point. He declared that if he had been able to do so the dispersion or capture of Hooker's army would have been certain. "For," said he, "my men sometimes fail to drive the enemy from their position, but the enemy are never able to drive my men from theirs." . . . General Stuart now departed from the plans of General Jackson by extending his right rather than his left, so as to approximate the Confederate troops on the southeast of Chancellorsville, under the immediate command of General Lee. Thus the weight of his attack was thrown against the southwest side of Hooker's position. General Jackson would rather have thrown it against the northwest. But the true design of the latter was to assume the defensive for a few hours on Sabbath morning, after occupying both the Orange turnpike and the road to Ely's Ford. He purposed to stand at bay there, and receive amidst the dense thickets the attack which he knew this occupation of his line of retreat would force upon Hooker, while General Lee thundered upon his other side. Then after permitting him to break his strength in these vain assaults he would have advanced upon his disheartened masses, over ground defended by no works, and Hooker would have been crushed between the upper and the nether millstones. To comprehend the plausibility of this design, it must be remembered that Chancellorsville, with its few adjoining farms, was an island, completely environed by a sea of forests, through whose tangled depths infantry could scarcely march in line, and the passage of carriages was impossible. Of the four roads which centred at the Villa General Lee held two, — the old turnpike and the plank road leading toward Fredericksburg. General Jackson proposed to occupy the other two. Had this been done, the strong defence of the surrounding woods, in which Hooker trusted, would have been his ruin, for he would have found his imaginary castle his prison. The necessity which compelled him again to take the aggressive in the leafy woods would have thrown the advantage vastly to General Jackson, by rendering the powerful Federal artillery, in which they so much trusted, a cipher, and by requiring the Federals to come to close quarters with the terrible Confederate infantry. And this was work always more dreaded by them than the meeting of a "bear bereaved of her whelps." But on the southwest side of his position, within the open farm of Chancellor, Hooker had constructed a second and interior line of works, upon the brow of a long declivity, consisting of a row of lunettes, pierced for artillery, and of rifle-pits. General Stuart's line of battle, after winning the barricade, once before won by General Jackson, and emerging from the belt of woods which enveloped it, found themselves confronted by these works, manned by numerous batteries, and hence the cruel loss at which the splendid victory of Sunday was won.

However presumptuous it may appear to say that *anything* was impossible to Jackson, the assertion is ventured that the successful execution of such a plan as that indicated by Dr. Dabney was not possible, and that had Jackson remained in command of his corps he must have adopted the plan which Stuart so successfully carried out.

To have gained the junction of the roads to Ely's and United States fords on the night of the 2d of May it would have been necessary for Jackson either to proceed along the plank road to Chancellorsville, turning thence northward, or to march his men through the dense and pathless forest for the distance of a mile, leaving Chancellorsville on his right hand, and still in the possession of Hooker. In the former case it would have been necessary for him to drive before him the entire Federal force then concentrated at Chancellorsville, still leaving open to it the line of retreat to the United States Ford. In the latter case, even if it had been possible for the infantry to have overcome the difficulties of such a march, Jackson, deprived of his artillery, would have found himself enclosed between Hooker, at Chancellorsville, and the 1st army corps, under Reynolds, which, fresh except from marching, reached the United States Ford at sunset, and, hurrying on toward the battle-field, took position before daylight on the very ground which Jackson would have covered. General Doubleday states that Hooker had 37,000 men who "were kept out of the fight, most of whom had not fired a shot, and all of whom were eager to go in. The whole of the 1st corps and three fourths of the 5th corps had not been engaged."[1]   Had Jackson been assailed by these troops, in front and rear, at the junction of the roads to the fords, the result must have been disastrous.

I am informed by Dr. Dabney that the statements which I have quoted from his " Life of Jackson " were made on the authority of the gentlemen of Jackson's staff who attended him during his last days.   There can, therefore, be no doubt of their accuracy, and no doubt of the fact that Jackson's original intention was to fight by his left rather than by his right.   But Jackson was too great a soldier to hold to a preconceived plan when the developments of the battle-field pointed in another direction.   Darkness had overtaken his incomplete victory.   He was ignorant of the topography of the battle-field, and really lost his life in the attempt to acquaint himself with it.   He was ignorant of the position held by Pleasonton and Sickles, so close to his right flank and on ground which commanded the whole field.   He was probably ignorant of the existence of a line of battle in his front, for General Rodes says that he satisfied himself that there was none, and so informed Colonel Crutchfield.   Perhaps he gave the same information to Jackson.   The events of the next few minutes must have disclosed the true state of affairs. Had Lane pushed " right ahead " he would have encountered two divisions of Federal infantry.   Had he been able to put these to flight, he would have been at once exposed to attack by Sickles' two divisions on his

---

[1] *Chancellorsville and Gettysburg*, p. 53.

right and rear, as well as to the fire of Captain Best's thirty-four guns in his front. This would have revealed the necessity of dislodging Sickles ; and when the battle was once joined on the right, it could not have been relaxed until a junction was effected with Anderson.

Almost immediately after the cessation of the battle at Chancellorsville, McLaws' division was sent towards Fredericksburg, to aid Early against Sedgwick. On the following day Anderson's division was sent in the same direction, leaving Stuart with Jackson's corps to watch Hooker at Chancellorsville. When the whole of the Federal army had retired across the Rappahannock, A. P. Hill resumed the command of Jackson's corps, and Stuart returned to his own division.

I am permitted to make the following extract from a letter written to me on the 16th of May, 1885, by General E. P. Alexander, whose distinguished abilities and eminent services give great weight to his utterances.

Stuart rode with the first battery we brought out of the woods, and I well remember his enthusiasm and delight in recognizing the Chancellorsville House from the plank road where it debouches on the edge of the woods.

Altogether, I do not think there was a more brilliant thing done in the war than Stuart's extricating that command from the extremely critical position in which he found it as promptly and as boldly as he did. We knew that Hooker had at least 80,000 infantry at hand, and that his axemen were entrenching his position all night; and in that thick undergrowth a very little cutting gave an abatis or entanglement that a rabbit could hardly get through. The hard marching and the night fighting and manœuvring had thinned our ranks to less than 20,000 ; and we had little chance in the night even to hunt for the best place to make our attack. But Stuart never seemed to hesitate or to doubt for one moment that he could just crash his way wherever he chose to strike. He decided to attack at daybreak ; and, unlike many planned attacks that I have seen, this one came off promptly on time, and it never stopped to draw its breath until it had crashed through everything and our forces stood united around Chancellor's burning house.

I always thought it an injustice to Stuart and a loss to the army that he was not from that moment *continued in command of Jackson's corps.* He had *won* the right to it. I believe he had all of Jackson's genius and dash and originality, without that eccentricity of character which sometimes led to disappointment. For instance: Jackson went into camp near Shady Grove Church before sunset on the 26th of June, 1862, when he might have participated in the battle of Mechanicsville. This, and his feeble action at White Oak Swamp, on the 30th of June, 1862, show that Jackson's spirit and inspiration were uneven. Stuart, however, possessed the rare quality of being always *equal to himself at his very best.*

That Sunday morning's action ought to rank with whatever else of special brilliancy can be found in the annals of the Army of Northern Virginia ; and as a test of the mettle of a commander it would be hard to conceive severer demands or more satisfactory results.

CHAPTER XV.

THE BATTLE OF FLEETWOOD.

A CONSIDERATION of the difficulties under which the cavalry of the Army of Northern Virginia labored will not be uninteresting to one who would form a true estimate of the services rendered by it.

At the beginning of the war, the Confederate government, charged as it was with the creation of an army and of war material of all kinds, felt itself unable to provide horses for the numerous cavalry companies which offered their services, especially from the State of Virginia. Many companies, organized as cavalry, were rejected. With those that were enrolled the government entered into contract, the substance of which was that the cavalrymen should supply and own their horses, which would be mustered into service at a fair valuation ; that the government should provide feed, shoes, and a smith to do the shoeing, and should pay the men a *per diem* of forty cents for the use of their horses. Should a horse be *killed in action*, the government agreed to pay to the owner the muster valuation. Should the horse be captured in battle, worn out, or disabled by any of the many other causes which were incident to the service, the loss fell upon the owner, who was compelled to furnish another horse, under the same conditions, or be transferred to some other arm of the service.

That the government should have adopted such a

policy at the beginning of the war was a misfortune ;
that it should have adhered to it to the very end was a
calamity against which no amount of zeal or patriotism
could successfully contend.

It is not in the spirit of unfriendly criticism that we
to-day proclaim the unwisdom of such a policy. At the
time, all acquiesced in it; the cavalryman most cheerfully of all.   Virginia was full of horses of noble blood.
The descendants of such racers as Sir Archy, Boston,
Eclipse, Timoleon, Diomede, Exchequer, Red-Eye, and
many others more or less famous on the turf, were
scattered over the State.   Gentlemen fond of following
the hounds had raised these horses for their own use.
They knew their fine qualities, their speed, endurance,
and sure-footedness, and they greatly preferred to in-
trust their safety in battle to their favorite steeds rather
than to any that the government could furnish.   But
the government might have purchased these horses at
the outset, and by suitable activity it might have provided for replenishing the losses incurred in the service.   The cavalrymen *were kept mounted,* but at an
enormous loss of efficiency in the army, and by a system of absenteeism which sometimes deprived the cavalry of more than half its numbers.   Why should it
have been thought that the people of Virginia would
hold back their horses, when they refused nothing else
to the government ?

The evil results of this system were soon apparent,
and rapidly increased as the war progressed.   Perhaps
the least of these was the personal loss it entailed upon
the men.   Many a gallant fellow whose horse had been
irrecoverably lamed for the want of a shoe, or ridden to
death at the command of his officer, or abandoned in
the enemy's country that his owner might escape capture, impoverished himself and his family in order that

he might keep his place in the ranks of his comrades and neighbors. Nor should it be a cause for wonder if this property question affected the courage of many a rider; for experience soon proved that the horse as well as the man was in danger during the rough cavalry *mêlée*. If the horse were killed the owner was compensated; but a wounded horse was a bad investment.

By far the greatest evil of the system was the fact that whenever a cavalryman was dismounted, it was necessary to send him to his home to procure a remount. To accomplish this required from thirty to sixty days. The inevitable result was that an enormous proportion of the command was continuously absent. Many of the men were unable to procure fresh horses within the time specified in their "details," and the column of " Absent without leave " always presented an unsightly appearance. To punish such men seemed an injustice, and the relaxation of discipline on this point was abused by some with impunity. We have already seen that Fitz Lee's . brigade, which should never have presented less than twenty-five hundred sabres in the field, was reduced to less than eight hundred at Kelly's Ford, on the 17th of March, and numbered less than fifteen hundred men at the time of the battle of Chancellorsville, when many of the absentees had returned.

Great as was this evil among the Virginia regiments, it operated with tenfold force upon the cavalry of Hampton's brigade. Think of sending a man from Virginia to South Carolina, North Carolina, Georgia, or Mississippi to procure a horse! Recruiting camps were established in Virginia and in North and South Carolina, and every means which the cavalry commanders could devise were used to ameliorate this state of affairs.

But the inevitable tendency was downwards; and in the last year of the war hundreds of men were gathered together in the "Dismounted Camp," or, as the men called it, "Company Q," in the vain attempt to utilize good, but misplaced material. Special officers were appointed for these men, and the attempt was made to use them, dismounted, in various ways; but with no success. The men were disheartened. *Esprit du corps* could by no possibility be infused into such an assemblage. Every man looked and longed for the time when his horse might be returned from the recruiting camp, or when some other kind providence might remount him and return him to his comrades. The penitentiary could not be more loathsome to him than his present condition, and yet even this was better than to give up all hope, and consent to a transfer to the infantry or artillery.

The want of proper arms and equipments placed the Southern cavalry at a disadvantage which can hardly be overestimated. At the beginning of the war the troopers furnished their own saddles and bridles. The English round-tree saddle was in common use, and sore-backed horses multiplied with great rapidity. After a time the government furnished an unsightly saddle which answered a very good purpose; for although the comfort of the rider was disregarded, the back of the horse was protected. Our best equipments were borrowed from our cousins of the North. The question of arming the cavalry was far more serious. Some of the more wealthy of the Virginia counties armed their cavalry companies with pistols when they were mustered into service, but whole regiments were destitute of them. Breech-loading carbines were procured only in limited quantities, never more than enough to arm one, or at most two squadrons in a regiment. The deficiency was made up, generally, by Enfield rifles. Robertson's two North Carolina regiments, which joined Stuart in May, 1863, were armed with sabres and Enfield rifles. The difference between a Spencer carbine and an Enfield rifle is by no means a mere matter of sentiment.

Horseshoes, nails, and forges were procured with difficulty; and it was not an uncommon occurrence to see a cavalryman leading his limping horse along the road, while from his saddle dangled the hoofs of a dead horse, which he had cut off for the sake of the sound shoes nailed to them.

On the 22d of May, General Stuart reviewed the three brigades of Hampton and the two Lees, on the broad open fields which lie between Brandy Station and Culpeper Court House. About four thousand men assembled on that day. Shortly afterwards Jones' brigade arrived from the Valley, and Robertson's brigade from North Carolina, doubling the force under Stuart's command. He appointed another review on the 5th of June, at which it was expected General R. E. Lee would be present. In this Stuart was disappointed; but, nevertheless, the pageantry of war proceeded. Eight thousand cavalry passed under the eye of their commander, in column of squadrons, first at a walk, and then at the charge, while the guns of the artillery battalion, on the hill opposite the stand, gave forth fire and smoke, and seemed almost to convert the pageant into real warfare. It was a brilliant day, and the thirst for the "pomp and circumstance" of war was fully satisfied. It was not esteemed a matter of congratulation when on the 7th of June notice was received that the commanding general desired to review the cavalry on the following day. The invitation could not be declined; and on the 8th of June the brigades were assembled

on the same field, and passed in review before the
great leader of the Army of Northern Virginia. Much
less of display was attempted on this occasion, for General Lee, always careful not to tax his men unnecessarily, would not allow the cavalry to take the gallop, nor
would he permit the artillerymen to work their guns.
He would reserve all their strength for the serious work
which must shortly ensue. The movement of his army
which resulted in the Gettysburg campaign had commenced. Longstreet and Ewell had already reached
Culpeper Court House, and he wished his cavalry to
move across the Rappahannock on the following day, to
protect the flank of these corps as they moved northward. In preparation for this movement the brigades
were, on the evening of the same day, moved down toward the river. Fitz Lee's brigade, commanded by Colonel T. T. Munford, having charge of the pickets on the
upper Rappahannock, was, with the exception of the 4th
Virginia Cavalry, moved across the Hazel River, and encamped in the vicinity of Oak Shade. W. H. F. Lee's
brigade was stationed near Welford's house on the road to
Welford's Ford ; Jones' brigade on the road to Beverly's
Ford ; while Robertson's brigade encamped between the
Botts and Barbour farms, picketing the lower fords.
Hampton's brigade returned to their camps between
Brandy Station and Stevensburg. One battery of horse
artillery was sent across the Hazel River with Fitz
Lee's brigade, while the other four accompanied Jones'
brigade to the vicinity of Saint James' Church. Orders
were issued to march at an early hour on the 9th, and,
ignorant of any concentration of the enemy's cavalry
on the opposite side, the battalion of horse artillery bivouacked in advance of Jones' brigade, on the edge of
the woods which skirt the large open field north of Saint
James' Church. This church stood, not upon the direct

road to Beverly's Ford, but about two hundred yards to the west of that road. Opposite to it toward the east, and on the east side of the Beverly's Ford road, stood an old brick house known as the Thompson or Gee House, which in the winter of 1863–64 was occupied as a Federal hospital. Around it was a considerable grove of trees; and the rise of the land gave it full command of the open field which extends on both sides of the Beverly's Ford road, for about five hundred yards toward the north. The 6th Virginia Cavalry encamped in this grove and in its vicinity. The camp of the horse artillery was in the edge of the woods beyond, but within sight and within supporting distance. Beyond the camp of the horse artillery unbroken woods extended on both sides of the road for more than a mile, and as far as the hill which overlooks the river low-grounds and Beverly's Ford. From this hill the ford is distant about a mile. The camp of Jones' brigade and the horse artillery was at least two miles distant from Beverly's Ford.

With all of his camp equipage — except two tent-flys — packed in the wagons and in readiness for an early start, Stuart himself bivouacked on the night of the 8th on Fleetwood Hill, so called from the name of the residence there situated. For some time past he had occupied this hill as his headquarters. It is half a mile east of Brandy Station and four miles from Beverly's Ford. It commands the open plain around it in every direction except toward the Barbour House, which stands on ground a little more elevated.

On the same evening General Pleasonton approached the northern bank of the Rappahannock, with the intention of effecting an early crossing on the morrow, and a reconnoissance in force as far as Culpeper Court House, if possible, to ascertain for General Hooker's information the truth of the reports that General Lee was moving his army westward and northward from Fredericksburg. He divided his command into two columns; one of which, consisting of the 2d and 3d cavalry divisions and General David Russell's brigade of infantry, and commanded by Brigadier-General D. McM. Gregg, was ordered to cross at Kelly's Ford, about four miles below the railroad bridge; the other, consisting of the 1st cavalry division, the reserve cavalry brigade, and General Adelbert Ames' brigade of infantry, all under the command of Brigadier-General John Buford, was ordered to cross at Beverly's Ford, about a mile and a half above the railroad bridge. General Pleasonton accompanied General Buford's column. No fires were allowed in the Federal bivouac, and the presence of this large force was perfectly concealed from the Confederate pickets.

At the very first dawn of day on the 9th of June, Colonel B. F. Davis, of the 8th New York Cavalry, led his brigade across the river at Beverly's Ford. Company A, 6th Virginia Cavalry, constituted the picket at the ford, and gallantly contested the enemy's advance, which, from the narrowness of the road and the wide ditches that crossed the low-grounds, was necessarily made in column of fours. This circumstance gave to the picket company some chance to delay the advance of the large attacking force, and Captain Gibson used his opportunity to the utmost. The picket was, however, steadily and rapidly pressed backward to the edge of the woods which skirted the open field already described north of Saint James' Church, when Major C. E. Flournoy, commanding the 6th Virginia Cavalry, having collected about one hundred men of his regiment, charged down the road. He was met by the 8th New York and the 8th Illinois Cavalry, and drove them

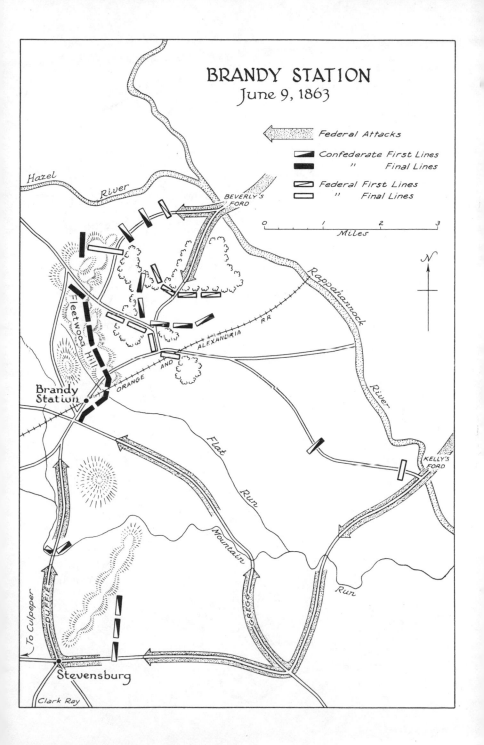

BRANDY STATION
June 9, 1863

Federal Attacks

Confederate First Lines
    "   Final Lines

Federal First Lines
    "   Final Lines

0   1   2   3
Miles

N

Hazel

River

Rappahannock

BEVERLY'S FORD

River

ALEXANDRIA   RR

ORANGE   AND

Fleetwood Hill

Brandy Station

Flat

Run

Mountain

Run

KELLY'S FORD

To Culpeper

DUFFIE

GREGG

Stevensburg

Clark Ray

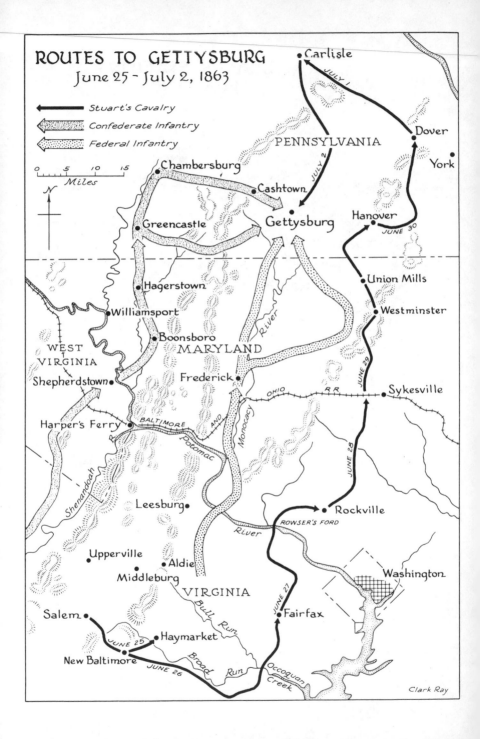

ROUTES TO GETTYSBURG
June 25 - July 2, 1863

Stuart's Cavalry
Confederate Infantry
Federal Infantry

0   5   10   15
Miles

N

PENNSYLVANIA

Carlisle
JULY 1
JULY 2
Dover
York
Chambersburg
Cashtown
Greencastle
Gettysburg
Hanover
JUNE 30

Hagerstown
Union Mills
Williamsport
Westminster
WEST VIRGINIA
Boonsboro
MARYLAND
JUNE 29
Shepherdstown
Frederick
OHIO   RR
Sykesville
Harper's Ferry
BALTIMORE   AND
JUNE 28
Potomac
Monocacy
River

Leesburg
Rockville
ROWSER'S FORD
River
Washington
Upperville
Aldie
Middleburg
VIRGINIA
Bull Run
Salem
JUNE 27
Fairfax
JUNE 25   Haymarket
New Baltimore   JUNE 26
Broad   Run
Occoquan Creek

Shenandoah

Clark Ray

back a short distance, with some loss in killed and prisoners. These gallant men certainly did their duty, for Major Flournoy reports a loss of thirty men in this encounter alone. Colonel B. F. Davis, commanding the Federal advance, was killed in this fight, and under the following circumstances. Lieutenant R. O. Allen, of company D, 6th Virginia Cavalry, had just returned from picket duty, when the advance of the enemy was reported. He joined in the charge which has been mentioned, and his horse was badly wounded. When Flournoy retired after having checked the enemy, Allen remained in the woods. Seeing an officer in the road, perhaps seventy-five yards in front of a column which was halted, Allen advanced upon him with his horse at a canter. The officer's attention was given to his own men, toward whom he was waving his sword as if to order them forward. Remembering that he had but one shot in his pistol, Allen reserved his fire until within sword's length of his foe. Perceiving his danger, Colonel Davis turned upon Allen with a cut of his sabre, which Allen avoided by throwing himself on the side of his horse. At the same moment he fired and Colonel Davis fell. He met a soldier's fate, and at the hands of one as brave, as daring as himself. Sergeant Stone, of company H, 6th regiment, and Private Larue, of company D, now came forward to the assistance of Lieutenant Allen. Others of the enemy advanced at the same moment. Sergeant Stone was killed almost instantly; and Allen and Larue, finding themselves alone in the presence of a large force, made a hasty retreat to their own lines.

During all this time the position of the horse artillery was critical in the extreme. There was nothing between the guns and danger but Flournoy's men. Captain [1] James F. Hart's battery had gone into camp

---

[1] Afterwards Major.

immediately on the road. Two guns from this battery were placed in position, and opened on the enemy, while the remainder of the battalion hastened back across the field to the line subsequently held at Saint James' Church. At this juncture General W. E. Jones brought up the 7th Virginia Cavalry, in hot haste, many of his men having mounted without their coats, and some even without waiting to saddle their horses.[1] A charge was instantly made to support Flournoy, but it was repulsed by the enemy, and in the recoil the 7th was carried back past the guns stationed on the road. These gallant cannoneers on two occasions during this memorable day proved that they were able to care for themselves. Although now exposed to the enemy, they covered their own retreat with canister, and safely retired to the line at Saint James' Church, where they found efficient support.[2] The delay caused by the fighting of Jones' two regiments and Hart's two guns was sufficient to give safety to the other guns of the battalion and to the transportation. No loss occurred worthy of mention, except that in the hurried flight the desk of Major Beckham, commanding the artillery, was jostled from his wagon, and fell into the enemy's hands.

The other regiments of Jones' brigade had now taken position on the left of Saint James' Church, and Hampton, with four of his regiments, had come in on the right. W. H. F. Lee, also, had advanced from Welford's down the river toward the firing, and had gained a strong position on the Cunningham farm, with excellent cover for his dismounted men behind the stone fence which runs northwest from near the overseer's house, with his artillery on the hill behind, near the Green House, and open ground around him

---

[1] Major James F. Hart, in the Philadelphia *Weekly Times*, 26th June, 1880.   [2] *Ibid.*

in every direction. The importance of this position, as affecting events which soon transpired on other parts of the field, will be noticed hereafter. A determined attack was made upon W. H. F. Lee by the enemy's dismounted men, and by cavalry; but it was repelled by the sharpshooters of the 9th Virginia Cavalry, aided by mounted charges made by the 10th Virginia and the 2d North Carolina regiments. The loss of the enemy at this point, especially in horses, is represented as having been unusually severe.[1] The enemy retired to the woods which covered the road to Beverly's Ford. The occasion now seemed favorable for an advance. General W. H. F. Lee's position seriously threatened the Federal right and rear, while Hampton had extended his right so as to partially envelop their left in the woods beyond the field in front of Saint James' Church. Both Hampton and Jones now advanced. The ground was, however, fiercely contested by the Federal cavalry, and a brilliant charge across the open field was made by the 6th Pennsylvania Cavalry, supported by the 6th Regulars. Major Hart thus describes the scene: —

From this time (near sunrise) until ten o'clock A. M., the engagement lingered along our front without anything noteworthy except the gallant charges of the 6th Pennsylvania and of

---

[1] In endeavoring to write a truthful narrative of the events on this part of the field, I meet with great discouragement. Neither General Buford nor any of his subordinates wrote reports of this engagement. Neither did General W. H. F. Lee nor any of his subordinates make report of their action. I have been compelled to rely upon a careful personal study of the battle-field, which I have twice visited for this purpose (once in company with General W. H. F. Lee), together with such facts as I could learn from the article of Colonel F. C. Newhall, published in the Philadelphia *Weekly Times,* and from personal correspondence with surviving officers of the Federal cavalry who took part in this engagement. General R. L. T. Beale, then colonel of the 9th Virginia Cavalry, has written out for me his recollections of this day. There is no doubt that a severe fight took place on the ground that I have described, and, as far as I can judge, I have stated the result correctly.

the Regulars, mentioned by Colonel Newhall in his careful narrative.   The latter of these charges was made over a plateau
fully eight hundred yards wide, and its objective point was the
artillery at the church.   Never rode troopers more gallantly
than did those steady Regulars, as under a fire of shell and
shrapnel, and finally of canister, they dashed up to the very
muzzles, then through and beyond our guns, passing between
Hampton's left and Jones' right.   Here they were simultane-
ously attacked from both flanks, and the survivors driven back.

Meanwhile the situation was becoming serious in
another direction, and that too while we were ignorant
of the danger.

Before sending Hampton into action Stuart had ordered that one of his regiments be detached to guard
our rear at Brandy Station.   Hampton had assigned
that duty to the 2d South Carolina Cavalry, commanded by Colonel M. C. Butler.   This regiment had
gone into camp the previous night on the road from
Brandy Station to Stevensburg, about half way between the two places.   Robertson had moved his
brigade at early dawn to the support of his picket at
Kelly's Ford, and soon reported the advance of the
Federal column upon Stevensburg.   Butler had hardly
reached Brandy Station with his regiment when he was
notified by the videttes, which he, with wise precaution,
had sent toward Kelly's Ford, that the enemy was advancing in force on that road.   Knowing that there
was nothing to prevent that column from marching
to Culpeper Court House, if so disposed, Butler, without
waiting for orders, started his regiment back, in all
haste, toward Stevensburg.   The 4th Virginia Cavalry,
Colonel W. C. Wickham, was shortly after sent by Stuart to his assistance.   These dispositions seemed to be
all that the circumstances required.   Robertson's brigade, with the 2d South Carolina and the 4th Virginia,

constituted a force of at least fifteen hundred men, and Stuart was justified in expecting them to protect his rear from attack by way of the lower fords.

Having made these dispositions, Stuart proceeded to the front, at Saint James' Church, to urge on the battle; and as the field was geographically so extensive, he stationed his adjutant (the author) upon Fleetwood Hill, directions having been given to the brigades and detached regiments to communicate with that point as headquarters. Every scrap of the camp was removed toward Culpeper Court House, and there remained nothing upon the hill except the adjutant and his couriers. A six-pounder howitzer, from Chew's battery, under charge of Lieutenant John W. Carter, which had been retired from the fight near the river because its ammunition was exhausted, was halted at the bottom of the hill; a circumstance which proved to be our salvation.

Perhaps two hours had elapsed since Stuart had mounted for the front when an individual scout from one of Robertson's North Carolina regiments reported to me that the enemy was advancing from Kelly's Ford, in force and unopposed, upon Brandy Station, and was now directly in our rear. Not having personal acquaintance with the man, and deeming it impossible that such a movement could be made without opposition from Robertson's brigade, I ordered the scout to return and satisfy himself by a closer inspection that he had not mistaken some of our troops for the enemy. In less than five minutes the man reported that I could now see for myself. And so it was! Within cannon shot of the hill a long column of the enemy filled the road, which here skirted the woods. They were pressing steadily forward upon the railroad station, which must in a few moments be in their possession. How could they be prevented from also occupying the Fleetwood Hill, the key to the whole position? Matters looked serious! But good results can sometimes be accomplished with the smallest means. Lieutenant Carter's howitzer was brought up, and boldly pushed beyond the crest of the hill; a few imperfect shells and some round shot were found in the limber chest; a slow fire was at once opened upon the marching column, and courier after courier was dispatched to General Stuart to inform him of the peril. It was all important to gain time, for should the enemy once plant his artillery on this hill it would cost many valuable lives to recover the ground, even if that could at all be accomplished. We must retain this position or suffer most seriously when enclosed between the divisions of Buford and Gregg. But the enemy was deceived by appearances. That the head of his column should have been greeted with the fire of artillery as soon as it emerged from the woods must have indicated to General Gregg the presence of a considerable force upon the hill; and the fact that his advance from Kelly's Ford had been entirely unopposed, together with his ignorance of what had transpired with Buford, must have strengthened the thought that his enemy, in force, here awaited an attack. In point of fact there was not one man upon the hill beside those belonging to Carter's howitzer and myself, for I had sent away even my last courier, with an urgent appeal for speedy help. Could General Gregg have known the true state of affairs he would, of course, have sent forward a squadron to take possession; but appearances demanded a more serious attack, and while this was being organized three rifled guns were unlimbered, and a fierce cannonade was opened on the hill.

My first courier found General Stuart as incredulous concerning the presence of the enemy in his rear as I had been at the first report of the North Carolina scout. Major Hart states that Stuart turned to him and ordered him to " ride back there and see what all that foolishness is about." But simultaneous with my second message — which was delivered by young Frank Deane, of Richmond, Va., one of my confidential clerks, and, in the field, one of our most trusted couriers — came the sound of the cannonading, and there was no longer room for doubt. The nearest point from which a regiment could be sent was Jones' position, one and a half miles distant from Fleetwood. The 12th Virginia, Colonel A. W. Harman, and the 35th battalion, Lieutenant-Colonel E. V. White, were immediately withdrawn from his line and ordered to meet this new danger. But minutes expanded seemingly into hours to those anxious watchers on the hill, who feared lest, after all, help *could* not arrive in time. But it *did* come. The emergency was so pressing that Colonel Harman had no time to form his regiment in squadrons or even in platoons. He reached the top of the hill as Lieutenant Carter was retiring his gun after having fired his very last cartridge. Not fifty yards below, Colonel Percy Wyndham was advancing the 1st New Jersey Cavalry in magnificent order, in column of squadrons, with flags and guidons flying. A hard gallop had enabled only the leading files of the 12th Virginia to reach the top of the hill, the rest of the regiment stretching out behind in column of fours. It was a trying position both to the pride and the courage of this regiment to be put into action in such manner that a successful charge seemed hopeless; but with the true spirit of a forlorn hope, Colonel Harman and the few men about him dashed at the advancing Federals.[1] Stuart

---

[1] The result of this charge was always a matter of mortification to this gallant regiment and its leader. It is but just that I should say, even at

reached the hill a few moments later, having ordered
Hampton and Jones to retire from the position at Saint
James' Church and concentrate on the Fleetwood Hill.
It would seem from Hampton's report that, before he
received this order, he himself perceived the danger in
our rear and had commenced the necessary withdrawal,
at the same time notifying Robertson, on the Kelly's
Ford road, that his rear would now be exposed.

And now the first contest was for the possession of
the Fleetwood Hill; and so stubbornly was this fought
on either side, and for so long a time, that all of Jones'
regiments and all of Hampton's participated in the
charges and counter-charges which swept across its
face. As I have already stated, the 12th regiment
reached the top of the hill just in time to meet the
charge of the 1st New Jersey. The 35th battalion was
not far behind, but these troops were so disordered by
their rapid gallop that, after the first shock, they recoiled and retired to reform. White's battalion seems
to have been cut into two parts, two of his squadrons
falling in with Colonel Harman on the eastern slope of
the hill, while the other two retired along the crest of
the ridge toward the Barbour House, in which direction
they were followed by a portion of the 1st New Jersey,
which now held the hill in temporary possession.[1] Colo-

this day, that the whole responsibility rested with me, and not with Colonel
Harman. The colonel was not aware of the extreme urgency of the case,
and his regiment was advancing only at a trot. Seeing this, I rode down
the hill to meet him, ordered the gallop, and put him into the fight in the
disorderly manner narrated. I have, however, always believed that the
circumstances justified the sacrifice of this regiment; for, had Colonel
Wyndham obtained undisputed possession of the summit, with time to make
arrangements for holding it, the subsequent fighting would probably have
had a different result.

[1] The Federal reports fail to make the proper distinction between the
Fleetwood Hill and that upon which stood the Barbour House. The latter
is distant from the former as much as half a mile and in a northwest direction. As regards Gregg's advance, it stood on his left and on the Confederate right.

nel Harman soon reformed his regiment, and, aided by
the two squadrons of the 35th battalion, regained the
hill for a short time. Colonel Harman was severely
wounded in a personal encounter with the officer leading the Federal cavalry. Lieutenant-Colonel White,
having reformed the two other squadrons of his battalion, swept around the west side of the hill and charged
the three guns which had been advanced to its foot.
The cavalry which supported these guns was driven
away. Not so, however, with the gallant gunners of
the 6th New York battery. They had already distinguished themselves at Chancellorsville on the 2d of
May, under General Pleasonton, and on this occasion
they stood by their guns with the most determined
courage. Lieutenant-Colonel White says in his report : —

There was no demand for a surrender nor offer to do so
until nearly all of the men, with many of their horses, were
either killed or wounded.

Captain J. W. Martin, commanding this battery, says
in his report : —

Once in the battery, it became a hand to hand fight with
pistol and sabre between the enemy and my cannoneers and
drivers, and never did men act with more coolness and bravery,
and show more of a stern purpose to do their duty unflinch-
ingly, and, above all, to save their guns ; and while the loss of
them is a matter of great regret to me, it is a consolation and
a great satisfaction to know that I can point with pride to the
fact that, of that little band who defended the battery, not one
of them flinched for a moment from his duty. Of the thirty-
six men that I took into the engagement, but six came out
safely ; and of these thirty, twenty-one are either killed,
wounded, or missing,[1] and scarcely one of them is there but

[1] Captain Martin doubtless means that twenty-one men out of thirty were
killed or wounded, and only nine missing or captured ; but I have not ventured to change the wording of his report without his consent, which I have
not been able to obtain.

will carry the honorable mark of the sabre or bullet to his grave.

Colonel White could not long retain possession of his trophies. He was soon surrounded by superior numbers, and was compelled to cut his way out with severe loss.

While these events were transpiring General Jones was withdrawing from Saint James' Church, with the 11th regiment, which was the only one of his brigade remaining on that line,[1] and Hampton was moving his brigade back toward Fleetwood. Hampton had formed his four regiments in column of squadrons, and, with everything well in hand for action, was moving forward briskly to the attack. He had already, in response to an order from Stuart, sent in advance of his brigade the 6th Virginia Cavalry, one of Jones' regiments, which had been acting with his line at Saint James' Church. Stuart had met this regiment and directed it to make a charge on the enemy's right, toward the east and south of the Fleetwood Hill. The result of Major Flournoy's charge may as well be given in this connection. He states in his report: —

I was then ordered by him (Hampton) to move quickly in the direction of Brandy Station, and while on the way I received orders from General Stuart to cut off three hundred Yankees who were near the Miller House. I moved across the railroad, and instead of three hundred, I met what prisoners reported as five regiments. I charged with my regiment, now reduced by casualties and the detachment of four of my companies, to two hundred and eight men. We drove back the whole force and had them in retreat, when we were attacked in rear and forced to fall back towards the Miller House, where the enemy opened on us with artillery. We charged and took the battery, but were unable to hold it. Having been charged

---

[1] The 6th regiment was with Hampton; the 7th, with W. H. F. Lee; and the 12th regiment and the 35th battalion were already at Fleetwood.

by five times our number, we fell back in confusion towards the hill in front of the Miller House, where the men rallied and reformed.

It is probably to this charge of the 6th Virginia Cavalry that Lieutenant J. Wade Wilson, commanding the left section of the 6th New York battery, refers in the following spirited extract from his report : —

Again, pursuant to orders from Colonel Kilpatrick, I limbered to the front and sought a position on the crest of the hill behind which the enemy was rapidly massing to force back the advance of Colonel Kilpatrick upon the house. Before reaching the crest, however, a halt was ordered by Colonel Kilpatrick, and, soon after, a retreat from that position, which was executed without panic and in admirable order. The enemy, perceiving the retreat, charged furiously up the hill and through the section fifty yards in rear of the pieces, charging desperately on the cavalry, some hundreds of yards in the advance of the pieces in retreat. The capture of the section seems to have been thought accomplished by the enemy, and the rebel line wheeled into column and pushed rapidly by the flanks, with the intent to turn the right of the 1st brigade, leaving, as they supposed, a sufficient force to secure the guns. At this time was displayed the heroism of the section, and valor of which any command and country may be justly proud. In reversing, one of the gun-limbers was nearly capsized, one wheel being in the air and the axle nearly vertical. Perceiving this, I ordered the cannoneers to dismount and restore to its position the limber. We were surrounded by a squad of rebel cavalry, firing with carbine and pistol. The order was scarcely needed, for the cannoneers had seen the peril of their gun, and, anticipating the order, had dismounted to restore it ; and with revolvers in hand, they defended the gun as if determined to share its destiny and make its fate their own. The bearer of a rebel battle-flag was shot by Private Currant, who would have recovered it but for the great difficulty of approaching the color with a lame and skittish horse upon which he was at the time mounted. The flag was taken by the 1st Maine Cavalry.

Following the sequence of events as nearly as may be possible, we must for a moment recall the position of the three guns of the 6th New York Battery under Captain Martin's command, which, following up the early successes of Wyndham's brigade, had been advanced to the foot of the Fleetwood Hill. Colonel H. S. Thomas, of the 1st Pennsylvania Cavalry, who was on staff duty during this day, tells us, in the Philadelphia "Weekly Times" of November 10, 1877, that

One gun did reach the crest of the hill mentioned, and fired two rounds of canister, but was dragged back to the foot, where some unknown officer had ordered the others to unlimber. Seeing the mistake that had been made, I hurried back from the charge in which I had taken part with the Jersey cavalry, but before the guns could be reached the drivers of the limber chests had taken flight with those who came back from the first charge, and were lost in the clouds of dust.

It was doubtless at the foot of the hill that these guns were reached in the charge made by Colonel E. V. White; and it was here that they were finally abandoned and fell into the hands of the men of Hart's battery, as the result of the charges made by Hampton's brigade, followed up as they were by a charge of the 11th Virginia Cavalry, under Colonel L. L. Lomax.

Let us now return to Hampton, remembering that most of the events already narrated had transpired before he came into the action at Fleetwood Hill. The magnificent order in which he advanced to the attack was the sure harbinger of success. I transcribe the following from Major J. F. Hart's narrative, premising only that the charge which he so graphically describes was made, as is clear from Hampton's report, by the 1st North Carolina Cavalry, Colonel L. S. Baker, supported by the Jeff Davis Legion, Lieutenant-Colonel J. F. Waring: —

. . . The battery I commanded moved abreast of Hampton's column in its gallop toward this new foe ; and as we came near Fleetwood Hill, its summit, as also the whole plateau east of the hill and beyond the railroad, was covered with Federal cavalry. Hampton, diverging toward his left, passed the eastern terminus of the ridge, and, crossing the railroad, struck the enemy in column just beyond it. This charge was as gallantly made and gallantly met as any the writer ever witnessed during nearly four years of active service on the outposts. Taking into estimation the number of men that crossed sabres in this single charge (being nearly a brigade on each side), it was by far the most important hand-to-hand contest between the cavalry of the two armies. As the blue and gray riders mixed in the smoke and dust of that eventful charge, minutes seemed to elapse before its effect was determined. At last the intermixed and disorganized mass began to recede, and we saw that the field was won to the Confederates.

We notice one omission in the narrative of Major Hart which must by all means be supplied. He makes no mention of the charge made by the Cobb Georgia Legion, Colonel P. M. B. Young, supported by the 1st South Carolina Cavalry, Colonel J. L. Black, which was made, as Hampton's report shows, at the same time, or a little in advance, of the charge of the 1st North Carolina and the Jeff Davis Legion. Colonel Young led this charge straight up the Fleetwood Hill from the northeast. His regiment used the sabre alone, and his movement was one of the finest which was executed on this day so full of brave deeds. Colonel Young says in his report : —

I immediately ordered the charge in close column of squadrons, and I swept the hill clear of the enemy, he being scattered and entirely routed. I do claim that this was the turning-point of the day in this portion of the field, for in less than a minute's time the battery would have been upon the hill. . . .

Scarcely had Colonel Young's command disappeared below the crest of the hill when Captain Hart galloped

his battery to the summit.   He was joined by a section
of McGregor's battery, and also, as Major Beckham
states in his report, by a part of Chew's battery.   And
now occurred one of the strangest events of the day.
A portion of the 1st New Jersey Cavalry still occupied
the extension of the ridge toward the Barbour House.
Pressed by Jones' regiments and isolated by the result
of Young's charge, it became necessary for this body
to cut their way through to their friends.   I borrow
again from Major Hart's narrative : —

Scarcely had our artillery opened on the retreating enemy
from this new position than a part of the 1st New Jersey Cavalry, which formed the extreme Federal left, came thundering
down the narrow ridge, striking McGregor's and Hart's unsupported batteries in the flank, and riding through between
guns and caissons from right to left, but met by a determined
hand to hand contest from the cannoneers with pistols, sponge-
staffs, and whatever else came handy to fight with.   Lieutenant-Colonel Broderick, commanding the regiment, was killed
in this charge, as also the second in command, Major J. H.
Shelmire, who fell from a pistol ball, while gallantly attempting to cut his way through these batteries.   The charge was
repulsed by the artillerists alone, not a solitary friendly trooper
being within reach of us.

In reference to this same charge, Major Beckham
says in his report : —

The charge was met by the cannoneers of the pieces.   Lieutenant Ford killed one with his pistol.   Lieutenant Hoxton
killed one ; and Private Sully, of McGregor's battery, knocked
one off his horse with a sponge-staff.

The Fleetwood Hill now seemed to be securely in
our possession, and Major Beckham speedily crowned
it with all his available artillery.   Hampton was pressing his advantage on the plain toward the railroad ;
but the enemy still held possession of Brandy Station,
and a few gallant men remained in the vicinity of Cap-

tain Martin's now silent guns, hoping that by some
means they might be saved. The hope was a vain one.
Stuart advanced Lomax's strong regiment, the 11th
Virginia, in the last charge which was made on this part
of the field. Lomax covered both sides of the road to
the station, rode over Martin's guns for the last time,
drove the enemy from the railroad station, and pursued
for some distance on the Stevensburg road. Hampton
states that he himself pressed the enemy until his advance was checked by the well-directed fire of Beckham's guns on the Fleetwood Hill. The dust and
smoke of the conflict was so great that it was impossible
at a distance, and difficult even near at hand, to distinguish between friends and foes. Colonel H. S. Thomas
tells us that in the confusion he picked up a Virginia
trooper, who remarked: "I can't tell you Yanks from
our folks."

Thus ended the attack of Gregg's division upon the
Fleetwood Hill. Modern warfare cannot furnish an instance of a field more closely, more valiantly contested.
General Gregg retired from the field defeated, but de-
fiant and unwilling to acknowledge a defeat. He reformed his division on the same ground on which he
had formed it to make the attack, and without further
molestation moved off to effect a junction with Buford's
division near Saint James' Church. He had been outnumbered and overpowered, but when the fighting was
over he retired from the field at his own gait.

It has, perhaps, occurred to the reader to ask how it
was possible for Stuart, in the presence of enterprising
officers, such as Pleasonton and Buford, to withdraw so
large a portion of his command from their front and
concentrate it upon Gregg's column. Lieutenant-Colonel
F. C. Newhall, assistant adjutant-general on the staff of
General Pleasonton, has published in the Philadelphia

" Weekly Times" of the 10th of November, 1877, an excellent article on that part of this battle which occurred near Beverly's Ford. Colonel Newhall's statements, when taken in connection with other facts, will give the necessary explanation. It will be remembered that W. H. F. Lee's brigade had taken position on the Cunningham farm, on the extreme Confederate left. He had repelled a strong attempt to dislodge him, and had formed a junction with Jones' line, making with it, as General Jones states, nearly a right angle. The 7th Virginia Cavalry, which formed the left of Jones' line, was somewhat separated from the rest of that brigade, but formed such close connection with Lee's line as really to constitute part of his battle. In the subsequent movements this regiment acted with Lee's brigade. This is shown by the reports of both General Jones and Colonel Thomas Marshall, then lieutenant-colonel commanding the 7th. W. H. F. Lee had therefore a strong force under his command. A glance at the map will show how threatening was the position which he occupied. He was within striking distance of the road by which Pleasonton had advanced from Beverly's Ford. Should he reach that road he would be full in the rear of the troops engaged at Saint James' Church, where the Confederates, at first acting on the defensive, now threatened to become the aggressors. General Buford therefore found it necessary, as Colonel Newhall states, to bring Ames' brigade of infantry into the battle near the church, and, replacing with it the reserve cavalry brigade, move the latter to meet the danger which threatened his right flank and rear. Of course, during such an operation, he was willing to be let alone; and it was just at this time that Stuart found it necessary to withdraw to meet Gregg. Before Buford's arrangements for an advance were completed,

Gregg's attack upon the Fleetwood Hill had been repulsed. As soon as General Gregg retired, Stuart formed a new line running almost north, on the eastern slope of the range of hills which, commencing at Fleetwood, extends in an irregular and somewhat broken manner to the river at Welford's Ford. Toward the northern end of this range, not upon the summit but in depressions between the hills, or upon the hill sides, are situated several houses ; most prominent among them Welford's house and Green's house. Thompson's house stands at the foot of the hills, just where they commence to rise from the level field of the Cunningham and Green farms. When General Jones withdrew the 11th regiment from Saint James' Church, he thereby uncovered a road leading to Green's house, which exposed W. H. F. Lee's right and rear. It was therefore necessary for Lee to withdraw to the west of this road. This he soon accomplished, bringing the 7th regiment with him. His line now occupied the hills overlooking Thompson's house. On his right, the 2d North Carolina Cavalry, dismounted, formed connection with General Jones, while the 9th, 10th, and 13th regiments extended the line, which, on the extreme left, was refused toward the west, facing Welford's house, which at this point is concealed from sight by intervening hills. Munford, with Fitz Lee's brigade, was momentarily expected on the field, and the direction of his march from Oak Shade would naturally bring him into position on the commanding ground about Welford's house.

The withdrawal of W. H. F. Lee's brigade from the open plain was, of course, in full view of the enemy, but was accomplished without provoking an attack until the new line was established, when a feeble charge in front was easily repulsed by the dismounted men.

This, however, was only the beginning of the real struggle. General Buford continued to extend his right until he had entirely enveloped the left of Lee's line, and was now prepared to make an attack from the high ground just south and west of Green's house. This, if successful, would have placed Buford in rear of the left of Stuart's line. An engagement of dismounted men — in which portions, at least, of the 2d Massachusetts and 3d Wisconsin infantry participated — was the prelude to a charge of the 6th Pennsylvania and the 2d United States Cavalry. This charge was met by the 9th Virginia, supported by the 10th and the 13th. General R. L. T. Beale, then colonel of the 9th Virginia Cavalry, in a description of this fight which he has kindly prepared for my use, claims that the 9th regiment broke the force which first attacked it, and drove it back across the stone fence in its rear. At this moment the 9th was attacked by a fresh regiment which came in on the flank, and was in turn driven back to the foot of the hill whence it had commenced the charge. Here the 9th was reinforced by the 10th and the 13th, and the tide of battle was finally turned against the Federal cavalry, which was driven back across the crest of the hill whence they had advanced. General Beale further states that having reformed his regiment after this action, he rode forward to reconnoitre before again advancing, when, to his surprise, he found the enemy moving back toward Beverly's Ford. A comparison of General Beale's statement with the narrative of Colonel Newhall indicates that this was the fight in which Adjutant Ellis, of the 6th Pennsylvania, was wounded, and in which General Wesley Merritt, then captain commanding the 2d Regulars, lost his hat in a sabre fight with a rebel officer. When the 9th Virginia first charged up the hill,

General W. H. F. Lee was upon its left flank, encouraging the men of his old regiment. Just before he reached the crest of the hill he was severely wounded and was carried from the field. Colonel Sol. Williams, of the 2d North Carolina Cavalry, had begged permission, inasmuch as everything was quiet on his line, to join in this charge. He went in on the right of the 9th, was shot through the head, and instantly killed. The command of the brigade now devolved on Colonel J. R. Chambliss, of the 13th Virginia Cavalry, who says in his report : —

About half-past four o'clock P. M. Brigadier-General W. H. F. Lee was wounded, and Colonel Sol. Williams, 2d North Carolina Cavalry, was killed, and I assumed command, having previously been in charge of three squadrons, dismounted as sharpshooters. Only a few shots were fired, and the action was virtually over when I assumed command.

While the attack upon the left of W. H. F. Lee's line was in progress, Colonel T. T. Munford arrived from Oak Shade with three regiments of Fitz Lee's brigade. He had been delayed in his march by a perplexing ambiguity in the orders which had been transmitted to him. Had he been able to reach the field of battle two hours earlier, and had he secured the hills commanding Green's house, more important results would perhaps have been secured. As it was, he was compelled to grope his way, in ignorance of what was transpiring to the left of W. H. F. Lee's line. Once in position, he performed effective service with three squadrons of sharpshooters from the 1st, 2d, and 3d Virginia Cavalry, aided by Breathed's battery. In these three squadrons, during the short time they were engaged, he lost three men killed and eighteen wounded.

Colonel Newhall tells us that while Buford's attack was in full progress, he was searching for Buford with orders from General Pleasonton to discontinue the attack and withdraw his division to the north side of the Rappahannock. Gregg had now effected a junction with Pleasonton at Saint James' Church. Duffié had come in from Stevensburg. The presence of Confederate infantry, supporting Stuart, had been definitely ascertained. Believing that he had accomplished the objects of the reconnoissance, Pleasonton determined to cross the river without delay. The reports of Stuart and of his subordinate officers show that no serious effort was made to impede his withdrawal.

We must now turn our attention toward Stevensburg, where events of less magnitude, but of equal interest, were transpiring.[1]

On the morning of the 9th of June the atmosphere was in a condition peculiarly favorable for the transmission of sound, and the firing of the pickets at Beverly's Ford aroused Stuart's entire command. At early dawn General Hampton rode in person to Colonel Butler's camp, and directed him to mount his regiment, move to Brandy Station, and there await orders. In executing this order Butler left Lieutenant W. W. Broughton, officer of the guard, with fourteen men, in charge of the camp, directing him to send two videttes to Stevensburg. Butler had hardly reached Brandy Station when Lieutenant Broughton reported that the enemy was advancing on the road near Stevensburg, and that the wagons of the regiment were in danger. Knowing that there was no force of cavalry between

---

[1] Senator M. C. Butler, of South Carolina, who on this day commanded the 2d South Carolina Cavalry, and General Williams C., Wickham, then colonel of the 4th Virginia Cavalry, have given me many of the facts upon which the following narrative is based. To the Hon. James W. Moore, state senator from Hampton County, South Carolina, then adjutant of the 2d South Carolina Cavalry, and to the Hon. John T. Rhett, mayor of Columbia, South Carolina, then a lieutenant in the same regiment, I am indebted for carefully written circumstantial narratives.

Stevensburg and Culpeper Court House, where lay General Lee with Longstreet's and Ewell's corps, Butler did not await orders, but moved at once to meet the danger. He sent forward, at a gallop, in advance of the regiment, Lieutenant-Colonel Frank Hampton, with twenty men, to observe and delay the enemy until the regiment could reach the range of hills known as Hansborough's Mount, where Butler wished to contest his advance. Colonel Hampton pursued the direct road to Stevensburg, and meeting Lieutenant Broughton's party learned that a squadron of the enemy had advanced through the town, and had again retired. As Hampton's party, now numbering thirty-six men, reached Stevensburg, he found this squadron drawn up in a position of observation on the east side of the town. He immediately ordered a charge, which the enemy did not wait to receive, but retired in the direction of their main body. Colonel Butler had, in the mean time, led his regiment on a by-road to the east of Stevensburg, and reached the main road just in rear of this retreating squadron, the pursuit of which was continued past Doggett's house to the wide stretch of open field beyond, over which the enemy was seen advancing in force. Judging that the attack would be made from the open field north of the road, Butler withdrew his regiment to the line of wooded hills already described. It was necessary for him to occupy a line from Doggett's house to Hansborough's, a distance of nearly a mile, and to cover this line he had less than two hundred men. Leaving the thirty-six men under Colonel Hampton to act mounted on the road, Butler deployed the remainder of his regiment on foot along the line on the north side of the road. Colonel Hampton was ordered to charge anything which might assail him.

It is now necessary to explain the presence of the

Federal cavalry at this point. The column under General Gregg had effected an easy crossing of the river at Kelly's Ford between the hours of five and eight o'clock A. M., for it was opposed by nothing but Robertson's picket, which retired toward his brigade in the direction of Brown's house, leaving General Gregg's advance entirely unobstructed and unobserved.[1] General Gregg left Russell's infantry brigade in the vicinity of Kelly's Ford, and pushed forward to Stevensburg the 2d cavalry division, 1,900 men, under Colonel A. N. Duffié, of the 1st Rhode Island Cavalry. Following Colonel Duffié's march as far as Willis Madden's, General Gregg turned the 3d cavalry division to the northwest, toward Brandy Station, where he made the attack, the result of which has already been narrated. Colonel Duffié's column continued to move toward Stevensburg. One squadron of his command entered the town without opposition, but retired on the main body when charged by Colonel Hampton.

The position in which Butler awaited attack was well chosen. The woods concealed the smallness of his numbers, and even on the road the sloping ground prevented the enemy from discovering any but the leading files of Hampton's mounted detachment. The enemy's advance was at first cautious, even timid. As Butler had anticipated, the first attempt was to break the line of his dismounted men, on his left, and two such attacks were made; but both were repulsed by the close fire of his Enfield rifles. The enemy now turned his attention to Hampton's position, and prepared to carry it by a direct sabre charge on the road, supported by squadrons on either flank. To meet this attack Colonel Hampton dismounted nearly one half of his men for the protection of his flanks, retaining but twenty to

[1] See Robertson's Reports, Appendix.

meet the enemy's mounted charge. Between Hampton's position on the road and the nearest point of the line of Butler's dismounted men was a considerable gap.

At this juncture Colonel Wickham arrived with the 4th Virginia Cavalry. He had been turned off from the direct road to Stevensburg by Captain W. D. Farley, volunteer aid-de-camp to General Stuart, and had been guided along the same obscure road by which Butler had advanced. He now found himself on the right of Butler's dismounted men, the head of his column resting on the main road east of Stevensburg, just in rear of the position held by Hampton's mounted detachment. The change in the direction of his march was most unfortunate, and was the real cause of the stampede which ensued. Had Wickham moved through Stevensburg, as he would have done had he not met Captain Farley, his regiment would have been in position to meet the enemy, whose advance might have been checked at the strong line occupied by Butler. The circumstances in which Wickham was placed were peculiar. His own regiment was in a position where it was impossible for it to act, enclosed as it was in a thick pine copse, on a narrow by-road, where even a column of fours could scarcely move. It was therefore necessary to turn the head of his column westward, toward Stevensburg, and after thus gaining the main road, to wheel about by fours, placing his left in front. Ignorant of the dispositions made by Butler, and of the events which had already occurred, Wickham naturally hesitated to give orders either to Butler or Hampton until he could survey the ground and bring his own regiment into action.

Major T. J. Lipscomb, commanding the 2d South Carolina Cavalry after Colonel Butler was disabled and

Colonel Hampton was killed, in an appendix to his report dictated by Colonel Butler, states that the command was turned over to Colonel Wickham by Colonel Butler, and that it was suggested that Colonel Hampton's position be strengthened by sharpshooters on the right, and by a mounted force in the road. The communication between Butler and Wickham was made though Lieutenant-Colonel W. H. Payne, of the 4th Virginia. Adjutant Moore states that in a brief interview between Colonel Hampton and Colonel Wickham, Hampton requested that both his right and left be strengthened by squadrons of sharpshooters, and that Wickham promptly acquiesced, and moved back toward his regiment to give the necessary orders. Captain John D. Hobson, of company F, 4th Virginia Cavalry, has recently assured me that the squadron, composed of his own company and Captain Strother's, was put in on Hampton's left, and that being soon separated from the rest of the regiment these companies acted with the 2d South Carolina during a considerable part of the rest of the day. This agrees with Major Lipscomb's report, and also with Colonel Wickham's. While these arrangements were being made the enemy was advancing a column on the road, supported by strong squadrons on either side, moving slowly, however, as they came under the fire of the few men dismounted on the road. The force of the enemy was so large that, in the opinion of both Adjutant Moore and Lieutenant Rhett, a charge by Hampton's twenty men, unsupported, would only have resulted in their destruction. Lieutenant Broughton informed Adjutant Moore that he delivered a message from Colonel Hampton to Colonel Wickham to the effect that he (Hampton) would close back upon the 4th regiment so as to make a charge in solid column. At this moment the rear of the 4th regiment was emerging upon the road from the woods, and the order " By fours, right about wheel," was heard. Whether this command was given by Colonel Hampton to execute the movement contemplated in the message delivered by Lieutenant Broughton, or whether it was given by some officer of the 4th regiment so as to bring the faces of his men toward the enemy, is entirely uncertain. The result was most unfortunate. Captain Chestnut and Lieutenant Rhett, at the head of Hampton's men, remained facing the enemy, to conceal, if possible, a movement which they felt must bring an attack upon them at once. But the enemy saw the wheel, and instantly ordered the charge. Colonel Hampton again ordered the right about wheel, and placed himself at the head of his men; but it was of no avail. In a moment they were swept to the side of the road, and the full force of the charge fell upon the 4th Virginia. Colonel Hampton, while engaging one of the enemy with his sabre, was shot through the body by another, and was mortally wounded. He succeeded in reaching the house of John S. Barbour, west of Stevensburg, where he died that night.

It cannot be a matter of surprise that the 4th regiment under such circumstances broke and ran. Had the regiment rallied quickly no blame would have attached to it. There was not a finer body of men in the service. They had frequently proved their valor on other battle-fields, and on many subsequent occasions they confirmed their good reputation. But on this day a panic possessed them. They did not respond to the efforts of their officers, and the enemy's pursuit was continued through the town of Stevensburg and beyond as far as Barbour's house, where Colonel Wickham and a few of his men threw themselves into a field on the road-side, and by the fire of their pistols checked further pursuit.

Very few of Hampton's men continued on the road with the 4th regiment. Most of them gave way to the left toward the line of the dismounted men of their own regiment. Simultaneous with the charge on the road, a squadron of the enemy had attacked the left of Butler's line, which was held by Lieutenant Markert; but this attack was readily repulsed, and Markert's line, still intact, offered a good rallying point for Hampton's men. Adjutant Moore says : —

I was told that some of the men, among whom was Lieutenant W. H. Waring, as soon as they got out of the road, stopped and began firing into the enemy, nor did they leave their position by the road until the head of the charging column had gone so far beyond them as to render them liable to be cut off and captured; that Lynch, of company H, knocked two dragoons off their horses with the butt of his rifle before he was surrounded and captured: and I remember that when I was engaged in rallying these men, Babb, of company E, brought me a prisoner whom he had captured after a hand to hand fight; and that I saw Pender, of company H, — who was badly mounted before the charge, — just afterwards on a fine horse, having killed the Federal dragoon who rode him.

Major Lipscomb's report narrates the events which now followed. He says : —

The enemy having gained possession of the road, and passed through Stevensburg on the road to Culpeper, the right of our line fell back obliquely to the road leading from Stevensburg to Brandy Station. They were rallied and formed by Colonel Butler between Stevensburg and Norman's Mill; but the columns of the enemy pouring out of the woods on his left, and threatening to gain his rear, compelled him to fall back beyond Norman's Mill and take a new position on the hill near Beckham's house. Colonel Butler ordered me to hold my position, and if they pressed on the right to move in that direction. The firing on the right gradually got to my rear, and I was in the act of moving when Captain Farley, of General Stuart's staff, brought to me a squadron of the 4th Virginia Cavalry, with orders to hold my position. I immediately put all the riflemen in position. About half an hour afterwards I received orders from Colonel Butler to retire with rapidity across Mountain Run. My line was extended, and by the time the riflemen were mounted the right and left of our line had both fallen back across Mountain Run. Having sixteen dismounted men with me, I was obliged to retire slowly to protect them. When I reached the open field I found a column of the enemy on either flank, from three to four hundred yards distant, and also moving towards Mountain Run. Our artillery fired two shots, which fell near me, and which, I think, caused the enemy to take me for one of their own columns, as they did not fire on me until after I had crossed the Run.

Butler had now secured a good position covering the road to Brandy Station, and where he might expect soon to be reinforced by the 4th Virginia Cavalry. Moreover, he threatened the enemy's flank should he advance towards Culpeper Court House. The one gun which had followed Colonel Wickham from Brandy Station was now available, and Butler proposed to make a stand. But while in the road, side by side with Captain Farley, their horses' heads in opposite directions, a shell from the enemy struck the ground near by, ricochetted, cut off Butler's right leg above the ankle, passed through his horse, through Farley's horse, and carried away Farley's leg at the knee.

The Hon. John T. Rhett addresses his narrative, from which I have already largely drawn, to the Hon. M. C. Butler; and thus describes a scene which for knightly courtesy and heroism cannot be surpassed.

After we crossed the stream the enemy placed a gun in position in full view of us all. While they were so doing you ordered us to retire. As we were moving off I was turned in my saddle looking backwards. I saw the artilleryman fire the gun, heard an exclamation, and saw that the shot had taken effect in the small group with you. Captain Chestnut and myself with a few men hastened to the spot. We first went to you, sending some men to aid Captain Farley. When we had placed you in a blanket you said to us, —

" I wish that you two gentlemen, as you have placed me in the hands of my own men, would go and take charge of Farley."

We went to Captain Farley, told him that you had sent us, took him out of a blanket, and placed him in an old flat trough. He was very cool, in fact pleasant and smiling, though evidently in great pain. Just as we were about to send him away, he called me to him, and pointing to the leg that had been cut off by the ball, and which was lying near by, he asked me to bring it to him. I did so. He took it, pressed it to his bosom as one would a child, and said, smiling, —

" It is an old friend, gentlemen, and I do not wish to part from it."

Chestnut and myself shook hands with him, bidding him good-by, and expressing the hope that we should soon again see him. He said, —

" Good-by, gentlemen, and forever. I know my condition, and we will not meet again. I thank you for your kindness. It is a pleasure to me that I have fallen into the hands of good Carolinians at my last moment."

Courteously, even smilingly, he nodded his head to us as the men bore him away. He died within a few hours. I have never seen a man whose demeanor, in the face of certain, painful, and quick death, was so superb. I have never encountered anything so brave from first to last.

Duffié's division, now far separated from the rest of the Federal cavalry, and recalled by repeated orders from General Gregg, did not press the advantage gained, but retired from Stevensburg in the direction of the railroad, where it effected a junction with Gregg's division, and recrossed the Rappahannock at the railroad bridge.

The severity of the fighting during this day is shown by the losses sustained in both commands. The total Confederate loss was 523 officers and enlisted men. As trophies of the fight there remained in Stuart's hands three pieces of artillery, six regimental and company flags, and 486 prisoners. The total Federal loss was 936 officers and enlisted men. Colonel J. Kilpatrick and Colonel P. Wyndham, commanding the two brigades of Gregg's division, each claim the capture of a Confederate battle-flag and of General Stuart's adjutant-general. Stuart did lose his aid, Lieutenant Goldsborough, who was captured while attempting to return to Brandy Station from Stevensburg ; but the report of the capture of the adjutant is a mistake.

The forces engaged were, on the Federal side, three divisions of cavalry, consisting of twenty-four regiments, and two brigades of infantry, consisting of ten regiments ; numbering in all, according to General Pleasonton, 10,981 effective men. All of these troops, except Russell's brigade of infantry, were more or less engaged in the battle. On the Confederate side there were five brigades of cavalry, containing twenty-one regiments, one of which was absent on picket duty, and not within reach of the battle-field. On the monthly return for May 31, 1863, these five brigades and the horse artillery reported an effective total of 9,536. The fighting on this day was done almost exclusively by fifteen regiments, — five of Hampton's, five of Jones', four of W. H. F. Lee's, and one of Fitz Lee's. Three squadrons of sharpshooters from Fitz Lee's brigade were engaged, late in the afternoon, on the Confederate left. Robertson's brigade was not engaged at any time during the day. General Robertson moved promptly to the support of his picket at Kelly's Ford, and discovered the movement of Gregg's division toward Stevensburg. He reported the facts to General Stuart, who was probably four miles distant, and asked for instructions. Meanwhile Gregg pursued his way unmolested.

General Robertson's movements are fully described in his report, which may be found in the Appendix.

The number of guns employed on either side was probably nearly equal, although the advantage of position was generally with the Confederates.

The results claimed by Federal writers as following from this battle seem extravagant. The information which General Pleasonton obtained was positive, as far as it extended, but after all was meagre. He developed the presence of the Confederate cavalry, and of a portion of the Confederate infantry at Brandy Station. Beyond this he learned nothing. Certainly General Hooker does not credit him with having penetrated General Lee's designs; for on the 12th of June he uses the following language in orders addressed to the commanding officer of the 1st corps : " In view of the position of affairs on the right, the absence of any specific information as to the objects, movements, and purposes of the enemy,"[1] etc., etc. Subsequent correspondence contained in General Hooker's testimony before the Committee on the Conduct of the War shows that uncertainty concerning General Lee's intentions existed both at Washington and at General Hooker's headquarters, as late as the 21st of June.[2] One result of incalculable importance certainly did follow this battle, — it *made* the Federal cavalry. Up to that time confessedly inferior to the Southern horsemen, they gained on this day that confidence in themselves and in their commanders which enabled them to contest so fiercely the subsequent battle-fields of June, July, and October.

There are two points in connection with this battle which, although proven incorrect, have been persistently repeated. It is asserted that General Stuart's

[1] *Conduct of the War*, vol. i. p. 158 *et seq.*   [2] *Ibid.*

headquarters, his baggage, and his papers were captured; and that Confederate infantry was seen debarking from the cars in the vicinity of Brandy Station while the fight with Gregg's division was in progress.

As regards the asserted capture of Stuart's baggage and papers, it is to be noticed that no official report on the Federal side makes any such claim; and it cannot be supposed that so important a fact would have passed without mention had it actually occurred. On the other hand, certain expressions in General B. H. Robertson's report caused General Stuart to explain, in his indorsement, that the Fleetwood Hill, where his headquarters had been located, was temporarily in the enemy's hands, but that his baggage had been sent off early to the rear. If necessary the testimony of every surviving officer of Stuart's staff can be produced, showing that long hours before Gregg's attack on the Fleetwood Hill, all of the headquarters' wagons had been sent to Culpeper Court House.

The assertion that Confederate infantry was seen debarking from the cars in the vicinity of Brandy Station has no better foundation. General Ewell's report, and the reports of General Rodes and his subordinate commanders, show that Ewell's corps marched to Stuart's assistance from a point on the Rixeyville road four miles north of Culpeper Court House, by way of Botts' farm, to Brandy Station; and that Rodes' division, which was in advance, did not reach Barbour's house until Pleasonton and Buford were in the act of retiring.

CHAPTER XVI.

ALDIE; MIDDLEBURG; UPPERVILLE.

AFTER the battle of the 9th of June, Longstreet remained at Culpeper Court House while Ewell pushed forward into the Valley and conducted those movements which resulted in the capture of Milroy's command at Winchester. On the 15th of June Longstreet moved from Culpeper to occupy Ashby's and Snicker's gaps, in the Blue Ridge, and Stuart placed three of his brigades, Fitz Lee's, W. H. F. Lee's, and Robertson's, in advance, and on the right of his column. Jones' brigade and Hampton's were left to guard the line of the Rappahannock until A. P. Hill's corps had passed northward. The movements of the cavalry did not bring Stuart in collision with the enemy until the evening of the 17th, when a severe engagement took place at Aldie. Fitz Lee's brigade, under Colonel Thomas T. Munford, had been sent forward to occupy the gap in the Bull Run Mountain at Aldie; while Colonel J. R. Chambliss, with W. H. F. Lee's brigade, reconnoitred toward Thoroughfare Gap. Robertson was held near Rectortown, so as to move to the assistance of either as occasion might demand.

Early on the morning of the 17th, Colonel Munford, with the 2d and 3d Virginia Cavalry, moved from Upperville through Middleburg, and having established his picket posts east of Aldie, crossed over to the Snicker's Gap road, and proceeded with these two regiments to procure corn at the house of Mr. Franklin Carter, about a mile distant. He expected to encamp that night in the vicinity of Aldie. Colonel Williams C. Wickham, with the 1st, 4th, and 5th Virginia Cavalry, the remaining regiments of the brigade, had moved from Piedmont through Middleburg and was about to place his men in camp at Dover Mills, near Aldie. The 5th regiment, Colonel Thomas L. Rosser, which arrived some little time after the 1st and 4th, was directed by Colonel Wickham to pass beyond Dover Mills, and select a camp nearer Aldie. In so doing Colonel Rosser encountered the enemy, who was rapidly driving back the pickets established by Colonel Munford.

The force of the enemy making this attack was the 2d cavalry division, commanded by General D. M. Gregg, and accompanied by Major-General Pleasonton. General Kilpatrick's brigade, consisting of the 2d New York, 1st Massachusetts, 6th Ohio, and 4th New York regiments, supported by the 1st Maine Cavalry, from Colonel J. I. Gregg's brigade, and by Randol's battery, appears to have done all the fighting. The two other brigades of General Gregg's division were closed up within supporting distance.

The arrival of Rosser's regiment was most opportune. By an immediate sabre charge he drove back the enemy's advance upon their main body in the town of Aldie. Having relieved the pressure on the pickets, Rosser stationed his sharpshooters, under Captain R. B. Boston, on the right of the Snickersville road, where a number of haystacks afforded some protection, and held the remainder of his small regiment ready for their support. Colonel Munford in the mean time arrived in person, and stationed Lieutenant William Walton, of the 2d Virginia Cavalry, with the reserve picket, fifteen men, behind a stone wall on the left of the Snickersville road, with orders to hold his position against any odds until the 2d and 3d regiments could come to his assistance. In the mean time, and while Colonel Wickham was stationing the 1st and 4th regiments and Breathed's battery to dispute any advance on the Middleburg road, Rosser, single-handed, had met and repulsed two charges which were made upon Captain Boston's squadron; and believing that he could be maintained there with advantage, had ordered Boston to hold his position at all hazards. The result proved that this disposition was unfortunate; for during the subsequent heavy fighting Boston was so far advanced as to be beyond the reach of support, and he and his squadron were captured.

During all this time there was no force on the left of the Snickersville road except the picket posted by Munford behind the stone wall. Munford therefore moved Rosser's regiment and the 4th Virginia Cavalry, with one gun from Breathed's battery, so as to command this road, leaving Colonel Wickham with the rest of the guns and the 1st Virginia Cavalry on the Middleburg road. In the mean time the enemy pressed heavily on Lieutenant Walton. He had repulsed two mounted charges, but being outflanked by dismounted men, had been withdrawn about fifty yards behind a house and orchard, in which position he commanded the only opening through which the enemy could attack. Here three distinct charges were met and repulsed in counter-charges by the 5th Virginia Cavalry, by the 3d squadron of the 4th regiment, led by Lieutenant A. D. Payne, and by the 2d and 5th squadrons of the same regiment, led by Captain W. B. Newton. These were the only squadrons of this regiment present at this battle, the 1st and 4th squadrons having been detailed early in the day to accompany General Stuart. In each of these charges the enemy had suffered severely at the hands of Lieutenant Walton's sharp-shooters, who poured volleys into their flank as they passed him in advancing and in retiring. As Walton's party was, however, evidently small, the enemy determined to dislodge him, and was preparing a considerable force for another attack, when the 2d and 3d Virginia Cavalry reached the field. Two squadrons of sharpshooters were at once dismounted and placed on the left of the road: the squadron from the 2d regiment under Captains Breckinridge and Graves, that from the 3d regiment under Captain George D. White. Their line was advanced to the stone wall from which Lieutenant Walton had been withdrawn. Colonel Munford now felt that his position was secure against an attack of cavalry, and there was nothing he more desired than that the enemy should wear himself out against it. His flanks were secured by the Little River and its tributaries. The enemy must necessarily attack his front. The road by which it was approached was worn, as it ascended the hill, into deep gullies, which compelled an attack in column of fours and prevented the enemy from spreading out his front. Munford's strong party of sharpshooters commanded the road. They were stationed in an enclosed field, with a stone wall in their front, a post and rail fence on their right, and another fence on their left. The fences to the rear were thrown down so as to give the cavalry access to the field. Munford felt that unless his cavalry failed in their duty his dismounted men were perfectly secure.

The 2d Virginia Cavalry, led by Lieutenant-Colonel J. W. Watts, now charged the advancing enemy, who had penetrated beyond the position of the sharpshooters. The heads of the columns met in the narrow road in a hand to hand sabre fight. While this was in progress, Captain Jesse Irving threw down the fence on the right of the road, and bringing his squadron to the front, opened fire on the enemy's left flank. Captain W. W. Tebbs executed a similar movement on the left of the road, while the sharpshooters were all the time firing into the enemy's rear. Their attack was completely broken, and their leading squadron almost destroyed. Another support moved up during the confusion, but was met and repulsed by Colonel Rosser. In this fight Lieutenant-Colonel Watts was wounded and permanently disabled. The command of the 2d regiment devolved on Major Cary Breckinridge, who moved the regiment off to the right to reform, carrying with him Colonel Louis P. De Cesnola and the colors of his regiment, the 4th New York Cavalry.

During all this time Captain Boston, of the 5th Virginia Cavalry, had been holding the haystacks, far in advance of his friends, where Colonel Rosser had placed him with such stringent orders. He was beyond the reach even of a recall, but had been doing his utmost to aid in the fight. He was now charged by the 6th Ohio Cavalry, under Lieutenant-Colonel William Stedman ; and after losing three of his officers, including his junior captain, and a third of his men killed and wounded, he surrendered to the odds brought against him.

The Federal cavalry were determined to carry the position if it were possible, and another charge was speedily organized. This was met by the 3d Virginia Cavalry, led by Colonel T. H. Owen, who took the road, supported on his right by the 2d regiment and on his left by the 5th. The sabre was the weapon used, and the enemy was again driven back. Colonel Munford pronounces this to be the most spirited charge of the day. Colonel Owen, however, pressed his success too far. He drove the enemy almost to the village of Aldie, where he was charged by a fresh regiment and driven back, losing many of the prisoners he had taken and some of his own men. Major Henry Carrington, of the 3d regiment, was captured at this point. Colonel Munford says in his report : —

Captain Newton, having rallied his small command and a good many men from other commands, was again ready to relieve Colonel Owen as he fell back, and by a timely charge repelled another effort to flank him. As the enemy came up again the sharpshooters opened upon him with terrible effect from the stone wall, which they had regained, and checked him completely. I do not hesitate to say that I have never seen as many Yankees killed in the same space of ground in any fight I have ever seen, or on any battle-field in Virginia that I have been over. We held our ground until ordered by the major-general commanding to retire, and the Yankees had been so severely punished that they did not follow. The sharpshooters of the 5th were mostly captured, this regiment suffering more than any other.

Colonel Munford reports that he captured 138 prisoners. His own total loss was 119, of which the 5th Virginia Cavalry lost 58, mostly from Captain Boston's squadron.

There is a significant absence of reports of this battle on the Federal side. General Kilpatrick made no report of it. General D. M. Gregg devotes one paragraph to it, in which, in general terms, he claims a victory over " the enemy, strongly posted, and in superior force to Kilpatrick's brigade." Lieutenant-Colonel William Stedman, commanding the 6th Ohio Cavalry, makes a particular report of the capture of Captain Boston's squadron, in which charge he lost " three men killed and eleven wounded, including Major Stanhope, who has since died of his wounds." Colonel

Stedman adds: "The enemy opened on us from the
hill beyond with grape and canister; but we held the
position until dark, when we were ordered to retire."
Colonel C. S. Douty, of the 1st Maine Cavalry, was
killed on the field. He was succeeded by Colonel C.
H. Smith, who, on the 31st of August, reports that "A
portion of the regiment, led by Colonel Douty, charged,
turned the enemy, and drove him from the hill and
his stronghold among the stone walls. The regiment
gained the position, secured our wounded, collected the
trophies of the field, and were burying the dead when
relieved just before dark. The casualties were as follows: killed, six; wounded, nineteen; missing, five."
No other statement of the Federal losses is to be found
in the reports; but the records of the Adjutant-General's Office show that the 1st Maine Cavalry and Kilpatrick's brigade (exclusive of the 1st Rhode Island
Cavalry, whose disaster at Middleburg will soon be noticed), lost 50 killed, 131 wounded, and 124 missing —
a total of 305. This excessive loss will perhaps account for the silence of the Federal officers. It certainly testifies to the gallantry of the regiments which
advanced so often against such a strong position held
by so determined a foe.

The disparity of numbers was in favor of the Federal cavalry, on whose part five regiments were actively
engaged. Only four regiments were engaged on the
Confederate side; and of these the 3d and 5th regiments were small. Two squadrons were absent from
the 4th regiment, and one from the 2d. The 1st Virginia Cavalry held the Middleburg road, but took no
other part in the battle. The fighting was done by
probably less than a thousand men on the Confederate
side. Munford retired from the field about dark, by
the Snickersville road, not because of any pressure that

was brought to bear on him by General Gregg, but in obedience to the orders of General Stuart, and in consequence of events which had occurred at Middleburg. He brought off from the field all of his dead, and all of his wounded who could be moved. He established his pickets about a mile from the battle-field, and these were not molested until the following morning.[1]

On this same afternoon events of considerable importance occurred at Middleburg, where Stuart had established his headquarters for the day.

Early in the morning Colonel A. N. Duffié, with the 1st Rhode Island Cavalry, had crossed the Bull Run Mountain at Thoroughfare Gap. His orders directed him to encamp at Middleburg on the night of the 17th, and to proceed the next day toward Noland's Ferry, extending his march to the west as far as Snickersville. These orders seem to have contemplated a somewhat extended scout by this regiment on the left flank of General Gregg's division, — a hazardous movement in the presence of an enterprising enemy. Colonel Duffié reached Thoroughfare Gap at 9.30 A. M., and was somewhat delayed in crossing the mountain by the picket from Chambliss' command. By eleven o'clock, however, he was fairly on his way toward Middleburg. At four o'clock P. M. he struck the pickets which Stuart had established for his own safety outside the town, and drove them in so quickly that Stuart and his staff were compelled to make a retreat more rapid than was

[1] Writers on the Federal side who have given narratives of this battle seem to have accepted as authority contemporary newspaper accounts, samples of which are preserved in Moore's *Rebellion Record*, volume VII. The official reports of Colonels Munford, Owen, Wickham, and Rosser, of Major Breckinridge, and of Captain Newton, on the Confederate side, are ignored. General A. Doubleday devotes pages 100 to 103 of his volume, *Chancellorsville and Gettysburg*, to this battle ; and it would be difficult to find *in any other* work claiming historical accuracy, within the same number of pages, an equal number of errors.

consistent with dignity and comfort. Having with him no force adequate to contest the ground with Duffié's regiment, Stuart retired toward Rector's Cross Roads. Munford was notified of his danger, and directed to withdraw from Aldie, and Robertson and Chambliss were ordered to move immediately upon Middleburg. The only hope for Duffié's regiment now lay in an immediate advance upon Aldie, where he might have created considerable commotion by attacking the rear of the 1st Virginia Cavalry on the Middleburg road. But he did not know this, and his orders were positive, requiring him to encamp for the night at Middleburg. He therefore made the best of his situation by dismounting one half of his regiment behind stone walls and barricades, hoping that he might be able to hold his position until reinforced from Aldie, whither he sent Captain Frank Allen to make known his situation at brigade headquarters. Captain Allen reached Aldie, after encountering many difficulties, at nine o'clock P. M. He says in his report : —

General Kilpatrick informed me that his brigade was so worn out that he could not send any reinforcements to Middleburg, but that he would report the situation of our regiment to General Gregg. Returning, he said that General Gregg had gone to state the facts to General Pleasonton, and directed me to remain at Aldie until he heard from General Pleasonton. I remained, but received no further orders.

Thus Colonel Duffié was left to meet his fate. At seven o'clock in the evening he was attacked by Robertson's brigade. His men fought bravely, and repelled more than one charge before they were driven from the town, retiring by the same road upon which they had advanced. Unfortunately for Duffié, this road was now closed by Chambliss' brigade, which surrounded him during the night, and captured, early the next morning, the greater part of those who had escaped from Robertson on the previous evening. Colonel Duffié himself escaped capture, and reached Centreville early in the afternoon, with four of his officers and twenty-seven men. He reports the loss in his regiment at twenty officers and two hundred and forty-eight men. This, however, was an exaggeration of the calamity; for other officers beside himself had taken to the woods, and succeeded in making their way back to the Federal lines on the 18th and 19th. Major Farrington, who was separated from his regiment on the night of the 17th, in Middleburg, thus brought in two officers and twenty-three men; Lieutenant-Colonel Thompson brought in eighteen men; Sergeant Palmer, twelve men; and Captain George N. Bliss, six men. Color - Sergeant Robbins, who was wounded and captured, was left in Middleburg and fell into the hands of his friends when Stuart retired from that place. This reduces the loss to two hundred. This regiment was composed of good materials, and it rapidly recuperated. On the 17th of August following it assembled three hundred men at Warrenton, and was attached to McIntosh's brigade of Gregg's division.[1]

It was doubtless Stuart's intention to occupy the gap at Aldie on the 17th, and there dispute any advance which the Federal cavalry might make. But it may be questioned whether he would have attempted to make a permanent stand on the line of the Bull Run Mountain, — a line which would have necessitated the

[1] For these facts I am indebted to Captain George N. Bliss, of Providence, R. I. There can be no doubt of their accuracy. I estimate the strength of the 1st Rhode Island Cavalry, from Colonel Duffié's report, at 300 officers and men. Colonel Duffié states his aggregate loss at 268. Four officers and twenty-seven men escaped with the colonel. This makes the strength of the regiment 300.

separation of the three brigades then available, to
guard as many gaps, upon any one of which the enemy
might concentrate and force a passage, — a line which
could, moreover, readily be turned by a movement toward the north.   The force at his command was inadequate to hold this line, and the advance of Gregg's division to Aldie, on the 17th, forced Stuart to adopt
perhaps the wiser plan of holding his command west
of the Bull Run Mountain, ready to oppose the enemy
wherever he might appear.

On the night of the 17th Robertson's brigade encamped about Middleburg, where Chambliss, with W.
H. F. Lee's brigade, joined it on the following morning.
Munford was drawn back on the road to Union to a
point about four miles distant.   Stuart's pickets east of
Middleburg were attacked and driven through the
town on the 18th ; but the enemy did not pursue beyond, and the pickets were reëstablished at night.   On
this day, Major John S. Mosby captured one of General
Hooker's staff who was bearing despatches to General
Pleasonton at Aldie.   These despatches informed Stuart
that he was confronted not only by the large cavalry
force commanded by General Pleasonton, but also by
General Barnes' division of infantry, three brigades
strong.   To oppose this force, Stuart had only two
brigades, or less than eight regiments, on the road from
Middleburg to Upperville, and one brigade of five regiments on the road to Union.

Early on the 19th Stuart's position on the Upperville turnpike was attacked by General D. M. Gregg's
division, Colonel J. I. Gregg's brigade being in the advance.   The attack was resisted for a long time ; but
when the enemy had gained a considerable advantage
on the Confederate right by a charge of dismounted
men supported by two regiments of cavalry, Stuart

withdrew to another line about a half a mile in his rear. This withdrawal was effected in good order, under the fire of the enemy's dismounted men and artillery, and no attempt was made to charge the retiring lines. During this movement Major Heros Von Borcke, an officer of the Prussian army, who was serving on General Stuart's staff, received a severe wound, which disabled him from future service. General Gregg claims to have captured a large number of prisoners, but makes no specifications. Colonel J. I. Gregg reports a loss of one hundred and twenty-seven officers and men from his brigade. No attack was made on Stuart's new position on this day, although hardly half of it was spent in this encounter.

Jones' brigade reached Stuart on the evening of the 19th, and was posted at Union ; Munford being moved still further to the left, to cover Snicker's Gap. Hampton arrived on the 20th, having met and repulsed, near Warrenton, a body of the enemy's cavalry which was making a reconnoissance in that direction. Hampton had been notified to expect a collision with the enemy, for the despatches captured by Mosby had indicated such a movement. Hampton was now stationed on the Upperville pike, and Chambliss was moved over to strengthen the line in front of Union. Although Stuart's five brigades were now in position, the necessity of guarding the three roads by which the mountain passes might be approached compelled him to divide his command into as many parts; and forewarned that the enemy's cavalry was supported by a strong force of infantry, he determined still to act on the defensive, and, if heavily attacked, withdraw toward the mountains, concentrating his cavalry at Upperville, after offering as much opposition as he could without involving his command in too serious a contest with superior numbers.

At about eight o'clock on the morning of Sunday, the 21st of June, the enemy moved out from Middleburg. Buford's division, three brigades, advanced on the road toward Union, endeavoring to turn Stuart's left flank; while Gregg's division, three brigades, supported by Vincent's infantry brigade, which alone numbered on the 19th of June an effective total of 1,545,[1] advanced on the Upperville pike. General D. M. Gregg states in his report that his advance was at first intended as a feint to occupy Stuart's attention in front, while Buford moved upon his left flank. But Buford found Chambliss, and Jones so strong that he could do no more than make a direct attack upon them. General Gregg's feint against Hampton and Robertson was, therefore, soon changed into a serious attack. Kilpatrick's brigade of cavalry and Vincent's brigade of infantry held the advance. Colonel Vincent, in his report, states with particularity the part taken by each of his four regiments up to a point west of Goose Creek, and reports a total loss of seven officers and men.[2] Pursuing the policy already indicated, Stuart directed Hampton and Robertson not to allow themselves to become too heavily engaged, and at the same time he ordered Chambliss and Jones to retire toward Upperville, as the artillery firing on the pike receded in that direction.

The first position held by Stuart was about three miles west of Middleburg. Here he delayed the enemy as long as prudence permitted, and then retired *en echelon* of regiments, covered by his artillery. This order of retiring was maintained throughout the entire day, and at no time was the enemy able to cause any serious disorder in his ranks. In leaving his first position a Blakely gun belonging to Hart's battery was aban-

---

[1] Records of the Adjutant-General's Office.   [2] *Ibid.*

doned. The axle had been broken by a shot from the enemy, and no means were at hand for its renewal. This was the first piece belonging to the horse artillery which had, up to that time, fallen into the enemy's hands, and the only one lost on that day.

The second position held by Stuart was on the west bank of Goose Creek, and here the enemy was delayed for several hours. At this point General Gregg's cavalry and Vincent's infantry were still further reinforced by the reserve cavalry brigade from Buford's division, and from this position Stuart again withdrew, to effect a junction at Upperville with Jones and Chambliss, who were retiring slowly before Buford's advance. As the battle approached Upperville the enemy pressed with renewed vigor. When within a mile of the town General Buford, believing from the appearance of the field that General Gregg was outnumbered, disengaged himself from Chambliss' front and moved rapidly to General Gregg's assistance. Having the shorter line to traverse, he thus cut off Jones and Chambliss from effecting a junction with Hampton and Robertson east of Upperville.

Perhaps the truest estimate of the situation north of the Upperville pike will be formed by a comparison of the reports of General John Buford and General W. E. Jones, proper allowance being made for the stand-points of these officers. General Buford says: —

When within a mile of Upperville I saw a large force in front of General Gregg, who appeared to be outnumbered. I resolved to go to his aid. The column struck a brisk trot, but ran afoul of so many obstructions in the shape of ditches and stone fences that it did not make fast progress, and got out of shape. While in this position I discovered a train of wagons and a few troops to my right, marching at a trot, apparently making for Ashby's Gap. I turned the head of my column toward them, and very soon became engaged with a superior force. The enemy brought four twelve-pounder guns into position, and made some excellent practice on the head of my regiments as they came up. The gunners were driven from their guns, which would have fallen into our hands but for two impassable stone fences. The enemy then came up in magnificent style from the direction of Snickersville, and for a time threatened me with overwhelming numbers. He was compelled, however, to retire before the terrific carbine fire which the brave 8th Illinois and 3d Indiana poured into him. As he withdrew, my rear troops came up, formed, and pressed him back to the mountains. He was driven over the mountains into the valley.

General Jones says : —

Having arrived in rear of Colonel Chambliss' position he was found retiring, and the advance of the enemy towards Upperville was such as to necessitate a deviation towards the mountain. This increase of distance rendered rapid movement necessary. The artillery of both brigades was put in the road, and the cavalry on the flanks, — Chambliss' to the left, and mine to the right, — approaching rapidly the elevation on which stands the house of Captain Gibson, to secure a position for our artillery. We found ourselves anticipated by the enemy, who, taking advantage of his shorter line, forced us into an engagement with Buford's whole division. The artillery, finding the struggle unavoidable, accepted with alacrity the part forced upon it by the enemy. The stone fence next the enemy was soon down, and the pieces in position were heard and felt by the enemy ; but the hostile cavalry pushing on, a charge became necessary to save the artillery. The 11th Virginia Cavalry, under Colonel O. R. Funsten (Colonel Lomax being still in charge of the rear-guard), made the attack, checking the advance until the artillery could cross the lane, where it again took position.

In the mean time the 7th Virginia coming up it was held in reserve. The leading squadron, under Captain H. R. T. Koontz, was sent to attack a body of the enemy approaching the road. The remainder of the regiment attacked the force to the front and left of the first position of our battery. The check thus given the enemy enabled our artillery and cavalry to cross the road.

By this time the enemy was massed in force in our front, and our cavalry having cleared our battery it played with fearful effect upon their men and horses. The punishment here inflicted, together with the difficulties of the ground, soon caused the enemy to abandon his intention of preventing a junction of our forces in Ashby's Gap. The difficulties of the ground brought Colonel Chambliss to my left in this engagement, our commands retiring together as soon as the pressure was removed.

While these events were occurring on the north of the Upperville pike, General Gregg was handsomely pushing his advance upon the town. Robertson's brigade held the road, and the open fields north of it. As he retired through the town one of his regiments was thrown into some confusion, which was, however, instantly relieved by the splendid conduct of Hampton's brigade, on the right. As the enemy followed Robertson on the road Hampton charged their flank with the Jeff Davis Legion. General Hampton gives the following account of this action: —

We repulsed the enemy, who threw a fresh regiment on the right flank of the Legion. I called up the right wing of the 1st North Carolina Cavalry, five companies, under Lieutenant-Colonel Gordon (afterwards brigadier-general), and in turn charged. Another regiment charged the North Carolinians, when Colonel Baker, with the remaining five companies, struck them upon the flank. Baker was charged by a fresh regiment. Then I put in the Cobb Legion and broke the attacking party. The Cobb Legion was again attacked, and again with the Jeff Davis Legion I turned the flank; and this series of charges went on until all of my regiments named had charged three times, and I had gained ground to the right and front of more than half a mile. At this moment the 2d South Carolina Cavalry was brought up in good order from the rear, and under its protection I reformed my command, and retired in column of regiments, at a walk and without molestation. In the mean time everything upon my left had given way, and the enemy were in Upperville. I came into the road beyond the village, and formed to support Robertson.[1]

Hampton brought off eighty prisoners from this fight. The enemy advanced but a short distance beyond Upperville. The last charge of the day was made by Colonel P. G. Evans' regiment of North Carolina Cavalry, of Robertson's brigade. This was the regiment which had become disordered in retiring through the town. Colonel Evans was determined to atone for this disgrace. Placing himself at the head of his column of fours in the narrow lane, and pointing with his drawn sabre toward the enemy, he cried, as with the voice of a trumpet, "Now, men, I want you to understand that I am going through!" He kept his word, but fell mortally wounded in the midst of the enemy, whose ranks he had penetrated too far for the recovery of his body. A feeble attempt to follow this regiment as it returned from the charge was checked by Hampton's brigade, and darkness closed down upon the scenes of this hard-fought day. Had a longer term of daylight permitted any further advance by the enemy they would have come into collision with Longstreet's infantry, which had come down from the gap to Stuart's aid. Of this reinforcement, however, General Pleasonton was ignorant. He acknowledges in his report that he was unable to follow Stuart into the gap, and, except that he assured himself "that the enemy had no infantry force in Loudon Valley," was able to transmit to army headquarters no other information as the result of this reconnoissance beyond that "given by the negroes here."

The Official Reports of Federal commanders and the

[1] Philadelphia *Weekly Times*, July 20, 1878.

narratives of Federal writers claim greater credit for the Federal cavalry than will be justified by a dispassionate study of *all* the records. The sum-total of results obtained in the way of information has already been indicated. As regards the fighting, it appears that Pleasonton, with superior force at his command, caused Stuart to retire over a distance certainly not greater than six miles, between eight o'clock in the morning and dark, on one of the longest days of the year. There is nothing in the details of the battle as given by the subordinate Federal commanders which would indicate any decided advantage gained by them in the fighting, and nothing which militates against the statement that Stuart's defensive policy was successfully carried out during the whole day, and that his withdrawal from one position to another was executed in uniformly good order. If victory in any passage at arms is to be claimed by either side, it must be accorded to Hampton's brigade, which at the close of the day relieved the pressure on Robertson's two regiments, drove back the forces opposed to it, regained more than half a mile of ground, and retired from the battle at a walk, and unmolested. This success was mainly due to that personal influence which both during and since the war has marked Hampton as a leader of men. When the Jeff Davis Legion was counter-charged, its position seemed perilous. Hampton saw the danger, and turned to Baker's regiment. Drawing his sabre, and raising himself to his full height, he cried, " 1st North Carolina, follow me ! " and those North Carolinians could as little resist that appeal as iron can fail to obey the magnet.

The duty devolving upon Stuart was one of the most difficult which belongs to the cavalry service, to retire in the presence of a superior force. He could oppose on either road only two brigades to the enemy's two divisions and their supporting infantry, and even the Federal reports, while claiming victory in general terms, show how stubbornly he contested the field.

There was one feature of Stuart's conduct on this day which attracted my attention. Until the battle reached Upperville he personally participated in it but little, remaining, however, in close observation of the field. I asked the reason of this unusual proceeding, and he replied that he had given all necessary instructions to his brigade commanders, and he wished them to feel the responsibility resting upon them, and to gain whatever honor the field might bring.

Stuart's loss in the battles of the 17th, 19th, and 21st of June was 65 killed, 279 wounded, and 166 missing ; a total of 510.

The Federal loss at Aldie and Middleburg, on the 17th of June, was 505. Colonel J. I. Gregg reports a loss of 127 in the battle of the 19th of June, and Generals Gregg and Buford report a loss of 188 on the 21st of June. Colonel Vincent lost 7 on the same day. The total Federal loss in these three engagements was, therefore, 827.

CHAPTER XVII.

GETTYSBURG.

EARLY on the morning of the 22d of June General Pleasonton retired from Upperville, and on the same day Stuart's headquarters were reëstablished at Rector's Cross Roads, with pickets well advanced toward Middleburg.

Colonel John S. Mosby has related in the Philadelphia "Weekly Times" of the 15th of December, 1877, how he submitted to General Stuart, on the 23d, a plan of crossing the Bull Run Mountain at Glasscock's Gap, and of passing through the centre of Hooker's army in Loudon and Fairfax counties, with the purpose of crossing the Potomac at Seneca. While General Stuart does not mention Mosby's name in this connection, there is evidence in his report that this, with some modifications, was the plan which he submitted for the approval of General Lee; for General Stuart states that, before moving from Rector's Cross Roads, he sent Mosby to reconnoitre within the enemy's lines, with orders to report to him on the 25th, near Gum Spring, Loudon County. It is also apparent from Stuart's report that he was not restricted to this one route, but was free to act as circumstances might direct; for he says : —

I submitted to the commanding general the plan of leaving a brigade or so in my present front, and passing through Hopewell, or some other gap in Bull Run Mountain, attaining the enemy's rear, and passing between his main body and Washington, to cross into Maryland and join our army north of the Potomac.

General Lee states in his report : —

Upon the suggestion of the former officer (General Stuart) that he could damage the enemy and delay his passage of the river by getting in his rear, he was authorized to do so.

And again : —

In the exercise of the discretion given him when Longstreet and Hill marched into Maryland, General Stuart determined to pass around the rear of the Federal army with three brigades, and cross the Potomac between it and Washington, believing that he would be able by that route to place himself on our right flank in time to keep us properly advised of the enemy's movements.

The circumstances under which Stuart received his orders well illustrate his spirit and hardihood as a soldier. The night of the 23d of June was most inclement. A pitiless rain poured without cessation from the clouds, and the land was drenched. Although the shelter of the old house at the Cross Roads was available, at bedtime Stuart ordered his blanket and oil-cloths to be spread under a tree in the rear of the house, and directed me to sleep on the front porch, where I could readily light my candle and read any despatches which might come during the night. I remonstrated with him upon this needless exposure, but his reply was: " No ! my men are exposed to this rain, and I will not fare any better than they." It was late in the night when a courier arrived from army headquarters, bearing a despatch marked "confidential." Under ordinary circumstances I would not have ventured to break the seal ; but the rain poured down so steadily that I was unwilling to disturb the general unnecessarily, and yet it might be important that he should immediately be acquainted with the contents of the despatch. With some hesitation I opened and read it. It was a lengthy communication from General Lee, containing the directions upon which Stuart was to act. I at once carried it to the general and read it to him as he lay under the dripping tree. With a mild reproof for having opened such a document, the order was committed to my charge for the night, and Stuart was soon asleep. It is much to be regretted that a copy of this letter cannot now be produced. A diligent search has failed to find it, and as General Stuart did not forward a copy of it with his report, I presume it was destroyed during our subsequent march. But I have many times had occasion to recall its contents, and I find that my recollection of it is confirmed by several passages in General Stuart's report.

The letter discussed at considerable length the plan of passing around the enemy's rear. It informed General Stuart that General Early would move upon York, Pa., and that he was desired to place his cavalry as speedily as possible with that, the advance division of Lee's right wing. The letter suggested that, as the roads leading northward from Shepherdstown and Williamsport were already encumbered by the infantry, the artillery, and the transportation of the army, the delay which would necessarily occur in passing by these would, perhaps, be greater than would ensue if General Stuart passed around the enemy's rear. The letter further informed him that, if he chose the latter route, General Early would receive instructions to look out for him and endeavor to communicate with him; and York, Pa., was designated as the point in the vicinity of which he was to expect to hear from Early, and as the possible (if not the probable) point of concentration of the army. The whole tenor of the letter gave evidence that the commanding general approved the proposed movement, and thought that it might be productive of the best results, while the responsibility of the decision was placed upon General Stuart himself. Well may General Longstreet say : " Authority thus given a subordinate general implies an opinion on the part of the commander that something better than the drudgery of a march along our flank might be open to him, and one of General Stuart's activity and gallantry should not be expected to fail to seek it." [1]

Having received his orders on the night of the 23d of June, General Stuart prepared on the 24th to execute them. The three brigades of Hampton, Fitz Lee, and W. H. F. Lee, the latter under the command of Colonel Chambliss, were ordered to rendezvous that night at Salem, and Robertson's and Jones' brigades, under command of Brigadier-General B. H. Robertson, "were left in observation of the enemy on the usual front, *with full instructions as to following up the enemy in case of withdrawal, and joining our main army.*" [2] I do not profess to give authoritatively the reasons which led General Stuart to make this disposition of his brigades, but there are some considerations which seem to lie upon the surface. Stuart was about to undertake a hazardous movement, in which he needed not only veteran troops, but officers upon whose hearty coöperation he could confidently rely. These qualities were united in the brigades and brigade commanders which he selected to accompany him. Moreover, by this division of his brigades he left in close communication with the army a force of cavalry nearly equal to that which he carried with him, for Jones' brigade was by far the largest in the division, and when joined to Robertson's

---

[1] Philadelphia *Weekly Times*, November 3, 1877.
[2] Stuart's Report.

two regiments, this command must have numbered more than 3,000 men, even after deducting the losses in battle since the 9th of June. This force, added to Jenkins' brigade, which constituted Ewell's advance in Pennsylvania, and which General Stuart estimated at 3,800,[1] he was justified in considering sufficient to fulfil every duty which might be required of the cavalry by the commanding general. Another consideration doubtless had weight. I have heard General Stuart pronounce in unqualified terms that he considered General Jones " *the best outpost officer* " in his command ; and that his watchfulness over his pickets and his skill and energy in obtaining information were worthy of all praise. General Stuart must, therefore, have considered that he was leaving in communication with the army an officer eminently qualified for the duty of observing and reporting the enemy's movements; and that the fact that his brigade constituted, perhaps, four fifths of the force employed would cause General Robertson, who commanded the two brigades, to give full weight to his suggestions and counsels.

I shall not be accused of attempting to detract from the good name of one of the most gallant, zealous, and efficient officers in the armies of Virginia, — one who proved his ability by his success in independent command, who possessed the confidence of General Robert E. Lee, and who sealed his devotion to his country in his own blood, — when I say that, in his intercourse with General Stuart, General William E. Jones well

---

[1] General Early has shown in the *Southern Historical Society Papers*, vol. iv. p. 245, that Stuart's estimate of the strength of Jenkins' brigade was excessive, and that it did not contain more than 1,500 or 1,600 men. But my object is to present the facts as they appeared to Stuart's mind when called upon to decide between the alternatives laid before him by General Lee's orders ; and, whether correct or not, he certainly at that time relied upon the information which caused him to estimate Jenkins' brigade at 3,800 men.

justified the sobriquet by which he was known among
his comrades in the old army — "Grumble Jones." In
the fall of 1861, soon after Jones had been promoted
and assigned to the command of the cavalry regiment
of which Stuart had been colonel, there was an unfortunate interruption of their personal relations, after
which kind coöperation between two such positive na-
tures was hardly possible. On several occasions General Stuart recorded his high estimate of Jones' abilities, and with equal clearness his protest against the
assignment or promotion of Jones under *his* command.
After Jones joined Stuart, in May, 1863, with his magnificent brigade, hardly a day passed without bringing
to Stuart's adjutant-general official papers containing
proof of Jones' idiosyncrasies. The disagreement between these two valuable men culminated, in the fall of
1863, in an official communication from Jones which
Stuart could not overlook. General Stuart ordered his
arrest and preferred charges against him. General
Jones was afterwards assigned to the command of the
department of Southwestern Virginia, where his distinguished services are a matter of history. Captain
Walter K. Martin, of Richmond, Va., so long and well
known as General Jones' assistant adjutant-general, has
given me the following incident: —

At the opening of the Wilderness campaign in May,
1864, General Jones was stationed at Saltville, Va.
The news of the earlier battles of that campaign had
spread through the country, and General Jones was
awaiting the result with the greatest anxiety. Returning to his camp after an absence of nearly the whole
day, he eagerly inquired of Martin what news had
been received. Martin replied: "General Stuart has
been killed." For many minutes Jones paced the floor
of his tent in silence, with eyes bent on the ground.
At length he said, with his own peculiar emphasis, —

" By G——, Martin! You know I had little love for Stuart, and he had just as little for me ; but that is the greatest loss that army has ever sustained except the death of Jackson." [1]

The three brigades selected to accompany Stuart rendezvoused at Salem during the earlier part of the night of the 24th, and at one o'clock on the same night marched out for Haymarket, passing through Glasscock's Gap early in the morning. As Stuart approached Haymarket it was discovered that Hancock's corps, marching northward, occupied the road upon which he expected to move. A brisk artillery fire was opened upon the marching column, and was continued until the enemy moved a force of infantry against the guns. Not wishing to disclose his force, Stuart withdrew from Hancock's vicinity after capturing some prisoners and satisfying himself concerning the movement of that corps. This information was at once started to General Lee by a courier bearing a despatch written by General Stuart himself. It is plain from General Lee's report that this messenger did not reach him ; and unfortunately the despatch was not duplicated. Had it reached General Lee the movement of Hancock's corps would, of itself, have gone far to disclose to him the intentions of the enemy as to the place where a passage of the Potomac was about to be effected.

It was now clearly impossible for Stuart to follow the route originally intended ; and he was called upon to decide whether he should retrace his steps and cross the Potomac at Shepherdstown, or by making a wider *détour* continue his march to the rear of the Federal army. He consulted with no one concerning the decision, and no one is authorized to speak of the mo-

---

[1] The reader will pardon this digression, the matter of which has seemed too important to occupy place in a foot-note.

tives which may have presented themselves to his mind. We may, however, fairly suggest the following considerations : Stuart's orders directed him to choose the most expeditious route by which to place himself on the right of Early's advance in Pennsylvania. Early was at Waynesboro', Pa., on the 23d of June, and his movements up to that day were of course known to Stuart, who did not leave Rector's Cross Roads until late in the afternoon of the 24th. Early's march to York, Pa., was indicated to Stuart in General Lee's orders, and York was named as the place where Stuart would probably find Early.[1] On the evening of the 25th, when Stuart drew back to Buckland out of the way of Hancock's corps, at least sixty miles of a mountainous road lay between him and Shepherdstown, the nearest ford of the Potomac west of the mountains. He could not hope to reach Shepherdstown with his artillery earlier than the evening of the 27th ; and he would have been more than fortunate could he have occupied the passes of South Mountain on the 28th. He would even then have been at least thirty miles from Gettysburg, and twice that distance from York. It should not therefore be wondered at if this consideration alone decided Stuart to persist in the movement already begun, especially when there was also the hope of damaging the enemy in his rear and thus delaying his movements. Moreover he had a right to expect that the information he had forwarded concerning the movement of Hancock's corps would cause Robertson and Jones to be active on their front, and would put General Lee himself on the alert in the same direction.

Stuart withdrew from contact with Hancock's corps to Buckland, from whence he marched on the 26th

[1] See Stuart's Report.

to the vicinity of Wolf Run Shoals, and on the 27th through Fairfax Court House to Dranesville, which he reached late in the afternoon of the 27th. General Hampton had a sharp encounter near Fairfax Court House with a squadron of cavalry from "Scott's Nine Hundred," commanded by Major Remington, which was on its way to Centreville. Major Remington and eighteen of his men escaped, but with a loss of eighty of his squadron.[1] This encounter cost Hampton's brigade the loss of a most gallant officer, Major John H. Whitaker, of the 1st North Carolina Cavalry, who was killed while leading the charge.

It had been necessary to halt the command several times since the 25th to graze the horses, for the country was destitute of provisions, and Stuart had brought no vehicles with him save ambulances. Upon reaching Dranesville Hampton's brigade was sent to Rowser's Ford, and made the passage early in the night; but the Potomac was so wide, the water so deep, and the current so strong, that the ford was reported impracticable for the artillery and ambulances. Another ford in the vicinity was examined, under circumstances of great danger, by Captain R. B. Kennon of Stuart's staff, but it was found to offer no better prospect of success, and Stuart determined to cross at Rowser's, if it were within the limits of possibility. The caissons and limber-chests were emptied on the Virginia shore, and the ammunition was carried over by the cavalry-men in their hands. The guns and caissons, although entirely submerged during nearly the whole crossing, were safely dragged through the river and up the steep and slippery bank, and by three o'clock on the morning of the 28th the rear-guard had crossed and the whole command was established upon Maryland soil. No

[1] Moore's *Rebellion Record*, vol. vii. p. 18.

more difficult achievement was accomplished by the cavalry during the war.   The night was calm and without a moon.   No prominent object marked the entrance to the ford on either side, but horse followed horse through nearly a mile of water, which often covered the saddles of the riders.   Where the current was strong the line would unconsciously be borne down the river, sometimes so far as to cause danger of missing the ford, when some bold rider would advance from the opposite shore and correct the alignment.   Energy, endurance, and skill were taxed to the utmost; but the crossing was effected, and so silently that the nearest neighbors were not aware of it until daylight.   Possession was immediately taken of the canal, which constituted one of the lines of supply for Hooker's army; a number of boats, some containing troops, were captured, and the canal was broken.   After the arduous labors of the night some rest was indispensable, especially for the artillery horses, and the sun was several hours high before the command left the Potomac for Rockville.   Hampton's brigade moved in advance by way of Darnestown, and found Rockville in the possession of a small force of the enemy, which was speedily scattered.

It was past noon when Stuart entered Rockville. While halting for the purpose of destroying the telegraph line, and to procure supplies, information was brought of the approach from Washington of a large train of wagons on the way to Meade's army.   Lieutenant Thomas Lee, 2d South Carolina Cavalry, with four men from his regiment, dashed along the train and routed its small guard.   Although some of the wagons in the rear had turned about and were moving rapidly toward Washington, Lee reached the one foremost in the retreat, and halted and turned it about within sight of the defences of the city.   Chambliss' brigade followed, and the whole train was secured. One hundred and twenty-five of the wagons, and all of the animals belonging to the train, were turned over to the chief quartermaster of the army at Gettysburg.

At this day we read the history of the minutest events connected with this campaign in the light of the final result. Had General Lee gained the battle of Gettysburg, as he said he would have done if Stonewall Jackson had been present,[1] the persistency with which Stuart held on to these wagons, and the difficulties he surmounted in transporting them safely through an enemy's country during the next three days and nights of incessant marching and fighting, would have been the cause of congratulation. But Gettysburg was lost to the Confederate arms, and not through Stuart's fault; and every circumstance which might have contributed to a different result will be judged in the light of the final catastrophe. Considered from this point of view, it must be acknowledged that the capture of this train of wagons was a misfortune. The time occupied in securing it was insignificant; but the delay caused to the subsequent march was serious at a time when minutes counted almost as hours. Had Stuart been entirely unimpeded he would have probably passed Hanover, Pa., on the 30th, before the arrival of Kilpatrick's division, and would have been in communication with General Lee before nightfall on that day. That this would have altered the result of the campaign is a matter of grave doubt; but it would certainly have relieved the movement of the cavalry around the rear of Meade's army of the disapprobation to which some have given expression.

Another cause of delay at Rockville was Stuart's

[1] *Personal Reminiscences of General R. E. Lee*, by Rev. J. William Jones, D. D., p. 156.

humanity towards his prisoners, of whom more than four hundred were in his hands. Among them were Major James C. Duane and Captain N. Michler, of the Engineer Corps, U. S. A. At the urgent solicitation of these officers, Stuart consented to a parole, and the whole of the night was consumed at Brooksville and much time the next morning at Cooksville in accomplishing this business, — a useless task; for the Federal authorities refused to acknowledge the parole, and returned officers and men immediately to duty.

While this parole was being transacted, Fitz Lee's brigade was moved northward towards the Baltimore and Ohio Railroad, which it reached soon after daylight on the morning of the 29th. Much time was necessarily consumed in tearing up the track at Hood's Mill, in burning the bridge at Sykesville, and in destroying the telegraph line; but this work was effectually accomplished, and the last means of communication between General Meade's army and Washington was destroyed. Stuart now pressed on to Westminster, which he reached about five o'clock P. M. Here his advance encountered a brief but stubborn resistance from two companies of the 1st Delaware Cavalry, commanded by Major N. B. Knight. This fight was more gallant than judicious on the part of Major Knight, for he reports a loss of sixty-seven men out of ninety-five.[1] Two officers of the 4th Virginia Cavalry, who were well known as among the best in the regiment, — Lieutenants Pierre Gibson and John W. Murray,— were killed in this affair. Stuart says in his report that the ladies of the town begged to be allowed to superintend their interment, and that the request was granted.

For the first time since the 24th an abundance of provisions for men and horses was obtained at West-

[1] *Official Records, Preliminary Print*, vol. xv. p. 929.

minster; and moving the head of his column to Union Mills, on the Gettysburg road, Stuart rested for the remainder of the night. Here he ascertained that the enemy's cavalry had reached Littlestown, seven miles distant, on the same evening, and had gone into camp. At this day we can see that it would have been better had Stuart here destroyed the captured wagons. Up to this time they had caused no embarrassment, for the necessary delay in destroying the railroad and telegraph on the previous day had given ample time for the movement of the train. But now the close proximity of the enemy suggested the probability of a collision on the morrow, and the separation of the brigades by the wide interval which the train occupied was a disadvantage which might well have caused its immediate destruction. But it was not in Stuart's nature to abandon an attempt until it had been proven to be beyond his powers; and he determined to hold on to his prize until the last moment. This was unfortunate. Kilpatrick's division, at Littlestown, was only seven miles from Hanover. His march would of course be directed upon that point early the next morning. To reach the same place Stuart must traverse more than ten miles; but an early start and an unimpeded march would have placed him in advance of his adversary. As it was he struck the rear of Farnsworth's brigade at about ten o'clock on the morning of the 30th, in the town of Hanover, and scattered one regiment, the 18th Pennsylvania Cavalry, inflicting upon it a loss of eighty-six officers and men.[1] The 2d North Carolina Cavalry, temporarily commanded by Lieutenant-Colonel W. H. Payne, of the 4th Virginia Cavalry, made this attack, which, if it could have been properly supported, would have resulted in the rout of Kilpatrick's com-

[1] *Official Records, preliminary print,* vol. xv. p. 167.

mand. But Hampton was separated from the leading
brigade by the whole train of captured wagons, and
Fitz Lee was marching on the left flank to protect the
column from an attack by way of Littlestown. There
was nothing at the front but Chambliss' small brigade ;
and before anything could be brought to the assistance
of the 2d North Carolina, General Farnsworth rallied
his regiments, and drove the North Carolinians from
the town. In this charge Lieutenant-Colonel Payne
was captured.

The road upon which this fight occurred debouches
from the town of Hanover toward the south, and at a
distance of perhaps three hundred yards from the town
makes a turn almost at right angles as it ascends the
hill beyond, enclosing a piece of meadow land, through
which flows a little stream, whose steep banks form a
ditch, from ten to fifteen feet wide and from three to
four feet deep. Stuart, with his staff and couriers,
occupied this field, on the side next the enemy.
When the 2d North Carolina broke and retreated
under Farnsworth's charge, this party maintained its
position for some moments, firing with pistols at the
flank of the enemy, who pursued the North Carolina
regiment on the road. The position soon became one
of extreme personal peril to Stuart, whose retreat by
the road was cut off. Nothing remained but to leap
the ditch. Splendidly mounted on his favorite mare
Virginia, Stuart took the ditch at a running leap, and
landed safely on the other side with several feet to
spare. Some of his party made the leap with equal
success, but not a few horses failed, and landed their
riders in the shallow water, whence by energetic scram-
bling they reached the safe side of the stream. The
ludicrousness of the situation, notwithstanding the peril,
was the source of much merriment at the expense of
these unfortunate ones.

Upon the repulse of the 2d North Carolina Stuart retired to the hills south and east of Hanover, which gave him such commanding position that the enemy declined further advance. Hampton, on his arrival, was moved to the right, and by means of his sharp-shooters dislodged the enemy from that part of the town. Fitz Lee in moving up on the left had encountered a part of Custer's brigade, and captured a member of Kilpatrick's staff and a number of other prisoners. In the mean time the wagons had been placed in close park, and preparation had been made to burn them should the necessity arise. But Custer's brigade, which had at first been placed on Kilpatrick's left, was subsequently moved to his right, and Hampton's success having relieved Stuart's right, he now determined to send Fitz Lee forward with the train, through Jefferson toward York, Pa., hoping thus to gain information which would guide his future movements. It was, however, late in the afternoon before this could be effected, and not until night had fallen did Stuart deem it prudent to withdraw from Kilpatrick, who still maintained his threatening position in front of Hanover. Kilpatrick showed no disposition to hinder Stuart's withdrawal, or to pursue him on the following day. He had been roughly handled during the short engagement at Hanover, and himself acknowledges an aggregate loss of 197. He moved as far northward on the next day as Abbottstown, and sent a detachment, under Lieutenant-Colonel A. J. Alexander, which followed Stuart's trail as far as Rossville, but neither of these movements came within Stuart's observation.

During the night march to Jefferson the wagons and prisoners were a serious hindrance. Nearly four hundred prisoners had accumulated since the parole at Cooksville. Many of these were loaded in the wagons;

some of them acted as drivers.   The mules were starving for food and water, and often became unmanageable.   Not infrequently a large part of the train would halt in the road because a driver toward the front had fallen asleep and allowed his team to stop.   The train guard became careless through excessive fatigue, and it required the utmost exertions of every officer on Stuart's staff to keep the train in motion.   The march was continued through the entire night, turning northward at Jefferson.   When Fitz Lee reached the road leading from York to Gettysburg he learned that Early had retraced his steps, and had marched westward.   The best information which Stuart could obtain seemed to indicate that the Confederate army was concentrating in the vicinity of Shippensburg. After a short rest at Dover, on the morning of the 1st of July, Stuart pressed on toward Carlisle, hoping there to obtain provisions for his troops, and definite information concerning the army.   From Dover he sent Major A. R. Venable, of his staff, on the trail of Early's troops, and at a later hour of the day Captain Henry Lee, of Fitz Lee's staff, was sent toward Gettysburg on a similar errand.   Stuart had reached Carlisle before either of these officers could return with a report.   He found the town in the possession of the enemy.   When the Confederate infantry had withdrawn from it General W. F. Smith had occupied the town with two brigades of militia, supported by artillery and a small force of cavalry.   General Smith was summoned to surrender, but refused.   While preparing to enforce his demand Stuart received, through Major Venable and Captain Lee, the first information of the location of the Confederate army, and orders from General Lee to move at once for Gettysburg.   Hampton's brigade had brought up the rear from Dover, and had not yet reached Dillsburg, at which place he was met and turned southward, with orders to proceed ten miles on the road toward Gettysburg before halting. After burning the barracks and throwing a few shells into the outskirts of the town, from which a constant fire of musketry had been maintained, Stuart withdrew from Carlisle and proceeded in the same direction. Hampton reached Hunterstown on the morning of the 2d of July, and was ordered to move thence to take position on the left of the Confederate infantry at Gettysburg. Before this movement was completed he received information of the advance of Kilpatrick's division upon Hunterstown, and was directed by Stuart to return and meet it. General Hampton states that after some skirmishing the enemy attempted a charge, which was met in front by the Cobb Legion, and on either flank by the Phillips Legion and the 2d South Carolina Cavalry, and that the enemy was driven back to the support of his dismounted men and artillery. He held the field until the next morning, when he found that the enemy had retired, leaving in Hunterstown some of his wounded officers and men. Lieutenant-Colonel W. G. Deloncy was wounded in this affair, and the Cobb Legion suffered other severe losses. On the other hand General Custer's report reads as follows : —

July 2d this regiment [the 6th Michigan Cavalry], being in advance, encountered the enemy's cavalry at Hunterstown. Here company A, Captain H. A. Thompson, charged a brigade of cavalry. Though suffering great loss he checked the enemy so as to enable our battery to be placed in position. The other squadrons of the regiment drove the enemy back, when the guns of the battery caused them precipitately to surrender the field.

General Kilpatrick states in his report that he was

attacked near Hunterstown by Stuart, Hampton, and Lee; that he drove the enemy from this point with great loss, and encamped for the night; and that the loss in Custer's brigade was thirty-two, killed, wounded, and missing.

Stuart himself, with Fitz Lee's and Chambliss' commands, reached Gettysburg on the afternoon of the 2d, and took position on the Confederate left. For eight days and nights the troops had been marching incessantly. On the ninth night they rested within the shelter of the army, and with a grateful sense of relief which words cannot express.

This movement of Stuart in the rear of the Federal army has been the subject of much discussion, and the prevalent opinion among writers, both Federal and Confederate, is that it was an error in strategy. General J. A. Early is, so far as I know, the only prominent Confederate general who has expressed the opinion that it was not a misfortune to the Confederate cause. He says, on page 270, volume IV., "Southern Historical Society Papers" : —

When Hooker was crossing the Potomac at Edwards' Ferry it was simply impossible for Stuart to cross that stream between that point and Harper's Ferry, as Hooker was keeping up his communications with that place, and the interval was narrow. Stuart's only alternatives, therefore, were to cross west of the Blue Ridge, at Shepherdstown or Williamsport, or east of Hooker's crossing. He selected the latter, in accordance with the discretion given him, and it is doubtful whether the former would have enabled him to fulfil General Lee's expectations, as Hooker immediately threw one corps to Knoxville, on the Baltimore and Ohio Railroad, a short distance below Harper's Ferry, and three to Middletown, in the Catoctin Valley, while the passes of the South Mountain were seized and guarded, and Buford's division of cavalry moved on that flank. It is difficult, therefore, to perceive of what more avail in ascertaining and reporting the movements of the Federal army Stuart's cavalry could have been if it had moved on the west of South Mountain than individual scouts employed for that purpose, while it is very certain that his movement on the other flank greatly perplexed and bewildered the Federal commanders, and compelled them to move slower.

We may dismiss at once the inconsiderate charge that Stuart disobeyed or exceeded the orders given to him by General Lee, for General Lee states that Stuart acted " in the exercise of the discretion given to him." Stuart had submitted his plans to his commander, in a personal interview. Those plans were approved, and he was authorized to carry them out if in his opinion it seemed best to do so. The responsibility of the movement, strategically considered, rests with General Lee. Many considerations may be urged in its favor. Two objects were placed before Stuart. He was desired to gain information of the enemy's movements, and to damage and delay him on his march. Let us consider the latter object. Among the direct results of Stuart's movement we find that Meade was deprived of the services of all of his cavalry except Buford's division until noon on the 2d of July, and that Buford's division was withdrawn from Meade's left on the second day of the battle at Gettysburg to protect the depot of supplies at Westminster, leaving unguarded the flank of Sickles' corps, to which circumstance is largely attributed the success of Longstreet's attack upon that corps.[1] A portion of French's command was also diverted eastward, to protect communication with Washington. Indeed, no one can read the despatches which passed between Meade and Halleck from the 28th of June to the 1st of July with-

[1] See Bates' *Gettysburg*, p. 111.

out noting the perplexity which existed in regard to
Lee's movements, and the wide divergence eastward of
Meade's corps, both caused by the presence of Stuart
in his rear. From this cause alone the 6th corps was
able to participate only in the battle of the last day.
It must, therefore, be acknowledged that in one respect
General Stuart's movement accomplished all that was
anticipated. General Lee expected that he would be
able to delay the movements of the enemy, and pro-
duce confusion and uncertainty in regard to the movements of his own army. This Stuart accomplished,
and it does not appear that he could have secured these
results by any other mode of operations; for had he
decided to cross the Potomac at Shepherdstown he
must have remained near Rector's Cross Roads until
the morning of the 26th, when the northward movement of Hooker's army would have been developed
to him. He could have crossed at Shepherdstown on
the 27th, but he could not have done more than
occupy the gaps of South Mountain with a portion
of his command on the 28th, even if unopposed.
These movements could hardly have been concealed
from the signal stations of the enemy, and would
have been met by corresponding movements of the
enemy's cavalry; for on the 28th Buford's division
was at Middletown and Kilpatrick's at Frederick, ready
to force a passage through the mountains and fall upon
Lee's trains. A concentration of these divisions upon
any one of the gaps would have enabled them to
accomplish this result, and with nothing to attract
attention on the other side of Meade's army there can
be but little doubt that some plan of this nature would
have been adopted. But on the 28th Halleck was
urging Meade to send cavalry in pursuit of the raiders,
and Gregg's and Kilpatrick's divisions were diverted

from Meade's left to protect his right and rear, while Buford was left to bear alone a two hours' conflict with the Confederate infantry at Gettysburg. The result shows that no better plan could have been adopted to secure Lee's right flank from annoyance.

It remains to consider whether Stuart made proper arrangements to obtain information concerning the enemy's movements during his separation from the army. Had he decided to follow Longstreet's crossing at Shepherdstown and operate on that flank, he could have attained this end only by using individual scouts or by making reconnoissances in force. For the latter purpose the force under Stuart's command was insufficient. After making the detachments which must necessarily have been made to observe or guard the passes of South Mountain, the handful of veterans left would have been unable to do more than hold their own in the presence of the Federal cavalry, which in recent encounters had proven itself an adversary by no means to be despised. Unless provided with an infantry support, Stuart could have made no reconnoissance which would have held forth any hope of piercing the cavalry which enveloped Hooker's advance. General Early speaks wisely when he says : " *It is doubtful whether the former* [alternative] *would have enabled him to fulfil General Lee's expectations.*"

It seems necessary to emphasize the fact that Stuart carried but a portion of his cavalry with him, and that he left in direct communication with the army a force numerically superior to that under his own immediate command. Jenkins' brigade and White's battalion from Jones' brigade, which accompanied the advance of the army in Pennsylvania, numbered not less than 1,800 men, while Robertson's and Jones' brigades, which remained on the front vacated by Stuart, numbered about

3,000. Mosby and Stringfellow, two of the best scouts
in either army, were, by Stuart's direction, operating
within the enemy's lines; but Mosby was paralyzed
by his failure to find Stuart in consequence of the
movements of Hancock's corps, and Stringfellow had
been captured and had allowed himself to be carried
to Washington, intending to make his escape thence
and return with the information he might gather.
He had succeeded in this plan on a former occasion,
but now was so closely guarded that he found no
opportunity to escape, and only rejoined Stuart after
the close of the campaign, and through the channel
of regular exchange. The arrangements which Stuart
made for obtaining information appear to have been
adequate to the occasion, and it seems strange that
General Lee did not use Robertson and Jones for this
purpose. He was aware that under the most favorable circumstances Stuart must be separated from the
army for at least three or four days, and that during
that time he must look to some one else for information; but although in daily communication with
Robertson, he does not appear to have called upon
him for such service; nor can it be discovered that
Robertson made effort in that direction. He remained
in the vicinity of Berryville until the 1st of July, on
which day he was ordered by General Lee to join the
army in Pennsylvania. It is to be regretted that Stuart did not assume the risk of taking Jones with him,
and that he did not leave behind him Hampton or Fitz
Lee; for it is inconceivable that either of these officers,
with or without orders, would have remained inactive
under such circumstances. It was not the want of cavalry that General Lee bewailed, for he had enough of it
had it been properly used. It was the absence of Stuart himself that he felt so keenly; for on him he had

learned to rely to such an extent that it seemed as if his cavalry were concentrated in his person, and from him alone could information be expected. Hampton or Fitz Lee, better than any one else, would have supplied Stuart's place to the commanding general.

On the morning of the 3d several hours were consumed in replenishing the ammunition of the cavalry. Jenkins' brigade, commanded by Colonel M. J. Ferguson, of the 16th Virginia Cavalry, was added to Stuart's command, but by some bad management was supplied with only ten rounds of cartridges to the man. At about noon Stuart, with Jenkins' and Chambliss' brigades, moved out on the York turnpike, to take position on the left of the Confederate line of battle. Hampton and Fitz Lee were directed to follow. Breathed and McGregor had not been able to obtain ammunition, and were left behind, with orders to follow as soon as their chests were filled. Griffin's 2d Maryland battery, which had never before served under Stuart, accompanied Jenkins and Chambliss. Stuart's object was to gain position where he would protect the left of Ewell's corps, and would also be able to observe the enemy's rear and attack it in case the Confederate assault on the Federal lines were successful. He proposed, if opportunity offered, to make a diversion which might aid the Confederate infantry to carry the heights held by the Federal army.

After marching about two and a half miles on the York turnpike, Stuart turned to his right by a country road which led past the Stallsmith farm to " a commanding ridge which completely controlled a wide plain of cultivated fields stretching towards Hanover on the left, and reaching to the base of the mountain spurs among which the enemy held position."[1] This ridge is

[1] Stuart's Report.

known as the Cress Ridge. Its northern end was covered with woods, which enveloped the road by which he approached it, and concealed his presence from the enemy. Near where the woods terminated on the southwest, and on the slope of the hill, stood a stone dairy, covering a spring. On the plain below, and not more than three hundred yards from the foot of the hill, stood a large frame barn, known as the Rummel Barn. A glance satisfied Stuart that he had gained the position he wanted. The roads leading from the rear of the Federal line of battle were under his eye and could be reached by the prolongation of the road by which he had approached. Moreover, the open fields, although intersected by many fences, admitted of movement in any direction. When Stuart first reached this place the scene was as peaceful as if no war existed. The extension of the ridge on his right hid from view the lines of the contending armies, and not a living creature was visible on the plain below. While carefully concealing Jenkins' and Chambliss' brigades from view, Stuart pushed one of Griffin's guns to the edge of the woods and fired a number of random shots in different directions, himself giving orders to the gun. This, quite as much as the subsequent appearance of Hampton and Fitz Lee in the open ground to the left, announced his position to the enemy's cavalry ; for General Gregg tells us that about noon he had received notice from army headquarters that a large body of cavalry had been observed moving toward the Confederate left. He was, therefore, on the alert before Stuart's arrival. I have been somewhat perplexed to account for Stuart's conduct in firing these shots ; but I suppose that they may have been a prearranged signal by which he was to notify General Lee that he had gained a favorable position ; or, finding that none of the enemy were within sight, he may have desired to satisfy himself whether the Federal cavalry was in his immediate vicinity before leaving the strong position he then held; and receiving no immediate reply to this fire, he sent for Hampton and Fitz Lee, to arrange with them for an advance and an attack upon the enemy's rear. In the mean time Lieutenant-Colonel Vincent Witcher's battalion, of Jenkins' brigade, was dismounted and sent forward to hold the Rummel barn and a line of fence on its right. Matters were not, however, allowed to remain in this position. Stuart's messenger was a long time in finding Hampton; and before he, in turn, could find Stuart, the condition of the field required his presence with his own brigade.

The first sign of activity on the Federal side came from a battery near the house of Joseph Spangler. This was horse battery M, 2d United States Artillery, consisting of six three-inch rifles, and commanded by Lieutenant A. C. M. Pennington. The fire of these guns was most accurate and effective. The first shot struck in Griffin's battery, and shot after shot came with such precision and rapidity that Griffin was soon disabled and forced to seek shelter. The enemy now advanced a strong line of dismounted men against Colonel Witcher's position, overlapping his right. Witcher was reinforced by a dismounted squadron from Chambliss' command, which took position on his left, and the line was still further extended in that direction by sharpshooters from Hampton's and Fitz Lee's brigades. The 2d Virginia Cavalry held the extreme left. Reinforcements were now added to the Federal line along the whole front. While these dispositions were being made, Witcher's battalion had been hotly engaged on the right, and so long as his ten rounds of cartridges lasted, he not only maintained his ground, but even gained on the enemy. The failure of his ammunition caused him to retire for a short distance just as the lines on his left closed in deadly fight. Here the charge of the Confederate sharpshooters was a success. The men sprang eagerly to their work, and the Federal line was driven back across the field for a long distance. It is either to this or to the mounted charge which next followed that Colonel J. Irving Gregg refers in the following extract from his report: " My command did not participate in the cavalry fight of July 3d, except one section of Captain Randol's battery, under command of Lieutenant Chaster, which was hotly engaged, and was obliged to retire about two hundred yards on account of a portion of General Custer's command giving way."

Up to this time no mounted men had been employed on either side ; but now the enemy brought forward a body of cavalry which rode through the Confederate line, drove it back, and captured a number of prisoners. This Federal charge was continued nearly to the original line held by the Confederates at the Rummel barn, where it was met by Chambliss' brigade, aided by the 1st Virginia Cavalry. The Federal cavalry was in turn forced back, but being reinforced, the tide was turned against Chambliss, and he was driven back to his starting-point. Just then Hampton arrived with the first North Carolina and the Jeff Davis Legion, and the battle was renewed back and forth across the plain until all of Hampton's brigade except the Cobb Legion, and all of Fitz Lee's brigade except the 4th Virginia Cavalry, were engaged in the fierce hand to hand *mêlée* which followed. For many minutes the fight with sabre and pistol raged most furiously. Neither party seemed willing to give way. The impetuous attack of the Federal cavalry was, however, finally broken ; and both parties withdrew to the lines held at the opening of the fight. During this conflict the artillery on either side had participated so far as the safety of their own troops would permit. Breathed and McGregor had reached the field, and had taken position near where Griffin's battery was originally posted. After the cavalry fighting was ended a fierce artillery duel ensued, in which the Confederate batteries suffered some severe losses. The inferiority of their ammunition was painfully evident. Many of their shells exploded before they had halfway crossed the plain. Breathed and McGregor, however, held their position until nightfall.

The result of this battle shows that there is no probability that Stuart could successfully have carried out his intention of attacking the rear of the Federal right flank, for it was sufficiently protected by Gregg's command. As soon as General Gregg was aware of Stuart's presence he wisely assumed the aggressive, and forced upon Stuart a battle in which he had nothing to gain but the glory of the fighting; while Gregg himself performed the paramount duty of protecting the right flank of the Federal army. At the close of the battle General Gregg had a reserve of one strong brigade which had hardly been engaged at all, and which was drawn up ready for action in full view of the Confederate position. Stuart had no fresh troops with which to renew the fight ; he therefore maintained his position until night, when he withdrew to the York turnpike, leaving the 1st Virginia Cavalry on picket on the field.

This battle has been described from the Federal stand-point by Colonel William Brooke - Rawle, in an address delivered at the dedication of the monumental shaft which marks the scene of the engagement. This address is characterized by a spirit of fairness and an accuracy of description which are worthy of imitation. It is only in regard to the result of the last *mêlée* that many surviving Confederate cavalrymen demand that I shall present their testimony. Colonel Brooke-Rawle says : —

As Hart's squadron and other small parties charged in from all sides, the enemy turned. Then there was a pell-mell rush, our men following in close pursuit. Many prisoners were captured, and many of our men, through their impetuosity, were carried away by the overpowering current of the retreat. The pursuit was kept up past Rummel's, and the enemy was driven back into the woods beyond. The line of fences, and the farm-buildings, the key-point of the field, which in the beginning of the fight had been in the possession of the enemy, remained in ours until the end.

I have not been able to find any Confederate who will corroborate this statement : on the contrary, all the testimony on that side indicates a result successful to the Confederates in the last charge. It is not just to say that this arises from a disposition on the part of the Southern cavalrymen to claim uniform victory for themselves; for they have put on record many instances of candid acknowledgment of defeat. Moreover, it is *improbable* that Federal skirmishers could have held possession of the Rummel barn : for that building was not more than three hundred yards from the woods from which Jenkins' and Chambliss' brigades debouched for the fight, and on the edge of which the Confederate cavalry and artillery held position until the close of the day. And yet it was more than half a mile from the Lott house, which was, perhaps, the nearest point where any Federal cavalry were visible. If Federal skirmishers held the Rummel barn they concealed their presence ; otherwise their capture would have been effected before aid could have been sent to them.

The testimony of many individuals is inconsistent with the idea of the Federal occupation of the Rummel barn. After the fighting had ceased, I accompanied Stuart as he rode over a part of the field in the vicinity of the barn, and often in close rifle range of it. We were the only horsemen visible on the plain. The fire from the opposing batteries passed over our heads; and we were so much endangered by the premature explosion of shells from our own guns, that I at length ventured to expostulate with him for what I considered an unnecessary exposure of his person. I may add that, attended by Private J. Thompson Quarles of our escort, I remained on the field until about ten o'clock at night, superintending the execution of some orders which had been intrusted to my care.

Dr. Talcott Eliason, Chief Surgeon of the cavalry division, writes to me in a letter of recent date that he remained in the vicinity of the Rummel barn, removing the wounded, a majority of whom were Federals, until half past seven or eight o'clock in the evening.

Colonel W. A. Morgan, of the 1st Virginia Cavalry, who was wounded in this battle, writes : —

The barn, a large frame one, was certainly held by a portion of my regiment during the fighting of the afternoon, and all night until our lines were called in, and the retreat began with our cavalry as rear-guard. My regiment held its line until recalled early the next morning.

The Rev. G. W. Beale, of Buchanan, Va., who, as lieutenant, commanded a squadron of the 9th Virginia Cavalry at Gettysburg, writes as follows : —

Our dismounted men were giving way on Jenkins' line, and a body of mounted men were dashing forward to force a rout, when we moved forward at a trot, passed Rummel's barn, and engaged the mounted men at close range across a fence. Some of our troops, dismounting, threw down the

344 MAJOR-GENERAL J. E. B. STUART.

fence and we entered the field. A short hand to hand fight ensued, but the enemy speedily broke and fled. Whilst pursuing them I observed another body of the enemy approaching rapidly from the right to strike us in the flank and rear. I bore off in company with a portion of our men to meet and check this force. We soon found ourselves overpowered, and fell back closely pressed on two lines which converged at the barn. I was by General Stuart's side as we approached the barn. My horse fell at this point, placing me in danger of being made a prisoner. At this moment General Hampton dashed up at the head of his brigade. He was holding the colors in his hand, and passed them into the hands of a soldier at his side just as he swept by me. The charge of his brigade, as far as I could judge, was successful in driving the enemy back from that part of the field. Our brigade reformed on the edge of the woods in which it stood before the charge was made, and this position was held until we were quietly withdrawn at night. Our position commanded an easy view of the barn and of the line our skirmishers assumed at the beginning of the battle. We were so near to the barn that I rode back to where my horse had fallen, to secure if possible the effects strapped on my saddle. Later in the evening I sent two of my men to the same spot to search for the body of Private B. B. Ashton, of my company, who was supposed to have been left dead on the field. These facts warrant me in the conviction that we were not driven from the field, as has been contended.

Among the incidents of this engagement I remember to have seen young Richardson, of company B, 9th Virginia Cavalry, the brother of our sergeant-major, fall on the fence as he was leaping into the field, mortally wounded by a piece of a shell. Corporal Caroll and Private Jett, of company C, after the hand to hand fight in the field, showed me their sabres cut off close to the hilt, and Caroll's forehead was gashed with a sabre.

Fitz Lee's brigade held the left of the Confederate line northeast of the Rummel barn. General Fitzhugh Lee writes : —

The position held by my cavalry at Gettysburg on the morning of the 3d was held by them at dark. They never left it except to go to the front in a charge. Such a condition of things could not have existed had other portions of the line been abandoned.

Private G. W. Gilmer, company C, 2d Virginia Cavalry, writes that he was twice wounded in the attack which his squadron made, as dismounted skirmishers, on the enemy's battery. He remained on the field where he fell for half an hour, after which he was conveyed by his own comrades to a farm-house in the rear. His wounds were too serious to permit his removal, and he fell into the enemy's hands on the following morning.

Lieutenant James I. Lee, company F, 2d Virginia Cavalry, writes: —

We were in a lane between two stake-and-rider fences. We were ordered to charge the enemy, which we did, and drove them for some distance. We had nearly reached their battery when we were charged by the enemy's cavalry, who were promptly met by our own, and a general fight began, which lasted only a short time, as the enemy withdrew and left us in possession of the field for the remainder of the evening. After the cavalry fight had ended, Lieutenant Baughn, of company C, and myself went back to our horse-holders leisurely, as did the rest of the command.

Similar testimony can be multiplied to an indefinite extent, and the high character of those who give it must command the careful consideration of one who would form a true judgment as to the result of the fighting in this battle.

In his official report General Gregg acknowledges an aggregate loss of 295 in his division. General Custer's report states the loss in his brigade at 542. This would put the entire Federal loss at 837, — a loss so excessive as to cause suspicion that error has crept into the statement. Through the kindness of Colonel Robert N. Scott, of the War Records Office, Washington,

D. C., I am enabled to state that the loss in Gregg's division was one killed, 24 wounded, and eight missing; and in Custer's brigade, 29 killed, 123 wounded, and 67 missing; an aggregate loss of 252. Colonel Scott states that he has proof that the statement in General Gregg's report includes the losses in his own division on July 2d and those in Custer's brigade on July 3d.

On page 398 of the preliminary print of Confederate reports of Gettysburg, Stuart states his loss at 181. This report does not include the losses in Jenkins' brigade and the horse artillery.

The regiments of Confederate cavalry present at this battle were as follows: in Hampton's brigade, the 1st North Carolina and the 1st and 2d South Carolina Cavalry regiments, the Cobb Georgia, the Jeff Davis, and the Phillips Georgia Legions; in Fitz Lee's brigade, the 1st, 2d, 3d, 4th, and 5th Virginia Cavalry regiments; in W. H. F. Lee's brigade, the 9th, 10th, and 13th Virginia Cavalry regiments, and the 2d North Carolina Cavalry; in Jenkins' brigade, the 14th, 16th, and 17th Virginia Cavalry regiments, and the 34th and 36th Virginia battalions. The 15th Virginia Cavalry, of W. H. F. Lee's brigade, was on detached service in Virginia. The 1st battalion of Maryland Cavalry, which on some returns appears as a part of Fitz Lee's brigade, had not yet joined Fitz Lee, but was serving with Ewell's corps. The 4th Virginia Cavalry guarded the Confederate left, at some distance from the battle-field, and did not participate in the fighting. All the Confederate regiments had been greatly reduced in numbers by the arduous services of the previous month. Some idea of this depletion may be gained from the following statement of Lieutenant G. W. Beale, of the 9th Virginia Cavalry: " My own company could muster for duty that morning only fifteen men, whose names I preserve. The 9th regiment was not more than one hundred strong, and the brigade could have hardly exceeded three hundred." The other regiments of Stuart's command were reduced in a similar proportion.

The Confederate batteries engaged were McGregor's, Breathed's, and Griffin's.

While Stuart was thus occupied on the Confederate left, Robertson's command was not inactive on the right. He had moved from the vicinity of Berryville on the 1st of July, and proceeding by way of Williamsport and Chambersburg, had reached Cashtown on the 3d. General Jones' brigade was reduced to three regiments, the 6th, 7th, and 11th. The 12th Virginia Cavalry had been picketing toward Harper's Ferry, and was left on that front, where, on the night of the 30th of June, Adjutant Harman and Lieutenant George Baylor captured a picket consisting of a lieutenant and nineteen men, one of the enemy being killed and one escaping.

At Cashtown orders were received from General Lee that a force of cavalry should be sent to Fairfield to protect the wagon trains. General Jones immediately proceeded in that direction with his three regiments. About two miles from Fairfield he encountered the 6th United States Cavalry. The opposing forces met in a lane, both sides of which were of post-and-rail fences too strong to be broken except with the axe. Although the country was open, the numerous small fields, divided by similar fences, rendered it difficult to bring into action more than a small body of men at one time. The 7th Virginia Cavalry made the first attack, but being met by a severe fire of dismounted men on either flank, the regiment broke and retired. General Jones says in his report: " A failure to rally promptly and renew the fight is a blemish in the bright history of this regiment. Many officers and men formed noble exceptions." Lieutenant - Colonel Thomas Marshall, commanding this regiment, admits this bad conduct with all frankness, but states that a portion of the regiment joined in the subsequent charge and contributed to the final result. The 7th regiment lost in this affair thirty men, only one of whom was captured.

The 6th Virginia Cavalry, under Major C. E. Flournoy, was now brought to the front and fully retrieved the fortunes of the day. An unhesitating charge broke the enemy and routed him. Major Samuel H. Starr, commanding the 6th Regulars, was wounded and captured, as was also his second in command, Captain G. C. Cram. General Jones states that he captured 184 prisoners. Colonel Marshall states the number at 220; while Lieutenant Nicholas Nolan, who commanded this regiment on the 27th of July, reports an aggregate loss of 298 officers and men and 292 horses.[1] Captain D. T. Richards, of the 6th Virginia, led this charge with his squadron. Adjutant John Allen was killed at the head of the regiment. Lieutenant R. R. Duncan, of company B, is mentioned by Major Flour-

[1] Captain G. C. Cram, commanding the 6th United States Cavalry, reports that he carried into the battle on the 21st of June 12 commissioned officers and 242 enlisted men. The records of the Adjutant-General's Office show that at that time over 400 men were absent from the regiment on "detached service." Between the 21st and 30th of June many of these absentees had been returned, so that at the latter date the regiment numbered 587 officers and men "present for duty." The actual loss of the regiment on the 3d of July, as shown by the records, was six men killed, five officers and 23 men wounded, and five officers and 203 men captured or missing; a total of 242. On the 7th of July the 7th Virginia Cavalry again encountered the 6th United States Cavalry, and inflicted upon it a loss of 59. In these two engagements this regiment lost 301 officers and men. Such a loss would almost have annihilated any one of the Confederate regiments; and accordingly we find that General W. E. Jones remarks: "The 6th United States Regular Cavalry numbers among the things that were." General Jones was mistaken. This regiment still kept the field with respectable numbers.

noy as " conspicuous for his daring." The loss in this regiment was 28, of whom five were missing.

After dark, on the 3d, Stuart withdrew his cavalry from the battle-field to the York road, where he encamped for the night. The main army was at the same time withdrawn to the ridges west of Gettysburg. Information of this movement did not reach Stuart, and it was only by a personal visit to army headquarters during the latter part of the night that he was made acquainted with it. His command was now in an isolated and exposed position, but it was successfully withdrawn early on the morning of the 4th.

Stuart's report thus continues the narrative of his movements : —

During the 4th, which was quite rainy, written instructions were received from the commanding general as to the order of march back to the Potomac, to be undertaken at nightfall. In this order two brigades of cavalry (Fitz Lee's and Hampton's) were ordered to move, as heretofore stated, by way of Cashtown, guarding that flank, bringing up the rear on the road *via* Greenwood to Williamsport, which was the route designated for the main portion of the wagon trains and ambulances, under the special charge of General Imboden, who had a mixed command of artillery, infantry, and cavalry (his own).

Previous to these instructions I had, at the instance of the commanding general, instructed Brigadier-General Robertson, whose two brigades (his own and Jones') were now on the right near Fairfield, Pa., that it was essentially necessary for him to hold the Jack Mountain passes. These included two prominent roads, — the one north and the other south of Jack Mountain, which is a sort of peak in the Blue Ridge chain.

In the order of march (retrograde) one corps (Hill's) preceded everything through the mountain ; the baggage and prisoners of war were escorted by another corps. Longstreet occupied the centre, and the 3d (Ewell's) brought up the rear. The cavalry was disposed as follows : two brigades on the Cashtown road, under General Fitz Lee ; and the remainder, Jenkins' and Chambliss', under my immediate command, was directed to proceed by way of Emmittsburg, Md., so as to guard the other flank. I dispatched Captain W. W. Blackford, of the engineer corps, to General Robertson, to inform him of my movement and direct his coöperation, as Emmittsburg was in his immediate front and was probably occupied by the enemy's cavalry. It was dark before I had passed the extreme right of our line, and having to pass through very dense woods, taking by-roads, it soon became so dark that it was impossible to proceed. We were in danger of losing the command as well as the road. It was raining, also. We halted several hours, when, having received a good guide, and it becoming more light, the march was resumed, and just at dawn we entered Emmittsburg. We there learned that a large body of the enemy's cavalry had passed through that point the afternoon previous, going toward Monterey, one of the passes designated in my instructions to Brigadier-General Robertson. I halted for a short time to procure some rations, and, examining my map, I saw that this force would either attempt to force one of the gaps, or, foiled in that (as I supposed they would be), it would either turn to the right and bear off toward Fairfield, where it would meet with a like repulse from Hill's or Longstreet's corps, or, turning to the left before reaching Monterey, would strike across by Oeiler's Gap toward Hagerstown, and thus seriously threaten that portion of our trains which, under Imboden, would be passing down the Greencastle pike the next day, and interpose itself between the main body and its baggage. I did not consider that this force could seriously annoy any other portion of the command under the order of march prescribed, particularly as it was believed that those gaps would be held by General Robertson till he could be reinforced by the main body. I therefore determined to adhere to my instructions and proceed by way of Cavetown, by which I might intercept the enemy should he pass through Oeiler's Gap.

In and around Emmittsburg we captured 60 or 70 prisoners of war, and some valuable hospital stores *en route* from Frederick to the army.

The march was resumed on the road to Frederick until we

reached a small village called Cooperstown, where our route turned short to the right. Here I halted the column to feed, as the horses were much fatigued and famished. The column, after an hour's halt, continued through Harbaugh's Valley, by Zion Church, to pass the Catoctin Mountain. The road separated before debouching from the mountain, one fork leading to the left by Smithtown, and the other to the right, bearing more towards Leitersburg. I divided my command, in order to make the passage more certain, — Colonel Ferguson, commanding Jenkins' brigade, taking the left road, and Chambliss' brigade, which I accompanied, the other. Before reaching the west entrance to this pass I found it held by the enemy, and had to dismount a large portion of the command and fight from crag to crag of the mountain to dislodge the enemy, already posted. Our passage was finally forced, and as my column emerged from the mountains it received the fire of the enemy's battery, posted to the left on the road to Boonsboro'. I ascertained too, about this time, by the firing, that the party on the other route had met with resistance, and sent at once to apprise Colonel Ferguson of our passage, and directed him, if not already through, to withdraw and come by the same route I had followed. Our artillery was soon in position, and a few fires drove the enemy from his position.

I was told by a citizen that the party I had just attacked was the cavalry of Kilpatrick, who had claimed to have captured several thousand prisoners and four or five hundred wagons from our forces near Monterey; but I was further informed that not more than forty wagons accompanied them, and other facts I heard led me to believe the success was far overrated. About this time Captain G. M. Emack, of the Maryland Cavalry, with his arm in a sling, came to us and reported that he had been in the fight of the night before, and partially confirmed the statement of the citizen, and informed me, to my surprise, that a large portion of Ewell's corps trains had preceded the army through the mountains.

It was nearly night, and I felt it of the first importance to open communication with the main army, particularly as I was led to believe that a portion of this force might still be hovering on its flanks. I sent a trusty and intelligent soldier (Private Robert W. Goode, 1st Virginia Cavalry) to reach the commanding general by a route across the country, and relate to him what I knew as well as what he might discover *en route*, and moved towards Leitersburg as soon as Colonel Ferguson came up, who, although his advance had forced the passage of the gap, upon the receipt of my despatch turned back and came by the same route I had taken, thus making an unnecessary circuit of several miles, and not reaching me until after dark.

The movements of the enemy referred to by Stuart need to be explained. On the morning of the 4th General Kilpatrick was ordered from Gettysburg to attack the trains which were moving on the road between Fairfield and Waynesboro'. He reached Emmittsburg at three o'clock in the afternoon, and joining Huey's brigade of Gregg's division to his own command, he moved on to the Monterey Gap. As has already been indicated in Stuart's report, two roads leading westward from Fairfield cross the mountains, the one on the north and the other on the south of Jack Mountain. The southern road intersects the road from Emmittsburg to Waynesboro' about six miles from Emmittsburg. Upon the northern road General Ewell's trains were passing. General Robertson lay in the vicinity of Fairfield with his own two regiments and three of Jones' brigade, with a picket at the intersection of the Emmittsburg road. When attacked by Kilpatrick this picket retired towards Fairfield, leaving no force on the road to Monterey Gap. Captain (afterwards Major) G. M. Emack, of the 1st Maryland Cavalry, had, however, been stationed by some one on this road, and was able to delay the enemy's advance from dark until three o'clock in the morning. General Kilpatrick seems to have considered that his command was in a perilous situation. He states that he brushed away a force of cavalry from his front, — probably Robertson's picket, — but was afterwards attacked, both in front and rear, on a rugged mountain-side, where the road was too narrow even to reverse a gun. He extricated himself from this dangerous position by a mounted charge of Custer's brigade. He reached the road upon which Ewell's train was moving, captured and destroyed a large number of wagons, and reached Smithfield early the next morning with 1,360 prisoners and a large number of horses and mules.

Major G. M. Emack, now residing near Versailles, Ky., has given me the following narrative of the events of this night : —

On the evening of the 4th of July, 1863, as Lee's army was on the retreat from Gettysburg, I was ordered to place a picket on the Emmittsburg road near Monterey. Selecting Sergeant Sam Spencer and six men for the post, the rest of my company, under Lieutenants Cook and Blackiston, were sent foraging. The advance picket had been on duty but a short time, when I was notified of the advance of a large body of Federal cavalry and artillery from the direction of Emmittsburg. I immediately returned to Ewell's wagon train, which was coming into the road in my rear, and going down the road half a mile, stopped the wagons from coming further, and started those in advance at a trot, so that, should the enemy break through my picket, they would find no wagons in the road. In doing this I came across a lieutenant of a North Carolina battery, who had but one gun and only two rounds of ammunition. With this he galloped up the road to my picket; and, placing him in position, I directed him to put both charges in his gun and await orders. Sergeant Spencer was placed in rear with five men, while I advanced down the road, accompanied by Private Edward Thomas, until I met the head of the enemy's column. It was then dusk and raining ; and as we wore our gum coats the Federal cavalry failed to recognize us. Without making any demonstration we turned and retreated before them at a walk, shielding the gun as much as possible as we neared it. As soon as we passed the gun the lieutenant fired into the head of the column. Taking advantage of the halt and confusion which followed this fire, I charged with my little party, in all only eight mounted men, and succeeded in driving them back for more than a mile, until they reached their artillery. From the shouting and firing among the retreating enemy we concluded that they had become panic-stricken and were fighting among themselves.

The firing brought up Lieutenant Blackiston with the rest of my company ; and dismounting the men, we formed line in some undergrowth on one side of the road. After fully an hour we heard the enemy advancing, this time with more caution and with dismounted skirmishers thrown out on each side of the road. Lying on the ground, we reserved our fire until they were within ten or fifteen paces of us, when we gave them a volley which caused another precipitate retreat. I now withdrew my men to another position, and formed them dismounted on either side of the road. Sergeant Spencer had charge of one squad and Sergeant Wilson of the other. Lieutenant Blackiston had charge of the horses and prisoners in the rear. Kilpatrick now commanded a general advance with mounted and dismounted men and with artillery, firing at every step, which to us was rather amusing, as we were about a mile distant and lying snugly on the ground. About midnight he reached Monterey, and opened a tremendous fire on us with artillery and dismounted men, to which we made but little answer.

In the mean time the wagons had commenced to run in on the road in my rear, and I again went back on the Gettysburg road and stopped them. They were soon started again, and on going back to ascertain the cause I was informed that they were moving by General W. E. Jones' orders. I found General Jones and told him that I had only a handful of men opposed to all of Kilpatrick's cavalry ; and I urged the importance of keeping the road clear, so that when the enemy broke through he would find nothing on it. The general said that the train must move on, and if I could hold out a little longer the 6th Virginia Cavalry would come to my assistance. I returned to my men and urged them not to yield an inch nor to

waste any ammunition (we had but little at the commence-
ment). The enemy now increased their fire until it seemed as
if nothing could stand before it. Still these men lay there
under it coolly, awaiting an opportunity to strike another blow.
The enemy's skirmishers at last walked into my line, and I
was told that one of them actually trod on private Key who
killed him on the spot. The enemy was again driven back.
My ammunition was entirely exhausted and some of my men
actually fought with rocks ; nor did they give back an inch.

The 4th North Carolina Cavalry now made its appearance
at the junction of the two roads in my rear, and after General
Jones and his staff had exhausted every means to get them to
my assistance, I finally succeeded in getting a lieutenant and
about ten men to dismount and advance to my line. The 6th
Virginia Cavalry, that I knew so well to be good fighters,
never made its appearance during the night. At about three
o'clock A. M., finding that he had no force of consequence
opposed to him, Kilpatrick advanced his cavalry to within
twenty yards of my position, and gave the order to charge. A
running fight now ensued amid wagons and ambulances. As
we passed out of the mountain we met Captain Welsh's company of the 1st Maryland Cavalry at the junction of another
road. Here the enemy was held in check for a moment, but
they soon swept us aside, and on they went until they had captured all the wagons found in the road. The two portions of
the train that I had cut off were not reached by the enemy ;
and I do not believe that we would have lost any of the train
had it not been started on the road after I had stopped it.

In this fight about half the men I had engaged were captured, and I myself was wounded. According to the official report of General Kilpatrick, his loss was five killed, 10 wounded,
and 28 prisoners, in all 43 men, or more than I had in the fight
including horse-holders.

General W. E. Jones says in his report : —

The evening of July 4th, when it was reported the enemy
were advancing in force on the Emmittsburg and Waynesboro' road, I saw that General Ewell's train (then on its way
to Williamsport) was in danger, and asked to go with my
command to its protection. I was allowed the 6th and 7th

regiments and Chew's battery; but the 7th was afterwards ordered back, and Colonel Ferebee's regiment (4th North Carolina Cavalry) allowed to take its place, the latter being then on this road. This narrow and difficult way, rendered doubly so by heavy rain just fallen, was so blocked by wagons as to render it wholly impracticable to push ahead the artillery or even the cavalry. With my staff I hastened on to rally all the stragglers of the train to the support of whatever force might be guarding the road. Arriving, I found Captain G. M. Emack's company of the Maryland Cavalry, with one gun, opposed to a whole division of Federal cavalry, with a full battery. He had already been driven back within a few hundred yards of the junction of the roads. Not half of the long train had passed. This brave little band of heroes was encouraged with the hope of speedy reinforcements, reminded of the importance of their trust, and exhorted to fight to the bitter end rather than yield. All my couriers and all others with fire-arms were ordered to the front, directed to lie on the ground and be sparing of their ammunition. The last charge of grape was expended and the piece sent to the rear. For more than two hours less than fifty men kept many thousands in check, and the wagons continued to pass long after the balls were whistling in their midst.

After Stuart had forced the passage of the mountains on the afternoon of the 5th, Kilpatrick retired to Boonsboro', where his prisoners were turned over to General French. On the next day, the 6th of July, Buford's division arrived at Boonsboro', and it was arranged between Buford and Kilpatrick that the former should attack the trains which were assembled at Williamsport, while the latter moved against Stuart at Hagerstown. General Stuart says in his report: —

Having heard from the commanding general about daylight the next morning, and being satisfied that all of Kilpatrick's force had gone towards Boonsboro', I immediately, notwithstanding the march of a greater portion of both the preceding nights, set out for Boonsboro'. Jones' brigade had now arrived by the route from Fairfield. Soon after night Brigadier-General Jones, whose capture had been reported by Captain Emack, came from the direction of Williamsport, whither he had gone with the portion of the train which escaped. The enemy's movements had separated him from his command, and he had made a very narrow escape. He informed me of Imboden's arrival at Williamsport.

Having reached Cavetown, I directed General Jones to proceed on the Boonsboro' road a few miles, and thence proceed to Funkstown, which point I desired him to hold, covering the eastern front of Hagerstown. Chambliss' brigade proceeded direct from Leitersburg to Hagerstown, and Robertson's took the same route, both together a very small command. Diverging from Jones' line of march at Cavetown, I proceeded with Jenkins' brigade by way of Chewsville towards Hagerstown. Upon arriving at the former place, it was ascertained that the enemy was nearing Hagerstown with a large force of cavalry from the direction of Boonsboro', and Colonel Chambliss needed reinforcements. Jenkins' brigade was pushed forward, and arriving before Hagerstown found the enemy in possession, and made an attack in flank by this road, Jones coming up further to the left and opening with a few shots of artillery. A small body of infantry, under Brigadier-General Iverson, also held the north edge of the town, aided by the cavalry of Robertson and Chambliss. Our operations here were much embarrassed by our great difficulty in preventing this latter force from mistaking us for the enemy, several shots striking very near our column. I felt sure that the enemy's designs were directed against Williamsport, where, I was informed by General Jones, our wagons were congregated in a narrow space at the foot of the hill near the river, which was too much swollen to admit their passage to the south bank. I therefore urged on all sides the most vigorous attack to save our trains at Williamsport. Our force was perceptibly much smaller than the enemy's, but by a bold front and determined attack, with a reliance on that help which has never failed me. I hoped to raise the siege of Williamsport, if, as I believed, that was the real object of the enemy's designs. Hagerstown is six miles from Williamsport, the country between being almost entirely cleared, but intersected by innumerable fences and ditches. The two places are connected by a lane, — a perfectly straight macadamized road. The enemy's skirmishers fought dismounted from street to street, and some time elapsed before the town was entirely clear, the enemy taking the road first toward Sharpsburg, but afterwards turning to the Williamsport road. Just as the town was cleared I heard the sound of artillery at Williamsport.

The cavalry, except the two brigades with General Fitz Lee, was now pretty well concentrated at Hagerstown, and one column, under Colonel Chambliss, was pushed directly down the road after the enemy, while Robertson's two regiments and Jenkins' brigade kept to the left of the road, moving in a parallel direction to Chambliss. A portion of the Stuart Horse Artillery also accompanied the movement. The first charge was gallantly executed by the leading brigade, the 9th and 13th Virginia Cavalry participating with marked gallantry. The column on the flank was now hurried up to attack the enemy, but the obstacles, such as post-and-rail fences, delayed its progress so long that the enemy had time to rally along a crest of rocks and fences, from which he opened with artillery, raking the road. Jenkins' brigade was ordered to dismount and deploy over the difficult ground. This was done with marked effect and boldness, Lieutenant-Colonel Witcher, as usual, distinguishing himself by his courage and conduct. The enemy, thus dislodged, was closely pressed by the mounted cavalry, but made one effort at counter-charge, which was gallantly met and repulsed by Colonel James B. Gordon, commanding a fragment of the 5th North Carolina Cavalry, that officer exhibiting under my eye individual prowess deserving special commendation. The repulse was soon after converted into a rout by Colonel Lomax's regiment, the 11th Virginia Cavalry of Jones' brigade, which now took the road under the gallant leadership of its colonel, and with drawn sabres charged down the turnpike under a fearful fire of artillery.

Lieutenant-Colonel O. R. Funsten behaved with conspicuous gallantry in this charge, and Captain S. Winthrop, a volunteer aid of Lieutenant-General Longstreet, also bore himself most gallantly.

The enemy was now very near Williamsport, and this determined and vigorous attack in his rear soon compelled him to raise the siege of that place and leave by the Downsville road. His withdrawal was favored by night, which set in just as we reached the ridge overlooking Williamsport. Important assistance was rendered by Brigadier-General Fitz Lee, who reached the vicinity of Williamsport by the Greencastle road very opportunely, and participated in the attack with his accustomed spirit.

General Kilpatrick describes this same affair in his report. He states that Stuart, at Hagerstown, was expecting him from the direction of Gettysburg ; but that he attacked Stuart from the direction of Boonsboro,' surprised him, routed him, and drove him in the direction of Greencastle and Gettysburg. Stuart, however, was not in Hagerstown at that time. The force which Kilpatrick attacked was Chambliss' and Robertson's brigades, which together hardly made one good regiment. Colonel J. Lucius Davis, of the 10th Virginia Cavalry, was captured in this fight. His horse was killed, and falling on him confined him to the ground until he was released by the enemy. Kilpatrick pressed Chambliss and Robertson back through the town until he encountered Iverson's brigade, which was marching with the trains for their protection. General Iverson says in his report : —

Reached Hagerstown next day, where I found the enemy engaged with our cavalry. Sent the train back to the rear, deployed skirmishers, fixed an ambuscade, and I believe killed, wounded, and captured as many of the enemy as I had men.

General Kilpatrick further states that, learning from prisoners belonging to Hood's division that their whole division was close at hand, he left one brigade, under Colonel Richmond, to hold the enemy in check at Hagerstown, while he, with the other two brigades, hurried on toward Williamsport in the hope that his command, united with that of General Buford, would be able to effect the capture and destruction of the Confederate trains before relief could reach them. He pushed Custer's brigade forward, and soon became hotly engaged on Buford's right, within less than a mile of Williamsport. When about to advance all of Custer's regiments, with prospect of success, he was informed by Colonel Richmond that the enemy had attacked him with infantry, cavalry, and artillery. At the same time he was made aware that a column of infantry was moving on his own right flank. "A few moments later General Buford sent a staff officer to say that he was about to retire; that he feared the enemy would move down on the Sharpsburg pike and intercept our retreat. My command was in a most perilous position; attacked in front, rear, and flank, and no prospect of a safe retreat till night. Slowly the regiments of each brigade fell back, taking up one position after another, repulsing each attack until night set in, and we formed a junction with General Buford, both commands going into camp near Jones' Crossing."

General Buford says in his report: —

While our hottest contest was in progress General Kilpatrick's guns were heard in the direction of Hagerstown, and as they grew nearer I sent word to him to connect with my right for mutual support. The connection was made, but was of no consequence to either of us. Just before dark Kilpatrick's troops gave way, passing to my rear by the right, and were closely followed by the enemy.

It now being dark, outnumbered, and the 1st and reserve brigade being out of ammunition, Devin was ordered to relieve Gamble and a portion of Merritt's troops. This being done I ordered the command to fall back, Devin to hold his ground until the entire road to the Antietam was clear. Devin handsomely carried out his instructions, and the division bivouacked on the road to Boonsboro'.

The expedition had for its object the destruction of the enemy's trains, supposed to be at Williamsport. This, I regret to say, was not accomplished. The enemy was too strong for me, but he was severely punished for his obstinacy. His casualties were more than quadruple to mine.

General Kilpatrick reports an aggregate loss of 185 in this engagement. Colonel Huey reports that his brigade lost one officer and 144 men between Emmittsburg and Williamsport. The greater portion of this loss of course occurred in the last battle. General Buford reports an aggregate loss of 72. The Federal cavalry, therefore, lost in this engagement nearly, if not quite, 400 officers and men. Stuart reports an aggregate loss of 254, exclusive of Jenkins' brigade, from which no report was received. These losses show the severity of the fighting. A comparison of the reports of Stuart, Kilpatrick, and Buford will show the result.

On the 7th of July Wofford's brigade of infantry was sent to Stuart's support, and was stationed by him at Downsville, on the road to Sharpsburg. The cavalry covered the rest of the front of the army. On this day the 7th Virginia Cavalry had another encounter with the 6th United States Regulars, which was more creditable to the 7th regiment than the affair at Fairfield on the 3d. Lieutenant-Colonel Thomas Marshall makes the following report of this fight: —

The enemy were reported advancing on Funkstown. I moved down immediately to support the advance picket, which had been driven in. After examining their position, which was very much obscured by woods and the crest of an intervening hill, I ordered companies F and G to advance upon them, and moved forward at a rapid trot. Their advance gave way after firing upon us, and fell back toward their reserve. I then ordered up our reserve at a charge, and moving F and G, or portions of them, on the right flank to clear the woods, while

Lieutenant Neff, with a small scouting party, was moving on the left, we drove the enemy before us, though they strove at first to make resistance. Our column pressed upon them with great rapidity, killing and wounding a number, and taking some sixty prisoners, capturing also a great many horses and a large number of rifles and revolvers. As I was mounted upon a recently-captured horse, about whose qualities I knew nothing, I did not endeavor to remain at the head of the column, but closed it up, sending back men when I found too many with the prisoners and urging forward those who were in rear.

Fearing (as eventually occurred) that in their eagerness our men would press the pursuit too far from our support, I sent two orders to the front to restrain them, but in vain. Coming up at length somewhere near the head of the column, I discovered that the enemy had rallied. I sent back immediately a reliable messenger to General Jones to make him aware of our position, and ordered all the men on jaded horses to go some distance to the rear, and form in a strong position to protect the portion of the column nearest the enemy. With a few better mounted men I awaited the development of the enemy's force and intentions. As the head of the column appeared we fired upon it. The enemy then charged vigorously upon us. Seeing our only hope was in a quick retreat, we double-quicked it as well as the condition of our horses would allow. I endeavored to rally the men when we came near the portion of the regiment which had been drawn up in a strong position, but to no purpose. One volley from this reserve brought down the leader of the enemy's column and several on the flank, but scarcely at all checked it.

In this return trip, in which we lost a portion of our laurels, we sustained the following loss in wounded and captured: total captured by the enemy, nine; wounded, two; horses captured by the enemy, nine; killed, one; wounded, four.

Privates Joseph S. Hutton and William L. Parsons, of company F, are spoken of by their captain as having made themselves particularly conspicuous for their gallantry.

Lieutenant Nicholas Nolan, commanding the 6th Regular Cavalry, makes report of this fight. He says: —

On the 7th instant the regiment was ordered to make a re-connoissance in the direction of Funkstown, under command of Captain Claflin. On arriving in the vicinity of the town we drove in the enemy's pickets, and immediately afterwards made dispositions of the regiment to resist the enemy, who was in force. The captain commanding proceeded to the front to reconnoitre, and when about 150 yards in front of the regi-ment (and with the advance-guard) was wounded in the shoul-der by one of the enemy's sharpshooters. I, being the senior officer with the regiment, again assumed command. I imme-diately proceeded to the front, where my advance-guard was posted, when I saw the enemy's cavalry preparing to charge my command. I then made preparations to meet them, but being overpowered by superior numbers was forced to fall back, inflicting, however, great damage to the enemy in a running fight of four and a half miles, my command losing fifty-nine men, in killed, wounded, and missing; ten of the above men were brought in dead by the 1st United States Cavalry the same afternoon.

Such agreement in the official reports, and such can-dor, are not always to be found. The history of the war could be written more easily and more accurately if we had a larger number of reports from regimental commanders.

From the 8th to the 12th of July Stuart covered the front of Lee's army, which had now taken a strong position, and was securely entrenched while waiting for the waters of the Potomac to fall. These days were occupied by severe fighting between Stuart's command and the divisions of Buford and Kilpatrick, at Boons-boro', Beaver Creek, Funkstown, and on the Sharps-burg front. The cavalry fought mostly dismounted, and was aided on either side by small bodies of infantry. It would be tedious to enter into all the details of these battles, in which both parties claim the victory, and with apparent sincerity. Stuart reports an aggregate loss of 216 in these engagements, while Generals Bu-

ford and Kilpatrick and Colonel Huey report a loss of
158. Stuart accomplished the object he had in view,
which was to delay the advance of the enemy until
General Lee was secure in his chosen position. On the
12th of July Stuart uncovered Lee's front, against
which the Federal army advanced, but found it so strong
that it declined to make an attack.

These days will be remembered by the members of
General Stuart's staff as days of peculiar hardship.
Scanty rations had been issued to the men, but nothing
was provided for the officers. The country had been
swept bare of provisions, and we could purchase nothing.
For four or five days in succession we received our only
food, after nightfall, at the hands of a young lady in
Hagerstown, whose father, a Southerner, sympathized
with the Confederacy. But for the charity of this
lady, whose name we shall always gratefully remember,
we would have suffered the pangs of severe hunger.
The attention of students of psychology is called to an
incident which occurred at this time. After a day of
incessant fighting Stuart and his officers reached the
house of this friend about nine o'clock in the night.
While food was being prepared Stuart fell asleep on the
sofa in the parlor. When supper was announced he
refused to rise. Knowing that he had eaten nothing
within twenty-four hours, and that food was even more
necessary for him than sleep, I took him by the arm
and compelled him to his place at the table. His eyes
were open, but he ate sparingly and without relish.
Thinking that the supper did not suit him, our kind
hostess inquired : —

"General, perhaps you would relish a hard-boiled
egg ? "

" Yes," he replied, " I 'll take *four or five.*"

This singular reply caused a good deal of astonishment on the part of all who heard it, but nothing was said at the time. The eggs were produced; Stuart broke *one* and ate it, and then rose from the table. When we returned to the parlor I sat down at the piano, and commenced singing, "If you want to have a good time, jine the cavalry." The circumstances hardly made the song appropriate, but the chorus roused the general, and he joined in it with a hearty good will. During all this time he had been unconscious of his surroundings, and when informed of the apparent discourtesy of his reply to our hostess, he apologized with evident mortification. Another incident, of a similar nature, occurred about this same time. It was probably on the night of the 11th or 12th of July that Stuart and myself were riding along one of the turnpikes, near Hagerstown, attended by only one courier. As we rode he dictated despatches which I was to write to two of his brigades and to the horse artillery, directing certain movements which were to be executed that night and the following morning. In order that I might have a light we dismounted at a toll-house, and asked to be provided with a lamp. The request was reluctantly granted. While I was writing, Stuart leaned forward his head and arms on the table, and fell fast asleep. When the despatches were completed I awoke him, that he might read them before they were sent. This was an almost invariable custom. The despatches to the brigades were read without correction being made, but when he revised that to the artillery he took out his pencil, erased the names of two places, and substituted the names Shepherdstown and Aldie. This was manifestly absurd, and I saw at once that he was unconscious of what he was doing. I aroused him with some difficulty, when my despatch was rewritten, approved, and sent off. These incidents seem to bear on the disputed question, whether the mind can act and yet be unconscious of its action.

General Stuart's report shall conclude the history of this campaign.

On the 12th firing began early, and the enemy having advanced by several roads on Hagerstown, our cavalry forces retired without serious resistance, and massed on the left of the main body, reaching with heavy outposts the Conococheague on the National Road. The infantry having already had time to intrench themselves, it was no longer desirable to defer the enemy's attack.

The 13th was spent in reconnoitring on the left, Rodes' division occupying the extreme left of our infantry, very near Hagerstown, a little north of the National Road. Cavalry pickets were extended beyond the railroad leading to Chambersburg, and everything was put in readiness to resist the enemy's attack. The situation of our communications south of the Potomac caused the commanding general to desire more cavalry on that side, and accordingly Brigadier-General Jones' brigade (one of whose regiments, the 12th Virginia Cavalry, had been left in Jefferson) was detached, and sent to cover our communication with Winchester. The cavalry on the left now consisted of Fitz Lee's, W. H. F. Lee's, Baker's (Hampton's), and Robertson's brigades, the latter being a mere handful.

On the 13th skirmishing continued at intervals, but it appeared that the enemy, instead of attacking, were intrenching in our front, and the commanding general determined to cross the Potomac. The night of the 13th was chosen for this move, and the arduous and difficult task of bringing up the rear was, as usual, assigned to the cavalry. Just before night (which was unusually rainy) the cavalry was disposed from right to left to occupy dismounted the trenches of the infantry at dark, Fitz Lee's brigade holding the line of Longstreet's corps, Baker's, of Hill's corps, and the remainder, of Ewell's corps. A pontoon bridge had been constructed at Falling Waters, some miles below Williamsport, where Longstreet's and Hill's corps were to cross, and Ewell's corps was to ford the river at Williamsport; in rear of which last, after daylight, the cavalry was also to cross, except that Fitz Lee's brigade, should he find the pontoon bridge clear in time, was to cross at the bridge, otherwise to cross at the ford at Williamsport.

The operation was successfully performed by the cavalry. General Fitz Lee, finding the bridge would not be clear in time for his command, moved after daylight to the ford, sending two squadrons to cross in rear of the infantry at the bridge. These squadrons, mistaking Longstreet's rear for the rear of the army on that route, crossed over in rear of it. General Hill's troops being notified that these squadrons would follow in his rear, were deceived by some of the enemy's cavalry, who approached very near in consequence of their belief that they were our cavalry. Although this unfortunate mistake deprived us of the lamented General Pettigrew, who was mortally wounded, the enemy paid the penalty of their temerity by losing most of their number in killed or wounded, if the accounts of those who witnessed it are to be credited. The cavalry crossed at the fords without serious molestation, bringing up the rear on that route by eight A. M. on the 14th.

The attack upon Pettigrew's brigade to which Stuart refers was made by General Kilpatrick at first, aided afterwards by General Buford. Kilpatrick claims to have captured 1,500 prisoners, two guns, and three battle flags. He says that he fought for two hours and thirty minutes, routed the enemy, and drove him towards the river. He lost in his own command 29 killed, 36 wounded, and 40 missing. General Buford states that he aided in this fight, and that " our spoils on this occasion were one ten-pounder Parrott gun, over 500 prisoners, and about 300 muskets." On the other hand, General Robert E. Lee states that two guns, which were abandoned because the horses could not draw them through the mire, fell into the enemy's hands; but that " No arms, cannon, or prisoners were taken by the enemy in battle." . . . Generals Meade and Kilpatrick, in reply to General Lee's statement, reaffirm the reports as quoted above.

General Stuart's report continues : —

To Baker's (Hampton's) brigade was assigned the duty of picketing the Potomac from Falling Waters to Hedgesville. The other brigades were moved back towards Leetown, Robertson being sent to the fords of the Shenandoah, where he already had a picket, which, under Captain L. A. Johnson, of the North Carolina Cavalry, had handsomely repulsed the enemy in their advance on Ashby's Gap, inflicting severe loss with great disparity of numbers.

Harper's Ferry was again in the possession of the enemy, and Colonel Harman, of the 12th Virginia Cavalry, had in an engagement with the enemy gained a decided success, but was himself captured by his horse falling.

Upon my arrival at the Bower that afternoon (15th), I learned that a large force of the enemy's cavalry was between Shepherdstown and Leetown, and determined at once to attack them, in order to defeat any designs they might have in the direction of Martinsburg.

I made disposition accordingly, concentrating cavalry in their front, and early on the 16th moved Fitz Lee's brigade down the turnpike towards Shepherdstown, supported by Chambliss, who, though quite ill, with that commendable spirit which has always distinguished him, remained at the head of his brigade. Jenkins' brigade was ordered to advance on the road from Martinsburg towards Shepherdstown, so as by this combination to expose one of the enemy's flanks, while Jones, now near Charlestown, was notified of the attack in order that he might coöperate. No positive orders were sent him, as his precise locality was not known.

These dispositions having been arranged, I was about to attack when I received a very urgent message from the commanding general to repair at once to his headquarters. I therefore committed to Brigadier-General Fitz Lee the consummation of my plans, and reported at once to the commanding general, whom I found at Bunker Hill. Returning in the afternoon, I proceeded to the scene of conflict on the turnpike, and found that General Fitz Lee had, with his own and Chambliss' brigades, driven the enemy steadily to within a mile of Shepherdstown, Jenkins' brigade not having yet appeared on the left. It, however, soon after arrived in Fitz Lee's rear, and moved up to his support. The ground was not practicable for cavalry, and the main body was dismounted and advanced in line of battle. The enemy retired to a strong position behind stone fences and barricades near Colonel A. R. Boteler's residence, and it being nearly dark, obstinately maintained their ground at this last point until dark, to cover their withdrawal.

Preparations were made to renew the attack vigorously next morning, but daybreak revealed that the enemy had retired towards Harper's Ferry.

The enemy's loss in killed and wounded was heavy. We had several killed and wounded, and among the latter Colonel James H. Drake, 1st Virginia Cavalry, was mortally wounded, dying that night (16th), depriving his regiment of a brave and zealous leader, and his country of one of her most patriotic defenders.

The commanding general was very desirous of my moving at once into Loudon a large portion of my command, but the recent rains had so swollen the Shenandoah that it was impossible to ford it, and cavalry scouting parties had to swim their horses over.

In the interval of time from July 16th to the 22d the enemy made a demonstration on Hedgesville, forcing back Baker's brigade. Desultory skirmishing was kept up on that front for several days, while our infantry was engaged in tearing up the Baltimore and Ohio Railroad near Martinsburg. . . .

It soon became apparent that the enemy were moving upon our right flank, availing themselves of the swollen condition of the Shenandoah to interpose their army, by a march along the east side of the Blue Ridge, between our present position and Richmond. Longstreet's corps having already moved to counteract this effort, enough cavalry was sent under Brigadier-General Robertson for his advance-guard through Front Royal and Chester Gap, while Baker's brigade was ordered to bring up the rear of Ewell's corps, which was in rear; and Jones' brigade was ordered to picket the lower Shenandoah as long as necessary for the safety of that flank, and then follow the movement of the army. Fitz Lee's, W. H. F. Lee's, and Jen-

kins' brigades, by a forced march from the vicinity of Leetown through Millwood, endeavored to reach Manassas Gap,
so as to hold it on the flank of the army; but it was already
in the possession of the enemy, and the Shenandoah, still high,
in order to be crossed without interfering with the march of
the main army, had to be forded below Front Royal.

The cavalry already mentioned reached Chester Gap early
on the 23d by a by-path, passing on the army's left; and with
great difficulty and a forced march, bivouacked that night
below Gaines' Cross Roads, holding the Rockford road and
Warrenton turnpike, on which, near Amissville, the enemy
had accumulated a large force of cavalry.

On the 24th, while moving forward to find the locality of
the enemy, firing was heard towards Newling's Cross Roads,
which was afterwards ascertained to be a portion of the enemy's artillery firing on Hill's column, marching on the Richmond road. Before the cavalry could reach the scene of action
the enemy had been driven off by the infantry, and on the
25th the march was continued and the line of the Rappahannock resumed.

CHAPTER XVIII.

THE BRISTOE CAMPAIGN.

AFTER the return from Gettysburg the cavalry occupied the line of the Rappahannock until the middle of September, while the main army withdrew behind the Rapidan. This was a period of rest and reorganization. Hampton and Fitz Lee were promoted as major-generals; and Colonels L. S. Baker, M. C. Butler, L. L. Lomax, and W. C. Wickham, were promoted as brigadier-generals. By Special Orders No. 226, from the headquarters of the Army of Northern Virginia, dated 9th of September, 1863, the cavalry divisions were arranged as follows: —

HAMPTON'S DIVISION.

Jones' Brigade. — Brigadier-General W. E. Jones.
6th Virginia Cavalry, Lieutenant-Colonel J. S. Green.
7th Virginia Cavalry, Colonel R. H. Dulaney.
12th Virginia Cavalry, Colonel A. W. Harman.
35th Battalion Virginia Cavalry, Lieutenant-Colonel E. V. White.

Baker's Brigade. — Brigadier-General L. S. Baker.
1st North Carolina Cavalry, Lieutenant-Colonel J. B. Gordon.
2d North Carolina Cavalry, Lieutenant-Colonel   Robinson.
4th North Carolina Cavalry, Colonel D. D. Ferebee.
5th North Carolina Cavalry,   Evans.

Butler's Brigade. — Brigadier-General M. C. Butler.
Cobb Georgia Legion, Colonel P. M. B. Young.
Phillips Georgia Legion, Lieutenant-Colonel W. W. Rich.

Jeff Davis Legion, Lieutenant-Colonel J. F. Waring.
2d South Carolina Cavalry, Colonel T. J. Lipscomb.

FITZ LEE'S DIVISION.

Lee's Brigade. — Brigadier-General W. H. F. Lee.
1st South Carolina Cavalry, Colonel J. L. Black.
9th Virginia Cavalry, Colonel R. L. T. Beale.
10th Virginia Cavalry, Colonel J. Lucius Davis.
13th Virginia Cavalry, Colonel J. R. Chambliss.

Lomax's Brigade. — Brigadier-General L. L. Lomax.
5th Virginia Cavalry, Colonel T. L. Rosser.
1st Battalion Maryland Cavalry, Lieutenant-Colonel Ridgley
    Brown.
11th Virginia Cavalry, Colonel O. R. Funsten.
15th Virginia Cavalry, Colonel W. W. Ball.

Wickham's Brigade. — Brigadier-General Wms. C. Wickham.
1st Virginia Cavalry, Colonel R. W. Carter.
2d Virginia Cavalry, Colonel T. T. Munford.
3d Virginia Cavalry, Colonel Thomas H. Owen.
4th Virginia Cavalry, Lieutenant-Colonel W. H. Payne.

This period of rest was broken on the 13th of September by the advance of the Federal army to occupy Culpeper County. Early on the morning of this day the Federal cavalry crossed at Kelly's and the other fords of the upper Rappahannock. General Stuart had received notice of this movement during the previous night, and was prepared for it. Dr. Hudgin, once a member of the 9th Virginia Cavalry, and afterwards employed on the surgeon's staff at cavalry headquarters, had been residing for some days at his home in Jeffersonton. His wife had recently died from fright caused by the conduct of some of Kilpatrick's men. Dr. Hudgin had good opportunity for observing the enemy's movements; and perceiving indications of an early

advance, he crossed the river at an obscure ford on
the night of the 12th, made his way with considerable
difficulty to General Stuart's headquarters at Culpeper
Court House, and laid his information before him. The
warning proved most timely. The wagons and disabled horses were immediately started toward Rapidan
Station, and thus escaped from the enemy, who attacked, as Dr. Hudgin had predicted, at daylight on
the 13th. Neither Stuart nor any of his subordinates
made report of the operations of this day, and the
forces engaged cannot be stated with certainty. Jones'
brigade, however, under Lomax, was occupied with the
enemy from Brandy Station back to Culpeper Court
House, where it was joined by W. H. F. Lee's brigade,
under Colonel R. L. T. Beale, of the 9th Virginia Cavalry. The enemy's cavalry was in large force, and
pushed their advance with great spirit and rapidity.
Until the battle had passed Culpeper Court House
Stuart himself did not take the field, but left the conduct of it to General Lomax. In retiring from the
vicinity of the Court House three guns of Thompson's
battery were captured by the enemy. Their support
had withdrawn without notifying Thompson, who was
so busily engaged in firing that he did not notice his
exposed position until he was charged by a body of the
enemy's cavalry. Seeing that it was impossible to
bring off his guns, Thompson ordered his gunners to
save themselves and their horses, and rode out alone
to observe the enemy's charge. The officer commanding the Federal company or squadron, secure of a rich
prize and carried away by his ardor, was riding more
than fifty yards in advance of his men. Thompson advanced upon him, and both commenced firing with their
pistols. Several shots were exchanged before one of
Thompson's bullets took fatal effect, and the Federal

officer fell dead from his horse, which, now riderless, continued to run toward Thompson, who caught the loose reins, and, turning his own horse, retreated in safety through the streets of the Court House, although closely pursued by the enemy.

Throughout the remainder of the day Stuart continued to retreat toward Rapidan Station, which he reached after nightfall. The enemy's advance reached the Rapidan River early the next morning, the 14th. There was but little activity on either side on this day. Just before night, Major Flournoy, of the 6th Virginia Cavalry, asked permission to cross the river and attack some squadrons of the enemy which were in sight on the other side. The permission was granted. Major Flournoy formed his regiment by squadrons on the north side of the river and advanced to the attack. The movement itself was of no consequence, and produced no result except, perhaps, the capture of a few prisoners; but Flournoy's charge was witnessed by a large number of spectators, both of the cavalry and of the infantry, and called forth many expressions of admiration at the skilful manner in which he handled his squadrons. After driving the enemy into the shelter of the adjacent woods, Flournoy reformed his regiment and returned at a walk.

On the 22d of September Buford's cavalry advanced from Madison Court House toward Liberty Mills. Stuart met him on the road near Jack's Shop, attacked him in several mounted charges, but failed to make any impression on his lines. A subsequent effort with dismounted men was equally unsuccessful. While Stuart was thus engaged in a severe fight he received information that a large body of the enemy's cavalry had turned his left and had gained possession of the road in his rear, thus cutting him off from the ford at Liberty

Mills. It was necessary to withdraw from Buford to meet this attack; but the moment that the withdrawal commenced Buford pressed on Stuart's lines with vigor. It seemed for a time that Stuart had at last been caught where he could not escape serious damage. Kilpatrick had already thrown a body of dismounted men across the road between Stuart and the ford, and he was thus enclosed in front and rear. Buford pressed so heavily that several mounted charges were necessary to hold him in check. The battle was soon brought within the compass of an open field, near the centre of which a little hill gave position for the Confederate artillery. The scene was now extremely animated. Stuart's artillery was firing in both directions from the hill, and within sight of each other his regiments were charging in opposite directions. If Kilpatrick could have maintained his position Stuart must at least have lost his guns; but two regiments were directed against him, and compelled him to relinquish his hold on the road and retire in the direction from which he had advanced. One of these regiments charged, mounted, up to the fence behind which Kilpatrick's men were dismounted, threw down the fence in their faces, and cleared the road for Stuart's retreat. Having effected this, Stuart withdrew rapidly from the engagement with Buford, and retired across the Rapidan at Liberty Mills, where he was soon reinforced by Wilcox's division of infantry. Stuart made no report of this action, and his losses cannot be stated.[1]

---

[1] For several weeks before this fight Lieutenant-Colonel George St. Ledger Grenfell, an Englishman and a soldier of fortune, had been serving, by assignment, on General Stuart's staff. It seems that he had previously held position in the western army, on the staff of General John H. Morgan, and is mentioned in that connection as having a reputation for gallantry. During his short stay with us his eccentricities were the source of much good-natured amusement. Stuart employed him somewhat as an inspector.

On the 9th of October, 1863, General Lee commenced that movement of his army around the right flank of the Federal army in Culpeper County which is known as the Bristoe campaign. It devolved upon Stuart to protect the line of march and conceal it from the enemy. Fitz Lee's division, supported by two brigades of infantry, was left at Raccoon Ford, while Stuart proceeded with Hampton's division to occupy the right flank of the army. General Hampton was absent, being still disabled by the severe wounds he had received at Gettysburg. In this campaign Jones' brigade was commanded by Colonel O. R. Funsten, and Butler's brigade was commanded by Colonel P. M. B. Young. Brigadier-General L. S. Baker had been severely wounded in one of the engagements in September, and being permanently disabled for the field, was assigned to the command of the second military district in the Department of North Carolina and South Virginia. Lieutenant-Colonel James B. Gordon had been promoted to brigadier-general, and now commanded the North Carolina brigade.

On the night of the 9th of October Stuart bivouacked at Madison Court House. On the morning of the 10th the march of the army was directed toward Woodville, on the Sperryville turnpike. Funsten's command was sent as an advance-guard in this direction, while Stuart, with Gordon and Young, crossed the Robertson

---

Grenfell became demoralized on this day. The fighting was closer and hotter than he liked. He was at my side when our regiments were attempting to force Kilpatrick from the road. Seeing one of them recoil from a charge, Grenfell concluded that the day was lost. He took to the bushes, swam the river, returned to Orange Court House, and reported that Stuart, his staff, and his whole command were surrounded and captured. When he found out his mistake, his mortification was so great that he did not again show his face in our camp. His subsequent history, which is a remarkable one, is related by Captain T. P. McElrath, of the 5th United States Artillery, in the Philadelphia *Weekly Times* of May 3, 1879.

River at Russell's Ford and pursued the direct road to James City. The enemy's picket at Russell's Ford was driven back to Bethsaida Church, where was stationed a reserve consisting of the 120th New York Infantry and a portion of Kilpatrick's cavalry.

While engaging the attention of the enemy in front with Gordon's brigade, Stuart led Young's command through the woods to their right and rear, and routed the whole line by one charge of the 1st South Carolina Cavalry. The rough and wooded character of the ground favored the escape of those who were disposed to run, but Young's brigade alone captured eighty-seven prisoners. Pressing on toward James City, now two and a half miles distant, Stuart encountered the main body of the enemy, which consisted of Kilpatrick's cavalry supported by infantry and six pieces of artillery. This force was strongly posted north of the town, upon hills which commanded the approach from our side. Having thus far accomplished his object of screening the movements of the army, Stuart made no further attack, but held his position in observation of the enemy throughout the remainder of the day. The opposing forces occupied the crests of two nearly parallel ranges of hills, between which, in an open valley, lie James City. The troops were hidden from view behind the swell of the hills, and an occasional shot from the opposing batteries was, for some time, the only sign of war. Once, during the afternoon, the enemy attempted to charge with cavalry two guns which Stuart had advanced to the edge of the village, but the charge was met by the sharpshooters of the 1st South Carolina Cavalry, under Captain Jones, and was easily repulsed.

During the night the enemy disappeared from Stuart's front, and early on the morning of the 11th, leav-

ing Young's brigade at James City, he pushed northward to the Sperryville turnpike, which he struck at
Griffinsburg. Here he found Funsten's brigade, from
which he sent one regiment, the 11th Virginia Cavalry,
Lieutenant-Colonel Ball commanding, to Rixeyville, on
the Warrenton road, and then, with Funsten and Gordon, pressed down the Sperryville turnpike toward
Culpeper Court House. The enemy's pickets were at
a distance of perhaps three miles from the town, and
were pursued so rapidly that Stuart found himself at
one time riding with one company of the 12th Virginia,
his advance-guard, in a line parallel with and opposite
to a considerable body of infantry which was endeavoring to join its friends. No other force being available, Stuart ordered his advance-guard and couriers to
charge. Lieutenant Baylor led his company most handsomely, but encountering a wide ditch and a stone wall,
was unable to reach the enemy, who delivered a harmless fire in his very face, and then retreated to Culpeper Court House. Before other troops could be
brought forward this regiment effected its escape. On
reaching the vicinity of Culpeper Court House, Stuart
found that Meade's infantry had retired beyond the
Rappahannock River, but that Kilpatrick's cavalry was
massed and in position to receive him. At a short distance from the Court House Captain Grigg's squadron
of the Harris Light Cavalry was encountered, and after
a most gallant resistance was driven by superior numbers through and beyond the town, with the loss, according to General Kilpatrick, of their leader and one
half the command.[1] Colonel Ferebee and Adjutant
Morehead, of Gordon's brigade, were wounded in this
action, and Lieutenants Baker and Benton were killed.
At this time Stuart had with him only five regiments,

[1] Philadelphia *Weekly Times*, August 23, 1879.

— two in Jones' brigade, and three in Gordon's. The other regiments of these brigades had been detached to accompany the advance of the main army. Fifteen hundred men would be an extreme estimate of the force present, while General Kilpatrick states his command at " less than four thousand, all told." [1] General Kilpatrick occupied the open ground east of the Court House, where it would have been folly to attack unless with some equality of numbers; and as Stuart had nothing to gain by such an encounter, he contented himself with a quiet observation of the enemy until the distant sound of artillery informed him that Fitz Lee was advancing from the Rapidan. He now determined to effect a junction with Lee at Brandy Station, and, if possible, to occupy the Fleetwood Hill, thus cutting off the cavalry at Culpeper Court House from their friends below. He therefore withdrew from Kilpatrick's front, and moved rapidly through farm roads in the direction of Brandy Station.

To rightly understand the events now transpiring it is necessary to follow General Fitz Lee's movements of this day, which are best described by an extract from his letter to the author published in the Philadelphia "Weekly Times," February 7, 1880. He says: —

When General Lee decided to push General Meade from his front on the Rapidan, he ordered me to hold his lines while he moved out and around Meade's flank. For this purpose two brigades of infantry were ordered to report to me, and with this force and my cavalry division I occupied the whole of General Lee's former extended front — the infantry upon the left of the line and my cavalry upon the right. Upon the day after General Lee's departure, gallant John Buford, who was at Stevensburg with his division of cavalry, moved up to the Rapidan, and crossed that stream below my right, on a forced reconnoissance. I attacked him at once with my cavalry alone, drove him back again across Raccoon Ford, and followed him up rapidly. He was dislodged, after severe combats, from the two positions where only he offered battle, namely, from Raccoon Ford and from Stevensburg. Expecting that Buford would make another stand at Brandy Station, I followed him to that point; but on arriving in its vicinity I ascertained that he had passed beyond it, toward the Rappahannock.

The country in which Stuart was operating was so open that his movement in withdrawing from the Court House could not long be concealed from Kilpatrick, who readily penetrated his design, and engaged with him in a race for Brandy Station. When Stuart reached the open plain near Slaughter Bradford's house, an animating sight presented itself. Dense columns of Federal cavalry were moving at a trot down the railroad, nearly parallel with his line of march. Below Bradford's the 1st North Carolina and the 12th Virginia were detached to attack two portions of the enemy's column which appeared to be separated from the main body. The hurry which seemed to pervade the Federal ranks, and the confusion which resulted from the charge of the 12th Virginia, promised good results, although the enemy's force was evidently much the greater. But while moving up in column of fours in a narrow farm lane to support the 12th Virginia, the 4th and 5th North Carolina Cavalry were suddenly opposed by a small body of the enemy, one batalion of the 5th New York Cavalry, charging in column of squadrons with drawn sabres. Huddled together in the lane, these regiments, which had on this same day done gallant service in previous charges, turned and ran from less than half their own numbers, nor could their flight be checked until a few determined officers, pressing their horses to the head of the column of fugitives, blockaded the road with drawn pistols. The success of the enemy

was, however, short lived ; for the opportune arrival of
the 7th Virginia Cavalry enabled Stuart to throw it
upon the flank of the attacking party, and many of
them were killed and captured. The time gained by
this diversion was of the greatest importance to the
Federal cavalry ; for it gave them possession of Fleetwood, which they occupied with artillery before the
arrival of either Fitz Lee or Stuart. Stuart's advance
throughout the day had been so rapid that his guns
could not keep to the front. He had, therefore, no
means of notifying Fitz Lee of his approach. In the
charges which had been made the fighting was done
with the sabre, and while the noise and cheering which
attended them was heard by Fitz Lee, it rather tended
to retard than to hasten his advance, producing upon
him the impression that the enemy in his front had
been reinforced, and Stuart's command was even subjected for a time to the fire of Lee's guns.

As Fitz Lee approached Brandy Station, following up
Buford's retreating column, he extended the 5th and
15th Virginia Cavalry and the 1st Maryland Battalion
across the railroad, facing the position which Buford
had now occupied on Fleetwood. The rear of these
regiments was of course presented to Kilpatrick, of
whose advance they were ignorant. The following extract from a letter to the author from General T. L.
Rosser, who then, as Colonel, commanded the 5th Virginia Cavalry, gives a vivid picture of the situation : —

My regiment, with the 1st Maryland and 15th Virginia Cavalry, extended across the road upon which these troops were
coming up in our rear. Not knowing who they were, I sent
to Fitz Lee to learn something about them, but before hearing
from him they came near enough for me to observe that they
carried the Federal flag ; and to prevent being crushed between
these two commands I withdrew my regiment, and advised the

other colonels to fall back so as to avoid the heavy blow in our rear. We did so, and reformed perpendicular to Buford and parallel to the direction of march of the advancing column from the rear, and we were in good order when the head of Kilpatrick's column got opposite us. These troops were moving at a full gallop; they were not charging upon us, for we stood in line off to one side, and for a moment I looked on in amazement at the performance. I soon concluded that they were being pursued, and charged them in flank. Never in my life did I reap such a rich harvest in horses and prisoners.

Stuart had now been disappointed in his expectation of delivering a serious blow upon Kilpatrick's cavalry. He could hardly have occupied Fleetwood, as events afterwards demonstrated, in advance of Buford's cavalry; and the bad behavior of the 4th and 5th North Carolina regiments had rendered him powerless to strike Kilpatrick as he passed on to join Buford. But when a junction was formed with Fitz Lee's division, Stuart attacked the enemy around Brandy Station, which was again the scene of a sanguinary cavalry battle. It was late in the afternoon. General Pleasonton, who had accompanied Kilpatrick's division from Culpeper Court House, assumed command of the united divisions of Buford and Kilpatrick, and handled his men as skilfully as he did on the 9th of June. Stuart extended Lomax's and Chambliss' brigades on the Confederate right, so as to pour a cross-fire upon the enemy's left flank, while the rest of the command attacked in front. It was no easy matter to dislodge the enemy from the woods about the station. They fought bravely, even desperately. Several times dismounted men, while eagerly pressing forward, were surrounded by the enemy's cavalry, and either fought their way out with their carbines and revolvers or were rescued by charges of their mounted comrades. Five times each did the 5th, 6th, and 15th Virginia Cavalry make distinct sabre charges, in one of which Colonel Harrison, of the 6th Virginia, was wounded. Despite all his efforts, the enemy was steadily pushed back to his position upon Fleetwood, in which he was so strong that Stuart declined to attack. Fitz Lee's division was now moved by the left past the Barbour House, as if to interpose between the enemy and the river, perceiving which Buford and Kilpatrick withdrew from their position, and protected by their artillery, which was handled with great skill, crossed the river after nightfall. Stuart's command bivouacked near Brandy Station, wearied with the hard conflicts of the day, but conscious that their efforts had been crowned with success.

Early on the 12th orders were sent to Colonel Young, at James City, to move Butler's brigade to Culpeper Court House. Leaving the 5th Virginia Cavalry, under Colonel T. L. Rosser, with one piece of artillery, to picket the Rappahannock, Stuart proceeded with the remainder of his command to gain the front of the army, now moving toward Warrenton.

Before following the movements of this column let us see what befell Rosser in his detached position. Stuart had succeeded in screening the march of Lee's army from the observation of the enemy. While Lee was hurrying northward Meade was under the impression that he had halted at Culpeper Court House, and on the afternoon of the 12th he countermarched the 2d, 5th, and 6th corps, with Buford's division of cavalry, intending to advance to Culpeper and there give battle to Lee if he could be found. This advance struck Rosser's regiment about two o'clock in the afternoon. He could, of course, do nothing but fall back, delaying Meade's march as much as circumstances would permit. So skilfully did he handle his men that it was nearly night when he reached the wooded ridge north of

Culpeper Court House, known as Slaughter's Hill.   To
this point Colonel Young had hurried forward his brigade from James City, bringing with him five pieces
of artillery.   Dismounting every available man, and
posting his guns in advantageous positions, he was enabled to display what seemed to be quite a formidable
line of battle ; and as Rosser's line joined with his own
the enemy was greeted with so severe a fire that he
declined to attempt a further advance that night.   Rosser and Young bivouacked on their line of battle, building extensive camp-fires.   Fortunately Young had with
him a regimental band.   This was moved rapidly from
point to point in the rear, and by its music tended to
exaggerate, in the enemy's estimation, the force at his
disposal.   Young, however, passed an anxious night,
anticipating a serious advance by the enemy in the
morning, which could not fail to disclose his real weakness.   But during the night Meade was made aware of
events, shortly to be related, which had transpired that
afternoon at Warrenton Springs, and hurriedly recalled
his army to meet Lee's advance upon the Orange and
Alexandria Railroad.,   Buford's movements in this
affair were doubtless rendered more cautious by the
severe handling which his men had received on these
same fields during the previous afternoon, and by the
knowledge that at that time certainly there was present
a large force of Confederate cavalry.   But this does not
detract from the credit due to Rosser and Young, by
whose bold management a small force was so magnified
in the eyes of the enemy as to cause him to move with
caution.

      Let us now return to the column operating under
Stuart.   Fitz Lee was sent to cross the river at Fox-
ville, while Stuart, with Funsten's and Gordon's brigades, moved on toward Warrenton Springs.   It will be

remembered that the 11th Virginia Cavalry, under Lieutenant-Colonel Ball, had been detached on the previous day from Funsten's command for service in this direction. While advancing, on the 12th, Colonel Ball encountered the enemy's cavalry, the 13th Pennsylvania and 10th New York regiments,[1] near Jefferson, and had unsuccessfully attempted to dislodge them from a strong position in the village. Upon Stuart's arrival the face of affairs was speedily changed. The 7th Virginia Cavalry was sent to the left and the 12th Virginia Cavalry to the right, with the intention of penetrating to the enemy's rear, and cutting them off from the fords. Colonel Funsten, with the 12th Virginia, soon encountered the 10th New York Cavalry, and, after a brief but severe struggle, drove them back toward the river. Meantime Colonel Ball had charged upon the 13th Pennsylvania Cavalry, in the town, and had succeeded in breaking their lines although they fought hard for their position. He had them in full retreat toward the river just as Colonel Funsten was reforming the 12th Virginia in their rear. Without delay Funsten charged the retreating column in flank, while Ball pressed heavily upon their rear. In a moment the rout was complete. The regiment broke and scattered. In this engagement the moral effect of superior numbers was of course upon the Confederate side, but the fighting was done by two regiments which could hardly have outnumbered the two to which they were opposed.

Sending two regiments to cross the Rappahannock higher up, Stuart proceeded to force the passage of the river at Warrenton Springs. Here the ford and bridge were commanded by rifle-pits, into which the enemy had thrown a considerable force of dismounted men, and these were supported by the mounted cavalry of

[1] Captain N. D. Preston, Philadelphia *Weekly Times*, November 23, 1878.

the 2d brigade of Gregg's division, and by artillery posted upon the hills beyond. In the absence of his own artillery Stuart applied for assistance to General Long, commanding the artillery of Ewell's corps. Eight guns were soon placed in position, and their fire silenced the enemy's battery and compelled the supporting cavalry to seek shelter.

Now the 12th Virginia was ordered to charge the bridge. Lieutenant Baylor's company still had the front. Darkness was settling down upon the field. Along a narrow causeway Baylor led his men in column of fours. In the face of a sharp fire from the rifle-pits he reached the very abutment of the bridge before he discovered that the planks had been removed, and that a crossing was impossible. He must retrace his steps and try the ford. There was no trepidation, no confusion. " By fours, right about wheel! Forward!" and in a moment he had descended from the causeway, and his column was plunging through the narrow ford, where hardly four could ride abreast. It was a gallant sight, and called forth wild huzzas from the Confederate infantry, many of whom were spectators of the scene. Up the hill went Baylor, and in a few moments the rifle-pits were cleared of the enemy and the approaches to the bridge were under our control. While the planks were hastily replaced the cavalry crossed at the ford and pressed the enemy steadily back to the Warrenton road. Although it was now dark Stuart ordered Funsten and Gordon to proceed to Warrenton, where they bivouacked. Funsten had several skirmishes on the road, and captured about fifty of the enemy, who in the darkness had by mistake fallen in with his rear.

On the morning of the 13th, while Lee's army was concentrating at Warrenton, Stuart was ordered to make a reconnoissance toward Catlett's Station. He received these orders about ten o'clock, and immediately sent forward Lomax's brigade. Funsten's and Gordon's brigades had been so constantly engaged with the enemy during the past four days that their ammunition was exhausted, and some unavoidable delay occurred while awaiting the arrival of their ordnance wagons. Lomax moved to Auburn, where he learned that the enemy occupied Warrenton Junction in force. Having gained this intelligence, he halted his command to await the other brigades. The proximity of the enemy rendered it likely that some severe fighting would occur on this reconnoissance, and Stuart carried with him seven pieces of artillery, under Major Beckham, and five ordnance wagons, that he might be prepared for any emergency. It was perhaps as late as four o'clock in the afternoon when Stuart joined Lomax at Auburn. A brief description of the roads in this vicinity is necessary for a correct understanding of the interesting and somewhat amusing events which now occurred.

Warrenton Junction is distant from Warrenton about eight and one half miles, and almost due southeast. The road between these places makes with the railroad nearly a right angle. Catlett's Station is nearly three miles from Warrenton Junction and nine miles from Warrenton. Five miles from Warrenton, on the road to Catlett's Station, is Auburn, a little hamlet, consisting of the residence of Stephen McCormick, a post-office, and a blacksmith's shop. It is situated at the crossing of Cedar Run. Intersecting the Warrenton road at this point is a road leading from Freeman's Ford on the Rappahannock, and Fayetteville, toward Greenwich. The country about Auburn is rough with hills, both clear and wooded, and the crossing of Cedar Run is rendered difficult not only by the steep descent to its bed, but also by the fact that the ford is common to the intersecting roads.

Leaving Lomax to guard his rear at Auburn, Stuart proceeded with the remainder of the command, including artillery and ordnance wagons, toward Catlett's Station. About three miles from Auburn the road debouches from the woods into the extensive open fields through which passes the Orange and Alexandria Railroad, and from this point the whole country between Catlett's Station and Hanover Junction is plainly visible. Here an exciting scene met the gaze of the Confederate horsemen. An immense park of wagons occupied the fields between the two stations; while infantry, artillery, and wagon trains were hurrying northward along the line of the railroad, at first in frequent detachments, afterward in steady columns. Hidden in the woods, Stuart remained in observation of the enemy for a long time. Satisfied that he was witnessing the movement of a large part of Meade's army, Stuart sent Major Venable, of his staff, to convey this information to General Lee, and to suggest an attack by the army upon the flank of this marching column. When Venable arrived within sight of Auburn he found it in the possession of the enemy; but making a *détour* to the northward, he avoided them, and continued his course to Warrenton, having first sent word to Stuart of the condition of things in his rear. The explanation of this surprising circumstance is this: the 3d army corps, which had been stationed at Freeman's Ford during the 12th, moved on the 13th to join Meade's army, marching by way of Auburn. The 2d army corps, recalled from its advance toward Culpeper, reached Fayetteville early on the morning of the 13th, and remaining there until the 3d corps had taken the advance, followed on the same road. Reaching Auburn

late in the afternoon, the advance of the 3d corps easily
brushed aside Lomax, who retired toward Warrenton.
This occurred immediately before Venable's arrival at
Auburn. Lomax had sent a messenger to Stuart with
this information, but he failed to reach him. Evening
was closing down when this state of affairs was announced, and, as any movement toward the railroad
was clearly impossible, Stuart retraced his steps to
Auburn, if perchance a passage might still be forced at
that point. A brief reconnoissance developed the fact
that he was securely enclosed between two large marching columns of the enemy, and that any attempt to force
his way through could be successful, if at all, only at a
great sacrifice. Concealment seemed impossible ; for
the advance was now skirmishing with the enemy at
Auburn, and an occasional shot in rear told that the
rear-guard had been observed by parties flanking the
march of the column on the railroad. Between the advance and the rear-guard stood the two brigades on the
road, in close column, wondering what would be the
result. Stuart hesitated not a moment. With all his
fondness for attack, he knew when to remain quiet as
well as when to act. Every available staff officer was
employed in withdrawing the command from the road
to the fields on its northern side. The advance and
rear-guards were drawn in, with orders on no account
to return the enemy's fire. As if by magic, the road
was cleared of horsemen, artillery, and wagons, and
darkness found us snugly sheltered beneath the hills
which raised their friendly crests between us and danger. How thankful we were for those hills! How
thankful for that darkness ! An hour of daylight would
have wrought our destruction ; for even with Lomax's
assistance on the opposite side, a passage of the difficult
ford would have been impossible in the face of War-

ren's infantry; and in no other direction could we look
with greater hope. The enemy enclosed us in front
and rear. Upon our right was a forest, upon our left
a mill-race.

Our guns were soon posted upon the crest of the hill
which overlooked the ford, and within three hundred
yards of the road along which the enemy was marching. And nothing now remained but to watch and
wait and keep quiet. Quiet? Yes, the men kept very
quiet, for they realized that even Stuart never before
had them in so "tight" a place. But many times did
we fear that we were betrayed by the weary, hungry,
headstrong mules of the ordnance train. Men were
stationed at the head of every team; but in spite of
all precautions, a discordant bray would every now and
then fill the air. Never was the voice of a mule so
harsh!

Though not without an admixture of the ludicrous,
those were anxious hours. This was the only occasion
on which I remember to have seen Stuart give outward
manifestation of his deep concern. So close were we
to the marching columns of the enemy that we could
distinctly hear the orders of the officers as they closed
up the column. We could even hear the voices of the
men in conversation, and could distinguish between the
passage of wagons and artillery by the noise of the
wheels. Throughout the whole night, and almost without interruption, did we listen to the sound of hostile
feet; and much did we rejoice that the noise of their
march rendered inaudible to them the sounds which
arose from our bivouac. Many were the plans of relief suggested and discussed. At one time it was proposed to abandon the artillery and wagons, mass the
cavalry, and, overriding all opposition, break a way
through the marching column. But Stuart would not

listen to a plan which involved the loss of a gun or a wheel. This might be adopted as a last resort, but that crisis had not yet arrived. Another plan, which his own mind suggested, nearly gained his approval. This was to turn off to the west the head of one of the wagon trains, as if by direction of some superior officer, then fall in with his own command and march the whole to a place of safety. Brilliant as such an achievement would have been if successful, and easy to accomplish with a small command, it seemed too hazardous to be attempted with two brigades. Moreover, Stuart still had hope that Lee would attack this column of the enemy, in which case he was in the best position to inflict damage. And so the night wore on. No break occurred through which it would have been possible to move, and our main hope of safety lay in the expectation that the rear of the enemy would have passed our position by dawn, or would have cleared the vicinity of Warrenton Junction, so as to admit of a *détour* in that direction. Should this fail, we had an abiding confidence that General Lee would send forces to our assistance ; for, during the night, Stuart had taken measures to inform him of our situation. As day began to dawn it was manifest that a collision of some kind was unavoidable. Upon the adjacent hill-tops and on the same side of Cedar Run with ourselves, but between us and the ford, a large force of infantry had halted, stacked arms, and were building camp-fires and preparing for breakfast. And now hearts beat quick with suspense, and saddle-girths were tightened, and arms were made ready ; for the moment of our discovery could not be far distant, and at that moment we must attack. Our seven guns were pushed a little further on the crest of the hill, so as fully to command the opposite bivouac ; and then we waited. As soon as it became light the infantry commenced to straggle in search of water, and some of them approached so near that they could not fail to recognize the Confederate uniforms. A few shots on the side of the enemy next to Warrenton informed us that some one was about to commence work there, and in an instant our seven guns were raining shell and canister upon the enemy. Never were men more completely surprised. Soon they recovered themselves, and a regiment or more was moved in line of battle, without skirmishers, directly upon the position of our guns; but their fire and that of the dismounted men who supported them was more than they could bear, and that line of battle sunk from sight below the crest of an intervening hill, and made its appearance no more. Our left flank, which extended across the road to Catlett's, was our weak point, and against this a strong attack was directed. It was all-important to repel this, for our only means of egress lay in that direction. Colonel Ruffin now led the 1st North Carolina Cavalry in a mounted charge. He rode over a strong line of skirmishers, most of whom surrendered; but his charge was broken by the close line of battle beyond, and his men returned and reformed for another attack, but left behind them for dead their gallant leader. The enemy's advance was checked, and, seizing the favorable moment, the artillery and wagons were withdrawn from the hills, and, passing in rear of the enemy's position, the whole command was extricated from its perilous situation. Stuart had expected when he commenced the attack that he would be aided by a vigorous movement of our troops from Warrenton, and he had hoped that the combined assault would inflict serious damage upon the enemy, and perhaps bring on a general engagement between the armies. General Lee had been fully informed of his situation by no less than six bold men, who, passing through the enemy's column while on the march, had carried verbal messages to the commanding general. A part, at least, of Ewell's corps had been moved down to his assistance, and had commenced an attack ; but as the fire of Stuart's guns, which were served with intensest energy, continued and increased, the fire of the infantry on the opposite side diminished to a weak skirmishing. They afterward complained that the shot from Stuart's guns, passing through and over the enemy, arrested their advance. Ignorant of what force was on the other side, and thinking that perhaps Lomax alone was endeavoring to do what he could for his relief, Stuart was compelled to abandon his attack, and at the first possible moment to provide for the safety of his men.

The advance of Lee's army ended with the fight at Bristoe Station, but Stuart continued to follow the withdrawing lines of the enemy, and had frequent collisions with their cavalry during the next three days, on Bull Run, at Manassas, Groveton, and Frying Pan Church. The result of these movements was that, on the night of the 18th, Stuart, with Hampton's division, was in position at Buckland, opposing Kilpatrick's cavalry and a large infantry support, which had been advanced from Fairfax Court House. Fitz Lee's division was within supporting distance at Auburn, and had orders to move to Buckland. Early on the 19th the enemy attempted to force the passage of Broad Run at Buckland, but were repulsed in every attempt. The morning was wearing away in the contest when Stuart received word from Fitz Lee that he was in motion to join him, and suggesting that Stuart should retire in Kilpatrick's front, drawing him on toward Warrenton, while he would attempt to interpose his

division between Kilpatrick and Broad Run.   If caught
in this trap, Kilpatrick would be likely to suffer.   Stuart at once adopted the suggestion and notified Lee
that he would turn upon Kilpatrick at the sound of the
first gun.   Halting Custer's brigade at Broad Run, to
guard his left flank and rear, Kilpatrick followed Stuart
with caution as far as Chestnut Ridge, about three miles
from Warrenton.

Meantime Fitz Lee had come up from Auburn, expecting to gain, unopposed, the rear of Kilpatrick's
entire division ; but he found Custer's brigade at Broad
Run ready to oppose him.   A fierce fight ensued.   Major P. P. Johnston, of the Stuart Horse Artillery, now
a resident of Lexington, Ky., who commanded at Buckland a section of Breathed's battery, and who was severely wounded in this engagement, makes to me in
substance the following statement : —

My battery was hotly engaged when Fitz Lee attacked Custer's brigade at Buckland Mills.   The battle was of the most
obstinate character, Fitz Lee exerting himself to the utmost to
push the enemy, and Custer seeming to have no thought of retiring.   Suddenly a cloud of dust arose on the road toward
Warrenton, and as suddenly everything in our front gave way.
The mounted cavalry was ordered forward, and I saw no more
of the enemy, although following as closely as my wounded condition would permit.

The first sound of Fitz Lee's guns roused Stuart from
his self - imposed inaction.   Instantly Hampton's division was faced about and hurled upon Davies' brigade.
Gordon's brigade, led by the 1st North Carolina, took
the road, and Young and Rosser charged on either
flank.   The attack was sudden and impetuous, and
although the enemy made resistance, their lines were
soon broken and routed.   Now commenced the race for
Buckland.   Routed in front, and admonished by the

artillery firing that an enemy had gained their rear, Kilpatrick's men ran in a manner worthy of the occasion. For nearly five miles the chase was continued without a pause. Naturally the crowd of fugitives, among whom all order was cast aside, made faster time than did the pursuing brigades. Colonel Young, who had led his brigade through the woods on the right of the road in the endeavor to reach the enemy's flank, was not able to get near enough to them to strike a blow, although he moved with all the speed that the nature of the ground permitted. Of course the stampede of Davies' brigade placed Custer in a critical position, and necessitated his precipitate withdrawal from Fitz Lee's front. But Custer was a hard fighter even in a retreat, and he succeeded in saving his artillery, and in recrossing Broad Run without any serious disorder. Some of the fugitives from Davies' brigade crossed at Buckland with Custer; the remainder, now cut off from that ford, continued their flight toward Haymarket.

In the rout of Davies' brigade Stuart captured two hundred and fifty prisoners, and eight wagons and ambulances, among them General Custer's headquarters' wagon, baggage, and papers. Fitz Lee now pushed down the pike toward Gainesville, while Stuart moved on the left toward Haymarket. On both roads the pursuit was continued until the lines of the 1st army corps were encountered. General Custer in his report [1] makes no mention of the stampede of Davies' brigade. General Kilpatrick has even attempted to deny it altogether.[2] But there are hundreds of eye-witnesses on either side yet living who can bear testimony to the substantial accuracy of this narrative.

[1] Moore's *Rebellion Record*, vol. vii. p. 561.
[2] Philadelphia *Weekly Times*, August 23, 1879.

On the night of the 19th Stuart bivouacked at Buck-land. On the next day he marched through Warren-ton on his way to rejoin Lee's army, which had again taken up the line of the Rapidan. His loss in killed and wounded during these operations was 408. The loss in missing is not stated, but was small. Major G. M. Ryals, provost - marshal of the cavalry, reports 1,370 prisoners captured from the enemy during these days. The losses of the Federal cavalry were 390 killed and wounded, and 885 captured or missing.[1]

[1] *Records of the Adjutant-General's Office.*

CHAPTER XIX.

THE WINTER OF 1863–64.

At the close of the Bristoe Campaign the Confederate army returned to Culpeper County, and encamped on either side of the Orange and Alexandria Railroad, holding the line of the Rappahannock. After rebuilding the railroad, which had been destroyed north of the river, the Federal army again advanced, and on the 7th of November forced the passage of the Rappahannock at Kelly's Ford and the railroad bridge, inflicting heavy loss at the latter place on the Confederate infantry. General Lee now withdrew his army beyond the Rapidan, and preparations were made for establishing winter quarters. This season of rest was, however, interrupted by the Mine Run Campaign. On the 26th of November General Meade put his army in motion, crossed the Rapidan at Germanna and Ely's Fords, and moved up the river in the direction of Orange Court House. Hampton's division, supported by the advance of Hill's corps, checked the enemy, on the 27th, near New Hope Church ; while Early, on the left, advanced as far as Locust Grove, where he found the enemy in force. Believing that it was the intention of General Meade to attack, General Lee withdrew, on the night of the 27th, to a strong position on the west side of Mine Run, where he intrenched himself. On the morning of the 28th Meade's army advanced to the Confederate position and threw up intrenchments. For four days the armies confronted each other, but on the night of the 1st of December General Meade withdrew and recrossed the Rapidan, after which the lines previously held were resumed by both armies. On the 27th of November General T. L. Rosser, who had been promoted and assigned to the command of Jones' brigade, attacked a wagon train in the rear of the Federal army, and made some important captures. On the 29th of November an engagement occurred at Parker's Store, between Hampton's and Gregg's divisions, in which the Confederate reports claim a success. It has not been convenient to obtain access to the Federal reports of these battles.

I desire to state one incident of this campaign which, so far as I know, has never been recorded. Hampton occupied the extreme right of the Confederate line. A personal reconnoissance on the 30th brought him into a position where he was in rear of the Federal left wing, which was fully commanded by his post of observation. Hampton was looking down on the rear of the Federal guns as they stood pointed against the Confederate lines. There seemed to be no reason why a heavy force could not be concentrated at this point, which might attack the Federal lines in reverse, and perhaps reënact some of the scenes of Chancellorsville. This information was quickly communicated to Stuart, who, after himself examining the ground, conducted General R. E. Lee to the same place. A council of war was held that night. The talk among the staff was that General Lee and General Stuart favored an immediate attack, but that Generals Ewell and Hill did not deem it best. General Lee made another personal reconnoissance on the 1st of December. He says in his report : —

Anderson's and Wilcox's divisions were withdrawn from the trenches at three A. M. on the 2d and moved to our right, with a view to make an attack in that quarter. As soon as it became light enough to distinguish objects it was discovered that the enemy's pickets along our entire line had retired, and our skirmishers were sent forward to ascertain his position. . . .

The movements of General Meade, and all the reports received as to his intention, led me to believe that he would attack, and I desired to have the advantage that such an attempt on his part would afford.

After awaiting his advance until Tuesday evening, preparations were made to attack him on Wednesday morning. This was prevented by his retreat.

During the month of February an expedition was projected by which it was expected that the capture of the city of Richmond and the release of the Federal prisoners there confined would be effected by a large body of Federal cavalry. The command of this expedition was intrusted to General Judson Kilpatrick. In order to cover this movement and increase the chances of success, a heavy demonstration was made on the Federal right. On the 28th of February the 6th corps and a portion of the 3d were thrown forward from Culpeper to Madison Court House. At about midnight General Custer left Madison Court House for Charlottesville. He commanded a body of 1,500 cavalry. There was nothing to interfere with his march, and he reached the vicinity of Charlottesville early in the afternoon of the 29th. Four batteries of horse artillery, Moorman's, Chew's, Breathed's, and McGregor's, were resting securely in their winter quarters, near the Rivanna River, about three miles from Charlottesville. Captain M. N. Moorman was in command of these batteries. He received the first information of the advance of the enemy at a little past midday on the 29th, from Lieutenant J. N. Cunningham, of the 1st Virginia Cavalry, who had been watching the column since it left Madison Court House. Captain Moorman at once sent out

pickets to the Rio Bridge, but before they could reach
that point they met the enemy and were driven back
and pursued into the camp.   There were no troops of
any kind at Charlottesville, for although a body of infantry was sent by railroad from Orange Court House
as soon as this movement was discovered, it did not
reach Charlottesville until after the enemy had retired.
Captain Moorman was compelled to rely on his own re-
sources.   In order to check the enemy he opened fire
from a portion of the guns of each battery, while the
drivers and the rest of the cannoneers caught up and
hitched the horses which were running loose in the
fields.   As fast as a carriage was horsed it was moved
to the rear, until only four guns remained in the
camp.   Lieutenant P. P. Johnston was placed in charge
of the guns which were retired, and he distributed
them along the road toward Charlottesville wherever
position could be obtained ; for it was the determination of these gallant artillerymen to dispute the ground
with the enemy, and to sell their guns at the dearest
price.   Captain Moorman says in his report : —

The enemy by this time had pressed back through camp the
line of skirmishers (unarmed except a few pistols) which I
had deployed in my front.   Having ordered all of my guns
back excepting two sections, I drew up behind each a mounted
support, placing the remainder of those mounted under Captains Chew and Breathed to guard my flank and manœuvre in
front, making a show of cavalry, in the execution of which
they deserve great credit.   Just at this moment, when the
enemy's column which had crossed at Cook's Ford had reached
and set fire to our camp, their right, which had crossed at Rio,
made a charge just in time to receive and mistake the explosion of one of Captain Chew's caissons for the reopening of
our guns (for they had just ceased firing at that point).   Each
column, mistaking the other for his enemy, fired into each
other and broke.   Captains Chew and Breathed, seeing their

mistake, charged with their squadrons, and drove the enemy
with such precipitancy that I presume they have never discovered their mistake, as they never ventured to return, but drew
up in line upon the opposite bank waiting the advance of the
Horse. They opened upon us two pieces of artillery, to which
I made no reply.

Captain Moorman enumerates his losses with great
particularity, the most serious of which were two men
and nine horses or mules captured. He states that the
men of Chew's and Breathed's batteries lost most of
their private effects in the burning of their camp, but
he rejoices that he was able to save his guns under
such circumstances.

For some reason, which cannot now be explained,
Stuart received tardy information of the march of the
enemy towards Charlottesville, and it was not until afternoon that he started in that direction with Wickham's
brigade. He had not marched many miles when the
sound of distant firing announced that the enemy had
reached Charlottesville. Still later the information was
received that the enemy had retired, and Stuart turned
his march northward in the hope of intercepting the
return of the raiders in the vicinity of Stannardsville.
The night was cold and rainy. As the rain fell it
froze, and covered the face of the earth with sleet.
Stuart reached the road on which the enemy was returning about daylight, and found that one detachment
had already passed on toward Madison Court House.
Here he awaited the arrival of the main body. For
two or three hours his men sat on their horses or on
the ground, exhausted, wet, and shivering. They had
no food, and no fires could be built. Under such circumstances men cannot fight. When Custer discovered that an enemy was in his front he ordered a
charge. His men, warm in the saddle, responded

promptly, and easily brushed aside the force which Stuart had posted along the road. Without attempting any pursuit, Custer continued his way to Madison Court House.

While these events were transpiring General Kilpatrick was marching upon Richmond. His force amounted to 3,582 men. Leaving Stevensburg on the night of the 28th, he marched to Ely's Ford on the Rapidan, where he succeeded in capturing the entire picket without giving any alarm. Soon after crossing the Rapidan he sent forward an advance column of 460 men, under Colonel Ulric Dahlgren, which passed through Spottsylvania Court House about three o'clock, A. M., and pushed rapidly forward in the direction of the Central Railroad, which they struck near Frederickshall about noon on the 29th. Here they captured a court-martial, consisting of eight officers. They also threatened the camps of the artillery of the 2d corps, commanded by General A. L. Long. Finding that General Long was prepared to offer resistance, they continued their march toward the James River. The papers found on the body of Colonel Dahlgren indicate that it was a part of the plan of this expedition that, if it were found possible to cross the James River, Dahlgren's command should be divided, and a portion of it should attack Richmond from the south side. General Kilpatrick's report indicates that it was his intention that the whole of Dahlgren's force should cross the James. It was hoped that a simultaneous attack by the main column under Kilpatrick and the detachment under Dahlgren would be successful in liberating the Federal prisoners, and in capturing Richmond. Colonel Dahlgren's command reached the James River in the vicinity of Dover Mills. Finding no means of crossing to the south side, he continued to march down the river toward Richmond, which he reached on the afternoon of Tuesday, the 1st of March, but not in time to give aid to Kilpatrick, or to receive assistance from him.

Following the route of his advance column to Spottsylvania Court House, General Kilpatrick, with the main body of his command, marched to Beaver Dam Station, on the Central Railroad, and thence to Ashland, on the Fredericksburg Railroad. He reached the outer defences of Richmond at about ten o'clock on Tuesday morning by the Brook turnpike. Colonel W. H. Stevens, commanding the defences of Richmond, had here about 500 men and six pieces of artillery. After engaging these troops until dark,[1] and hearing nothing from Dahlgren, Kilpatrick withdrew by the Meadow Bridge road, and encamped for the night near Atlee's Station. This withdrawal was effected not far from the time when Dahlgren made his attack upon the intrenchments of Richmond by the river road.

During this day Hampton had moved down from Hanover Junction with 306 men of Gordon's North Carolina brigade, under the command of Colonel W. H. Cheek. He reached Hughes' Cross Roads after dark, and, discovering the camp-fires of Kilpatrick's men near Atlee's Station, he dismounted 100 men, brought his artillery up to close range, attacked the camp, and drove Kilpatrick from it. Kilpatrick's men made but little resistance. Eighty-seven prisoners, 133 horses, and a number of arms and equipments were captured. Hampton was joined the following morning by Colonel Bradley T. Johnson, who with forty men of the Maryland cavalry had followed the enemy from Beaver Dam, and who also had captured a number of prisoners. After being driven from his camp Kilpatrick continued

[1] Kilpatrick's report.

his march during the night, and made his escape to Williamsburg.

The most important result of the night attack made by Hampton was that it caused Colonel Dahlgren, with a considerable portion of his command, to make a wide *détour* in the effort to reach Gloucester Point. He had succeeded in crossing both the Pamunkey and the Mattapony, although his march was watched and harassed by small bodies of cavalrymen, who were at home recruiting. On Wednesday night, the 3d of March, he fell into an ambuscade near King and Queen Court House, which had been laid in his path by Lieutenant James Pollard, of company H, 9th Virginia Cavalry. Lieutenant Pollard was aided by Captain W. M. McGruder, of the 42d Virginia battalion, and by Captains Bagby, Halbach, and Todd, of the Home Guards. Just before the action occurred Captain E. C. Fox, of company E, 5th Virginia Cavalry, arrived with 28 men of his company, and assumed command of the whole force, which now amounted to about 150 men. The fire of the ambush was reserved until the enemy had approached to close quarters. Colonel Dahlgren fell at the first fire. His men were surrounded in such a position that escape was impossible. At daylight they surrendered to Lieutenant Pollard, who reports the capture of 40 negroes and 135 soldiers.

Upon the body of Colonel Dahlgren were found papers which disclosed the objects of his expedition. An address which was to be delivered to his troops, and which was signed with his official signature, directed that the city of Richmond should be burned and destroyed, and that President Davis and his cabinet should be killed. Another paper, containing special orders and instructions, but without signature, made provision for the same course of conduct. Photographic copies of these papers were transmitted under flag of truce by General Lee to General Meade, and the inquiry was made whether the United States government or Colonel Dahlgren's superior officers approved and sanctioned such orders. In his reply General Meade denies that the United States government, himself, or General Kilpatrick authorized, sanctioned, or approved the burning of the city of Richmond and the killing of Mr. Davis and cabinet, or any other act not required by military necessity and in accordance with the usages of war. General Kilpatrick further states that the officers of Colonel Dahlgren's command all testify that he issued no address whatever. General Kilpatrick adds: —

Colonel Dahlgren, one hour before we separated at my headquarters, handed me an address that he intended to read to his command. The paper was indorsed in red ink "approved," over my official signature. The photographic papers referred to are true copies of the papers approved by me, save so far as they speak of exhorting the prisoners to destroy and burn the hateful city, and kill the traitor Davis and his cabinet, and in this, that they do not contain the indorsement referred to as having been placed by me on Colonel Dahlgren's papers. Colonel Dahlgren received no orders from me to pillage, burn, or kill, nor were any such instructions given me by my superiors.

CHAPTER XX.

THE DEATH OF STUART.

On the morning of the 4th of May, 1864, commenced the Wilderness campaign.

As soon as intelligence was received that the enemy had crossed the fords of the Rapidan, Stuart proceeded to his picket line, accompanied by only one courier, leaving his staff to break up the pleasant camp near Orange Court House which had been our home during the winter. Later in the day we joined him at the front, and bivouacked that night just in rear of the picket reserve, and some distance beyond the lines of the infantry. Meantime the cavalry was moving up on the right to envelop the enemy.

On the morning of the 5th Stuart in person conducted the advance of A. P. Hill's corps on the plank road until the enemy's lines were reached and the battle was joined. On this day Rosser had a severe and successful encounter with Wilson's division of cavalry, on the right, beyond Todd's Tavern.[1]

On the 6th the battle was renewed in the Wilderness, and was continued throughout the day with great intensity. On the 6th and 7th the cavalry of both armies was engaged in severe conflicts on the Confederate right. On the night of the 7th General Grant commenced to move his army by the left flank, in the endeavor to interpose it between General Lee and Rich-

[1] Moore's *Rebellion Record*, vol. xi. p. 452.

mond. The movement was discovered in time, and Fitz Lee's division was thrown in front of the Federal column, to delay it until Longstreet's corps, under Anderson, could reach Spottsylvania Court House. This was accomplished, although it entailed on Fitz Lee's division one of the severest conflicts in which it was ever engaged. Torbert's cavalry, commanded by Merritt and backed by the 5th corps, attacked before daylight. Fitz Lee employed his whole command dismounted, and presented so solid a front that the Federal cavalry found it difficult to move him; and having forced him slowly back beyond the forks of the road west of Alsop's, they were, at Merritt's suggestion, relieved by a line of battle from the 5th corps.[1] General Grant bears testimony to the character of the fighting when he says in his report:—

On the 8th General Warren met a force of the enemy which had been sent out to oppose and delay his advance, to gain time to fortify the line taken up at Spottsylvania. This force was steadily driven back on the main force within the recently constructed works, after considerable fighting, resulting in severe loss to both sides.

Fitz Lee was greatly aided in this battle by his battery, now commanded by Captain P. P. Johnston, Breathed having been recently made major of the battalion. His last position was close to Spottsylvania Court House, and immediately in front of a portion of Anderson's corps, which was drawn up in line of battle,

---

[1] It was in this action that Captain Joseph P. Ash, of the 5th United States Cavalry, was killed. This young officer is frequently mentioned in the reports of his superiors as a model of gallantry. An interesting incident occurred some months after his death. A sergeant of the 5th Cavalry who had served in the old army under Fitz Lee was captured and brought into his presence. During the conversation which ensued, Fitz Lee asked the sergeant why the old Rifles did not stand to their work better than they had done recently; and the sergeant replied that since Captain Ash was killed they had n't had any one to lead them right in a charge.

behind cover, and concealed from the view of the enemy
by the crest of an intervening hill, which was held by
Johnston's battery to give the led horses and dismounted men time to retire. Both Breathed and Johnston were present. A strong line of battle soon made
its appearance on the edge of the opposite woods, and,
seeing no support to the battery, pressed eagerly forward to capture it. The fire of the battery was maintained as long as possible, when Breathed directed
Johnston to retire the left section, leaving the right to
him. Johnston declined to leave while his battery was
engaged, but retired three of his guns, one piece at a
time, when he himself was shot through the shoulder,
and followed the third from the field. Before any of
the guns had left position the enemy had approached
so near that they felt secure of capturing the battery,
and the demand to surrender was heard from all sides.
Breathed was now alone with the last gun. The cannoneers had limbered up the piece and had mounted their
horses to retire; but before the gun could be moved,
the drivers and horses of the lead and swing teams were
killed or wounded, and Ryan, the driver of the wheel
team, had his arm shattered by a bullet. As if unconscious of the presence of an enemy, Breathed jumped
from his horse, cut loose the teams that were struggling
on the ground, mounted a wheel horse, and brought off
the gun almost as by a miracle. The enemy pressed on
with loud cheering. As they crossed the crest of the
hill they met the fire of Anderson's men at short range.
Staggered by it, they fell back and did not renew the
charge.

Up to this time only a portion of Anderson's corps
had reached the Court House. A few moments later
Stuart arrived with the remainder. At General Anderson's request he extended the left of the infantry

with his dismounted cavalry, and remained in command of the left of Anderson's line for several hours, until the arrival of the rest of the army relieved the cavalry and enabled it to withdraw.

While Stuart was thus engaged, brisk skirmishing was continued along the line. He exposed himself to fire with more than his usual disregard of danger, in spite of the repeated and earnest remonstrances of several of the infantry officers. I was the only member of his staff present. Not even a courier attended us. He kept me so busy in carrying messages to General Anderson, and some of these messages seemed so unimportant, that at last the thought occurred to me that he was endeavoring to shield me from danger. I said to him : " General, my horse is weary. You are exposing yourself, and you are alone. Please let me remain with you." He smiled at me kindly, but bade me go to General Anderson with another message.

During this day, the 8th, the enemy's cavalry was concentrated in rear of the army and moved to the vicinity of Fredericksburg. On the morning of the 9th General P. H. Sheridan, with about twelve thousand cavalry and a large force of artillery, moved to Hamilton's Crossing, thence to the Telegraph Road, and on toward Richmond. He thus avoided all but the outer line of the Confederate pickets and patrols. The movement was promptly reported, and within two hours after his column had passed Massaponax Church Wickham's brigade was in pursuit. Wickham struck the enemy at Jarrald's Mill, and drove in the rear-guard, the 6th Ohio Cavalry,[1] taking a number of prisoners. Here the enemy left the Telegraph Road, taking that to Beaver Dam. The 6th Ohio was now reinforced by the 1st New Jersey Cavalry,[2] and the rear-guard, thus strength-

[1] Moore's *Rebellion Record*, vol. xi. p. 453.   [2] Ibid.

ened, made a determined stand near Mitchell's Shop.
Wickham attacked promptly, but made no impression.
One or two of his regiments had recoiled from the
charge, when he called for Matthews' squadron of the
3d Virginia, with the remark, "I know he will go
through." Matthews led his column of fours down the
narrow lane and pierced the enemy's lines, but he did
not return. The heavy force of the enemy closed upon
the head of his column, killed five, wounded three, and
captured ten men of his company. Matthews' horse was
killed. While fighting on foot with his sabre, he was
shot from behind and mortally wounded. His gallantry
excited the admiration of his enemies, who carefully
carried him to a neighboring farm-house, leaving with
him one of his company who had been captured in the
charge. He died that night.

At this point Stuart and Fitz Lee joined Wickham,
with Lomax's and Gordon's brigades. These three brigades numbered between four and five thousand men.
Leaving Fitz Lee to follow the enemy's rear toward
Chilesburg, Stuart marched in the night, with Gordon's
brigade, to Davinport's Bridge, where he crossed the
North Anna the following morning. The brigades were
united at Beaver Dam Station, where the enemy's rear
was again encountered. While his troops were at
Beaver Dam, Stuart snatched a few minutes to visit the
residence of Colonel Edmund Fontaine, in the immediate vicinity, to ascertain the safety of his wife and children, who were visiting there at that time. Having
satisfied himself that his family had escaped the danger
to which they had been exposed, and having learned that
the main column of the enemy had passed southward
toward Negro Foot, with the intention of striking the
Louisa or Old Mountain Road, Stuart divided his command, sending Gordon's brigade to follow the rear of the

enemy, while he himself, with Fitz Lee's two brigades, marched to Hanover Junction, on his way to interpose between the enemy and Richmond. He reached the Junction some hours after dark, and proposed to prosecute his march without a stop. But Fitz Lee's men were thoroughly worn out. At the urgent request of General Lee, Stuart consented that the command should rest until one o'clock; and calling me to him, he ordered me to accompany General Lee to his bivouac, and not to close my eyes until I saw his command mounted and on the march at the appointed hour. When the troops had moved out I returned to Stuart and awoke him and the staff. While they were preparing to move I lay down, to catch, if possible, a few minutes' rest. The party rode off as I lay in a half-conscious condition, and I heard some one say : " General, here 's McClellan, fast asleep. Shall I wake him ? "

" No," he replied; " he has been watching while we were asleep. Leave a courier with him, and tell him to come on when his nap is out."

I gratefully accepted this unusual and unlooked-for interposition in my behalf, and after a short but most beneficial rest I succeeded in rejoining the general just after he had passed the road leading to Ashland. Here I learned that a squadron of the 2d Virginia Cavalry had encountered a body of the enemy in the town of Ashland, and had driven them from it with considerable loss. In this fight Lieutenant E. P. Hopkins, of the 1st Massachusetts Cavalry, son of Professor Albert Hopkins of Williams College, was killed. Stuart's march was now directed toward the Yellow Tavern, at the intersection of the Telegraph and Old Mountain roads. As I rode by his side we conversed on many matters of personal interest. He was more quiet than usual, softer, and more communicative. It seems now that the shadow of the near future was already upon him.

He reached the Yellow Tavern at about ten o'clock, and found himself in advance of the enemy's column, and in full time to interpose between it and Richmond. Not knowing what troops were at the disposal of General Bragg, he was uncertain whether to take position in front of the enemy or to remain on the flank of his march, near the Yellow Tavern. He preferred the latter course if he could be satisfied that there was sufficient force in Richmond to hold the trenches. To ascertain this he sent me to General Bragg. I was informed by General Bragg that he had irregular troops to the number of about four thousand, and that three brigades had been ordered from the army at Petersburg, and were hourly expected. He thought he could hold the fortifications. On my return I found that the enemy held the Brook turnpike, south of the Yellow Tavern, and I was compelled to make a *détour* through the fields to avoid capture. This somewhat delayed me, and I did not reach Stuart until after two o'clock. He told me that a heavy fight had taken place during my absence. The enemy had attempted to drive him from the Telegraph Road, but had been repulsed, after a most desperate and hand to hand fight, by the sharpshooters of Fitz Lee's brigade. The losses had been heavy. Among the killed was Colonel H. C. Pate, of the 5th Virginia Cavalry. Stuart spoke of the great gallantry he had exhibited under his own observation. He was pleased with the information I had brought from Richmond, and expressed the intention of retaining his position on Sheridan's flank, and the hope that, aided by a strong attack by the infantry in Richmond, he might be able to inflict serious disaster on the enemy's cavalry. Thus we sat talking for more than an hour, near one of our batteries on the right of our line, north of Half-Sink. Wickham held the right, and

Lomax the left. Lomax's line extended along the Telegraph Road for a short distance, then crossed it to a hill on the left, where was posted a piece of artillery. Two guns were placed immediately in the road. The whole command was dismounted except a portion of the 1st Virginia Cavalry, which was retained as a mounted reserve.

I quote the following passage from a letter which I wrote to Mrs. Stuart soon after the general's death, which was published, by her authority, in the seventh volume of the " Southern Historical Society Papers : " —

" About four o'clock the enemy suddenly threw a brigade of cavalry, mounted, upon our extreme left, attacking our whole line at the same time. As he always did, the general hastened to the point where the greatest danger threatened, — the point against which the enemy directed the mounted charge. My horse was so much exhausted by my severe ride of the morning that I could not keep pace with him, but Captain G. W. Dorsey, of company K, 1st Virginia Cavalry, gave me the particulars that follow.

" The enemy's charge captured our battery on the left of our line, and drove back almost the entire left. Where Captain Dorsey was stationed — immediately on the Telegraph Road — about eighty men had collected, and among these the general threw himself, and by his personal example held them steady while the enemy charged entirely past their position. With these men he fired into their flank and rear as they passed him, in advancing and retreating, for they were met by a mounted charge of the 1st Virginia Cavalry and driven back some distance. As they retired, one man who had been dismounted in the charge, and was running out on foot, turned as he passed the general, and discharging his pistol inflicted the fatal wound. When Captain Dorsey discovered that he was wounded he came at once to his assistance, and endeavored to lead him to the rear; but the general's horse had become so restive and unmanageable that he insisted upon being taken down, and allowed to rest against a tree. When this was done Captain Dorsey sent for another horse. While waiting the general ordered him to leave him, and return to his men and drive back the enemy. He said he feared that he was mortally wounded, and could be of no more service. Captain Dorsey told him that he could not obey that order; that he would rather sacrifice his life than leave him until he had placed him out of all danger. The situation was an exposed one. Our men were sadly scattered, and there was hardly a handful of men between that little group and the advancing enemy. But the horse arrived in time; the general was lifted on to him, and was led by Captain Dorsey to a safer place. There, by the general's order, he gave him into the charge of private Wheatly, of his company, and returned to rally his scattered men. Wheatly procured an ambulance, placed the general in it with the greatest care, and, supporting him in his arms, he was driven toward the rear. I was hastening toward that part of the field where I had heard that he was wounded when I met the ambulance. The general had so often told me that if he were wounded I must not leave the field, but report to the officer next to him in rank, that I did not now presume to disregard his order, and the more so because I saw that Dr. Fontaine, Venable, Garnett, Hullihen, and several of his couriers were attending him. I remained with General Fitz Lee until the next morning, when he sent me to the city to see General Bragg, and I thus had an opportunity to spend an hour with my general."

As he was being driven from the field he noticed the disorganized ranks of his retreating men, and called out to them : —

" Go back ! go back ! and do your duty, as I have done mine, and our country will be safe. Go back ! go back ! I had rather die than be whipped."

These were his last words on the battle-field, — words not of idle egotism, but of soldierly entreaty. The shadow that for days had hung over his joyous, earnest life was deepening with the mist from out the dark valley, and ere the chill night closed in he would once again urge to effort, once again cheer to the charge, the comrades he had loved and led so well. But a few months later came the answering echo from the lips of his great commander, who would gladly have shared with him a soldier's grave, " My men, I have done my best for you."

While yet in the ambulance Dr. Fontaine and Lieutenant Hullihen turned the general over on his side, in order that an examination of the wound might be made. While this was in progress he spoke to Hullihen, addressing him by the pet name which he usually employed : —

" Honey-bun, how do I look in the face ? "

" General," replied Hullihen, " you are looking right well. You will be all right."

" Well," said he, " I don't know how this will turn out; but if it is God's will that I shall die I am ready."

In order to avoid the enemy, who now held full possession of the Brook turnpike, it was necessary for the ambulance to make a wide *détour* to reach Richmond, and it was some time after dark when the general arrived at the residence of his brother-in-law, Dr. Charles Brewer. The long ride caused him great suf-

fering.   On the morning of the 12th, after delivering
General Fitz Lee's message to General Bragg, I repaired to the bedside of my dying chief.   He was calm
and composed, in the full possession of his mind.   Our
conversation was, however, interrupted by paroxysms
of suffering.   He directed me to make the proper disposal of his official papers, and to send his personal
effects to his wife.   He then said : —

"I wish you to take one of my horses and Venable
the other.   Which is the heavier rider ? "

I replied that I thought Venable was.

"Then," said he, "let Venable have the gray horse,
and you take the bay."

Soon he spoke again : —

"You will find in my hat a small Confederate flag,
which a lady of Columbia, South Carolina, sent me,
with the request that I would wear it upon my horse
in a battle and return it to her.   Send it to her."

I was at loss how to interpret these instructions ; for
I had never seen any such decoration upon his hat.
But upon examining it the flag was found within its
lining, stained with the sweat of his brow ; and among
his papers I found the letter which had conveyed the
request.

Again he said : "My spurs which I have always
worn in battle I promised to give to Mrs. Lilly Lee, of
Shepherdstown, Virginia.   My sword I leave to my
son."

While I sat by his side the sound of cannon outside
the city was heard.   He turned to me eagerly and inquired what it meant.   I explained that Gracy's brigade and other troops had moved out against the enemy's rear on the Brook turnpike, and that Fitz Lee
would endeavor to oppose their advance at Meadow
Bridge.   He turned his eyes upward, and exclaimed

earnestly, " God grant that they may be successful."
Then turning his head aside, he said with a sigh, —
" But I must be prepared for another world."

The thought of duty was always uppermost in his
mind ; and after listening to the distant cannonading
for a few moments, he said : " Major, Fitz Lee may
need you." I understood his meaning, and pressed his
hand in a last farewell.

As I left his chamber President Davis entered. Taking the general's hand, he asked : " General, how do
you feel ? "

He replied : " Easy, but willing to die, if God and
my country think I have fulfilled my destiny and done
my duty."

The Rev. Mr. Peterkin visited him, and prayed with
him. He requested Mr. Peterkin to sing " Rock of
Ages," and joined in the singing of the hymn.

During the afternoon he asked Dr. Brewer whether
it were not possible for him to survive the night. The
doctor frankly told him that death was close at hand.

He then said : " I am resigned if it be God's will ;
but I would like to see my wife. But God's will be
done."

Again he said to Dr. Brewer : " I am going fast
now ; I am resigned ; God's will be done."

And thus he passed away.

APPENDIX.

REPORTS OF BRIGADIER-GENERAL B. H. ROBERTSON, C. S. ARMY, COMMANDING BRIGADE, OF ENGAGEMENT AT BRANDY STATION.

HEADQUARTERS CAVALRY BRIGADE, *June* 12, 1863.

MAJOR : — On 9th instant, according to orders, my brigade proceeded to within two miles of Kelly's Ford to check the enemy's advance upon the railroad, near which our forces were engaged. I dismounted a portion to oppose the enemy's infantry in the woods. The enemy's cannon had just opened when several orders were received to fall back rapidly to Brandy Station, the Yankees being in my rear.

I had reported their advance upon Stevensburg and Brandy, and was ordered, through Lieutenant Johnston, to hold the ground in my front. One regiment of my brigade was then ordered to move rapidly to the general's headquarters. The other was instructed to cover the right and rear of Hampton's brigade. Both regiments were subsequently drawn up in line of battle to repel the advance of the enemy's columns, which finally moved to the left. One of my regiments was then ordered in that direction. I accompanied it, and, in accordance with instructions, deployed it as skirmishers to hold that wing until reinforcements should arrive. The other regiment remained with Hampton.

My command, although opposed to the enemy during the entire day, was not at any time actively engaged. Will make a detailed report.   Very respectfully,

B. H. ROBERTSON,
Brigadier-General Commanding Cavalry.

Major H. B. McClellan,
Assistant Adjutant-General, &c.

HEADQUARTERS CAVALRY BRIGADE, *June* 13, 1863.

MAJOR : — In answer to yours just received, I have the honor to make the following statement : —

About two miles this side of Kelly's Ford, at Brown's house, I think, I met Captain White falling back from his picket line. He reported that five regiments of infantry and a large amount of cavalry had crossed the river, and were slowly advancing towards the railroad. Just then the enemy's line of skirmishers emerged from the woods, and I at once dismounted a large portion of my command and made such disposition of my entire force as seemed best calculated to retard their progress. I immediately sent scouting parties to my right, and went forward myself to ascertain what was transpiring there. I soon learned that the enemy was advancing upon the Brandy Station road, and despatched Captain Worthington with the information. Soon afterwards the enemy was reported marching upon Stevensburg in large force. I ordered Lieutenant Holcombe to report the fact to the major-general commanding, who informed me that a force had been sent to Stevensburg, and that troops were at Brandy Station. Before receiving this message I had contemplated making an attack in rear should it meet the general's approval. I therefore sent Lieutenant James Johnston to report to General Stuart, who sent me orders to hold my front. A division of my force was impossible, as I needed them all.

I consider it extremely fortunate that my command was not withdrawn from the position it occupied (which was a very strong one), as the enemy's force, consisting of infantry, artillery, and cavalry, were marching directly upon the right flank of our troops engaged in front of Rappahannock Station. I had not force sufficient to hold in check (and it was vitally important to do so) this body, and at the same time follow the flanking party. All the facts may be summed up as follows : Before my arrival the enemy's cavalry had turned off to the points upon which they intended to march. They had posted artillery, cavalry, and infantry so as to cover this movement, or if unopposed march upon the railroad. Had I pursued the flanking party, the road I was ordered to defend would have been left utterly exposed. I acted according to orders and the dictates of judgment.

I came to this army resolved that my official conduct should meet the approbation of my military superiors, and whenever in their opinion I deserve censure I shall most cheerfully submit to official investigation.   Very respectfully, major,

Your obedient servant,

B. H. ROBERTSON,
Brigadier-General Commanding Cavalry.

Major H. B. McCLELLAN,
Assistant Adjutant-General, Headquarters Cavalry Division.

[Indorsement.]

HEADQUARTERS CAVALRY DIVISION, *June* 15, 1863.

Respectfully forwarded. It is very clear that General Robertson intended to do what was right. At the time Lieutenant Johnston reported to me it was too late for any movement to have been made from General Robertson's front, and it would have been extremely hazardous for him to have interposed his command between the enemy's infantry and artillery and the column of cavalry that had already passed on his right flank. At the time he arrived on the spot it is presumed he could have made the detachment to get to the front of the flanking column and delay its progress.

J. E. B. STUART,
Major-General.

HEADQUARTERS CAVALRY BRIGADE, *June* 15, 1863.

MAJOR:— Early on the morning of the 9th instant Captain White, commanding outposts, reported the enemy crossing in force at Kelly's Ford with cavalry and infantry, three regiments of the latter having passed at the time this despatch was written. I immediately announced this intelligence to the major-general commanding, and shortly afterwards received instructions to proceed with my command in that direction, to hold the enemy in check, and protect the right flank of our forces, then engaged between Rappahannock and Beverly fords. Another courier from Captain White informed me that five regiments of infantry, several regiments of cavalry with artillery, had crossed and were moving slowly up the river. I at once despatched this information to headquarters.

About two miles from Kelly's I met Captain White, and learned that the enemy was then occupying a piece of woods directly on our front. Dismounting a portion of my men and deploying them as skirmishers, I made such disposition of the remainder as in my judgment would successfully resist the enemy's further advance. I then reconnoitred his position, and ascertained that some of his cavalry had gone in the direction of Brandy Station, which fact I communicated to Major-General Stuart through Captain Worthington, of my staff.

Upon further investigation I learned that several cavalry regiments had taken the road to Stevensburg via Willis Madden's, and reported the same through Lieutenant Holcombe, from whom I learned that a force to meet them had been sent in the directions above stated. I therefore determined to hold the ground in my front should the infantry attempt to advance upon the railroad, and placed my skirmishers behind an embankment (parallel to a ditch) to protect them from the artillery which had been opened from the woods.

Soon after firing commenced I received orders to fall rapidly back towards Brandy, as the enemy was in my rear and had probably turned my left. When I reached the railroad I discovered on my right a considerable force of the enemy's infantry. At this point a courier from the major-general commanding directed me to advance rapidly with one regiment and report to him, as the enemy had possession of his headquarters. I selected the 63d, which was in front, and pushed rapidly forward, sending instructions to Colonel Ferebee to cover my rear and right.

The enemy having retired before my arrival, I was ordered to support General Hampton, who was making preparations to pursue. Soon afterwards, the enemy displaying a large force in our immediate front, apparently with the intention of attacking, I drew my two regiments up in line of battle and awaited his advance. His columns advancing to our left, one of my regiments was ordered in that direction. I accompanied it and deployed it as skirmishers dismounted, to hold that end of the line in case it should be pressed. The other regiment I instructed to report to Brigadier-General Hampton.

When General Lee was wounded I was ordered to command the left wing, and saw nothing more of my brigade. Although in sight of the enemy for many hours and exposed to the fire of his artillery, my command was not at any time actively engaged. With the exception of four horses mortally wounded or totally disabled, I have no casualties to report. Very respectfully, major,

Your obedient servant,

B. H. ROBERTSON,
Brigadier-General Commanding Cavalry.

Major H. B. McCLELLAN,
Assistant Adjutant-General, Headquarters Cavalry Division.

[Indorsement.]

HEADQUARTERS CAVALRY DIVISION ARMY OF
NORTHERN VIRGINIA, *June* 20, 1863.

Respectfully forwarded to accompany my report of the battle of Fleetwood. The enemy having been reported moving by Madden's to Stevensburg, two regiments (2d South Carolina and 4th Virginia) were sent to the latter place, but a portion of the enemy was detached from this column and sent to Brandy, where, as at Fleetwood, they were soon routed by Jones' and Hampton's brigades. Nothing of any value was at Brandy. My own headquarters' baggage having been sent off early to the rear, the place spoken of as my headquarters was a high hill (Fleetwood), where they had been, but had early in the day been transferred to the field, — everything packed and sent off. General Robertson's report appears satisfactory.

J. E. B. STUART,
Major-General.

EDITOR'S NOTES.

—·—

CHAPTER 1

Page 3. McClellan erred in enumerating the children of Archibald and Elizabeth Stuart, according to General Stuart's granddaughter, Mrs. Virginia Waller Davis of Alexandria, Va. Her statement to the editor, in 1956, was that there were eleven, and not ten, children.

Page 7. Emory & Henry College, Emory, Va., does not now have Stuart's academic records, but the U. S. Military Academy, in records of 1850-54, has a complete Stuart file. Some samples:

At the end of his plebe year, Stuart was eighth in a class of 71 in general merit; eighth in mathematics, fifteenth in French, twelfth in English. In conduct he stood No. 82 among 229 cadets, with only 43 demerits. The second year saw little change.

"Delinquencies for the Year of 1853" show Stuart at play: Loudness and boisterousness, bedding out of order, improper uniform, tardiness for drill, taking civilians on sentry posts (perhaps girls), "raising hands at parade," "swinging arms marching," dirty shoes, untidy room, and "loitering" were all listed as his military sins.

In addition to the comments of Fitz Lee cited by McClellan, Robert Lee's talented nephew wrote of Jeb: " 'Beauty' Stuart he was then universally called, for however manly and soldierly in appearance he afterwards grew, in those days his comrades bestowed that appellation upon him to express their idea of his personal comeliness in inverse ratio to the term employed."

Many letters from Stuart to a kinswoman, Bettie Hairston, and others, during the West Point years are in Louis R. Wilson Library, University of North Carolina, the Southern Historical Collection. Among them are his first known pledge of support to the Democratic Party and States' Rights, and a revealing statement on his future as a soldier: "Had you not rather see your cousin a bold Dragoon than a petty-fogger lawyer?"

CHAPTER 3

Page 19. Stuart's courtship of Flora Cooke was brief; he wrote her his first note on July 25, asking her to go horseback riding with him near Fort Riley, and they were married on November 14. In the interim, Jeb wrote a Virginia cousin: "I'm bound to be married before I am 23."

Page 20. Not only did Stuart meet John Brown in Kansas; he became acquainted with Henry Clay Pate, who was deeply involved in the struggle over slavery in that state, and was later to ride with Stuart's cavalry. Among 1st Cavalry officers to rise to prominence in the Civil War were Edwin V. Sumner, Joseph E. Johnston, John Sedgwick, and George B. McClellan.

CHAPTER 4

Page 28. Stuart's saber attachment was Patent No. 25,684, of October 24, 1859. Another military invention of his, a "Lightning Horse-Hitcher," evidently was not patented.

Page 29. Invaluable light on Stuart's personality and his views on slavery is shed by a New York *Herald* report on the John Brown raid, published October 21, 1859. Stuart twice broke into the interview between the wounded captive, Brown, and Virginia leaders who interrogated him:

Brown: "I hold that the Golden Rule, 'Do unto others as you would have them do unto you,' applies to all who would help others to gain their liberty."

Stuart: "But you don't believe in the Bible."

Brown: "Certainly I do." . . .

Brown: "I was chosen . . . commander-in-chief."

Sen. J. M. Mason: "What wages did you offer?"

Brown: "None."

Stuart: "The wages of sin is death."

Brown: "I would not have made such a remark to you, if you had been a prisoner and wounded in my hands."

One result of Stuart's experiences at the capture of Brown was his letter to Virginia's Governor Henry Wise, pointing out "the exposed situation of Virginia to attack from the North," and urging him to provide uniforms for militia companies.

CHAPTER 5

Page 31. Stuart did not wait, as McClellan intimates, for the secession of Virginia before casting his lot with the South. In January, 1861, before he was aware of the resignation of Jefferson Davis from the U. S. Senate, he wrote him "as one likely to exercise a large control in the organization of the Army of the South," asking that he save him a place, and put his application on file.

He also wrote a brother, William Alexander Stuart, on January 18: "Events are transpiring rapidly that furnish so little hope of perpetuating the Union, that I feel it incumbent upon me to tell you my course of conduct in such an emergency. Of course I go with Virginia, whether she be alone or otherwise."

In a later letter to William, he added: "If no war ensues upon Virginia's secession, I will quit the army, and if I can obtain no desirable position in her [Virginia's] regular army, I will resign and practice law in Memphis, Tenn. . . . I had rather be a private in Va.'s army than a general in any army to coerce her."

Pages 35-40. McClellan, relying upon Early, may have overstated Stuart's claim to fame as a factor for Confederate victory at First Manassas; yet there is no contradictory evidence, and the rout of the New York Zouaves contributed to Federal flight, if it did not initiate it. Readers should consult W. W. Blackford's *War Years with Jeb Stuart* (New York, 1946), pp. 23-41.

Pages 41-46. Most of Stuart's contributions to Confederate cavalry success date from the months following First Manassas, when he taught green troops bold tactics, the secrets of survival in the field, gathering intelligence, and screening the infantry. Especially enlightening is the testimony of a trooper, George C. Eggleston (in *A Rebel's Recollections,* pp. 110 ff., and *Recollections of a Varied Life,* pp. 78 ff.).

From his handling of the training cadres, it is obvious that Stuart's concept of cavalry was in the classic tradition, and that he did not, as did a few contemporaries, regard the arm as mounted infantry. It is possible to argue that Stuart's orthodox view of the uses of cavalry resulted in the failure of that arm to achieve decisive strategic objectives for the Army of Northern Virginia.

CHAPTER 6

McClellan makes no mention of Stuart's difficulties with Richmond during the war; in this winter of Confederate withdrawal Jefferson Davis was sharply critical of the cavalryman, and after one complaint by the infantryman, General D. H. Hill, the President wrote Joseph Johnston: "The letter of General Hill painfully impresses me with that which has heretofore been indicated—a want of vigilance and intelligent observation on the part of General Stuart. The officers commanding his pickets should be notified of all roads in their neighborhood, and sleepless watchfulness should be required of them." (*Official Records,* Vol. 5, p. 1063.)

Page 47. The winter months were vital to Stuart, since it was then that he acquired his Horse Artillery and some young gunners who were to become famous, especially Major John Pelham and Captain James Breathed. He also acquired in this period several scouts who would render fine service, including William D. Farley and Redmond Burke.

Page 49. The skirmish between Colonel Goode's scouting party and the Federals is detailed in the thinly-disguised fictional account by John Esten Cooke in *Wearing of the Gray,* with the role of William Farley featured on pp. 146, 411, and 437. In this account Farley is called "Darrell." A few hours after the brush with enemy cavalry, Farley led an impetuous charge of Confederate infantry on the overgrown battlefield of Williamsburg.

Page 51. Stuart made a report of sorts on Williamsburg in a letter to his wife, a document evidently not available to McClellan. It said in part: "Blessed be God that giveth *us* the victory. The battle of Wmsburg was fought and won on the 5th. A glorious affair. . . . On the 4th my Brigade distinguished itself, and on the 5th by its attitude and maneuvering under constant fire prevented the enemy's leaving the woods for the open ground—thus narrowing his artillery scope of fire. . . . For *myself* I have only to say that if you had seen your husband you would have been proud of him. I was not out of fire the whole day."

Page 51. McClellan dismisses the battle of Seven Pines with such haste that he does not chronicle the wounding of General J. E. Johnston, whom Stuart thought "head and shoulders above every other" Confederate general, and his "dearest friend." With Johnston's wounding, Robert E. Lee took command of the Army of Northern Virginia. A few weeks earlier Stuart had written of his new chief: "With profound personal regard for General Lee, he has disappointed me as a General."

CHAPTER 7

Pages 52-53. There were two preliminaries to the order from R. E. Lee to Stuart which resulted in the breath-taking raid around McClellan's army. One, documented only by a participant, Colonel John S. Mosby, was an exploratory scout by Mosby and a small party, on Stuart's orders. The second was a proposed plan of battle from Stuart to Lee (the original is in Confederate Memorial Institute, Richmond), which resembled the final plan only in boldness of spirit. Stuart wrote in part: "We have an army far better adapted to attack than defense. Let us fight at an advantage before we are forced to fight at a disadvantage. It may seem presumption in me to give these views but I have not thus far mistaken the policy and practice of the enemy. At any rate, I would rather incur the charge of presumption than fold my arms in silence and indifference to the momentous crisis at hand. Be assured, however, General, that whatever course you pursue you will find nowhere a more zealous and determined cooperator and supporter. . . . "

Pages 54-67. Though McClellan got excitement into his narrative of this raid, readers seeking the color of eyewitness reports should see Heros von Borcke (in *Memoirs of the Confederate War for Independence*), John Esten Cooke (in *Wearing of the Gray*), John S. Mosby (in his *Memoirs*), and the *Official Records,* Vol. 11, Parts 1 and 3. The latter source contains scores of accounts, and the Federal entries, in particular, highlight the drama of the chase of Stuart by his father-in-law, General Philip St. George Cooke, who commanded on the sector involved.

Page 55. "Adjutant Robbins" was properly Lieutenant W. T. Robins, who won Stuart's praise for gallantry in his report on this raid.

Page 68. The most accurate source known to the editor on the burial of Captain Latané is a memoir of Mrs. Kate B. Newton Christian, a granddaughter of an eyewitness. It is owned (1958) by J. Ambler Johnston, of Richmond, Va.

Pages 69-70. Stuart's report of the raid is in *Official Records,* Vol. 11, Part 1, pp. 1038 ff. Lively and unique details are in the war diaries of John Esten Cooke, in Duke University Library, Durham, N. C.

In an interesting footnote to this raid by Stuart, the exact route was traveled by the Richmond Civil War Round Table by automobile in October, 1956. The logged distance was 100.1 miles.

CHAPTER 8

Pages 72-74. McClellan, with the 3rd Virginia Cavalry, was again left behind when Stuart joined Jackson on the upper wing of Lee's audacious attack, and in consequence added little to the sketchy narrative of Jeb's role around Totopotomoy Creek. The skirmishing of cavalry was brief and light.

John Esten Cooke, who was at Stuart's side during June 27, wrote of "shelling hotter than I ever knew it . . . I followed Stuart here, there, everywhere." And, near the end of the day, when Federal infantry was hurled back: "Musketry terrible. Artillery duel in full roar. . . . Enemy trying it last time. . . . Stuart and Jackson in thickest of it. . . . Went forward. . . . Our guns belching flame, and throwing shovelsful of fiery cinders from muzzles. Enemy's batteries silenced. Found Stuart, rode forward with him."

There was a brief cavalry action in a field near Gaines' Mill, in which Stuart routed some Union Lancers. Major von Borcke described the charge: "But before our Virginia horsemen got within fifty yards of their line, this magnificent regiment . . . turned tail and fled in disorder, strewing the whole line of their retreat with their magnificent but inconvenient arms. The entire skirmish was over in less time than is required to record it; and I do not believe that out of the whole body of 700 men more than twenty retained their lances."

Page 76. The nature of the ground of the Seven Days' fighting probably doomed cavalry to a secondary role; in any event, Stuart was away from headquarters from June 28 until the morning of July 2, when he came into position near Jackson at Malvern Hill.

Surviving records do not present a thorough résumé of Stuart's role of the week. It appears that he left the main army on the orders of R. E. Lee, to pass Ewell's infantry as it moved down the Chickahominy. Whether his subsequent further forays were on his own initiative is not clear.

One witness with a view otherwise unsupported is J. Churchill Cooke, in *Confederate Veteran,* July, 1931, p. 248: "The morning after the battle of Mechanicsville, Jackson ordered me to find General Stuart and order him to report immediately. . . . I had not the least idea where to find him. . . . A cavalryman told me he had gone to the White House. . . . I reported to General Jackson. He became very angry and said he would dismount every cavalryman and put them in the ranks."

None of this is reflected in reports on the week's fighting —though this is almost the only phase of the Confederate operations on which there was not bitter controversy.

Pages 83-85. Criticism of Stuart's attack at Evelington Heights seems to have originated with Colonel Walter Taylor. McClellan's stout defense of his chief might have been strengthened by citing the records in detail, for Stuart advised R. E. Lee of the situation when he opened fire on the exposed Federal camp, around 9 A.M. of July 3, and was told that the infantry of Jackson and Longstreet would support him. At 2 P.M., when artillery ammunition was depleted, Stuart learned that Longstreet's men had taken the wrong road, and were yet six miles away. Thus Stuart abandoned the hill which was the key to the riverside position of the Federal army.

CHAPTER 9

Page 88. When Mosby was captured he carried a letter from Stuart to Jackson as recommendation: "General—The bearer, John S. Mosby, late 1st Lieutenant of 1st Virginia Cavalry, is en route to scout beyond the enemy's lines toward Manassas and Fairfax. He is bold, daring, intelligent and discreet. The information he may obtain and transmit to you may be relied upon, and I have no doubt that he will soon give additional proofs of his value. . . ."

Mosby's capture gave him an opportunity to spy on Federal troop movements from Fortress Monroe, and he was at least a factor in R. E. Lee's shrewd transfer of infantry strength from the Richmond front to Northern Virginia, where he would smash the invasion attempt led by John Pope. See Mosby's *Memoirs,* pp. 130 ff.

Page 89. McClellan does not mention the battle of Cedar Mountain, or Slaughter Mountain, fought by Jackson against Pope's vanguard on August 9. Stuart's role here was as an observer during a truce, and an inspector of cavalry which, under General Beverly Robertson, had caused Jackson concern. Stuart on the field of truce was sketched by George Alfred Townsend, a reporter for the New York *Herald,* who thought Jeb had a kind of "airiness," and was prone to speak of his own prowess. Townsend's observations are in *Rustics in Rebellion*, p. 241; other details of Stuart on this day are recorded by Captain C. M. Blackford, in *War Letters From Lee's Army*, p. 110, and Captain W. W. Blackford, in *War Years with Jeb Stuart*, p. 98, note.

Pages 89-91. The Verdiersville escapade, one of the minor highlights of Stuart's war career, is reported in detail by Mosby in his *Memoirs* and other accounts, by von Borcke, by J. E. Cooke in *Wearing of the Gray*, pp. 204 ff.—and by Stuart in *Official Records*, Vol. 12, Part 2, p. 275. The accounts of Mosby and von Borcke, in particular, are in direct conflict, but from all these sources a lively narrative can be constructed. For a synthesis, see Davis, *Jeb Stuart: The Last Cavalier*, pp. 161 ff.

Pages 94-95. The raid to Catlett's Station, as R. E. Lee wrote Jefferson Davis, "accomplished some minor advantages, destroyed some wagons, and captured some prisoners."

Stuart's own view of it went into his report: "What a demoralizing effect the success of this expedition had upon the army of the enemy, shaking their confidence in a general who had scorned the enterprise and ridiculed the courage of his adversaries. . . . It compelled him to make heavy detachments from his main body. It inflicted a mortifying disaster upon the general himself in the loss of his personal baggage and part of his staff."

Perhaps the most telling summation of Stuart's work at Catlett's Station was set down by George Neese, a young gunner, in his *Three Years in the Confederate Horse Artillery* (p. 102): "Raiding with General Stuart is poor fun and a hard business. Thunder, lightning, rain, storm nor darkness can stop him when he is on a warm fresh trail of Yankee game. This morning our battery, guns, horses and men look as if the whole business had passed through a shower of yellow mud last night."

Pages 96-104. The Stuart-Trimble controversy, which raged in the following winter, looms strangely large in the eyes of modern readers. After all, the army swept Pope's forces out of Virginia, so that almost everyone soon forgot Bristoe Station and the details of that raid.

After Second Manassas, Stuart wrote of Trimble's official report that it "does the cavalry injustice. . . . There seems to be a growing tendency to abuse and underrate the services of that arm by a few officers of infantry, among whom I regret to find General Trimble. Troops should be taught to take pride in other branches of service than their own."

Pages 104-107. The role of Stuart's cavalry at Groveton and Second Manassas was minor, though on the first day when Jackson faced the enemy alone, Major John Pelham and the Stuart Horse Artillery won Stonewall's heart, and a place of honor in his report. Stuart added: "Pelham is always in the right place at the right time."

During the night of August 30-31 Stuart came under enemy fire and, according to Major von Borcke, narrowly escaped. In the severe fighting of the thirtieth, Longstreet observed with amazement as Stuart reported to R. E. Lee at head-quarters, and, when asked to wait: "Turned round in his tracks, lay down on the ground, put a stone under his head and fell instantly asleep." (*Battles & Leaders,* Vol. 2, p. 525.)

Cavalry aided at the end of Second Manassas, when the combined strength of Jackson and Longstreet drove Pope from the field, and Stuart wrote with characteristic verve: "About 3 P.M. our right wing advanced to the attack. I directed Robertson's brigade and Rosser's regiment to push forward on the extreme right, and at the same time all the batteries that I could get hold of here advanced at a gallop to take position to enfilade the enemy in front of our lines. This was done with splendid effect, Colonel Rosser, a splendid artillerist as well as a bold cavalier, having the immediate direction of the batteries.

"The fight was of remarkably short duration. The Lord of Hosts was plainly fighting on our side, and the solid walls of Federal infantry melted away before the straggling but determined onset of our infantry columns."

Stuart thought a final swoop of Robertson's troopers after the fleeing enemy gave them "a claim for courage and discipline equal to any cavalry in the world."

Page 109. On September 4 Stuart wrote his wife, in part: "Long before this reaches you I will be in Maryland. I have not been able to keep the list of battles, much less give you any account of them. Our present position on the banks of the Potomac will tell you volumes. . . . all the officers on the other side speak kindly of me. May God bless you.

"I send $200 in draft and $50 in notes. Can you pay my tailor bill?

"The Horse Artillery has won imperishable laurels!"

CHAPTER 10

Page 111. McClellan does not mention one of the most ingratiating scenes of Stuart and his staff at war—the famous dance at Urbana on September 8 which was interrupted by a Federal raid, and continued after midnight despite the necessity for a second roundup of Urbana ladies. This dance, held in an abandoned academy building, was ended at last by the arrival of Confederate wounded on stretchers. Women left the dance floor to nurse the casualties. William Blackford and von Borcke left detailed accounts of the evening.

Page 113. "Gov. Curtain" is Alexander Curtin.

Pages 116-18. The natural confusion of a rearguard action along mountain peaks obscures events involving Stuart here. General D. H. Hill was surprised that Stuart did not hold all the assigned passes, and Jeb's own report has a defensive ring as he attempts to explain his withdrawal which permitted Federal attacks: "This was obviously no place for cavalry operations, a single horseman passing from place to place on the mountain with difficulty."

After the fighting at Crampton's Gap, however, Stuart fought his handful bravely in open country just to the west, and when he got word of Jackson's conquest of Harper's Ferry, took them gaily over the river. Von Borcke wrote of the moment: "Stuart now came back to us, and was so delighted that he threw his arms around my neck and said. 'My dear Von, isn't this glorious? You must gallop with me to congratulate old Stonewall.' "

Pages 126-27. According to William Blackford (in *War*

Years, p. 148), R. E. Lee began his defense at Sharpsburg by ordering Stuart to probe Federal skirmish lines on his left. Stuart in turn sent Blackford with a few men, who found the enemy advancing in earnest.

Stuart's part in Sharpsburg was limited to fighting twenty-five guns of his Horse Artillery on Jackson's front, and to leading a small reconnaissance party to the river on the Confederate left, in a vain effort to launch a flanking attack for Stonewall.

Stuart's report after Sharpsburg said in part: "My command did not suffer on any one day as much as their comrades of other arms, but theirs was the sleepless watch and the harassing daily *petite guerre*, in which the aggregate of casualties sums up heavily. There was not a single day, from the time my command crossed the Potomac . . . . that it was not engaged with the enemy."

CHAPTER 11

Page 136. By this time Confederate gossips were whispering tales of Stuart, his officers, and the young women who attended parties and dances at cavalry headquarters, but William Blackford wrote: "Though he dearly loved to kiss a pretty girl, and the pretty girls loved to kiss him, he was as pure as they . . . I know this to be true, for it would have been impossible for it to have been otherwise and I not to have known it."

Pages 142-47. This appears to be one of the rare instances in which McClellan withheld evidence which might tend to put Stuart in an unfavorable light. The cited source of A. K. McClure is his *Lincoln and Men of War Times*, p. 372, and in addition to the scene chosen by McClellan, McClure reported that Hugh Logan told him he was not safe on his parole. When McClure protested that Wade Hampton had given his word, Logan replied: "Hampton gave it to you. And if you are arrested and can reach Hampton, he will parole you, for he's a gentleman. But Jeb Stuart wants you, and I'm not sure he would let you go on parole."

An addition to McClellan's reports on behavior of Confederate troops in Chambersburg was made by Lieutenant Channing Price, the acting adjutant, who outfitted himself anew from a Federal depot there. (Price left the most valuable source on the entire raid, in a letter to his mother, now in the Southern Historical Collection, L. R. Wilson Library, University of North Carolina.

A Gettysburg newspaper report added: "The whole town was converted into one vast dressing room. On every hotel porch, at every corner, on the greater portion of the street doorsteps, might be seen Rebel cavalry donning Yankee uniforms, and throwing their own worn out and faded garments into the street. Each took as many coats, hats and pairs of pants as he could conveniently handle." (From J. Melchoir Sheads, "Border Raids into Pennsylvania during the Civil War," unpublished history thesis, Gettysburg College, 1933; this cites the Gettysburg *Compiler*, no date.)

Page 147. McClellan neglected to record that the expedition failed in one of its important objectives, the destruction of a railroad bridge over the Conococheague, which turned out to be built of iron, and was impervious to the axes and torches of Stuart's raiders.

Page 168. The "Capt. McClellan" referred to here is the author's brother, Captain Carswell McClellan.

Chapter 12

Page 177. A personal tragedy for Stuart is omitted by McClellan here. On November 1 he learned from his brother-in-law, Dr. Charles Brewer, that his daughter, young Flora, was seriously ill, and wrote his wife: "I was at no loss to decide that it was my duty to you and to Flora to remain here. I am entrusted with the conduct of affairs, the issue of which will affect you, her, and the mothers and children of our whole country much more seriously than we can believe.

"If my darling's case is hopeless there are ten chances to one that I will get to Lynchburg too late; if she is convalescent why should my presence be necessary? She was sick nine days before I knew it. Let us trust in the good God, who has blessed us so much, that he will spare our child to us, but if it should please Him to take her from us, let us bear it with Christian fortitude and resignation." (*Southern Historical Society Papers,* Vol. 8, p. 454.)

Page 190. Early in the fighting at Fredericksburg Stuart sent a report to Robert Lee: "Jackson has not advanced, but I have, and I am going to crowd them with artillery." (J. E. Cooke in his *Stonewall Jackson,* p. 375.) After this ringing announcement Jeb sent Major John Pelham into the open with two guns, only one of which survived, and the young gunner made his most famous appearance of the war, as sketched by McClellan on pages 193-95.

Page 195. Captain Charles Blackford, in *Mines Eyes Have Seen the Glory,* by L. Minor Blackford, p. 209, reports that Stuart ordered a rash cavalry charge at Fredericksburg which Charles Blackford and Fitz Lee thought would become "a second Balaklava"—and that it was cancelled by Stonewall Jackson, who feared every man involved would be killed.

CHAPTER 13

Page 211. The meager account of Pelham's death given here should be supplemented by Harry Gilmor's *Four Years in the Saddle,* pp. 64 ff; and by H. H. Matthewe in *Southern Historical Society Papers,* Vol. 38, p. 379.

Blackford, writing not long before Pelham's death, saw Stuart's affection for the young gunner: "Stuart loved him like a younger brother, and could not bear for him to be away from him." Pelham had, in fact, literally run away from cavalry headquarters when he stumbled onto the scene of fighting at Kelly's Ford.

A minor error in McClellan's account (p. 211) is that "Major Fuller" was Major J. W. Puller, a casualty of the day.

Page 217. Stuart's most impassioned orders went to the cavalry after Pelham's death: "He fell the noblest of sacrifices on the altar of his country." And to his wife he wrote: "You know how his death distresses me. He was noble in every sense of the word. I want Jimmie to be just like him." Writing of Pelham and his own baby boy seemed to stir Stuart to even stronger emotions, for he added : "I wish an assurance on your part in the event of your surviving me—*that you will make the land for which I have given my life your home and keep my offspring on Southern soil.*"

(In after years "Jimmie," who was J. E. B. Stuart, Jr., spent most of his life in New York City, and his son, J. E. B., III, was in 1958 an engineer there with Consolidated Edison.)

CHAPTER 14

Page 218. Stuart was acutely conscious of his weakness at this period, since a total of 2,700 troopers covered the front "from the Chesapeake to the Blue Ridge," as he put it. Hundreds of men were at home, as far away as Mississippi, seeking new mounts for the spring campaign.

Stuart confided his outlook for the future to John Esten Cooke : "If there is a Spring campaign, it will last through the year, and if so, it will go on to the end of Lincoln's time."

Pages 227-29. Stuart's vigilance at the opening of Chancellorsville was questioned by no major critics, but the cavalryman himself may have felt his shortcomings. His letter to R. E. Lee which prompted the following reply from the commander-in-chief is believed to be lost, but the text leaves little to the imagination : "As regards the closing remarks of your note, I am at a loss to understand their reference or to know what has given rise to them. In the management of the difficult operations at Chancellorsville, which you so promptly understood and creditably performed, I saw no errors to correct, nor has there been a fit opportunity to commend your conduct. I prefer your acts to speak for themselves, nor does your character or reputation require bolstering up by out-of-place expressions of my opinion."

Page 232. Evelina Wellford, who lived near the spot of Price's wounding, described in a letter the officer's arrival at her house. Price died there at midnight of April 30, and though officers said Stuart was too grief-stricken to rest, Evelina Wellford wrote : "General Stuart and his staff remained until after breakfast next morning. They slept under the trees in the yard and seemed to have a good time." The letter is owned by McDonald Wellford of Richmond, Va.

Page 233. The flank march of Jackson, one of the war's most decisive, is sketchily presented here. Stuart's role in the movement was to help find a route, and, through Fitz Lee, to fix the position of the exposed Federal flank. Other than this, and the support of Horse Artillery in the opening of the attack, the cavalry did not aid in Jackson's coup.

Page 236. Stuart had his first order from R. E. Lee about daylight of May 3: "It is necessary that the glorious victory thus far achieved be prosecuted with the utmost vigor, and the enemy given no time to rally. As soon, therefore, as it is possible, they must be pressed, so that we may unite the two wings of the army. Endeavor, therefore, to dispossess them of Chancellorsville, which will permit the union of the whole army."

In the light of subsequent criticism of the recklessness of Stuart's infantry attacks against the village of Chancellorsville, Lee's order seems vital. It left no recourse but immediate attack.

Stuart, in his first and only major infantry command, led with such daring as to astonish witnesses. Colonel W. L. Goldsmith of the Georgia troops thought Jeb's dash "the bravest act I ever saw."

Page 256. R. E. Lee praised Jeb Stuart, though he did not agree with Alexander as to Stuart's future value as an infantry commander. Stuart wrote his wife: "God has spared me through another bloody battle and given us the victory yesterday and the day before. I commanded Jackson's corps."

When he was told by Colonel Thomas Rosser that the dying Stonewall Jackson had asked that Stuart succeed him, Jeb said: "I would rather know that Jackson said that than to have the appointment."

CHAPTER 15

From this point McClellan was an intimate witness at cavalry headquarters. He had been Assistant Adjutant

General since April 20, but with the death of Channing Price he took over duties which made him the equivalent of the modern chief of staff.

Page 261. The relative inefficiency of Confederate cavalry resulting from poor horses and arms was growing rapidly more evident in 1863, as a result of the farsighted policy of the Union army, whose horses were furnished by the government. This at first worked in favor of the South, for the limited supply of fine blooded plantation horses was the best stock on the continent, and Virginia cavalrymen, in particular, were superbly mounted in the early months of fighting. Now, in May, 1863, Stuart's regiments rode the last of the serviceable mounts from farms of the South.

Pages 261-62. This is the most famous of Stuart's wartime reviews, which won for him warm praise and bitter criticism. His gunner, George Neese, sketched the cavalry chief on the first day of the parading squadrons: "He was superbly mounted and his side arms gleamed in the morning sun like burnished silver. A long black ostrich plume waved gracefully from a black slouch hat cocked up on one side, held with a golden clasp. . . . He is the prettiest and most graceful rider I ever saw. I could not help but notice with what natural ease and comely elegance he sat his steed as it bounded over the field . . . he and his horse appeared to be one and the same machine."

Neese thought the review "one grand magnificent pageant, inspiring enough to make even an old woman feel fightish."

Page 264. McClellan's narrative tends to obscure the extent to which Stuart was surprised by Federal attacks over the Rappahannock early on June 9. Two boy soldiers in the front ranks whose memoirs are of value are Luther Hopkins (*From Bull Run to Appomattox*) and George Neese (*Three Years in the Confederate Horse Artillery*).

A few days after the battle the tart Richmond *Examiner* said: "The more the circumstances of the late affair at Brandy Station are considered, the less pleasant do they appear. If this was an isolated case, it might be excused under the convenient head of accident or chance. But this puffed up cavalry of the

Army of Northern Virginia has been twice, if not three times, surprised since the battles of December, and such repeated accidents can be regarded as nothing but the necessary consequences of negligence and bad management. . . . "

Page 295. Though Stuart saved his headquarters baggage, as McClellan says, he was forced to move his tents from Fleetwood Hill, which was littered with corpses of men and horses and swarming with flies.

Casualties of this greatest of the war's cavalry engagements were some 900 for the Federals and over 500 for Stuart. Stuart's resulting order to his men regarded the affair as a triumph and took no note of the fact that he had been taken by surprise: "Comrades, two divisions of the enemy's cavalry and artillery, escorted by a strong force of infantry, 'tested your metal' and found it 'proof steel'. . . . Your saber blows, inflicted on that glorious day, have taught them again the weight of Southern vengeance. . . . Nothing but the enemy's infantry strongly posted in the woods saved his cavalry from capture or annihilation. An act of rashness on his part was severely punished by rout and the loss of his artillery. With an abiding faith in the God of battles and a firm reliance on the saber, your success will continue."

CHAPTER 16

Page 303. In one of his books Colonel Mosby gave a glimpse of Stuart in Middleburg this day, when the cavalryman was surrounded by women in the street: "The scene looked like a dance around a maypole. It lasted an hour or so until they heard the guns." (*Stuart's Cavalry in the Gettysburg Campaign,* p. 62.)

Page 307. The wounding of von Borcke is graphically described by William Blackford in *War Years* (pp. 218 ff.), and his work, with that of Mosby cited above, supplements McClellan's fine narrative of this mountain fighting. The detailed movements of troops presented by McClellan should not obscure the larger picture—the vital matter was that Stuart was screening Lee's infantry by holding the passes of the Bull Run Mountains and the approaches to the Blue Ridge, which lay just to the west.

CHAPTER 17

Pages 315-17. These days of late June, 1863, are vital in a study of Stuart, or of Gettysburg. In general, the difficult situation of the Confederate command was this:

Lee's infantry was beginning to cross the Potomac into Maryland, toward an as-yet-unselected target to the north. Lee was himself west of the Blue Ridge, near the river; Longstreet was behind him, and Stuart still farther behind on the hills of the infantry's eastern flank.

Federal forces were in general east of the Bull Run Mountains, thought to be moving on a parallel route northward toward the Potomac.

Lee's concern for the moves of General Joseph Hooker (in his last days of command of the Army of the Potomac) were made clear in all dispatches to Stuart. The orders, however, passed through Longstreet's hands as senior commander of the front, a further complication.

On June 22 Lee wrote Stuart, via Longstreet, warning the cavalryman not to allow the enemy to cross the Potomac before him, and to watch Hooker with care: "Do you know where he is and what he is doing? I fear he will steal a march on us, and get across the Potomac before we are aware. If you find that he is moving northward, and that two brigades can guard the Blue Ridge and take care of your rear, you can move with the other three into Maryland and take position on General Ewell's right, place yourself in communication with him, and guard his flank."

In an accompanying note Longstreet approved this plan, but added that the cavalry might cross the river with greater safety by moving in the *rear* of the Federal army, rather than in its front—this, of course, would place the enemy between Stuart and Lee's infantry, a fact evidently appreciated by no one on this day. Ewell, with whom Stuart was to maintain contact, was already far north, moving on Greencastle, Pennsylvania.

On the day of this exchange, Stuart wrote his wife, who had been anxiously inquiring of his safety at army headquarters: "Don't be telegraphing General Lee's Staff or anybody else. If I am hurt you will hear of it very soon."

Page 317. The dispatch from Lee which McClellan failed to find is in *Official Records,* Vol. 27, Part 3, p. 923. Its vital paragraphs are:

"If General Hooker's army remains inactive, you can leave two brigades to watch him, and withdraw with the three others, but should he not appear to be moving northward, I think you had better withdraw this side of the mountains tomorrow night, cross at Shepherdstown next day, and move over to Frederickstown.

"You will, however, be able to judge whether you can pass around their army without hindrance, doing them all the damage you can, and cross the river east of the mountains. In either case, after crossing the river, you must move on and feel the right of Ewell's troops, collecting information, provisions, etc.

"I think the sooner you cross into Maryland, after tomorrow, the better. ... Be watchful and circumspect in all your movements."

In short, though he warned Stuart of virtually every danger to be faced, Lee gave him discretion. The added admonition of Longstreet that Jeb should move only by rear of the enemy made it almost inevitable that Stuart would take the longer, more exposed, route which would lead him far from the main army and make necessary a wide and long-remembered detour. Whether Stuart's absence from Gettysburg during July 1 and early on July 2 was decisive is uncertain despite generations of controversy.

Page 323. Captain Kennon's narrative of the cavalry's crossing, an exciting though brief document, is in the Virginia State Library, Richmond.

Page 331. The condition of Stuart's wagoners on the ride from Carlisle to Gettysburg is thus described by Colonel R. L. T. Beale of the 9th Virginia: "The drivers, suffering in agony for sleep, lay on the road with bridles in hand, some

on rocks, and others on the wet earth, slumbering soundly."
When Stuart ordered an all-night march and Beale protested,
Jeb relented and there was a brief rest. John Esten Cooke
reported that Stuart halted for an hour's rest, sleeping against
a tree trunk in his cape, to mount again "as fresh, apparently,
as if he had slumbered from sunset to dawn."

Page 370. McClellan's vigorous defense of Stuart throughout this chapter (especially in citing the furiously partisan
Jubal Early) goes further than modern critics. Stuart's report
on the battle was written late, despite urging from Lee's staff,
and was in controversy from the moment of its appearance.
Colonel Charles Marshall made no secret of his opinion that
Stuart had failed to obey Lee's instructions. Stuart's staff
regarded Marshall as an enemy to their chief.

Perhaps R. E. Lee hoped to close the controversy over the
campaign when he told General Eppa Hunton (cited in
Hunton's *Autobiography,* p. 98): "It took a dozen blunders
to lose Gettysburg, and I committed a good many of them."

CHAPTER 18

Page 371. Unmentioned here in the shuffling of Stuart's
commanders was the transfer of Beverly Robertson, with
whom Stuart's relations had been none too smooth; Robertson
went to the rear to train new troopers.

A flurry of excitement followed the passing over of W. E.
(Grumble) Jones as division commander. Jones evidently
cursed Jeb, and was arrested. Lee briefly reported to
Jefferson Davis: "I consider General Jones a brave and intelligent officer, but his feelings have become so opposed to
General Stuart that I have lost all hope of his being useful
in the cavalry here. . . . He has been tried by court martial
for disrespect. . . . I understand he says he will no longer
serve under Stuart and I do not think it would be advantageous for him to do so."

Jones went to command in Southwest Virginia, and was
replaced by Thomas Rosser.

Page 371. The minor omissions in rosters on this page are:

Lieutenant Colonel William G. Robinson, 2nd North Carolina; and Colonel Peter G. Evans, 5th North Carolina.

(For some reason the role of North Carolina regiments, particularly cavalry, is relatively little known, though these squadrons were numerous and reliable, often called up in emergencies. Many are concealed in records under the names of Virginia regiments. Valuable research could be done in the field; some historians rank the 1st North Carolina Cavalry, for example, as the finest in Confederate service, yet it is little known.)

Page 375. Stuart's failure to report this sharp fight is unfortunate, for it was one of his most trying days, when disaster seemed near, and lack of an official report tends to reflect discredit on the cavalry commander. R. E. Lee's complaint to Stuart of a few days earlier may contain the reason for Jeb's increasing difficulties: "I think your dismounted men should be speedily organized, and thoroughly drilled as infantry, and armed to be used as infantry, until they can be mounted."

Lee had also written Jefferson Davis: "The cavalry also suffer, and I fear to set them at work. Some days we get a pound of corn per horse and sometimes more; some none . . . You can judge of our prospects."

At Jack's Shop, as McClellan makes clear, Stuart was fortunate to emerge with his skin, and was saved only by the reckless daring of young commanders and hard-riding troopers.

Page 376. On October 9, the day Stuart began the Bristoe Campaign, his third child was born; he named her Virginia Pelham. A day later, after the clash at Culpeper Courthouse which both sides claimed as a victory, the Federal cavalry withdrew north of the Rappahannock, and Stuart led Lee's flanking movement upstream.

Pages 387-93. The amusing episode of Stuart's entrapment at Auburn and his escape is another typical incident in his career. His daring led him into the predicament and his talents extricated him, yet the result was only an embellishment of the Stuart legend; there were no Confederate gains, tactical or strategic.

Stuart did not share this view. In his report he protested

the failure of Lee to push up his infantry to aid the cavalry: "A vigorous attack with our main body at the time that I expected it would have assured the annihilation of that army corps."

Pages 393-96. A far more successful use of Stuart's squadrons was the clever ambush of Federal troopers at "The Buckland Races," a decided setback for Kilpatrick's bluecoat riders. In fairness, however, it must be said that it was Fitz Lee who conceived the trap and made possible its springing.

CHAPTER 19

Page 398. A kindred incident of the Mine Run campaign was related by William Blackford, who, when he took word to Lee that the enemy was moving, saw the commander-in-chief in one of his rare moods of anger. "Captain, if they don't attack us today, we must attack them!" Lee said. "We must attack them, sir! And you young men must exert yourselves!" Lee stamped his foot impatiently. (Blackford in *War Years,* pp. 245-46.)

Page 399. A saddening loss at cavalry headquarters in this period was the death of Sam Sweeney, Stuart's banjoist and leader of his crude "jazz band" composed of bones, fiddles, banjo and guitar. Sweeney died of smallpox. He was a native of Appomattox, Va., one of the earliest blackface minstrels, and brother of Joe Sweeney, the "inventor" of the modern banjo.

Von Borcke was still recuperating from his severe throat wound, and in January Captain Blackford left Stuart for service with the engineers.

CHAPTER 20

Page 409. A glimpse of Stuart on May 8 by George Neese is revealing. One of the artillery drivers was grumbling because he got no breakfast, when Stuart rode by with his staff. Rather than thundering his wrath, as Neese expected, Jeb pulled two biscuits from his own haversack and passed them to the hungry man.

Stuart acted as an infantry officer most of this day, putting into line the regiments of Anderson.

Pages 409-10. Movements of Stuart's cavalry are not quite clear in this narrative. At 8 A.M. on May 9 Stuart wrote R. E. Lee: "There is a demonstration of the enemy's cavalry on the Fredericksburg road about one mile and a half from Spotsylvania Courthouse. If it amounts to anything serious I will be sure to inform you in time to change your dispositions. I have sent a regiment down to engage them and see what it means."

This was the advance of Sheridan on the raid toward Richmond, from 12,000 to 15,000 troopers, stretching for thirteen miles on the Telegraph Road, going south toward the Confederate capital. Stuart, with a handful of his men already attacking, rode eastward across country in an effort to block the raid.

Wickham was in the Federal rear, and Rosser must be left with R. E. Lee's infantry. Thus Stuart had with him only Fitz Lee, and the brigades of James Gordon and Lunsford Lomax. All told, including Wickham's rear-guard force, there were no more than 4,000 Confederate troopers available.

Page 410. The only witness to Stuart's last visit with his wife at Beaver Dam was Major Reid Venable of his staff, whose account is in a letter to Fitz Lee of 1885 date; the original is in the Virginia Historical Society. Venable wrote: "Mrs. Stuart came out, and after a few words of private conversation, the General (not dismounting) bade her a most affectionate farewell."

A few moments afterward, Stuart told Venable he did not expect to live through the war, and that if the South were to be conquered, he did not want to live.

Page 411. Stuart's attitude in the desperate situation may be read in a dispatch he sent General Braxton Bragg in Richmond late on May 10, in which he said of the vastly superior enemy: "I hope to be able to strike him if he endeavors to escape."

Page 412. A dispatch, Stuart to Bragg, at 6:30 A.M., May

11, included the now famous defiance: "My men and horses are all tired, hungry and jaded, but all right."

While McClellan was off in Richmond to carry Stuart's message, Major Theo Garnett of the staff overheard Jeb scold a brigadier who despaired of overtaking Sheridan: "No! I would rather die than let him go!"

For a more detailed account of Yellow Tavern see Davis, *Jeb Stuart: The Last Cavalier*, pp. 395 ff. In particular, the identity of Stuart's probable killer, John A. Huff, Company E, 5th Michigan Cavalry, should be of interest to readers.

Pages 415-17. Other, more complete, versions of Stuart's wounding, his ride into Richmond, and death scene, are in Reid Venable's cited letter to Fitz Lee; von Borcke, Vol. 2, p. 310; *Southern Historical Society Papers*, Vol. 7, p. 140; and T. S. Garnett's *Jeb Stuart*. A brief sketch of Stuart's funeral, though far from satisfactory, is in *Southern Historical Society Papers*, Vol. 7, p. 109.

INDEX.

Peterkin, Rev. Joshua, 417
Pettigrew, Gen. Johnston, CSA, 367
Pleasonton, Gen. Alfred, USA, 110-11, 115, 135, 150-51, 153, 156, 162, 171, 173-74, 179, 180, 237-40, 263, 294, 297, 312-13
Pollard, Lt. James, CSA, 404
Poolesville, Md., 110, 154-55, 160
Pope, Gen. John, USA, 87
Porter, Gen. Fitz John, USA, 60, 72
Posey, Col. Carnot, CSA, 185
Potomac River, 110, 113, 130, 133, 150, 169, 315, 323
Price, Lt. R. Channing, CSA, 191-95; death, 231
Puller ("Fuller"), Maj. J. W., CSA, 211

Quarles, Pvt. J. Thompson, CSA, 343

Radford, Col. R. C. W., CSA, 40
Rapidan River, 92, 226, 374, 376, 406
Rappahannock River, 93-95, 187, 190, 197, 204-206, 218-26, 260-64, 372, 385, 397
Reynolds, Gen. J. F., USA, 63
Richards, Capt. D. T., CSA, 348
Richmond, Va., 403, 412, 415-17
Richmond and Fredericksburg R.R., 219, 403
Robertson, Gen. Beverly H., CSA, 87, 92, 109, 268-69, 318, 336, 347, 349
Rockville, Md., 324-25
Rodes, Gen. Emmett, CSA, 236, 240, 247-48, 254
Rosser, Gen. Thos., CSA, 93, 103, 106-108, 115, 178-79, 180, 194, 198, 211, 297-300, 381-83, 394, 398, 406
Royall, Capt. W. B., USA, 54-58
Rowser's Ford, Va., 323
Rush, Col. Richard, USA, 152-53, 190

Savage Station, Va.; battle of, 79
Scheibert, Major Justus ("I"), CSA, 229n
Second Manassas, battle of, 95-108
Sedgwick, Gen. John, USA, 28
Seven Days' Battles, 72-85
Seven Pines, Va., battle of, 51
Shepherdstown, W. Va., 133
Sharpsburg (Antietam), Md., battle of, 116-35
Sheridan, Gen. Philip H., USA, 409-12
Shiver, Lt. Robt., CSA, 138
Sickles, Gen. D. E., USA, 232, 237
Simonson, Gen. John S., USA, 10-11, 17-19
Smith, Capt. B. H., Jr., CSA, 168
Smith, Col. C. H., USA, 302
Smith, Gen. G. W., CSA, 50-51
Smith, Gen. W. F., USA, 330
South Mountain, Md., 115
Southall, Capt. F. W., CSA, 149, 152, 155
Spencer, Sgt. Sam, CSA, 353-54
Spotsylvania Courthouse, Va., 402, 407-409
Starr, Maj. Samuel H., USA, 348
Stedman, Col. Wm., USA, 300-302
Stoneman, Gen. Geo., USA, 48, 73, 77, 151, 154, 218-23
Strange, Capt. J. W., CSA, 221
Stringfellow, Scout Frank, CSA, 336
Stuart, Alexander, Sr., 1
Stuart, Alexander, II, 2
Stuart, Archibald, Sr., 1
Stuart, Archibald, II, 2-3, 7-9, 19
Stuart, Elizabeth P., 3
Stuart, Flora Cooke, 19, 66, 410, 413
Stuart, J. Hardeman, 107-108
Stuart, Gen. James Ewell Brown, CSA
aggressiveness, 8, 33, 52-58, 76-78, 82-85, 92-93, 152, 156, 173, 318, 338-41, 386-94, 398, 415

Other titles of interest

**A BIRD'S-EYE VIEW
OF OUR CIVIL WAR**
Theodore Ayrault Dodge
376 pp., 47 maps and charts
80845-5 $15.95

**THE LIFE OF GENERAL
ALBERT SIDNEY JOHNSTON
His Services in the Armies of the
United States, the Republic of
Texas, and the Confederate States**
Colonel William Preston Johnston
New introd. by T. Michael Parrish
807 pp., 9 illus., 9 maps
80791-2 $19.95

**CHANCELLORSVILLE AND
GETTYSBURG**
General Abner Doubleday
New introduction by
Gary W. Gallagher
269 pp., 13 maps
80549-5 $13.95

**THE ANNALS OF THE
CIVIL WAR
Written by Leading Participants
North and South**
New introd. by Gary W. Gallagher
808 pp., 56 illus.
80606-1 $21.50

ADVANCE AND RETREAT
General John Bell Hood
New introduction by
Richard M. McMurry
376 pp., 6 illus.
80534-0 $14.95

**GENERAL LEE
A Biography of Robert E. Lee**
General Fitzhugh Lee
Introduction by
Gary W. Gallagher
478 pp., 2 illus., 3 maps
80589-8 $15.95

**THE WARTIME PAPERS OF
ROBERT E. LEE**
Edited by Clifford Dowdey and
Louis H. Manarin
1,012 pp.
80282-1 $19.95

**THE CIVIL WAR DAY BY DAY
An Almanac 1861–1865**
E. B. Long with Barbara Long
1,135 pp., 8 pages of maps
80255-4 $24.50

**FROM MANASSAS TO
APPOMATTOX**
General James Longstreet
New introduction by
Jeffry D. Wert
760 pp., 30 illus., 16 maps
80464-6 $18.95

**MILITARY MEMOIRS
OF A CONFEDERATE
A Critical Narrative**
Edward Porter Alexander
New introduction by
Gary W. Gallagher
658 pp., 13 maps
80509-X $17.95

**THE STORY OF THE
CONFEDERACY**
Robert Selph Henry
Foreword by
Douglas Southall Freeman
526 pp.
80370-4 $14.95

**STONEWALL JACKSON AND
THE AMERICAN CIVIL WAR**
G. F. R. Henderson
New introduction by
Thomas L. Connelly
740 pp.
80318-6 $17.95

**THE RISE AND FALL OF THE
CONFEDERATE GOVERNMENT**
Jefferson Davis
New foreword by
James M. McPherson
Vol. I: 636 pp., 10 illus.
80418-2 $17.95
Vol. II: 696 pp., 26 illus.
80419-0 $17.95

Available at your bookstore

OR ORDER DIRECTLY FROM

DA CAPO PRESS, INC.

1-800-321-0050